Women and Inequality in the 21st Century draws from the best traditions of feminist scholar-activism, while reorienting focus toward topics and groups that to date have received less attention in the scholarship on gender inequality than is warranted, and indeed necessary. With chapters spanning a unique range of formats—from interviews with prominent gender scholars, to novel empirical studies and self-reflexive narratives—the text is at once accessible, theoretically nuanced, and highly engaging. Slatton and Brailey have generated an innovative volume from an incredible diversity of scholars addressing the many margins and complex positionalities that constitute contemporary womanhood today.

Jennifer Mueller, *Assistant Professor of Sociology and Director of the Intergroup Relations Program, Skidmore College*

WOMEN AND INEQUALITY IN THE 21ST CENTURY

Recent books have drawn attention to an unfinished gender revolution and the reversal of gender progress. However, this literature primarily focuses on gender inequality in the family and its effect on women's career and family choices. While an important topic, these works are critiqued for being particularly attentive to the concerns of middle-class, heterosexual, White women and ignoring or erasing the issues and experiences of the vast majority of women throughout the United States (and other countries).

Women and Inequality in the 21st Century is an edited collection that addresses this dearth in the current literature. This book examines the continued inequities navigated by women occupying marginalized social positions within a "nexus of power relations." It addresses the experiences of immigrant women of color, aging women, normative gender constraints faced by lesbian and gender non-conforming individuals assigned the female gender at birth, religious constraints on women's sexual expression, and religious and ethnic barriers impeding access to equality for women across the globe. Contributors to this collection reflect varying fields of inquiry—including sociology, psychology, theology, history, and anthropology. Their works employ empirical research methods, hermeneutic analysis, and narrative to capture the unique gender experiences and negotiations of diverse 21st-century women.

Brittany C. Slatton is Associate Professor of Sociology at Texas Southern University. Dr. Slatton's recent books include *Mythologizing Black Women* (2014) and *Hyper Sexual Hyper Masculine? Gender, Race, and Sexuality in the Identities of Contemporary Black Men* (2014). You can find her scholarly articles in journals such as *Sociology Compass*, *Socius*, and *Genders*. In 2017, she served as the prestigious Langston Hughes Visiting Professor at the University of Kansas.

Carla D. Brailey currently serves as Assistant Professor of Sociology at Texas Southern University. In addition to teaching and research, Dr. Brailey participates in New Leaders Council (NLC), Houston Chapter, serves as the Chair of KeyPac and on the Advisory Council for Sankofa Institute, and was recently selected for Leadership Houston's Class XXXIV. Dr. Brailey also served in the former Mayor Adrian Fenty's Cabinet as the Executive Director of Community Affairs and Senior Advisor for Religious Affairs for the District of Columbia.

NEW CRITICAL VIEWPOINTS ON SOCIETY SERIES
Edited by Joe R. Feagin

VIOLENCE AGAINST BLACK BODIES
Edited by Sandra Weissinger, Elwood Watson and Dwayne A. Mack

RACISM IN THE NEOLIBERAL ERA
A Meta History of Elite White Power
Randolph Hohle

LEADING A DIVERSITY CULTURAL SHIFT IN HIGHER EDUCATION
Comprehensive Organizational Learning Strategies
Edna Chun and Alvin Evans

KILLING AFRICAN AMERICANS
Police and Vigilante Violence as a Racial Control Mechanism
Noel A. Cazenave

WHEN RAPE WAS LEGAL
The Untold History of Sexual Violence During Slavery
Rachel A. Feinstein

LATINO PEOPLES IN THE NEW AMERICA
Racialization and Resistance
Edited by José A. Cobas, Joe R. Feagin, Daniel J. Delgado and Maria Chávez

WOMEN AND INEQUALITY IN THE 21ST CENTURY
Edited by Brittany C. Slatton and Carla D. Brailey

For more information about this series, please visit www.routledge.com/ New-Critical-Viewpoints-on-Society/book-series/NCVS

WOMEN AND INEQUALITY IN THE 21ST CENTURY

Edited by Brittany C. Slatton and Carla D. Brailey

Routledge
Taylor & Francis Group

NEW YORK AND LONDON

First published 2019
by Routledge
52 Vanderbilt Avenue, New York, NY 10017

and by Routledge
2 Park Square, Milton Park, Abingdon, Oxon, OX14 4RN

Routledge is an imprint of the Taylor & Francis Group, an informa business

© 2019 Taylor & Francis

The right of Brittany C. Slatton and Carla D. Brailey to be
identified as the authors of the editorial material, and of the authors
for their individual chapters, has been asserted in accordance with
sections 77 and 78 of the Copyright, Designs and Patents Act 1988.

Library of Congress Cataloging-in-Publication Data
Names: Slatton, Brittany C., editor. | Brailey, Carla D., editor.
Title: Women and inequality in the 21st century / [edited] by
Brittany C. Slatton and Carla D. Brailey.
Description: 1 Edition. | New York : Routledge, 2019. | Series:
New critical viewpoints on society series
Identifiers: LCCN 2018060671 (print) | LCCN 2018061335
(ebook) | ISBN 9781315294971 (e) | ISBN 9781138239777
(hardcover) | ISBN 9781138239784 (pbk.) | ISBN
9781315294971 (ebk)
Subjects: LCSH: Women—Social conditions—21st century. |
Sexism. | Sex discrimination against women. | Sex role.
Classification: LCC HQ1155 (ebook) | LCC HQ1155 .W646
2019 (print) | DDC 305.4009/05—dc23
LC record available at https://lccn.loc.gov/2018060671

ISBN: 978-1-138-23977-7 (hbk)
ISBN: 978-1-138-23978-4 (pbk)
ISBN: 978-1-315-29497-1 (ebk)

Typeset in Bembo
by Swales & Willis Ltd, Exeter, Devon, UK

CONTENTS

CONTENTS

CONTENTS

CONTRIBUTORS

Abiola Akiyode-Afolabi, is a lecturer with the University of Lagos, Faculty of Law, the National Coordinator of Women Advocates Research and Documentation Center (WARDC), is a former student leader and dedicated human rights defender, with specialization in gender and international human rights law. In recognition of her commitment and efforts on behalf of her fellow citizens, particularly women, the International League for Human Rights named her a recipient of the 1999 Defenders' Day Awards. Abiola, received the award at an impressive ceremony in New York City on December 9, 1999, the first anniversary of the United Nations Defenders Declaration. Abiola earned her Master's Degree in International Human Rights Law from the University of Notre Dame Law School, Center for Civil and Human Rights, Indiana, USA. Abiola has led several coalitions and has worked extensively on gender, human rights, law, democracy, and peace building, and has produced several research materials and publications on these areas. Abiola has also worked as a consultant to local and international organizations on several projects.

Rasha Aly is a graduate student with the University of Cincinnati's Sociology Department. Her dissertation focuses on how domestic violence shelter environments influence the identities of the women who live within them. She received her Master's Degree in Criminal Justice from the University of Cincinnati. She also has years of hands-on experience working as a domestic violence shelter advocate. In addition, she has also served as an instructor, teaching at the University of Cincinnati, Chatfield College, and Cincinnati State University.

Jacqueline F. Ballou graduated from Howard University's School of Divinity with a Master's Degree in Religious Studies with a concentration in Ethics. She also holds a Master's Degree in Business Administration from Duke University, the Fuqua School of Business where she was a Rollins Fellow, concentrating in Corporate Finance and Strategic Management. She received her Bachelor of Science degree in Accounting from North Carolina Agricultural and Technical State University where she graduated Salutatorian. She is also a Certified Public Accountant. Jacqueline has aspirations to one day obtain her Ph.D. in Christian/Social Ethics and become a professor and writer while continuing to give back to the community through focused efforts on the education and empowerment of young women of color.

Ellen Benoit is a sociologist and principal investigator at National Development and Research Institutes, Inc., in New York, NY. Her research is primarily qualitative and concerns HIV/STI risk and substance use in vulnerable populations, with a special interest in structural contexts of behavior. With Dr. Eloise Dunlap, she is a principal investigator on a study of substance use and HIV risk among heterosexual Black women with multiple partners, funded by the National Institutes of Health. Dr. Benoit's other work includes studies with behaviorally bisexual and high-risk heterosexual Black men and a critical-consciousness based intervention

Stephanie Campos has a Ph.D. in Anthropology from The Graduate Center, City University of New York. Her dissertation, titled "'Small Village/Large Hell': Cocaine and Incarceration in Lima, Peru," explores the ways in which the Santa Monica women's prison in Lima both reflects and reconstructs intersecting inequalities of race, class, gender, and citizenship. She was awarded the Carolyn G. Heilbrun Dissertation Prize for the "outstanding feminist dissertation in the humanities" by the Women's Studies Certificate Program at The Graduate Center. Dr. Campos is an Investigator at National Development and Research Institutes, Inc., where she is receiving training support through the Supplements to Promote Diversity in Health-Related Research sponsored by the Eunice Kennedy Shriver National Institute of Child Health and Human Development. She has also taught courses in Latin American studies, anthropology, sociology, and women's studies.

Rosalind S. Chou is a native of Florida, where her parents emigrated from Taiwan in the 1970s. She attended Florida State University earning a Bachelor's Degree in Sociology, and then spent six years working for Eckerd Youth Alternatives at Camp E-Nini-Hassee, a non-profit therapeutic wilderness camp for at-risk girls, before moving to Texas in 2005 for graduate school at Texas A&M University. She co-authored the book, *The Myth of the Model Minority: Asian Americans Facing Racism*, in 2008 with Joe R. Feagin, and published the second edition in 2014. She completed her Ph.D. in Sociology with an emphasis on race, ethnicity, gender, and sexuality in May 2010, and then was the 2010–11 Samuel Dubois Cook Postdoctoral Fellow at Duke University. She is an Associate Professor of Sociology at Georgia State University and her second book, *Asian American Sexual Politics: The Construction of Race, Gender,* *and Sexuality*, was published in 2012 by Rowman and Littlefield. Her third book, *Asian Americans on Campus*, was published in August 2015.

Colleen Denney is Professor of Art History in the Gender and Women's Studies Program at the University of Wyoming, where she teaches courses on visual activism, gender and the humanities, Victorian Women, and the History of Women Artists, among others. Her research specializes in representations of women, including *Representing Diana, Princess of Wales* (Associated University Press, 2005) and *Women, Portraiture and the Crisis of Identity in Victorian England: My Lady Scandalous Reconsidered* (Ashgate, 2009). She has twice been named "Top Prof" at her university, is past Director of her program, has received her university's Seibold Fellowship, and also has held a Yale Center for British Art Fellowship.

Melissa K. Ochoa Garza is a Sociology doctoral candidate at Texas A&M University, College Station, Texas. Her main focus is race and gender; her advisors are Dr. Joe Feagin and Dr. Jane Sell. She has a Women's and Gender Studies certificate from Texas A&M University. She graduated from Purdue University, West Lafayette in 2009 for her undergraduate degrees, Psychology, and Public Relations and Rhetorical Advocacy. Melissa's research seeks to understand the contexts in which sexism is experienced among different racial groups and genders through daily interactions. Melissa's research connects the micro-level displays of power in gender to a larger, oppressive system. Systemic forms of sexism have continued for thousands of years ensuring women's lower status in society, although these forms have varied throughout time and culture. She is specifically looking to understand the normalization of sexism by studying not just the contexts, but also investigating which actors embrace, perpetuate, and contribute to these sexist frames and the ways in which they do it.

Daniella Graves has had seven years of experience in higher education administration and instruction. She is currently an Academic Dean at a business college in southern California, and teaches courses in Sociology, Leadership, and Management. Daniella earned her Ph.D. in Organizational Leadership from the Chicago School of Professional Psychology. She earned both a B.A. and M.A. in Sociology from UCLA and the California State University at Northridge, respectively. Her research interests include gender norms, social constructionism, and leadership, and her dissertation explored the social construction of women's leadership identity.

Elizabeth Gregory directs the Women's, Gender & Sexuality Studies Program at the University of Houston, where she is a Professor of English. Her research interests include 20th-century poetry and the intersection of fertility and women's work in contemporary life. Both strands of her work explore issues of aging. Her books include *Ready: Why Women Are Embracing the New Later Motherhood*; *Quotation and Modern American Poetry: "'Imaginary Gardens with Real Toads'"* and two edited collections. She is now completing projects on the later poetry of Marianne Moore, on the lack of "School/Work Synchrony" and its effect on gender dynamics, and on the interactions of fertility and work in the US economy. Her blog, *Domestic Product: Later Motherhood & the Politics & Economics of Women's Work*, is online at www.domesticproduct.net.

Chien-Juh Gu is an associate professor in the Department of Sociology at Western Michigan University. She specializes in gender, social psychology, and immigration. Gu has received numerous awards and grants. She is the first winner of the Gender Scholar Award at WMU. She has also received, among other recognitions, the Junior Scholar Grant from the Chiang Ching-kuo Foundation and the Faculty Research and Creative Activities Award from WMU. On students' nomination, she received a 2015–16 College of Arts and Sciences' Faculty Achievement Award in Teaching, and a 2016–17 College of Arts and Sciences' Faculty Achievement Award in Research and Creative Activity.

Erin Heisler recently graduated from the University of Saint Thomas in Saint Paul, Minnesota with a Master of Arts in English. She currently works in online communications at the Children's Home Society of Minnesota. Erin's passion for feminist activism was ignited when she first performed in *The Vagina Monologues* in 2004. Since then, she has been constantly considering the ways in which activists can be empowered and newly engaged citizens can be called into action. In 2014, she was awarded the Luann Dummer Center for Women's Graduate Research Fellowship to support her research in online feminism.

Dresden N. Lackey is a first-generation doctoral student at Georgia State University. She received her Bachelor of Arts degree in Psychology and Sociology at Appalachian State University, and her Master of Science degree in Applied Psychology at the University of Baltimore. Prior to beginning her studies at Georgia State, Dresden worked for the National Institute of Health, Johns Hopkins University, and the University of Baltimore. Her current research interests include racial and gender microaggressions, social stratification, and Asian American oppression. When she is not conducting academic research, Dresden volunteers with the House Rabbit Society.

Martin J. Leahy has 30 years' experience as an organizational and leadership consultant and is Professor, Ph.D. Organizational Leadership Program, at the Chicago School of Professional Psychology. He serves on the school's Academic Affairs Leadership Council, The President's Council, and is Chair of the National Faculty Council, representing faculty at all four campuses. He has taught leadership and qualitative research methods to doctoral students since 2003. Dialogue (Buber, Rogers) is his area of practice, research, and writing; he advocates a relational approach to leadership and research methods. He serves on the boards of the American Catholic Council and the Gestalt Therapy Institute of Philadelphia.

Alexandra C. H. Nowakowski is an Assistant Professor of Geriatrics and Behavioral Sciences at the Florida State University College of Medicine. Dr. Nowakowski's work examines the experience and management of chronic health conditions across the life course. Using mixed methods and diverse literatures, Nowakowski explores how people age with, and adjust to, persistent health challenges.

Candace Nunag Tardío is Trotter Multicultural Center's Operations and Event Coordinator and joined the team in February 2018. Candace holds a Bachelor of Arts degree in International Affairs from the University of Colorado Boulder, as well as Master of Social Sciences degree in Women's and Gender Studies from the University of Colorado Denver. Prior to working at the University of Michigan, Candace worked as a Multicultural Program Coordinator at the University of Colorado, Boulder.

Dean Ohmsford is a trans man and Allen S. Wilber Scholar from the University of Kansas, where he graduated with a B.G.S. in Sociology with a minor in Psychology. His focus as a doctoral student is on the construction of identity, with interests in gender, race and ethnicity, surveillance, and critical theory. Previous research includes a sociological examination of the use of achieved versus ascribed identity on social media, and its effects on at-risk populations, and a study of the ways in which transgender and cisgender women buy into, or reject, feminine norms. He is currently exploring TSA agents' thoughts and feelings on their use of biometric surveillance devices to screen air travelers, with a focus on their interpretations of the screening process. Outside of academia, Dean's interests include drawing, hiking, writing fiction, performing in a darkwave band, and taking entirely too many pictures of his cat.

Kimberly Brown Pellum maintains an ongoing mission to help people accurately understand their place in American history and the world. With a doctoral degree in United States history earned at Howard University, she has worked as a Multicultural Fellow at the Smithsonian Institution National Museum of American History. The Montgomery Improvements Association (founders of the famed 1955 Bus Boycott) and the Birmingham Civil Rights Institute are among a number of groups and organizations that have called upon her leadership and expertise to guide community-based preservation projects, commemorative programs, and educational initiatives. For two consecutive years, she served the United Negro College Fund as both moderator and panelist for its nationwide "Empower Me Tour." She has made presentations for the Buffalo Soldiers National Museum, the Baylor College of Medicine Office of Institutional Diversity, as well as the American Historical Association's Texas Conference on Introductory History Courses. She is the author of two history books for children, founder of the non-profit Education Like Me and was recently promoted graduate faculty at Texas Southern University where she teaches courses in US, African American, and Women's History.

Susan Rasmussen, Professor of Anthropology within the Department of Comparative Cultural Studies at the University of Houston, has conducted field research in rural and urban Tuareg communities of northern Niger and Mali and among African immigrants in France. Her interests include religion, healing and healing specialists, possession, gender, aging and the life course, verbal art performance, and African humanities. She has written a number of articles and five books. Her published authored books include *Spirit Possession and Personhood among the Kel Ewey Tuareg, The Poetics and Politics of Tuareg Aging, Healing in Community, Those Who Touch: Tuareg Medicine Women in Anthropological Perspective*, and *Neighbors, Strangers, Witches, and Culture-Heroes: Ritual Powers of Smith/Artisans in Tuareg Society and Beyond*. Current projects include a book manuscript on urban Tuareg play performances in northern Mali and manuscripts on conversion experiences among Kabyle in France.

Sarah V. Suiter, Ph.D., M.S., is an Assistant Professor of the Practice in Human and Organizational Development, and the Director of the Community Development and Action M.Ed. program at Vanderbilt University. Prior to coming to Vanderbilt, Dr. Suiter was a Senior Program Evaluator at Centerstone Research Institute. Dr. Suiter received her Ph.D. from Vanderbilt University in Community Research & Action, and completed a postdoctoral fellowship at the Center for Spirituality, Theology & Health at Duke University Medical Center. Dr. Suiter's work engages community-based responses to promoting human health and well-being. She has conducted community-based research with health and human development organizations around the globe, including PRODEPINE in Ecuador; Casa de Galilea in Buenos Aires, Argentina; Magdalene House in Nashville, Tennessee; Southlight in Raleigh, North Carolina, and two federally funded System of Care sites in central Tennessee. Dr. Suiter's first book, *Magdalene House: A Place About Mercy*, was published in 2012.

Kesslyn Brade Stennis, M.S.W., M.Div., Ph.D., serves as the current Chair of the Department of Social Work at Coppin State University in Baltimore, Maryland, Director of the Dorothy Height Center for the Advancement of Social Justice and is the first African American female

Board President for the North American Association of Christians in Social Work. She has published in several peer-reviewed journals and been a reviewer, editorial consultant and/or guest editor for journals including *Social Work, Journal of Social Work Education, Social Work and Christianity, Journal of Religion and Spirituality in Social Work,* and *Journal of Family Violence.* She has also worked on various violence-related and community-based grant projects associated with Oakwood University, Georgetown University, Howard University and Coppin State University.

J. E. Sumerau is an Assistant Professor of Sociology at the University of Tampa, Florida. Dr. Sumerau's teaching and research focuses on the intersections of sexualities, gender, religion, and health in the historical and interpersonal experiences of sexual, gender, and religious minorities. For publications to date and teaching materials, see www.jsumerau.com. To date, Sumerau's work has focused on, for example, the experiences of Christian sexual minorities, gender and sexualities in Mormonism, gender and sexual health disparities; and transgender religious experience. Zir work has been published in many books and journals, including but not limited to *Gender & Society, Symbolic Interaction, Sexualities, Journal of Contemporary Ethnography, Men and Masculinities, Sociology of Religion, Sociological Spectrum* and *Journal of Sex Research.*

Omar Swartz (Ph.D., Purdue University, 1995; J.D., Duke University, 2001, magna cum laude) is Associate Professor and Director of the Master of Social Science program in the College of Liberal Arts and Sciences at the University of Colorado Denver, where he has also coordinated the Law Studies minor for the past twelve years. His primary areas of research and teaching are law and diversity, mass media law and policy, cultural criticism, and philosophical problems in the social sciences. Specifically, his work focuses on the intersections between the US legal system, the history of social injustice and intellectual intolerance in the United States. He is the author or editor of twelve books and nearly a hundred essays, book chapters, and reviews.

Arthur L. Whaley is an independent consultant in research design/program evaluation. He received a Ph.D. in Clinical Psychology from Rutgers University in 1986 and a Dr.P.H. in Epidemiology from Columbia University in 2000. He has been a professor or research scientist at several institutions of higher education over the past 25 years. Dr. Whaley also was a community mental health practitioner working with children, adolescents, and their families in poor communities of New York City. He was a Visiting Scholar at the Russell Sage Foundation and the recipient of the National Alliance of Research on Schizophrenia and Depression (NARSAD) Young Investigator Award. His research involves the study of the role of cultural and cognitive factors in the etiology, diagnosis, and treatment of mental disorders in ethnic/racial populations, with a particular focus on African Americans.

Evelyn B. Winfield-Thomas is the Executive Director of Institutional Equity and Special Assistant to the President at Western Michigan University (WMU) where she has worked for the last 15 years. She also holds rank and tenure as an associate professor at WMU and is a licensed clinical psychologist in Michigan. Dr. Winfield-Thomas earned a B.A. degree in Psychology from Dillard University, a M.A. degree in Psychology from the University of Northern Iowa, and a Ph.D. in Clinical Psychology from Southern Illinois University at Carbondale. For the past five years, she has focused her efforts on developing partnerships and organizational capacity to lead campus climate and strategic diversity change initiatives in higher education. Her primary research interest is the impact of sociocultural factors and experiences on identity development, behavior, and well-being, with a primary focus on African American/Black women.

INTRODUCTION

Inequality and the Complex Positionalities of 21st-Century Women

Brittany C. Slatton and Carla D. Brailey

The gender revolution resulted in women having access to birth control, employment opportunities in male-dominated jobs, greater access to college education and political office, legal bans on gender discrimination in the workplace, and a host of other changes since the 1960s.[1] However, change in the "gender system has been uneven—affecting some groups more than others and some arenas of life more than others."[2] Social inequities intersect to "create complex positionalities" for women within a society's social power relations.[3] Thus, women have varying experiences of oppression and dominance,[4] barriers and access. In the fight for equality and democracy, cisgender, heterosexual, middle- and upper-class White women have been and continue to be the primary beneficiaries of privileges and rights gained by the women's rights movement and via existing racist and heterosexist social structures. Marginalized groups of women have experienced much slower progress because they were excluded from the early fight for democratic change and because privileges for dominant groups—such as access to outsourced care work—often come at their expense.[5] However, all women in the 21st century—to different degrees and within varying contexts—continue to encounter barriers to full democratic inclusion and equality.

A review of recent data illustrates a series of setbacks in pertinent areas integral to women's full access to rights and opportunities in society. At least nine states have passed the "Abortion Insurance Opt-Out Act" which bans all public and most private insurance plans from covering abortion—even for women pregnant due to incest or rape.[6] Federal policy changes under the Trump administration bolster states' ability to defund Planned Parenthood, an act that disproportionately limits access to reproductive and preventative health care for women who are low income, living in rural areas, and/or women of color.[7] Despite technological advancements, the United States has the highest rate of maternal death of all industrialized countries. Particularly atrocious is that African American women are a staggering 243 percent more likely to die due to pregnancy- and childbirth-related issues than White women, a disparity that holds even when education and socioeconomic status are accounted for.[8] The gender wage gap continues to threaten women's economic opportunities. A recent study finds women workers must have an additional academic degree to earn the same salary as men.[9] Similarly, women lag behind men in the ownership of assets, a gender wealth gap that is particularly shaped by race. While single white women have a median wealth of $41,500, single Black and Hispanic women have a median wealth of only $100 and $120 respectively.[10]

Perhaps the ascension of Mr. Donald Trump to the presidency of the United States best illustrates the systemic nature of gender inequality. He has a long history of judging women's physical appearance, criticizing women when they do or say something he disagrees with, and upholding the system of patriarchy. To give a few examples, Mr. Trump blamed sexual assault in the military on cohabitation, stated women who get abortions should be punished (although he later recanted this statement), and contended that Mrs. Hillary Clinton would be incapable of satisfying the country because she is incapable of satisfying her husband.[11] Most egregious are the accusations of sexual assault and harassment against Mr. Trump.[12] Speaking to former *Access Hollywood* host Billy Bush in a 2005 audio, he admitted that because of his celebrity he can do anything to women: "I just start kissing them. It's like a magnet. Just kiss, I don't even wait. And when you're a star, they let you do it. You can do anything. Grab 'em by the pussy. You can do anything."[13] Several women have come forward alleging Mr. Trump indeed kissed or grabbed them without consent. Mr. Trump's status as President sanctions his behavior at the highest office in the country, making his election a most important contemporary representation of the stall in women's access to equality.[14]

Sheryl Sandberg's *Lean In: Women, Work, and the Will to Lead* (2013), Paula England's "The Gender Revolution: Uneven and Stalled" (2010), and Ann-Marie Slaughter's "Why Women Still Can't Have It All" (2012) and *Unfinished Business: Men, Work, Family* (2016) are recent influential works that have importantly drawn attention to an unfinished gender revolution and the reversal of gender progress. While these works are integral in bringing attention to continued gender inequality, there is still much to be learned about the inequities experienced by diverse women in society. The aforementioned literature primarily focuses on gender inequality in the family and its effect on women's career and family choices. While an important topic, these works[15] are critiqued for being particularly attentive to the concerns of middle-class, heterosexual, white women and ignoring or erasing the issues and experiences of the vast majority of women throughout the United States (and other countries).[16] A volume of work on the continued inequities navigated by women occupying marginalized social positions within a "nexus of power relations"[17] reflects a dearth in the current literature.

Women and Inequality in the 21st Century addresses this gap by featuring topics currently limited in the gender inequality literature. This book examines the experiences of immigrant women of color, aging women, normative gender constraints faced by lesbian and gender non-conforming individuals assigned the female gender at birth, religious constraints on women's sexual expression, and religious and ethnic barriers impeding access to equality for Nigerian and North African Kabyle women, amongst other topics. Contributors reflect varying fields of inquiry—including sociology, psychology, theology, history, and anthropology. Their works employ empirical research methods, hermeneutic analysis, and narrative to capture the unique gender experiences and negotiations of 21st-century women.

The organizational structure of *Women and Inequality* was developed to address several key concerns including the limited democracy in which diverse women live, key arguments/critiques in women's inequality, the inequitable terrain women negotiate, its psychosocial effects, and the resistance and activism strategies employed by women and their allies. The book is divided into five parts. Each part begins with a Gender Scholar Spotlight feature, where established and up-and-coming scholars in the field of women and gender studies completed interviews that address several key issues, theories, and approaches within their field.[18] These interviews showcase the work of gender/women's studies scholars, underscore the importance of this type of research, and present pertinent topics for future research in the field.

Part I, "An Unrealized Democracy," introduces readers to the ways in which intersecting systemic inequalities historically and presently preclude women from full democratic realization. Brown-Pellum starts this collection off by examining how deeply racialized and sexualized American-made images of women uphold white supremacy and capitalism. She provides a historical context for how American labor, politics, and entertainment manipulate and exploit women's images in ways that obstruct them from securing full equality. In Chapter 2, Swartz and Nunag-Hicks connect historical legal doctrine grounded in difference to women's contemporary experiences of inequality. This chapter illustrates the breadth of gender discrimination and problematizes postfeminist arguments. In Chapter 3, Gregory illustrates how patriarchy and racism shape who has access to economic and civic power to define how paid and unpaid work is assigned and what work is valued and compensated in society.

Part II, "Negotiating Inequitable Terrain," gives specific examples of women's everyday experiences of inequality and the ways in which their complex positionalities shape the type of inequality they encounter. Chapter 4 begins with Garza's examination of systemic sexism. Collecting and analyzing journal entries of detailed accounts, stories, or daily events experienced by women of various racial/ethnic backgrounds,

Garza finds men's everyday interactions with women reproduce gender inequality and perpetuate discrimination against women. In Chapter 5, Gu relies on 45 life-history interviews with middle-class Taiwanese immigrant women to examine how they navigate everyday encounters of discrimination and negotiate their American identity. Chapter 6, by Lackey and Chou, examines the types of harassment experienced by queer and gender non-conforming women. Drawing on in-depth interviews, they present data on dimensions of familial approval and disapproval in respondents' identities as queer women and their experiences of gender-conforming expectations. Building on Lackey and Chou's work, Omshford provides a personal narrative in Chapter 7 that details unique forms of discrimination experienced by a gender non-conforming individual assigned the female gender at birth. Attention is given to the ways in which hegemonic gender norms are maintained through surveillance and gatekeepers. In Chapter 8, Graves and Leahy examine how women organizational leaders negotiate societal gender expectations in their presentation of self and impression-management strategies. This part ends with a chapter on diasporic North African Kabyle people's use of religion to negotiate gender constructs and relations between men and women.

Part III, "Psychosocial Effects of Inequality," examines the effects of inequality on women's mental and emotional well-being and social functioning in society. Chapter 10 addresses Whaley and Winfield-Thomas' investigation of "hair stress," which they define as the physical and mental health correlates of unnatural hair care and styling practices among African American women. Their findings suggest a health cost to African American women who reject their natural hair and emulate Eurocentric standards of beauty. In Chapter 11, Sumerau and Nowakowski explore the obligation to have sexual intercourse among older women. Drawing on nationally representative data from the National Social Life, Health, and Aging Project, the authors capture feelings of sexual obligation as well as the ways such feelings vary in relation to social factors. They find that arthritis may be deeply related to gendered experiences of such pressures in later life and that significant variations arise in relation to respondent's racial, class, age, and ability statuses. This part ends with Brade-Stennis and Aly's chapter on the impact of identity and stigma on domestic violence survivors.

In Part IV, "Key Debates in Women's Inequality," authors problematize key arguments and practices restricting women's rights and freedoms, and propose possibilities for women's potential liberation. Ballou's chapter, "Is there Liberation for the Single, Saved, and Sexually Repressed?" opens this part. She employs a womanist biblical hermeneutic to analyze scriptures used by many Christian Churches to repress unmarried women's sexual desires and condemn their sexual behavior outside of marriage. Her examination offers an interesting debate on the interpretation of scriptural text by the

4

early Christian Church and is particularly concerned about what these texts mean for African American Christian women because of their increasing improbability of marriage. In Chapter 14, Suiter explores current debates around sex work through the lenses of three feminist political theories of freedom in an attempt to understand the ways in which inequalities related to gender, race, class, and sexuality express and perpetuate themselves for women who trade sex for money. And in Chapter 15, Akiyode-Afolabi examines how conflicting religious and ethnic positions in Nigeria pose a threat to the acceptance of women's human rights protocols.

The chapters in the final part, "Pushing Back: Resistance and Activism," illustrate women's active resistance strategies, assess current forms of activism, and propose techniques for improving the established ways in which women *push back*. In Chapter 16, Campos and Benoit examine sexual assertiveness among Black women as a form of resistance to limited means of social mobility and cultural images that emphasize control over their sexuality. They contend that while these women's experiences may not portend structural changes, their stories reject victimization and highlight their power and agency. Chapter 17, "Raise Your Banner High! Mounting a Take Back the Night Event," Denney provides an example of feminist service learning and civic engagement among college students. Denney uses this service learning project as a tool to teach students about women's historic activism. Lastly, in Chapter 18, Hiesler employ's Nancy Fraser's theory of justice to argue that Eve Ensler's *The Vagina Monologues* is unsuccessful in combatting women's oppression—which it successfully brings attention to—because it silences the voices of marginalized women. Hiesler contends an intersectional approach that explores the ways in which women are simultaneously oppressed by racism, capitalism, gender binarism, and nationalism can develop the play into a tool with the potential for ending gender violence for all women.

Notes

1 Paula England, "The Gender Revolution: Uneven and Stalled," *Gender & Society* 24 (2010): 149–166.
2 England, "The Gender Revolution," 149–166.
3 Laura Dean, Rachel Tolhurst, Renu Khanna, and Kate Jehan, "'You're Disabled, Why Did You have Sex in the First Place?' An Intersectional Analysis of Experiences of Disabled Women with Regard to their Sexual and Reproductive Health and Rights in Gujarat State, India," *Global Health Action* 10 (2017): 1.
4 Dean et al., "You're Disabled," 1.
5 Catherine Rottenberg, "Neoliberal Feminism and the Future of Human Capital," *Signs: Journal of Women in Culture and Society* 42, no. 4 (2017): 329–348.
6 Nicki Rossoll, "9 States Where You Might Need 'Abortion Insurance'" *ABC News*, December 13, 2013, http://abcsnews.go.com/Politics/states-abortion-insurance/storu?id=21197679
7 Jessie Hellman, "Trump Administration Rescinds Obama Guidance on Defunding Planned Parenthood," *The Hill*, January 19, 2007, www.google.com/

amp/thehill.com/policy/healthcare/369723-trump-administration-rescinds-guidance-protecting-planned -parenthood%3famp

8 Nina Martin, "Black Mothers Keep Dying After Giving Birth. Shalon Irving's Story Explain Why," *NPR*, December 7, 2017, www.npr.org/2017/12/07/568948782/black-mothers-keep-dying-after-giving-birth-shalon-irvings-story-explains-why

9 Anthony P. Carnevale, Nicole Smith, and Artem Gulish, "Women Can't Win: Despite Making Educational Gains and Pursuing High-Wage Majors, Women Still Earn Less than Men," *Georgetown University*, accessed April 18, 2018, https://cew-7632.kxcdn.com/wp-content/uploads/Women_FR_Web.pdf

10 Mariko Change and Meizhu Lui, "Lifting as We Climb: Women of Color, Wealth, and America's Future," *Insight*, accessed, April 18, 2018, www.mariko-chang.com/LiftingAsWeClimb.pdf

11 Claire Cohen, "Donald Trump Sexism Tracker: Every Offensive Comment in One Place," *Telegraph*, July 14, 2017, www.google.com/amp/s/www.telegraph.co.uk/women/politics/donald-trump-sexism-tracker-every-offensive-comment-in-one-place/amp/

12 Jeremy Diamond and Daniella Diaz, "Trump on Sexual Assault Allegations: I am a Victim," *CNN*, October 15, 2016, www.cnn.com/2016/10/14/politics/donald-trump-sexual-assault-allegations/index.html

13 David A. Fahrenthold, "Trump Recorded Having Extremely Lewd Conversation about Women in 2005," *Washington Post*, October 8, 2016, www.washingtonpost.com/politics/trump-recorded-having-extremely-lewd-conversation-about-women-in-2005/2016/10/07/3b9ce776-8cb4-11e6-bf8a-3d26847eeed4_story.html?noredirect=on&utm_term=.9168a6d28e25

14 It should be noted that White women were instrumental in Trump's election. Fifty-three percent of White women voted for Mr. Trump. Whereas 94 percent of Black women and 68 percent of Latina women voted for Mrs. Clinton. According to certain arguments, this disparity is due to some White women seeking to sustain privileges derived from the existing patriarchal system for themselves, their husbands, and their children and because they do not view the concerns of other racial/ethnic/religious groups of women as their own. See Phoebe Lett, "White Women Voted Trump. Now What," *New York Times*, November 2016, www.nytimes.com/2016/11/10/opinion/white-women-voted-trump-now-what.html; also see Laura Morgan Roberts and Robin J. Ely, "Why Did So Many White Women Vote for Donald Trump? *Fortune*, November 2016, http://fortune.com/2016/11/17/donald-trump-women-voters-election/

15 This critique is particularly so for the works of Sandberg and Slaughter.

16 Catherine Rottenberg, "The Rise of Neoliberal Feminism," *Cultural Studies* 28, no. 3 (2014): 418–437; Rottenberg, "Neoliberal Feminism," 329–348.

17 Dean et al., "You're Disabled," 1.

18 The Gender Scholar Spotlight Feature and the interview questions derive from the excellent Spotlight on Research feature in Mindy Stombler, Dawn M. Baunach, Wendy Simonds, Elroi J. Windsor, and Elisabeth O. Burgess (eds.), *Sex Matters: The Sexuality & Society Reader* (New York: W.W. Norton, 2013).

Part I

AN UNREALIZED DEMOCRACY

GENDER SCHOLAR SPOTLIGHT: INTERVIEW
WITH AMRITA CHAKRABARTI MYERS

Amrita Chakrabarti Myers is Ruth N. Halls Associate Professor of History and Gender Studies at Indiana University. She earned her doctorate in US History from Rutgers University and has been the recipient of several awards for scholarship, teaching, and activism, including a 2017 fellowship from the American Council of Learned Societies, the 2012 Julia Cherry Spruill Book Prize from the Southern Association of Women Historians, and the 2016 Martin Luther King, Jr. Building Bridges Award from Indiana University. Her first book, *Forging Freedom: Black Women and the Pursuit of Liberty in Antebellum Charleston*, was published in 2011. Myers is currently writing her second book, *Remembering Julia: A Tale of Sex, Race, Power, and Place*.

What led you to begin studying women's inequality?

I began studying women's inequality because of the gender dynamics I witnessed growing up in my own household. While both my parents worked long hours outside the home, and my mother earned more money than my father did after a certain point, she was still expected to perform all the domestic labor inside the home . . . simply because she was a woman. Whereas my father came home from work and sat in his easy chair, watching TV while waiting for dinner to be served, my mother came home after work and began preparing our dinner. These types of scenarios frustrated me as a child, and shaped my early interest in gender inequities.

How have your lived experiences shaped your research interests?

Growing up as a woman of color with immigrant parents in a predominantly White nation deeply shaped my research interests. I always felt like an outsider, both at home and at school and work. At home, I was daily chastised for being "too western" in my thoughts and behaviors, while out in the real world, my Canadian-ness was always in question because of the color of my skin and my "unusual" name. It is no surprise, then, that I gravitated towards studying Black women's history. The field gave me a better understanding of my own history, provided me with the language to name the things that happened to me and around me, and explained my constant feelings of being an outsider, or what W.E.B. DuBois called "double consciousness."

In your opinion, what scholarly works have been most impactful in your research on women and inequality?

The scholarly works that I found, and still find, most impactful in my own work on Black women include Deborah Gray White's *Ar'n't I a Woman?: Female Slaves in the Plantation South*, Darlene Clark Hine's *Hine Sight: Black Women and the Reconstruction of American History*, Tera W. Hunter's *To 'Joy My Freedom: Southern Black Women's Lives and Labors After the Civil War*, and Stephanie Camp's *Closer to Freedom: Enslaved Women and Resistance in the Plantation South*.

What has been most challenging about your field of work?

My field of work has presented me with several challenges. It meant leaving my home, family, friends, and country, for starters, and moving to the United States, first to attend graduate school and then, eventually, to pursue my career. It currently means extensive time away from home to do archival research in various facilities around the nation, an endeavor both costly and tiring. The kind of work I do takes a long time (I have been doing research on my new book on and off since 2010), real patience, and willingness to pursue every lead and not leave any stone unturned. It is definitely not for those looking for quick finishes and regular pats on the back.

Why is your work on women important?

I believe my work on women is important because it brings Black women to the center of US history. Not only does this reshape the narrative of our history and bring us closer to the "truth" of what happened, and what role people of color played in building this nation, it also gives young Black girls and boys a real sense of pride when they see their ancestors' stories and voices in our history books. This makes them feel like they belong here, that they are a part of this nation, and that they, too, can help to move us forward and make this country a better place. I also believe that without

8

historical context, we simply cannot comprehend what is happening in the world around us. In order to understand our current political moment, we must understand the path that brought us here. Black women's history is this fundamental to understanding current, critical issues including the existence of rape culture, state-sanctioned violence against people of color, generational poverty, and more.

Which scholar(s) (and why) has been most influential in developing your perspective?

The scholar that I think has been most influential in developing my perspective on race and gender inequality is Kimberlé Crenshaw. Her pioneering work on, and coining the term, "intersectionality" is foundational to how I think and write about Black women, and how I understand the structural inequities I see around me in the very fabric of this nation. I also admire her for being both a scholar and an activist and am trying to follow in her footsteps as best I can.

What theoretical approach best guides your research?

My research is guided by a blend of theoretical approaches, particularly those of social history, Black feminist theory à la bell hooks, and critical race theory via Kimberlé Crenshaw and others.

What pedagogical approaches have you found most effective when teaching on women and inequality?

Over fifteen years of full-time teaching, I have found that small-group work is the most effective way to help students come to grips with issues of gender and race inequality and truly absorb, retain, and understand the material. I assign readings, provide contextual information via short lectures, and then have students work through each reading as a group, guided by pre-set discussion questions. We then come back together as a large class to address any confusions or questions that arose during small group time. While this method requires much more from the students, and from me, the result is papers that reflect a deeper and more nuanced understanding of women and issues of inequality than simple rote memorization.

In your opinion, what are the most pertinent issues facing the women in your area of research today?

The most important issues facing Black women in the US today are sexual assault, domestic violence, HIV-AIDS, drug addiction, state-sanctioned police violence, systemic poverty, and a lack of access to quality health care. All of these problems are bolstered by a national, stereotyped image of Black women as loud, angry, ugly, lazy, unintelligent, gold-digging, amoral, hypersexual Jezebels who are bad mothers, an image crafted during slavery and continually reinforced through to the present by the media, educational structures, and popular culture.

1

BEAUTY AND THE BEAST OF INEQUALITY

A Historical Synopsis of Women's Images as Barriers in American Labor, Politics, and Entertainment

Kimberly Brown Pellum

"The stronger women became politically, the heavier the ideals of beauty would bear down on them, mostly in order to distract their energy and undermine their progress." Naomi Wolf, feminist writer and former advisor to President Bill Clinton, published this poignant observation in her sociological critique *The Beauty Myth: How Images of Beauty are Used Against Women* (Wolf 1990). Wolf's text assists in recognizing the beauty ideal, together with its unattainability, as a political apparatus designed to tighten around the necks of women as they advance in society. Consequently, as recent years have extended new privileges and higher platforms to women, the chokehold of the beauty ideal and its oppressive disadvantages have in many ways intensified for the contemporary woman. As evidence of the severity of the phenomenon, Wolf points to the long-lasting and rapidly expanding dieting industry, an increased number of women who undergo elective surgery for facial and body enhancements, and those with eating disorders that have led to death (Wolf 1990).

Ironically, feminist scholar bell hooks, once named Wolf a symbolic beneficiary of America's racially driven and size-sensitive beauty caste. hooks remarked, "[As a White woman,] Naomi Wolf is allowed to be both intellectual and sexy. Whenever a Black woman is attractive and sexy, she must be a whore" (Trescott 1999). Today, even as a renowned African American author, hooks remains convinced that publishers and audiences perceive her very differently from Wolf, as a consequence of her image first and then perhaps the content of her writings. Negative perceptions lead to palpable challenges, professional and otherwise, not just for hooks, but for women from all walks of life. The phenomenon is not new, but rather carries origins in the nation's founding. In fact, critics of Wolf's work found her challenging of the beauty ideal "not only unfeminine but almost un-American" (Wolf 1990). This chapter provides historical context essential to explicating how a general public could arrive at such a limiting conclusion and how femininity and American identity became so intricately linked. It will also integrate and expand hooks's argument that American-made images are deeply racialized and sexualized for the purpose of upholding both White supremacy and capitalism. Finally, it will succinctly consult the spheres of American labor, politics, and entertainment in which women's images, and the manipulation and exploitation thereof, have obstructed them from securing full equality since the formation of the United States until now.

hooks's *Black Looks: Race and Representation* summarizes, "From slavery on, white supremacists have recognized that control over images is central to the maintenance of any system of racial domination" (hooks 1992: 7). Indeed, early America's constitutional structure and economic livelihood rested on racial domination, and history proves the entire system was framed by patriarchy. Thomas Jefferson, and similarly minded White men, inserted these constructs into their crafting of the Declaration of Independence, which states, "All men are created equal," but offers no consideration to women. According to historian Kenneth Hafertepe, Jefferson's "aesthetic theory was informed by his understanding of the human mind" (Hafertepe 2000: 216–231). In Jefferson's only book, *Notes on the State of Virginia*, written in 1781, he broadcast his thoughts on "the circumstance of superior beauty" (Jefferson 1787). He identified color as a primary factor in distinguishing value between the races. He designated Europeans' "flowing hair and more elegant symmetry of form" as reasoning for what he believed was Africans' "own judgment in favor of the whites, declared by their preference of them." Jefferson stretched his beauty hypothesis further, stating that there existed a "preference of the orangutan for the Black women over those of his own species" (Jefferson 1787). Although it is a ludicrous assertion meant to equate African women with animals, acceptance of the image itself was critical in enforcing and standardizing breeding norms at the expense of Black women for the purpose of driving the nation's principal moneymaker: slavery. Even those founding fathers such as John Adams, who avoided direct ownership of Africans, led efforts normalizing these ideas. In 1765, Adams had written that God had never intended the American colonies "for Negroes . . . and therefore never intended us for slaves" (Hine et al. 2007: 7). The textbook *African American Odyssey* contends, "Jefferson, Adams, and other Patriot leaders were so convinced that Black people could not claim the same rights as white people, they felt no need to qualify their words proclaiming universal liberty" (Hine et al. 2007: 73). Jefferson commented, "I advance it therefore as a suspicion only, that the blacks, whether originally a distinct race, or made distinct by time and circumstances, are inferior to the whites in the endowments both of body and mind" (Jefferson 1787). His inclusion of the "body" is of sobering importance as a marker

12

for establishing White superiority, since the "mind" in many circumstances might prove more difficult to substantiate as a European advantage. Here, the body operates as an easily readable visual aid to hierarchal ideology.

The most impolite deliberations on beauty and ugliness, such as those in Jefferson's *Notes* that likened some women to monkey species, stress the female gender, which literally leaves *men free*. While assigning African women to the lowest end of ugliness and White women to the highest end of beauty, White men altogether escaped serious unwarranted societal ridicule and constant critique, and instead experienced the privilege of upward mobility without those handicaps. As for White women in both colonial and antebellum America, they found themselves confined by men's manufacturing and regulation of their image too. Men regularly projected both their idealistic aesthetic, sexual, and behavioral expectations for women into public discourse. In 1789, a male essayist proclaimed modesty "adds charms to their beauty and gives a new softness to their sex" (Norton 1980: 112). Another postulated, "When a woman loses her native modesty . . . she loses all her charms, she loses all her virtue, and is undone forever" (Norton 1980: 112). Such severe cautions burdened women to chase perfection lest they be otherwise banished from societal acceptance, and media influencers of the period worked to engrain these messages. In 1790, an author writing in the *Massachusetts Magazine* warned that the "minutest speck" upon the surface of a woman "will obscure almost all its luster." Such unfortunate specks, as laid out by scholar Mary Beth Norton in *Liberty's Daughters* (1980), included an "ungraceful walk, a careless choice of clothing, a slovenly hairdo, an injudicious conversation, and even an elevated tone of the voice" (Norton 1980: 112). Women were made to literally quiet and cover and adorn themselves according to the requirements of men. Otherwise, in a society that forced their financial dependency, they might risk the protection and provision they received in exchange.

Within the context of slavery, White women suffered at the hands of sexism, but rather than align themselves with subjugated Black women, they, so constricted by images and ideals, functioned as agents of White male domination. Professor Thaviola Glymph skillfully details the contentious relationship between the two women groups in *Out of the House of Bondage* (2008). She removes "the elegance of manners" often ascribed to White women and posits them as wielders of "the power of slave ownership." While husbands, brothers, and sons were often away from plantations conducting human sales and negotiations business and related endeavors, White women "owned slaves and managed households in which they held the power of life and death" (Glymph 2008: 4). Author Jacqueline Jones notes, "White women devised barbaric forms of punishment that resulted in the mutilation or permanent scarring of female slaves" (Jones 1985: 23). Glymph describes them as "so handicapped by patriarchy and paternalism that their lives more closely resembled those of enslaved women" (2008: 2) than their White male counterparts. Yet, they too depended on the slave society and therefore perpetuated it. They enjoyed the monetary profits as well as the elevated image that the degradation of African women afforded. Thus, many participated in the whippings and general dehumanization process. Given the common reoccurrence of such violent episodes, how then could White women live out the daintiness of disposition patriarchy demanded of them? Fascinatingly, images require little to no attachment to reality; hence image-makers can simply imagine and invent them.

After slavery, White men ensured their highly crafted woman's image remained intact by hooking it into the larger American imagination through film. This way, whether or not White women actually stepped outside of boundaries of restrictive ideals was less of a concern. Even when they did, as was the case when they brutalized Black women and children, they were pressured to step back into and remain inside idealistic lines (or at least pretend to) because prevailing beliefs about who they were and who they should be were now re-inscribed, in many ways, heightened, and certainly, intertwined with notions of natural American identity. This was the power of movies. The 1915 transformative film *Birth of a Nation* exposed the South's resolve to resuscitate itself from the tremendous loss of the Civil War, interpreted by Southern men as an assault on their collective identity and the future of the country. It imagined their worst fears of reckless African Americans assuming political power and soiling pure White women, but also responded to these fears by portraying themselves as sophisticated protectors and saviors.

Both *Birth of a Nation* and *The Clansman*, the book which inspired the movie, were produced by men. Here again, they publically directed women's images in order to solidify their own. *Birth of a Nation*, a national sensation, pictured White women as well dressed and privileged, but soft and endangered. Once more, as a symbol of America itself, their safety and wholeness lay in the strength of men, especially those willing to suppress African Americans and other ethnic groups in the name of patriotism. Other women, such as Latinas and Native Americans, were either ignored or reduced to sexualized varieties of general stereotypes of their race. Writers in the *Oxford Journal*, in an article titled "Colonialism, Racism and Representation," conceded, "Mexicans were reduced to greasers in films like *Tony the Greaser*" (Stam 2017). The article continued, hundreds of Hollywood westerns made "Native Americans appear to be intruders on what was originally their land, and provided a paradigmatic perspective through which to view the whole of the non-white world" (Stam 2017).

Perhaps the weight of these kinds of images would be less relevant if they reached only a few people. However, these images became dangerously normal after permeating the population. In an issue of *American Quarterly*, historian Everett Carter called the imprint of *Birth of a Nation* "enormous." In addition to Woodrow Wilson hosting a screening, making it the first film ever presented at the White House, "by January 1916 it had given 6,266 performances in the area of greater New York alone" (Carter 1960: 347). A conservative estimate of five hundred persons at each performance would support an "astounding total of over three million residents of and visitors to New York who saw the picture, and forever viewed themselves and their country's history through its colorations" (Carter 1960: 347). Millions also consumed the very similar feminine trope in 1933's *King Kong*. Although women earned the right to vote thirteen years earlier, they remained disenfranchised in American deed and thought. The Ann Darrow character of *King Kong* is penniless and vulnerable. She is also thin and blonde, which producers intended as a contrast to the dark and threatening giant gorilla who sought to capture her. A handsome White man, unsurprisingly, rescues her from the monstrous animal's grasp at the Empire State Building, emblematic of American world dominance. Symbolically, the ability for White men to secure global victory, then, depended on weakened ideas and images of women and national acceptance thereof.

The 1939 blockbuster *Gone with the Wind* departed only slightly from its predecessors, presenting a faintly more complex version of White women. Perhaps its origins as a book written by a woman afforded the complexity. Although black-haired and exuding a spicier countenance, Scarlett O'Hara, *Gone with the Wind's* main protagonist, boasts a small waist and draws the attention of men mesmerized by her beauty much like the other formulaic women in film. Predictably, she enjoys the plantation wealth of her Southern family and exudes all the charms and Victorian manners the men of colonial America called for a century earlier. In keeping with the pattern, Scarlett finds herself in a financial conundrum when her father (a White man) becomes ill and the Civil War (resulting in freed African Americans) disrupts their aristocratic lifestyle. Once she realizes dependency on her father is no longer an option, she turns for security to Rhett Butler, a younger, stylish, handsome White man with wealth. However, by the movie's end, Rhett leaves and Scarlett is left alone and without stability. It shamelessly suggests that national unrest, expressed by Scarlett's frantic behavior, is imminent without the leadership of fine White men. Movies seared these fragile and underdeveloped caricatures of women deeply into the American psyche by employing them repeatedly and disseminating them widely on screen. The pale, frail, and frightened beauty symbols appeared so frequently, audiences eventually named those acting in horror films "scream queens." Furthermore, since several of the most influential movies were anchored in historical events, viewers often read the stories and the stereotypes within as factual.

Interestingly, stereotypes, although distinct from fact, require updating to meet the needs of history's reality. World War II evidenced this, particularly in the area of labor. Considering World War II was a total war, compelling the entire American population to contribute to the effort, the United States government actively encouraged women to work in factories and perform necessary production and assembly-line jobs while men engaged in combat overseas. The global war, which penetrated every aspect of society, thus necessitated a new image of women. The Office of War Information (OWI) and the magazine industry collaborated to launch massive propaganda campaigns to address labor shortages in multiple industries. Maureen Honey illuminated the frenzied state and America's prescription for it in *Creating Rosie the Riveter.* "Through psychological manipulation and emotional appeals, propaganda could perhaps accomplish what registration and enrollment drives were failing to do: make more orderly the relationship between labor supply and demand" (Honey 1984: 29). President Franklin Roosevelt implemented the OWI to specifically influence press and advertising. Posters and ads communicated that the women who had earlier been conscribed to domesticity should now demonstrate empathy for men at war by seeking industrial employment outside of the home. In 1942, the Westinghouse Company's War Production Coordinating Committee hired illustrator J. Howard Miller to produce a poster series, out of which came the iconic "We Can Do It" image. Later called "Rosie the Riveter," the poster posited the upper body of a straight-faced woman with her hair tied and apparently ready to work. Accented by bold hues of red, white, and blue, she is rolling her shirtsleeve back to expose a flexed and exaggerated muscle while her eyes pierce straight forward. Although the total war depended on the contributions of African American, Latino, Asian, and other women workers, the period's many "Rosie the Riveter" interpretations always featured fit White women.

Revealingly, World War II's pro-work messages nudged women to seek this shift only temporarily, as a sacrifice only to later return to the ideal American life and their role in it. A Monsanto ad proclaimed, "There'll come a day . . . when a lot of the good new things of peacetime will become important to Rosie the Housewife" (Honey 1984: 123). Likewise, the Thermos Bottle company showed a war worker with its product pouring coffee for herself at a factory in one picture and serving coffee to her husband and friends in another as she muses: "This is what I'm working for—the carefree home parties we used to have" (Honey 1984: 123). In both, the woman is in servitude, albeit voluntary and seemingly content, to her country and her husband, often one and the same in the American media. According to the *Encyclopedia of American Economic History* (2017), "Rosie the Riveter" stimulated an increase of working American women to 20 million by 1944, a 57 percent increase from just three years prior.

War industries represented one of several that manipulated and then monetized women's images. Unfortunately, the progression of time failed to stall this national trend and automatically generate job access and equality for women. In *Jet Sex: Airline Stewardesses and the Making of an American Icon* (2013), scholar Victoria Vantoch argues, "Beauty, an aspect of femininity, was a critical qualification for stewardess work." In the 1950s and '60s, not only did strict airline requirements concerning age, weight, hair, and charm hamper how women employees were viewed and treated, they also prevented women who fell outside of narrow beauty ideals from securing work in the air carrier business. This included both White women considered unattractive and non- White women in general. Vantoch states that while airline hiring practices appeared race-neutral when they called for "wholesome" and "virginal" applicants, the implied meanings were implicitly White since African Americans were read as "sexually promiscuous in mainstream American culture" (Vantoch 2013: 73). Hiring managers repeatedly interpreted Black physical features as supporting evidence of the sexualized stereotypes; for example, Northwest Airlines once rejected an African American applicant because "her bust measurements appeared to be abnormally large" (Vantoch 2013: 73).

These discriminatory practices led African American women to file suit against the companies. The court cases called into evidence all manner of bodily examinations, even including ankle measurements. When Black women and their lawyers successfully proved that they in fact met the airlines' physical beauty standards, hiring supervisors would often call "femininity" into question instead. In one particular case, Northwest representatives claimed they rejected Marlene White, not because she was African American, but because she was "ill-groomed, had an arrogant attitude, and lacked the personality for stewardess work." Officials also described her as, "aggressive, argumentative, and masculine." In response to White's discrimination claim, Northwest stated the complaint itself was "evidence of an antagonistic attitude" (Vantoch 2013: 73). Once more, women, as defined by American standards, were to be inaudible. In not conforming, one lost her claim to her born identity.

Effectively banned from the airline services industry, African American women also found themselves wanting for work in the same Hollywood that maintained narrow entryways and character possibilities even for White women. Certainly, neither group had yet accessed the ranks as any more than on-screen talent. Writers, producers, and studio authorities were men. As White women struggled to break free from one-dimensional "damsel" roles, African Americans had been traditionally barred completely from performance, except in silent buffoon or servitude roles. Studios passed over Black actresses even when the script called for someone of color. Producers for 1951's *Show Boat* selected Ava Gardner over *café-au-lait*-hued Black starlet Lena Horne, who embodied "Black femininity," according to women's performance studies authority Kirsten Pullen (Pullen 2014: 74). In the relatively few instances in which African American women professionals in entertainment secured Hollywood contracts, they usually played domestic servants and regretfully accepted lower pay rates compared to other supporting cast members. Walter White, Chief Secretary for the National Association for the Advancement of Colored People, and Lena Horne collaborated to successfully secure an unusual MGM contract, which stipulated

17

her exemption from maid-type or demeaning roles. White hoped the breakthrough deal with Horne, specifically, would transform opportunities for Blacks in Hollywood (Janken 2003).

Surely, the challenges women faced in labor and entertainment reflected the nation's political landscape, and surely again, the nation's political landscape reflected its institution of inequality. Even a cursory comparison of Franklin D. Roosevelt and his wife Eleanor evidences the imbalance of opportunity. President Roosevelt, despite functioning with a physical handicap, and often immobile due to polio, enjoyed public adoration throughout four terms in the White House. Rather than scorn him or rule him incapable, office staff, health care assistants, and lovers worked to help him conceal his illness and fervently supported and respected his position as leader of the free world. Meanwhile, researcher Eric Burns reveals Eleanor maintained a lifelong insecurity about her looks. As a result of vocal ridicule from adults, she grew up "convinced she was physically ugly . . . with a mouth full of teeth so prominent that they gave a look of weakness to her chin" (Burns 2017). Even as an adult and First Lady of the United States, she often cracked self-deprecating jokes and recalled, "I knew I was the first girl in my mother's family who was not a belle, and though I never acknowledged it [to any potential suitors] at the time, I was deeply ashamed" (Burns 2017). Undoubtedly, a woman could not be president, and a woman considered unattractive was undeserving of much.

It is likely that this situation contributed to her overlooking her husband's liaisons with other women, as much as possible. Instead, she deeply embedded herself in international reform and civil rights causes. She was central to the establishment of the National Youth Administration and became the first US delegate to the United Nations, as well as chairing the committee which drafted the Universal Declaration on Human Rights. Her contributions, including critical support for the Tuskegee Airmen program in World War II, are innumerable. She befriended African American women's activist, college founder, and political strategist Mary McLeod Bethune and enthusiastically supported her work. Bethune, like Roosevelt, was considered uncomely and experienced an unsuccessful marriage. Robustly built with ebony skin and kinky hair, Bethune fit neither the Hollywood standard for starlets, nor the airline prerequisite for stewardesses. According to Bethune scholar Ida Jones in *Mary McLeod Bethune in DC*, Bethune, like her comrade Eleanor Roosevelt, found liberation in social uplift, the education of others and serving as a voice for her own people (Jones 2013). In fact, Bethune advised four US presidents, including Franklin Roosevelt, and used her platform to advocate for African American causes. Given both women's breadth of accomplishments, in another time, and perhaps in another universe where beauty is irrelevant, they would have experienced widespread public adoration for their work and become presidents themselves, as opposed to wives and advisors to men.

Eight years after Bethune's death, President John F. Kennedy signed the Equal Pay Act of 1963. Women, despite America's imagination of them, were a major workforce demographic, but *because* of America's imagination of them as subordinate, collected substantially less pay. As a consequence of decades of pressure from groups such as Bethune's National Council of Negro Women and others, the president legislated correction of the 60 percent women received as compared to the wages of men. In the same year, Betty Friedan published her seminal work, *The Feminine Mystique* (1963), which challenged the housewife image created by both the education system and advertising industry, Kennedy announced the following:

I am delighted today to approve the Equal Pay Act of 1963, which prohibits arbitrary discrimination against women in the payment of wages. This Act represents many years of effort by labor, management, and several private organizations unassociated with labor or management, to call attention to the unconscionable practice of paying female employees less wages than male employees for the same job. This measure adds to our laws another structure basic to democracy. It will add protection at the working place to the women, the same rights at the working place in a sense that they have enjoyed at the polling place.

(Kennedy 1963)

The foundational work of women like Eleanor Roosevelt and Mary McLeod Bethune precipitated the continued ascension of women's voices in the political sphere during the last quarter of the 20th century. African American voting rights activist Fannie Lou Hamer's voice shook the nation in 1964 when she told her story of terror upon attempting to register to vote in Mississippi. Her speech before the Democratic National Convention Credentials Committee led to her seat four years later as the first African American official delegate at a national-party convention since Reconstruction, and as the first woman delegate from Mississippi. New York African American Congresswoman Shirley Chisholm launched her presidential campaign in 1972 as the first Black person to run and the first woman to attempt to gain the Democratic Party's presidential nomination. Houston-born Barbara Jordan altered the course of history as the first African American elected to the Texas Senate since Reconstruction. In her powerful 1974 opening statement during the House Judiciary hearings on the Richard Nixon impeachment process, she reviewed women's progress toward equality in the political arena:

"We, the people." It's a very eloquent beginning [to the Constitution]. But when that document was completed on the seventeenth of September in 1787, I was not included in that

"We, the people." I felt somehow for many years that George Washington and Alexander Hamilton just left me out by mistake. But through the process of amendment, interpretation, and court decision, I have finally been included in "We, the people."

(Jordan 1974)

Still, even in proving themselves advantageous to the American democratic process, women paid dearly both when they did not mirror beauty ideals *and* when they did. None of the names mentioned above fit within the tightly established silhouette of feminine attractiveness. As history unravels, necessary questions rise: To what extent did their distance from the beauty ideal help them secure a space in government? Did constituents and public audiences take them more seriously because they were not perceived as traditionally soft and dependent? Is unattractiveness a political strength for women? Is beauty a disadvantage? Sara Palin, a self-professed "hockey mom" who wears lipstick, drew widespread criticism during her 2008 bid for the vice-presidency of the United States. As a candidate, she embraced skirts, heels, both flowing hairstyles and polished updos, and adopted a "country first" patriotic persona. She typified modern femininity, often bringing her children and husband onto her campaign stages and posing in loving photos with them. While criticism and opposition to her policy positions were expected and acceptable, political pundits and media influencers concentrated heavily and unnecessarily on her appearance. Opponents unrelentingly questioned her ability to hold office and be a mother. Meanwhile male politicians, many of whom were parents, never grappled with such skepticism. Disturbingly, a few years after her run, one comedian remarked that Palin was "good masturbation material" (McGlynn 2011). Was this her compensation for adhering to the national image for women?

If so, Hillary Clinton departed from it and espoused a different, less "feminine" approach to public life. In her husband's 1992 bid for the presidency, her vocal temperament and vigorous political career, separate from her husband's, further aggravated traditionalists already unnerved because of the era's culture wars. Moreover, she stirred existing controversy about her audacity when she quipped, "I suppose I could have stayed home, baked cookies and had teas" (Nicks 2015). According to *TIME* magazine, the assertion enraged conservative voters. One responded, "If I ever entertained the idea of voting for Bill Clinton, the smug bitchiness of his wife's comment has nipped that notion in the bud" (Nicks 2015). Was this her compensation for years of public service and developing a proud identity apart from the presidential candidate? Nevertheless, Bill Clinton still won both of his presidential campaigns. Without a doubt, advisees counseled Hillary Clinton to soften her image. More than a decade later, during a stop on her own presidential campaign, she briefly, sincerely, and openly wept about caring deeply for the country and the future of its children. Media headlines marked her as experiencing a "breakdown" and commentators called her "bewildered," suggesting she could not handle high-pressure politics. Both in 2008 and in 2016, she lost to different men, experiencing the highest point of her career as Secretary of State (2009–13), a position to which she was appointed by a man. Was this her compensation for being human, with emotion, who happened to be a woman?

Further inquiry and deeper studies on beauty and image will continue to emerge. Direct confrontation of new, more unique, and more complex challenges will also be required for women to dismantle inequality and chart self-determined identities in a global world. Can or should stereotypes of ethnic women be undone as television shows showcasing poor behavior of such groups reach international audiences? How can institutions like the Smithsonian, which prominently displays the dresses of first ladies and marginally discusses their work, be more responsible *and* appeal to the general public? How does sexy modeling in social media and pornography in the digital realm fit into conversations about technology, employment, and empowerment versus objectification? Is it possible to reconfigure Google search results for the term "beauty" to be more inclusive? Should women's groups of today like Mary McLeod Bethune's National Council of Negro Women advance their rich legacy by contesting the Federal Reserve's recent decision to "honor" Harriet Tubman featuring her image on one side of the twenty-dollar bill, while Andrew Jackson remains on the other? Do the two faces on either side of the bill evoke equality or reinforce notions of "secondary-ness" and servitude? In the Donald Trump era of anti-immigration, will foreign women living within US borders feel more pressure to physically alter themselves? Consider the growing double-eyelid operation trend targeted toward Asians. How will traditional Muslim women address their religious and gender identities tied to their hijabs? As transgender public figures such as Laverne Cox and Caitlyn Jenner gain notoriety, will notions of femininity change? Is there a need to revisit and expand feminist Naomi Wolf's concern for elective surgeries, with new consideration toward black-market buttock enhancements that have led to death? To what extent is the Black Lives Matter Movement and police aggression toward non- White bodies an issue of beauty? When a man, infamous for his recorded trivialization of physical vulgarity and lack of self-control around women ("grab 'em by the pussy," he said), ascends to the highest position in the world as President of the United States, where does that leave concepts of women's safety? How likely is a thoughtful reconsideration of rape culture and victim blaming? Furthermore, how will scholars make sense of the convoluted nature of the same man as a leader in women's image-making as a one-time owner of the Miss Universe corporation (which he later sold to another male business tycoon, Ari Emanuel)? Will White, African American, Latina, Asian, and other women engage in collective activism on the basis of common identity? These are problems the 21st century must answer. The intellectually strongest men must acknowledge their role and work alongside women to destroy image-based barriers and defy the status quo. All, as citizens desiring and moving toward true freedom, might consider the words of Mary McLeod Bethune as an incremental barometer for losses and gains until equality arrives: "A woman is free if she lives by her own standards and creates her own destiny, if she prizes her individuality and puts no boundaries on her hopes for tomorrow."

Discussion Questions

1 Is it possible to reconfigure Google search results for the term "beauty" to be more inclusive?
2 In the Donald Trump era of anti-immigration, will foreign women living within US borders feel more pressure to physically alter themselves? Consider the growing double-eyelid operation trend targeted toward Asians. How will traditional Muslim women address their religious and gender identities tied to their hijabs?
3 As transgender public figures such as Laverne Cox and Caitlyn Jenner gain notoriety, will notions of femininity change?
4 To what extent is the Black Lives Matter Movement and police aggression toward non- White bodies an issue of beauty?
5 How will the #MeToo Movement influence public and private projections of, performances of, and responses to beauty?

Suggested Readings

1 Wolf, Naomi. *The Beauty Myth: How Images of Women Are Used Against Women*. New York: Harper Collins, 1990.
2 hooks, bell. *Black Looks: Race and Representation*. Boston, MA: South End Press, 1992.
3 Norton, Mary Beth. *Liberty's Daughters: The Revolutionary Experience of American Women, 1750–1800*. Boston, MA: Little Brown, 1980.
4 Glymph, Thavolia. *Out of the House of Bondage: The Transformation of the Plantation Household*. Cambridge: Cambridge University Press, 2008.
5 Honey, Maureen. *Creating Rosie the Riveter: Class, Gender and Propaganda in World War II*. Amherst, MA: University of Massachusetts, 1984.

References

Burns, Eric. "Introduction." In *Someone to Watch Over Me: A Portrait of Eleanor Roosevelt and the Tortured Father Who Shaped Her Life*. Pegasus Books, 2017.
Carter, Everett. "Cultural History Written with Lightening: The Significance of Birth of a Nation." *American Quarterly* 12, no. 3 (1960): 347–357.

Friedan, Betty. *The Feminine Mystique*. New York: Norton, 1963.

Glymph, Thavolia. *Out of the House of Bondage: The Transformation of the Plantation Household*. Cambridge: Cambridge University Press, 2008.

Hafertepe, Kenneth. "An Inquiry into Thomas Jefferson's Ideas of Beauty." *Journal of the Society of Architectural Historians* 59, no. 2 (June 2000): 216–231.

Hine, Darlene Clark, William C. Hine, and Stanley Harrold. *The African-American Odyssey: Combined Volume*. Upper Saddle River, NJ: Pearson Prentice Hall, 2007.

Honey, Maureen. *Creating Rosie the Riveter: Class, Gender and Propaganda in World War II*. Amherst, MA: University of Massachusetts, 1984.

hooks, bell. *Black Looks: Race and Representation*. Boston, MA: South End Press, 1992.

Janken, Kenneth R. *Walter White: Mr. NAACP*. Chapel Hill, NC: University of North Carolina Press, 2003.

Jefferson, Thomas. *Notes on the State of Virginia*. London: John Stockdale, 1787.

Jones, Ida E. *Mary McLeod Bethune in Washington, D.C.: Activism and Education in Logan Circle*. Charleston, SC: The History Press, 2013.

Jones, Jacqueline. *Labor of Love, Labor of Sorrow: Black Women, Work, and the Family from Slavery to the Present*. New York: Basic Books, 1985.

Jordan, Barbara. "Statement on the Articles of Impeachment." *AmericanRhetoric.com* Accessed May 1, 2017, www.americanrhetoric.com/speeches/barbarajordanjudiciary statement.htm

Kennedy, John F. *The Public Papers of the Presidents of the United States*. Washington, DC: White House, 1963.

McGlynn, Katla. "Tracy Morgan: Sarah Palin is Good Masturbation Material." *Huffington Post*, January 28, 2011.

Nicks, Denver. "This Was the Hillary Clinton Comment that Sparked Leah Dunham's Political Awareness." *TIME*, September 29, 2015.

Norton, Mary Beth. *Liberty's Daughters: The Revolutionary Experience of American Women, 1750–1800*. Boston, MA: Little Brown, 1980.

Pullen, Kirsten. *Like a Natural Woman: Spectacular Female Performance in Classical Hollywood*. Brunswick, NJ: Rutgers University Press, 2014.

"Rosie the Riveter." *Gale Encyclopedia of U.S. Economic History*. Encyclopedi.com. Accessed May 1, 2017, www.encyclopedia.com/history/encyclopedias-almanacs-transcripts-and-maps/rosie-riveter-0

Stam, Robert. "Colonialism, Racism and Representation." Academia.edu. Accessed April 2017, www.academia.edu/12180023/Colonialism_Racism_and_Representation

Trescott, Jaqueline. "What bell hooks Had to Say About the State of Feminism in 1999." *Washington Post*, February 9, 1999.

Vantoch, Victoria. *The Jet Sex: Airline Stewardesses and the Making of an American Icon*. Philadelphia, PA: University of Pennsylvania Press, 2013.

Wolf, Naomi. *The Beauty Myth: How Images of Women Are Used Against Women*. New York: Harper Collins, 1990.

2

PROPTER DEFECTUM SEXUS

Male Privilege over a Woman's Body

Omar Swartz and Candace Nunag Tardío

> *The physical handicap which nature places upon women cannot be removed even by constitutional amendment, and the laws and customs of civilization recognize this handicap and seek to protect women from dangers and hardships that may result from it. The kind of legislation that assists in this beneficent purposes rests upon the difference between woman and men, and a system of law which refused to recognize this difference would be cruel to women. There are various forms of protection that women need and that men do not need*
> (Lukens 1925: 646)

This opening quotation by attorney Edward C. Lukens in 1925 argues against extending the suffrage to woman, illustrating attitude toward women in law, medicine, and custom in Anglo-American history until the early 1970s. Following the religious biases of the time, women were defined as weak, juvenile, and unpredictable, and thus subject to patriarchal control for their own good and for the good of the species. They had to be carefully watched and managed by men who frequently exerted an ownership right over their wives and daughters, for example, as stated by an English court in a 1685 homicide case, the recognition that "adultery is the highest invasion of property." A man, consequently who kills the lover of his wife "cannot receive a higher provocation" and was thus immune from criminal prosecution.[1]

Before discussing the long and fraught history of male legal privilege over a woman's body, it behooves us to take a closer look into the cultural beliefs of our *current* times pertaining to feminism and women's issues. As mentioned before, the medical, juridical, and customary paradigm that has informed the status and attitude toward women has changed a great deal since the feminist movements of the 1960s and '70s. The successes of these feminisms have, however, lent themselves to a relatively new ideology that juxtaposes itself with women's movements: "postfeminism."

Postfeminism is described as a process, an ideology, a backlash, or a sentiment that points to a clear and definitive "end" of feminism. We are using the term "postfeminism" to describe a widespread cultural belief that the goals of the feminist project or movement have been met, thus rendering feminism redundant in the present. Though postfeminist is not an identity category, we can understand postfeminists as having taken "the achievements of earlier feminists for granted" in the sense that they believe that women and men have achieved "equality" (Gray and Boddy 2010). The vague notion of "equality of the sexes" underpins much of postfeminist thought, while at the same time lends itself to an ideology that privileges individualism, agency, and personal choice.

Ostensibly, postfeminism signals an end for feminist activism (since the difference and divide between men and women seems to have closed, so why keep fighting?). Why not turn to individual people for explanations of injustice? Perhaps in a time of equality, these questions would be legitimate. Alas, the fact of the matter is, contrary to postfeminist belief that the sexes are equal in the eyes of the Constitution, men and women are both *different* and *unequal*. As it turns out, and as we will discuss in this chapter, the equality that postfeminists take for granted has *never* existed.

Constitutionally, historically, philosophically, socially, economically, and biologically, women have never been the same as or equal to men. Though the idea that we live in a country and world that no longer needs feminism sounds tempting, the reality is that the long history of women's subordination to men cannot be brought to justice or erased in only a few decades' time. Furthermore, male superordination over women in the United States, and the West more broadly, has been fortified, legitimized, and substantiated in our laws and practices, and has yet to be changed.

While the legal and social status of women has changed for the better since the 1970s, many of the sentiments that can be found during this period still exist through significant segments of the American population. Most telling on this point is that, with the *defeat* of the Equal Rights Amendment (ERA) in 1982, the rights, liberties, and protections granted women after many decades of struggle receive something less than full constitutional protection. To this day, women and men are treated differently in the eyes of the Constitution, and this condition exists largely because most Americans still believe that women and men are, in fact, *different*.

Gains in the civil and human rights of women in the United States, while real and important, still have not gone far enough, and can be reversed, particularly in regards to *reproductive* freedom. Here, we define reproductive freedom in two ways. The first being a freedom of women's bodily integrity, or the idea that individual women must be in control of their bodies and procreative capacities. In other words, women are capable and responsible for bodily self-determination. The second way that we define reproductive freedom is in observance of the social construction of gender and the implicit gendered division of labor embedded within that social construction and hierarchy. Reproductive freedom is accordingly defined by women's roles as mothers and caretakers; seeing as how women are relegated to these specific laborings, they alone should be able to make decisions pertaining to birth control, abortion, and raising children (Petchesky 1980). These two ideas of reproductive freedom culminate to illustrate a larger point, particularly in regard to American juridical practice: without full reproductive freedom, women cannot achieve equality with men.

The most controversial aspect of women's reproductive freedom in the United States is women's right to have an abortion without the risk of being criminalized or so regulated that the right becomes, in practice, unattainable. With the aforementioned definitions of reproductive freedom in mind, the right to procure an abortion is an essential constituent of women's bodily self-determination. On a larger scale, when abortion access is limited or cut off, everyone suffers, not just women.

We disagree with the court in *Bray v. Alexandria Women's Health Clinic* which argued that "the disfavoring of abortion . . . is not *ipso facto* sex discrimination."[2] Nothing can be further from the truth. To deny a woman authority over her own body is, *ipso facto* what, in common language, we mean by slavery. It is the contention of many people, including ourselves, that disfavoring abortion is sex discrimination in that it denies women autonomy as human beings. Men do not get pregnant, and thus there are no debates about their bodily autonomy, nor is there constant undermining of their reproductive self-determination. The fact that, nearly fifty years after the momentous *Roe v. Wade* decision, we are fighting for the basic human right to abortion, means that we are all vulnerable to having our liberties taken away.[3]

With the widespread proliferation of local- and state-level restrictions and the non-stop violence, vandalism, and arson to family planning healthcare facilities, it has become apparent that there are certain liberties that some Americans believe that we can do without. One of the covert ways in which the right to have an abortion is being skirted is with the widespread proposals for "fetal personhood." Fetal personhood is a branch of anti-choice rhetoric that takes the focus away from women's reproductive freedom and, instead, posits that unborn fetuses are "people" who should be endowed with the rights, privileges, and dignity of human beings. In the state of Colorado alone, there have been three different personhood amendments on the ballot in the last seven years. Though the rhetoric of dignity and humanity is tempting, it is in many ways insidious and deceptive. Implicit in personhood rhetoric is that women are criminals (murderers, specifically), along with the doctors who provide their care if they terminate a pregnancy. The personhood movement is just one of the many ways that women's reproductive freedom is not only impinged upon, but belittled and effaced. What is pertinent about these amendments is that they directly affect women's reproductive freedom and serve as a greater reminder that the clock can be turned back on reproductive freedom and equality for women. Moreover, the backlash to *Roe* can be recognized simply and distinctly as sex discrimination, albeit like the Hydra, with many separate and constantly sprouting heads.

Of course, there are other issues and interests in the debate over abortion, but that does not change the fact that equality for woman means freedom to make this choice, even if that choice is fraught with difficulty (see Luker 1984).[4] Women, like men, have to live with the consequences of their choice, be it positive or negative. However, the greater concern with abortion and reproductive freedom is not whether it is bad or good for women, or whether a fetus is a person or not, it is simply this: without the right and access to abortion without risk, women are undeniably slaves to their reproductive capacities, and society as a whole suffers for it.

Women in the United States have known for a long time how important bodily autonomy is, and accordingly, developed the Equal Rights Amendment (ERA) in an attempt to secure its namesake for women. The ERA had three brief sections, the pertinent one being: "Equality of rights under the law shall not be denied or abridged by the United States or by any State on account of sex." At first glance, such language seems unremarkable. How could this in any way be controversial; every schoolchild learns that *all* Americans are entitled to equal protection of the law. Few ideas in the American pantheon of virtues is more fundamental than this. How could this be something *rejected* in 1982? How can this be something that is still not part of the Constitution today? All things considered, this is a significant oversight, and yet people do not realize it; and if they do realize it, they do not see it as a problem.

The first question is easy to answer. The ERA had been proposed more than 70 years earlier because, in fact, women and men were treated differently in the eyes of the law, with women being legally, socially, and economically subordinated to men. To be a woman was to live with significant legal disabilities. It took 70 years and hard work for the political mood of the different states and the federal government to become agreeable to change. Change only came as the result of the difficult process of trying to ratify the amendment, and they failed. All the while, women kept fighting for civil rights on other fronts and, as a result, most of those legal disabilities, particularly the harshest ones, have been abolished by legislative action. A good example of this are the various Married Women's Property Rights Acts passed by the states during the nineteenth century. Although uneven, these Acts were intended to grant the control of certain property to women who were otherwise losing it to their husbands (see Chused 1985).[5] In more modern times, legal disabilities for women have been abolished through judicial intervention, starting with *Reed v. Reed* in 1971 where the Court for the first time applied the equal protection clause of the Constitution to discrimination based on gender, holding that the administrators of estates cannot be named in a way that discriminates between the sexes.[6]

While positive movement at the levels of the legislatures and the courts are welcome developments, they are *not* the same thing as full legal equality, and men and women *to this day* are *not* similarly situated in the eyes of the law as well as in much social practice. This is wrong, even outrageous. Without the ERA protections for women, they rely on the goodwill of the legislature and the courts to construct and interpret statutes that recognize and enforce equality for women. Thankfully, such goodwill has existed in the last couple of decades. They are grounded in the liberal trends that swept across this nation in the 1960s and 1970s that have, alas, long since dissipated:

> But to a degree that has been insufficiently appreciated and is in some ways barely believable, the contemporary federal courts are fundamentally different from the federal courts of just two decades ago. What was then the center is now the left. What was then the far right is now the center. What was then on the left no longer exists.
>
> (Sunstein 2005: 10)

Clearly, there is no reason to believe that, unattended, any goodwill will continue in future generations on these issues. The backlash against such liberalization has been severe and successful on many levels. Many politicians and judges today are poised to turn back the clock on much social progress and may only be an election or two away from succeeding.

The second question is harder to answer: Why does this situation continue to exist? These rights that we have depend upon what women and men themselves *do*. If more women acted as if they were entitled to greater freedom, and if more men acted similarly toward the freedom and autonomy of women, the more freedom would be in fact created and the less need for the law to compensate. But because people are often compliant with the status quo, and because the status quo benefits influential stakeholders, we often need to change the law, constricting discriminatory behavior—with the hope that attitudes will change over time. Often, they do change and, years later, we wonder why the laws were necessary in the first place. Without civil rights legislation to point the way forward morally, prejudicial attitudes tend to harden. Regardless, freedom is not a *status*; it is an *action*, so no matter what the law says, it remains up to us to enact the freedom by which we experience our lives.

However, herein lies one of the most difficult issues of gender equality and the law: social sentiments about the difference between men and women are so deeply entrenched from centuries of practice and unquestioned belief, that men and women, for all intents and purposes, *are* different. Attitudes about men and women's difference are not only hardened, they are seemingly wrought into stone, and many other paradigms agree with this difference. The medical, scientific, and religious ideologies which inform large swaths of society agree with the juridical ideology that men and women are somehow different. But, perhaps, the issue of difference is a red herring; difference really is not a bad thing on its own. The problem with difference, particularly *essential* difference as postulated by patriarchy, is that it inevitably leads to a hierarchy, and in this case, gender discrimination.

Central to the subordination of women—legal or not, was the doctrine of *propter defectum sexus* ("on account of defect of sex"). In a nation founded on liberty of the individual and on the "inalienable rights of man," women were defined as *defective men* and, therefore, excluded from just about anywhere in the public sphere and controlled by men at home. While it would be incorrect to write that this is the dominant view today in the United States, it is a view grounded in the belief in *difference* and in the imagined significance of that difference, and that difference remains as salient today as it did when this nation was founded. Simply, the law, following much in our religious heritage, treated women as not being men and, thus, a dual series of expectations became codified that cut on strict gender lines, that are largely arbitrary, capricious, and cause much avoidable harm. More specifically, as individuals today, we need to be aware of this history because, in some sense, it is not merely history. Our present is rooted, directly, in this past. By looking at the past, we can see the ways in which it differs from the present and thus we benefit from a nearly unlimited amount of perspectives, across all of human experience, that we can draw upon to displace the normative assumptions we make about the present. In the following section, we address the historical limitations placed on women, by focusing on the doctrine of coverture, which placed women under the control of a man for their "protection."

Woman, Under the Cover (and in the Bed) of a Man: Historical Limitations Placed on Women

The legal doctrine of coverture is encapsulated by the Latin phrase *propter defectum sexus.* Upon marriage, a woman's legal rights were subsumed by those of her husband. She was, in effect, a "covered woman" (often a "smothered" women). As such, she was not recognized as existing independently of her husband—a woman's existence was incorporated into that of her husband's, who then had authority over her. The wife and husband were one person, and that person was the husband (this is also known as the Doctrine of Marital Unity). As the influential English jurist William Blackstone explained:

> By marriage, the husband and wife are one person in law: that is, the very being or legal existence of the woman is suspended during the marriage, or at least is incorporated and consolidated into that of the husband: under whose wing, protection, and cover, she performs every thing; and is therefore called in our law-French a *femme-covert;* is said to be *covert-baron,* or under the protection and influence of her husband, her baron, or lord; and her condition

during her marriage is called her *coverture*. Upon this principle, of a union of person in husband and wife, depend almost all the legal rights, duties, and disabilities that either of them acquire by the marriage.

(Blackstone 1765: 442; in Mansfield 1845)

As a citizen, as a person, a woman was legally inconsequential. For instance, women were prohibited (or strongly discouraged) from, among other things, voting, owning or inheriting property (their goods were transferred to her husband), keeping their own wages, serving on juries,[7] going to college, and practicing most professions. Married women did not have equal rights to manage community property,[8] had to assume her husband's last name,[9] and live where the husband decided to live.[10] For a time, when an American woman married a foreigner, she would automatically lose her U.S. citizenship. For instance, in *Mackenzie v. Hare*, the Supreme Court upheld Congress's power to expatriate under the Citizen Act of 1907. As a result of this decision, U.S.-born female citizens could lose their citizenship by a marriage to any non-citizen. If the husband was not eligible for nationalization, the wife lost her citizenship, even if she had been born a U.S. citizen. The Court argued that such "expatriation" was justified under a type of national security rationale:

We concur with counsel that citizenship is of tangible worth, and we sympathize with plaintiff in her desire to retain it and in her earnest assertion of it. But there is involved more than personal considerations. As we have seen, the legislation was urged by conditions of national moment. And this is an answer to the apprehension of counsel that our construction of the legislation will make every act, though lawful, as marriage, of course, is, a renunciation of citizenship. The marriage of an American woman with a foreigner has consequences of like kind, may involve national complications of like kind, as her physical expatriation may involve. Therefore, as long as the relation lasts, it is made tantamount to expatriation.[11]

The rights of husbands approached that of a sovereign and covered areas that today would be unthinkable. Wives were required to live in the home of the husband. Runaway wives could be charged with a crime, as well as people who harbored her. The husband had the ability to sue for money if another man slept with his wife (i.e., "criminal conversation," discussed below). If his wife ran off with his children, the husband had the power to compel the police to return the children (see McFarlane 2007).[12] Wives and children could be institutionalized in mental hospitals on the word of their husbands if he deemed them "incorrigible."[13] Up until relatively recently, women were treated as infantile and unable to exert agency of their lives, and in particular, their sexuality. For example, the infamous Mann Act, passed in

1910, exemplifies the notion that women have to be protected from sexual activity. The Act assumes that women are naturally chaste and virtuous and cannot become a "whore" unless she has been raped, seduced, drugged, or deserted. Similarly, statutory rape laws were intended, and enforced, against men to "protect" the virginity of women. Their purpose has been to protect the virginity (i.e., property) of women from being taken advantage of by "bad" men. A woman had to be protected from losing her virginity to a man who would not marry her. The assumption here is that young women made poor judgment, and could not be responsible for the most precious property they owned: virginity. Here, it is important to note that women themselves were not protected; rather, chastity, honor, and virginity were protected. Non-virginal women were considered fair game for unwanted sexual advances, including rape, and men could defend against this charge by pointing to the fact that the victim was not a virgin. Even today, the vestiges of this harmful and paternalistic rhetoric remain in our cultural repertoire, as we frequently see victim blaming in rape and sexual assault trials, in which women are asked questions about their sexual proclivities, drinking habits, or even what they were wearing at the time of the attack.

We will now discuss two examples of women being treated as the property of men in practice and reinforced by the law. The first is the "Marital Rape" exception which prohibited the law from charging married men with the rape of their wives. The second is the doctrine of "Reasonable Chastisement" and its implications for contemporary domestic violence against women.

Marital Rape: It's Not Rape if You are Married to the Rapist (or if He Then Married You)

Women have been raped by their husbands for a long time, for as long as there has been marriage, except we usually do not call it "rape." In fact, the common-law definition of rape excluded this very situation, as the crime of rape was defined as a "male engaging in forcible sexual intercourse with a female not his wife, without her consent." Rather to call it rape, courts, and society more generally, referred to it as "conjugal duty," the responsibility of the wife to please her husband sexually and to produce a male offspring. Women are expected to have sex with their husbands, whether they want to or not.

Consider some of these high-profile remarks from distinguished elected and/or public leaders. Charles Burt, President of the Oregon State Bar, claimed in 1978 in response to the first nationally publicized marital rape trial that "a woman who is in marriage is presumably consenting to sex. Maybe this is the risk of being married, you know." "Any woman who claims she has been raped by her spouse has not been properly bedded" (Hines and Malley-Morrison 2005: 42).[14] Senator Bob Wilson (D-CA) asked in 1979 that "if you can't rape your wife, who can you rape?" (Waterman 1988: 611). Lest one suspects that this is merely the rationalization of men, we find a similar sentiment expressed by conservative icon and anti-ERA champion Phyllis Schlafly who declared that "by getting married, the woman has consented to sex, and I don't think you can call it rape" (Hananoki 2016).

As Schlafly suggests, rape is such an ugly term that we reserve it for something done as an *illegitimate* use of male power. It denotes unjustified access to and control over a woman's body. It is a way of conserving the sexuality of woman in the service of the state. Rape laws were ways for men to protect their interests and power over a particular woman. Rape, in this context, was harm done to another man's property (Brownmiller 1995).[15] As a weapon against women, rape is an act that transcends the individual because, due to its prevalence, it restricts the freedom of all women. As Andrea Dworkin notes:

All men benefit from rape, because all men benefit from the fact that women are not free in this society; that women cower; that women are afraid; that women cannot assert the rights that we have, limited as those rights are, because of the ubiquitous presence of rape.
(Dworkin 1993: 142)

At the common law, the concept "marital rape" (i.e., spousal rape and conjugal rape) was a legal impossibility. An early legal authority for this principle can be found in Sir Matthew Hale who wrote in 1736 that such a rape could not be recognized by the law. He reasoned that "the husband cannot be guilty of a rape committed by himself upon his lawful wife, for by their mutual matrimonial consent and contract the wife hath given up herself in this kind unto her husband which she cannot retract" (Hale 1847). Not only were women erased as individuals upon marriage, but the marriage bond was for all practical purposes indissoluble.

While, over time, statutes were passed to alleviate some of the worst burdens on women, the bar was set extremely high. Take, for example, the grounds of *intolerable cruelty* in the context of a fault-based divorce. Because patriarchal rights were a given, spousal rape was not considered "bodily harm" severe enough to constitute cruelty. In one well-known case, a wife sued her husband for divorce on the grounds that he had repeatedly raped her while she was in "delicate and feeble health." While she suffered physical harm because of this, the harm was deemed by the court as "unintentional." The husband in this case merely insisted on his "marital rights," that is, sexual intercourse with his wife. The trial court found that "the act was injurious to her health and endangered it," but the appellate court did not find that the husband knew that harm would be the consequence. "Are we to allow nothing to the frailty of human nature, excited by passion?" asked the court in explaining its ruling.[16] Cruelty as grounds for divorce had to be extreme and repeated: "Our divorce laws do not compel a separation of husband and wife, unless the conduct of husband be so cruel as to render the wife's condition intolerable." This could be defeated if the wife "provoked" the violence or condoned it by not leaving.[17]

Not only does the husband have a right to his wife's body regardless of her wishes, but the law recognized it as a property right against other men. This was called "criminal conversation," a euphemism for adultery but one in which the husband is permitted to sue the man who had sex with his wife without his permission for damages to the husband. As a court explains:

The foundation of the husband's right of action is the wrong done him by the defendant in violating his personal rights. The husband has the right to the conjugal fellowship of his wife, to her society, her aid, and her fidelity in every conjugal relation. Any act of another by which he is deprived of this right constitutes a personal wrong, for which the law gives him a redress in damages.

Moreover:

Her sexual intercourse with another is an invasion of his rights, and it is immaterial whether this invasion is accomplished by force or by the consent of the wife. As the right belongs to the husband, it is no defense to his action for redress that its violation was by the consent or procurement of the wife, for she is not competent to give such consent. And it is not necessary that the husband should show that it was by force or against her will. The wrong to the husband consists in the carnal intercourse with his wife by another, and it is immaterial whether this intercourse is accomplished by persuasion or by force. His right of action is established upon proof of the intercourse, and the means by which this intercourse was effected are but incidents to increase or mitigate his damages.[18]

In 1977, Oregon became the first state in the U.S. to reject the marital rape exception through legislative action. However, a year later, this law was tested when John Rideout was charged for the rape of his wife Greta Rideout. In the case, a circuit court judge declared that he would not rule out the common law in the case; he would consider the concept of "marital privilege" in the case. In other words, he would consider the precept of common law stating that when a woman marries a man, she gives sexual consent to her husband. While Greta's neighbors stated that John Rideout did beat his wife, they questioned Greta's motives for accusing John of rape. Ultimately, a jury of eight women and four men found John Rideout not guilty of rape.[19]

The Doctrine of Reasonable Chastisement

Because women were considered to be disabled and dependent, both emotionally and legally, husbands had great power over them, such as the power of "reasonable chastisement," a form of corporal punishment intended to discipline or control a dependent. Indeed, this is the same power that parents have over their children, or by extension the school standing in *parens patriae*, as sanctioned by the U.S. Supreme Court in *Ingraham vs. Wright*.[20]

According to William Blackstone, a husband "might give his wife moderate correction. For, as he is to answer for her misbehavior, the law thought it reasonable to entrust him with the power of restraining her, by domestic chastisement." Such reasoning is circular. Why does he have to answer for her? If she was her own person legally, her bodily integrity would be respected. After all, the power to prevent abortion is the power to chastise a woman for being out of control of some male authority. This plays out in other ways as well, dealing with "unruly women." For example, there was once something called the Muncy Act, a 1913 statute requiring courts to assign women (but not men) an indeterminate sentence if convicted of a crime punishable by more than one year. For example, Jane Daniel was convicted of robbery in 1966 and had her sentence enhanced significantly under the Muncy Act because she was a woman in need of additional reformation. A similarly situated male defendant would have had a sentence for at most half as long. When challenged, the court denied that this was an infringement of her rights, stating that the inherent physical and psychological differences between the sexes justified differential treatment (Armstrong 1977). Or consider the 1840 case of *Re Cochrane* in which a woman left her husband without cause and was forcefully returned by her husband and trapped in the house.[21] She asked the courts for help but the court concluded that "the husband hath by law power and dominion over his wife and may keep her by force within the bounds of duty, and may beat her, but not in a violent or cruel manner." The wife could regain her freedom, the court noted, if she wished, by cheerfully performing her part of the marriage contract.

In *State v. Black*, the North Carolina Supreme Court ruled that a husband cannot be convicted for physical abuse of his wife unless he inflicts permanent injury on her or uses excessive force or cruelty. The Court reasoned:

> A husband is responsible for the acts of his wife and he is required to govern his household, and for that purpose the law permits him to use towards his wife such a degree of force as is necessary to control an unruly temper and make her behave herself; and unless some permanent injury be inflicted, or there be an excess of violence, or such a degree of cruelty as shows that it is inflicted to gratify his own bad passions, the law will not invade the domestic forum, or go behind the curtain.[22]

To do so is to expose a harm that should be left secret; publically, "it can do no good" but merely widens the breach between the couple. The courts refuse to exert jurisdiction here "unless there is a permanent injury or excessive violence or cruelly indicating malignity and vindictiveness."

Additionally, provocation was a defense:

> if what is complained of as cruelty is the result of the complainant's own misconduct, it will not furnish ground for the proceeding. The remedy is in her own power; she has only to change her conduct; otherwise the wife would have nothing to do but misconduct herself, provoke the ill treatment and then complain.[23]

For example, in *Robbins v. State* the wife's provocation can be shown in mitigation of husband's fine for assault:

> if the husband was at the time . . . provoked to this unmanly act by the bad behavior and misconduct of his wife, he should not be visited with the same punishment as if he had without provocation wantonly and brutally injured one whom it has his duty to nourish and protect.[24]

Even so, other barriers to redress existed. Women could not sue or press charges against their husbands and they would be dependent upon the State to initiate such action. In *Self v. Self*, a California Supreme Court decision, the court explained that a spouse's right to sue would "destroy the peace and harmony of the house."[25] This refusal to take violence against women seriously can be seen, to some extent in recent years, in a string of cases— *State v. Norman, State v. Stewart, State v. Barry*, and *United States v. Morrison*, where the U.S. Supreme Court ruled that Congress overstepped its power by enacting a federal civil remedy for victims of gender-motivated violence (see Dressler 2006).

Without doubt, the most obnoxious privilege afforded a husband was the court's understanding that a man can turn murderous with rage upon the sight of catching his wife in the act of adultery. The existence of this rage, or perhaps the belief that such rage was "understandable" often resulted in, if not a complete exoneration for murder, at least justification for reducing the charge. For example, on October 17, 1994, the trial judge sentenced Sandra Peacock's killer, her husband, to 18 months in jail for the murder. The defendant had arrived home unexpectedly to find his wife in bed with another man. After grabbing a shotgun, the defendant drove away his wife's lover, and then shot her. Outrageously, the killer was allowed to plead guilty to voluntary manslaughter. In sentencing the defendant, the judge expressed sympathy for him; he could not imagine a situation that would "provoke an uncontrollable rage greater than this . . . for someone who is happily married to be betrayed in your personal life, when you're out working to support the spouse." He added, "I seriously wonder how many men married five, four years would have the strength to walk away without inflicting some corporal punishment" (Lewin 1994).

Conclusion: Beyond Postfeminism

Propter defectum sexus is not only a juridical trope, but is also indicative of a long-standing tradition in Western thought and culture suggesting that gender difference is undeniable and essential, as well as a justification for hierarchy, discrimination, violence, rape, and oppression. Through tracing the ideology of paternalism, misogyny, and essentialism, we can now behold the breadth and tremendous reach of gender discrimination against women. Moreover, we can better understand how difficult it is to dislodge sexism from the schema of our culture, as it has been so deeply embedded and reinforced by not only laws, but also the majority of Western philosophy.

This chapter aimed to reposition women's status as defective men in the eyes of the law with the postfeminist phenomenon. In no way are we discounting the social sentiment that the work of women's movements is no longer necessary; on the contrary, we celebrate the great strides that feminism has made, so much so that there has been a change in the lived experiences of both women and men that would prompt them to believe in postfeminism. However, as we demonstrated in this chapter, there is still so much work to be done in terms of achieving full legal equality for women. With the ERA's failure to ratify, coupled with new and insidious amendments aimed at destroying women's reproductive freedom, we seem to be perpetually making the same demands that feminists have been making for decades. It is in this sense that we maintain that, while there remains *any* threat to women's reproductive self-determination, there will always be a need for feminism. Thus, we deny the sentiment propagated by postfeminism as we assert that, while the laws and rights of women are different and unequal to men, feminism will remain an ongoing project.

Although the many examples of the harsh, obnoxious, or absurd limitations upon women in this chapter seem outlandish at best, we aim to highlight that these laws and practices are not a part of our distant past; rather, they are inextricably tethered to our present. Juridical and ideological changes in the last half-century make reasonable chastisement look archaic if not savage, but we encourage readers to keep in mind that the perpetuation of the belief of essential gender difference is rooted in these brutal practices. In other words, though legally sanctioned violence against women is no longer, the notion that women and men are *different* and, subsequently, *unequal* is the toxic part of this practice that has seeped into the present. Gender essentialism is part and parcel of the oppressed and sometimes violent realities of women, and moreover, it is the largest constituent part of paternalistic ideology that must be challenged and dismantled in order for women and men to become equals in the eyes of the law and the minds in our society.

Discussion Questions

1   What is the postfeminist movement? Why is this movement problematic?
2   According to the authors, why have people adopted postfeminism?
3   What is the doctrine of coverture?
4   Describe two historical limitations placed on women. Do these examples compare to modern-day discrimination women experience? Please explain.

Suggested Readings

1   Petchesky, Rosalind P. "Reproductive Freedom: Beyond 'A Woman's Right to Choose,'" *Signs* 5, no. 4 (1980): 661–685.
2   Gray, Mel and Boddy, Jennifer. "Making Sense of the Waves: Wipeout or Still Riding High?" *Affilia* 25, no. 4 (2010): 368–389.
3   Hines, Denise A. and Malley-Morrison, Kathleen. *Family Violence in the United States: Defining, Understanding, and Combating Abuse.* Thousand Oaks, CA: Sage, 2005.

Notes

1 See *Regina v. Mawgridge* in *The English Reports*, volume 84 (Edinburgh: William Green & Sons, 1908), 1107–1115.
2 See 506 U.S. 263 (1993).
3 Many women *have* already lost their right to reproductive freedom, as states are attacking it with what has been called "death by a thousand cuts." Hundreds of laws regulating reproductive health are being introduced and enacted, many which facially go against *Roe v. Wade* and its progeny, as states get ready for what they hope is the law's ultimate repeal at the hands of the U.S. Supreme Court.
4 We think the traditional argument that the two sides do not agree on the basic premises—is it a "baby" or a "fetus" is the wrong way to look at it. We are militantly pro-choice but we are willing to concede every point of the opposition. We are talking about babies, we are talking about life, and we are talking about killing. All that is important, yes, but it does not outweigh the interests of the mother. It is her choice alone.
5 Yet, as one court complained, the Married Woman's Property Act went too far: "towards clothing one class of females with strange and manly attributes." See *Norval v. Rice*, 2 Wis. 22, 31 (1853).
6 The *Reed* case concerned a legal presumption that privileged males over females for be named administrator of an estate.
7 See *Hoyt v. Florida*, 368 U.S. 57 (1961).
8 It was not until 1979 that Louisiana, under pressure from the Supreme Court, became the last state to treat spouses equally to manage community property. See *Kirchberg v. Feenstra*, 450 U.S. 455 (1981).
9 Women were required to assume her husband's name upon marriage. See *Whitlow v. Hodges*, 539 F.2d 582 (1976). In reviewing the common law, the *Chapman* court

wrote: "For several centuries, by the common law among all English speaking people, a woman, upon her marriage, takes her husband's surname. That becomes her legal name, and she ceases to be known by her maiden name. By that name she must sue and be sued, make and take grants and execute all legal documents. Her maiden surname is absolutely lost, and she ceases to be known thereby" (449). See *Chapman v. Phoenix National Bank*, 85 N.Y. 437 (1881).

10 See *Hair v. Hair*, 10 Rich (S.C.) 163 (1858).

11 See 239 U.S. 299 (1915), 312.

12 *Olmstead v Olmstead*, 27 Barb 9, 31 (N.Y. Sup. Ct. 1857) granted fathers habeas corpus remedy against mother and mother-in-law to obtain custody of child.

13 The case of Elizabeth Parsons Ware Packard is illustrative here. In 1860, after challenging her husband's views on religion, slavery, and child rearing, he had her placed in Jacksonville Insane Asylum where she was held against her will for three years. The expose of her ordeal, *The Prisoners' Hidden Life, Or Insane Asylums Unveiled* was published in 1868 and helped lead to the changing of such laws that oppressed women in this manner.

14 This quote is widely attributed to an unnamed Maine legislator who resisted abolishing the marital rape exception in that state.

15 See also *State v. Smith*, 148 N.J. 219 (1977) which discusses the history of marriage being a defense to a charge of rape.

16 See *Shaw v. Shaw*, 17 Conn. 189 (1845).

17 See *State v. Rhodes*, 61 N.C. 453(1868), 455.

18 *Bedan v. Turney*, 34 P. 442 (1893), 443.

19 See *Oregon v. Rideout*, 108,866 Circuit Court, County of Marion Oregon (1978).

20 See 430 U.S. 651 (1977).

21 See 8 Dow PC 630.

22 See 60 N.C. 266 (1864), 267.

23 See *Knight v. Knight*, 31 Iowa 451 (1871).

24 See 20 Ala. 36 (1852), 39.

25 See 58 Cal.2d 683 (1962). In *Drake v. Drake*, 177 N.W. 624 (Minn. 1920), the court held that wives were barred from suing husbands for intentional torts. They worried that family relations would be disturbed by court proceedings and in which the "nagging, ill-tempered wife" would air "matters of no serious moment" that should be "permitted to slumber in the home closet" and "silently be forgiven or forgotten."

References

Armstrong, Gail. "Females under the Law—'Protected But Unequal.'" *Crime & Delinquency* 23, no. 2 (April 1977): 190–120.

Blackstone, William. *Commentaries on the Laws of England, 1765–1769 Vol. 1.* Chicago, IL: University of Chicago Press, 1765 [1979].

Brownmiller, Susan. *Against Our Will: Men, Women and Rape.* New York: Simon & Schuster, 1995.

Chused, Richard H. "Late Nineteenth Century Married Women's Property Law: Reception of the Early Married Women's Property Acts by Courts and Legislatures." *American Journal of Legal History* 29 (1985): 3–35.

Dressler, Joshua. "Battered Women and Sleeping Abusers: Some Reflections." *Ohio State Journal of Criminal Law* 3 (2006): 457–471.

Dworkin, Andrea. *Letters from a War Zone.* New York: Lawrence Hill Books, 1993.

Gray, Mel and Jennifer Boddy, "Making Sense of the Waves: Wipeout or Still Riding High?" *Affilia* 25, no. 4 (2010): 368–389.

Lewin, Tamar "What Penalty for a Killing in Passion?" *New York Times*, October 21, 1994, accessed March 2, 2018, www.nytimes.com/1994/10/21/us/what-penalty-for-a-killing-in-passion.html?pagewanted=print&src=pm

Hale, Matthew. *History of the Pleas of the Crown, Vol.* 1, 1847.

Hananoki, Eric "Trump Rallies with 'Great Lady' Who Doesn't Believe Wives Can be Raped by Husband," *Media Matters for America*, March 11, 2016, accessed March 2, 2018, www.huffingtonpost.com/entry/conservative-activist-phyllis-schlafly-dead-at-92_us_57ce0171e4b0a22de096adfe

Hines, Denis A. and Kathleen Malley-Morrison, *Family Violence in the United States: Defining, Understanding, and Combating Abuse*. Thousand Oaks, CA: Sage, 2005.

Lukens, Clark Edward. "Shall Women Throw Away Their Privileges?" *American Bar Association Journal* 11, no. 10 (October 1925): 645–646.

Luker, Kristin. *Abortion and The Politics of Motherhood*. Berkeley, CA: University of California Press, 1984.

Mansfield, Edward *The Legal Rights, Liabilities and Duties of Women*. Salem, MA: Jewett and Co, 1845.

McFarlane, Richard. "There is No Substitute for a Mother's Love: The Rise and Fall of the Tender Years Doctrine in California." *California Legal History*, 2 (2007): 165–182.

Petchesky, Rosalind P. "Reproductive Freedom: Beyond 'A Woman's Right to Choose.'" *Signs* 5, no. 4 (1980): 661–685.

Sunstein, Cass R. *Radicals in Robes: Why Extreme Right-Wing Courts are Wrong for America*. New York: Basic Books, 2005.

Waterman, Sally Fry. "For Better or for Worse: Marital Rape." *Northern Kentucky Law Review*, 15 (1988): 611.

3

DEMOCRACY, POWER, AND WORK

Elizabeth Gregory

Though we think of ourselves as individuals, we are all products of the economic, social, and ecological systems we live in. Our identities are shaped within those systems, which we embody and carry forward. Part of the creation of our identities connects to the work we are being prepared to do and the social roles we will play as adults. Social class has a big role in determining whether people are funneled into well-paid, middle-paid, or low-paid tasks.[1] Gender and race also directly affect the kinds of jobs open to many workers. Both factors have historically served as work-assignment systems in the U.S., and only recently have the limitations built into those systems begun to be challenged. Though some change has occurred that has opened up new options to some, many inequalities of education, access to jobs, pay scale, and influence on policy remain between women and men. Likewise, many inequalities remain between women of different races, which are also often linked to class and to differences in educational opportunities (U.S. Census 2016),[2] as well as to continuing bias (see Lee 2017).[3]

Though it has improved from the 1960s and 1970s when the average woman made 59 cents to the average man's $1, the gender wage gap has persisted into the 21st century (National Committee on Pay Equity n.d.). In 2017 in the US, according to the Institute for Women's Policy Research, full-time working women earned 80.5% of what full-time working men earned (down 1.1% from 2016). Intersectionally, the rate varies by race: White women earned 77% of what White men earned, Black women earned 60.8% of White men's annual pay, Hispanic/Latina women earned 53.0%, and Asian women earned 85.1%. (Black and Hispanic men make less than White men on average, but more than women in their own racial groups, and Asian men make more than White men and more than Asian women, on average.) Since in order to care for their families large numbers of women do not work full time, overall women earn about 49% of what men earn. This chapter will explore the factors behind these pay inequities, as well as some means of addressing them.

Gender, Work, and Identity

Gender and work form major parts of people's identities. Sex is often the first thing known about a person: "It's a girl," or "It's a boy!" (whether announced upon delivery or earlier in the examination process). And gendering follows directly upon that announcement—with color-coded clothing and expectations about the ways children will behave: boys will be active and assertive; girls will be more passive and other-focused. This early gender training directly affects the kinds of work that women and men will be channeled into later in life. Though there's been room for some variation, children who differed much from those "norms" have historically gotten a lot of pushback from adults and peers. This is now changing to some extent, as the culture has come to recognize that by coding certain kinds of work as "unfeminine" they effectively limit the talent pool of engineers and scientists, as well as, conversely, that of caregivers of all kinds when that work is coded as "unmasculine." The effort to undo this kind of gender coding requires a culture-wide reboot. Such a loosening of gender norms is occurring, and connects to the concept of personal "gender fluidity." Both question the assumption that there should be clear, gendered rules not just about the work a person does but also about how a person should behave or look, or about one's choice of sexual partners. All of these factors are linked, and they are all in motion.

As an adult, if people are asked what they "are," they often answer with their profession or major activity: "I'm a doctor," "I'm a student," "I'm a clerk," etc. But many people do multiple kinds of work, including care work for members of their families, emotional work for people they are close to, and civic work as citizens of their communities. In the big picture, *work* comprises all forms of effort that serve the functioning of the group a given person works within. That includes *paid work* of all kinds (including *legal and illegal* activities). It also includes *"reproductive" labor*—which means not just sex and fertility (physically producing the bodies of the next generation), but also the care work associated with keeping people going from day to day, like cleaning, cooking, childcare, and other "housework" done for no pay, often within families, and the *emotional work* of keeping people balanced enough to move forward "productively."

Of course, gender and work are directly linked. *Gender* has historically been the backbone of society's work-assignment system, both in public and in the home. It has divided up the kinds of tasks that males and females are allowed to do within society, marked them as "masculine" and "feminine," and set their pay scales. Though women have made inroads into "male" professions, and to a lesser degree men have moved into some "female" professions (like nursing), the old divisions often still hold.

Much of the reproductive labor done in our society falls to women, and has long been known in Western culture as both "women's work" and "not work" (as in "I don't work, I'm just a housewife"). Not only are these tasks assigned to people who are female, but doing the tasks has often defined a person as "feminine"; men who do them have been seen as compromised, as are women who do "male" tasks or exhibit "masculine" characteristics. The mockery that often follows serves as means of forcing those norm-challengers back into their assigned roles. But the reproductive work that women have done has always been essential to society, so essential that the low self-esteem and self-abnegation that have often been taught as part of women's upbringing may be understood as essential to getting women to do this essential work. If they thought better of themselves, they might a) question why they should be limited to low paid work, and b) question why this important work was so low paid and associated with so little cultural influence. They might demand better, more equitable treatment—something like what is beginning to happen today.

Work that is "gendered" rather than "sexed" is assigned to one group or the other not based on nature but on custom. While women are physically structured to do the labor of child-bearing, they have no inherent ability to cook or clean, nor do men have inborn skills at truck-driving. Other physical characteristics also affect work choice, but it is sometimes difficult to distinguish physical and cultural differences. While men within a given ethnic group are often bigger or stronger than women in that same group and thus may seem suited to different tasks, differences in strength or dexterity may also be expanded by social encouragement of exercise and weight-training among men and not women, and attention to detail among women and not men. A cultural preference for less strong women may have affected the ongoing evolution of both sexes, leading to current patterns of physical difference. Which is to say that while there are some physical differences that lead certain people to be better at certain jobs than other people, the degree to which these are either true across the board or permanent is in question.

Race, Class, and Work

In economics, *class* is often discussed as the means by which people are sorted into task assignments—the "lower" classes have historically been given less education, limited to manual labor and excluded from policy-making roles (policy being the means by which it's determined what kind of education is provided to various groups or neighborhoods, and not coincidentally the policy-makers provide better education opportunities to their own children). But *race*, which often overlaps with class in our society, has also served as a means of task assignment.

In the United States, race has been part of the work-assignment system since early days. The enslavement of Africans to work in the sugar industry (initially) and later in cotton and other industries used "otherness" as a warrant for robbing those workers of their right to determine whom to work for and for what pay. Though no longer enslaved, a disproportionate percentage of African Americans continue to be impoverished, having been limited in their access to education and to the vote and thus to fair representation in the legislative system, for generations. While in 2016, 25% of Whites were lower income, 49% of Blacks and 53% of Hispanics were, per a Pew research Centre communication. While numbers in the middle-Income bracket were closer (50% of Whites, 40% of Hispanics, and 42% of Blacks), there were more than twice as many White families in the upper-Income bracket (26% of Whites, 10% of Blacks and 8% of Hispanics). In addition, many Black men have been imprisoned, both because they were pushed into crime due to lack of other options and due to imbalanced sentencing practices (Blacks are incarcerated at five times the rate of Whites, and the percentage of Black women in prison is twice that of White women) (NAACP 2018).[4] As prisoners, their forced labor is sold for low wages, and again the profit goes to others. All of these factors shape the way citizens are allowed to contribute their talents to the national labor pool and to be compensated.

Current patterns of growing inequality mean that the middle class is shrinking, and this decline affects Blacks and Hispanics more than it has Whites. In 2017, the average overall wealth of White families in the US was 10 times greater than that of Black families and 8 times greater than that of Hispanic families, in large part because they were in less precarious circumstances to begin with, and so could better weather recessions and other financial hardships (Kochhar and Cilluffo 2017).

Though gender and race still largely inform what kinds of work people are allowed to do, increasingly those divisions are being questioned. This is due to at least two major factors: the invention and availability of hormonal birth control, and the unrolling logic of democracy.

Gradual Democracy

Democracy is a radical concept, and while endorsed in principle in 1776, it has taken a while to advance even to the limited point currently achieved in the United States (along with other global democracies). Though the U.S. Declaration of Independence includes the assertion that the country is based on the understanding that "All men are created equal," slavery was legal in 1776 and continued to be so through the Emancipation Proclamation in 1863. The phrase itself also includes a clear sex bias—though the term "men" is now understood to refer to all "humans," not just the male sex, women did not have the vote (also known as *suffrage*, or *the franchise*) in 1776. Social equality is most clearly demonstrated by access to the vote, and through that to policy-making roles. At the nation's start, only White male property owners could vote. The vote was extended to all White male citizens in the ensuing decades. Black men won their suffrage via the 15th Amendment in 1870, though they were often prevented from actually voting thereafter, via poll taxes, literacy tests, and other means of disenfranchisement, especially in the South, until the Voting Rights Act was passed in 1965, which improved things. Though there were efforts to extend the vote to women starting in 1848, women did not win the right to vote until 1920, and like Black men, Black women were often prevented from voting until 1965. Though they had been citizens prior, Native Americans only got the vote in all states in 1962, Chinese Americans were made voting citizens in 1943, and all Asian Americans got the right to become citizens and vote in 1952, while citizens residing in Washington, DC only won the vote in 1961 (Al Jazeera 2016). Poor citizens of all races have often been prevented from voting by lack of education about the voting system, lack of faith in the possibility of change, and difficulty in getting to the polls when they work multiple jobs (or on Tuesdays). At various times and locations, the rights of certain citizens to vote have continued to be blocked. Thus, democracy in America is and has always been limited.

Though they have differences, race discrimination and patriarchy have in common that both force certain groups of people (based on physical characteristics) to do specific kinds of work for reduced (or no) pay, apart from the minimal support required to keep those workers functioning, in order that others may profit from that work. Both exclude groups of citizens from participating in democratic decision- and policy-making, in business and government. Although it is clear that slavery and race discrimination exploit people to their detriment (arguments for slavery's benevolence were never convincing), the patriarchal system has sometimes been seen as "natural," and women are often understood to profit with their male family members from the success of the family overall, trading the benefits of independence for those of subordination with some rewards. But though many world cultures involve patriarchy—defined as the "rule of the fathers" over the women and children, other types of societies have also existed in which women were also included among the cultural decision-makers, making it clear that patriarchy is not "natural," but a system imposed by some members of a group on others (Goettner-Abendroth 2012). The intersection of race and gender creates a power grid that means that Black and Hispanic women are more underrepresented in leadership roles and underpaid at all levels of employment. Position on the grid is at least in part linked to the education level of each group, itself linked to education funding in home districts, which of course depends on who is in the legislature, setting tax rates and education budgets.

Fertility, Under/Representation, and Subordination

In contemporary society, many citizens and activists are working to imagine political, social, and economic structures in which democracy is fully realized and people of all races and genders get equal access to power. This would include economic and civic power, so that all can have a voice in shaping the policies that dictate how work is assigned, what work is valued, and society's overall foci. But we're far from that goal.

Historically, women's relationship to work has been directly linked to the physical labor of child-bearing. Although logic might have held that since women bear the children, men should raise them, instead the care and feeding of children and of the entire household has fallen to women in patriarchy. The linkage of sexuality with the fertility that follows from it has been the means of keeping women in service roles, assigned the care of children and of the whole family, and available at any moment to "fix a plate" for any male who requests it. Female subordination has been utilized to subordinate men as well: Men of all classes have traded off their own submission to classes above them for dominance over the women in their homes—a dominance that also assists business/capital since men's sexual intercourse with women creates more workers. As part of the trade-off for dominance, men have also often sacrificed their own emotional expression and involvement with children and caregiving.

While White women and people of color can now vote, they are not proportionately represented in state, local, and national legislatures and executive offices, and thus have not made the substantial changes in the operation of society that would be required to create an equal playing field for all. In 2019, women make up 50.8% of the population but only 23.7% of the US Congress—23 Senators and 102 Representatives. Of those, 47 (8.7% of the total) are women of color (22 Black, 13 Latina, 9 Asian/Pacific Islander, 2 Native American, 1 Middle Eastern/North African, and 1 multiracial. Women hold 28.7% of state legislature seats, 20.9% of mayoral seats (in cities over 30,000), though only two of the largest five cities have ever had female mayors (Chicago 1979–83; Houston 1982–92; 2011–16). The year 2020 will be the Women's Suffrage Centennial, marking 100 years since US women were granted the vote in the 19th Amendment to the Constitution.

Though members of one group may represent the interests of constituents of different gender and race, if no or few members of those different gender and race groups are in the rooms where decisions are made, the positions that best serve them are unlikely to be even introduced into discussion let alone endorsed by the majority, if they challenge the status quo. Conversely, people of a given race or gender may work against positions that best serve those groups' interests, especially if they are elected to represent parties opposed to those interests. But overall, direct election of representatives of all constituencies in numbers proportionate to their presence in the wider population is important to full and fair discussion and decision-making about social policy.

Though majority rule is an established voting principle, it too can be unfair—in that if 51% of a population holds all the seats in a governing body, 49% of the population's interests may go unrepresented. This "tyranny of the majority" is avoided in a number of nations worldwide through *proportional representation* (the form of representation advocated in the 1990s in the U.S. by Lani Guinier), which guarantees that all points of view will be represented in the room where decisions are made (Guinier 1995). Even if their proponents do not hold a majority, the presence of those representatives of alternative views in the discussion may evolve the views of others and lead to compromises that address the needs and interests of the full population.

In business, women hold just 5.8% of CEO positions in S&P 500 companies (in 2019 none is a woman of color), though women make up 44.7% of employees and fill 26.5% of executive and senior managerial posts. Again, the absence of women in the rooms where policy is made affects the fact that policy does not support people who are responsible for family. It's a vicious circle: because the support infrastructure hasn't changed, women haven't yet been able to move in sufficient numbers into positions where they could change it. But some progress is occurring, perhaps due to changes in the expectations for equity of younger workers.

If there are fewer women than men in leadership positions, then, predictably, women outnumber men at the bottom of the scale. For instance, in 2018 12% of women lived in poverty, compared to 9% of men. This is due to many factors that add up over a lifetime: occupational segregation into low-wage jobs, the overall gender wage gap, the absence of a social safety net for many elderly, lack of affordable childcare, family care responsibilities (which may cause women to skip work), social patterns of violence and abuse of women, the greater longevity of women, etc. (Legal Momentum 2018). Many of these same factors limit women's ability to climb executive leadership ladders to date and explain the continuing gender wage gap.

Factors that particularly affect that gap

Occupational Segregation

Women have tended to be socialized and educated to work in service and helping professions, many of which pay less than job types into which men are socialized and educated. Likewise, the culture of "male" occupations often is or has been hostile to women, as has been demonstrated by recent discussions of Silicon Valley and of STEM fields, pushing women out (Benner and Isaac 2017; Bennet 2017). Efforts are being made to change these cultures, in order to make them more woman and family friendly. Such changes would expand the talent pool for these industries and introduce new perspectives and insights. On the other side, work that has traditionally been marked feminine and paid less (the pool of workers there being artificially inflated because all women were restricted to those areas), like teaching, secretaries and assistants, nursing, cooking, cleaning and other care work, has to begin to be paid more in order to attract qualified male workers who might enjoy that work more but find the wages too low.

Lack of Affordable Care and Inadequate School Hours

Studies show that employers tend to give women smaller raises and fewer promotions. This seems to be because they can predict that many women will step out of work at some point in order to care for children, and thus be "unreliable workers" over the long term (this is the backstory for the TV show *Younger*). Though the assumption that stepping out of the workforce means that when they return women will not be able to catch up to the skills of their co-workers is questionable, it nonetheless affects employers' judgments. But the reason many women step out is not their desire to do so, but the failure of the school schedule to mimic the work schedule. School lets out at 3 p.m. (though work ends at 5 or later); it closes on many holidays not taken by employers—including a three-month summer break! In addition, there is no school coverage in many districts before age 5 (though some cities do offer some preschool for 4-year-olds). This unsupported time often creates a need for a parent to step out to care for kids, and that is generally the lowest-earning person in the couple. This is most often the female, if she has been given lower raises and promotions because her employer expects her to be unreliable: a self-fulfilling prophecy.

This failure of the school infrastructure to support working families (which directly affects the careers of the women who step out, but in so doing also affects the wages of the entire family) is a major factor in the gender wage gap and in women's failure to advance in the workplace. A responsible system would provide full-day care from 8 a.m. to 6 p.m., from age 0 to 18. The additional hours could be optional, so families that didn't want to utilize them, needn't. Instead of focusing on making parents' work schedules "flexible" in order to accommodate school, a system that reversed the picture and made school more consistent, would accommodate women's work and provide early childhood education to the huge proportion of our children currently in bad care or at home with parents who cannot provide them with the resources they need to enter kindergarten well prepared. The cost would be covered by the taxes paid by women who worked more consistently, and by those paid by the increased numbers of educated teachers who would have to be employed at good wages to fill the childcare, after-school and summer positions.

Salary Negotiation

Evidence shows that men are more likely than women to negotiate better terms after receiving an initial salary offer. This can affect long-term salary. Some evidence also shows that women may refrain from negotiating because they understand that will be perceived as "unladylike," or too aggressive, potentially leading to loss of a job offer. The AAUW Start

Smart Salary Negotiation Workshop teaches women how to research their salary needs and the salary norms for their field and level of experience within the geographical area where they seek work, and to remind themselves of their own skills and the value they will bring to their new employer, so they can present that data as part of their negotiation. In that way, they will not risk seeming merely to be asking for more than they deserve.

Discrimination

A recent AAUW report found that even childless women fresh out of school make 7% less than their male peers in the first year in equivalent jobs. Ten years later, the differential among full-time male and full-time female workers not attributable to personal choices or occupation choice and has increased even further (Corbett and Hill 2012). Representative examples of the percentage of full-time men's average salaries made by full-time women in equivalent jobs include: accountants 70.6%; elementary-school teachers 87.1%; nurses 90.6%; financial managers, 69.3%; managers, 77%; retail salespersons, 70.4% (Hegewisch and Williams-Baron 2017).

Change

When women entered the workforce in large numbers (specifically middle-class White women), the work they had been doing at home did not go away. Newly employed women in the 1960s and after faced a "second shift" at home, because men expected them to continue doing housework, which was still gendered feminine. Sons of more recent generations, raised by their working mothers with the expectation of equality, tend to share the housework much more than their fathers did, as their working wives and partners expect (Altintas and Sullivan 2016). Egalitarian marriage comes with the added benefit for men of having equally educated peers as wives (Schwartz 1994), who understand their work lives and can share the burden of income responsibility, and of being more involved in the lives of their children.

At the same time, women are choosing to have fewer children—or at least to delay children until they can afford good childcare. Increasingly, they wait until after they have finished their schooling, established at work, and taken some time to rise in the ranks to a position of some experience and authority that would allow them some flexibility at work (see Gregory 2012). With births at an all-time low in 2017, employers and policy-makers of all kinds have to consider whether it's time to make families more affordable and workable, by taking some of the cost off the shoulders of working families. In the context of declining births and women's increasing roles in policy discussions, the movements to deny access to birth control and abortion look more and more like efforts by old-school patriarchs to push back the clock and limit change, by thrusting babies onto parents who don't want or can't afford them. Such babies are generally delivered at the expense of the state, through Medicaid. This kind of fertility manipulation doesn't promise the kind of educated population that the technology challenges on the horizon demand.

The needs of the immediate future would seem to call for a world in which the talents of all members of society are identified, nourished, and utilized. Some, like social theorist Kathi Weeks (2011), propose a basic wage for all (rather than allowing all the wealth created by the economic environment in which we all participate to flow to the few while many suffer), as a basis for a democracy that does not discriminate by gender, class, race, sexuality, age, or dis/ability.

Discussion Questions

1 How has gender shaped the work options (paid and unpaid) of women and men, historically and now?
2 How have race and gender historically intersected to determine who is assigned what task, and how has that changed in recent decades?
3 How do access to the polls and voting rights affect wages?
4 How could changes in family-friendly policy affect women's participation in the paid and unpaid workforces?
5 What is patriarchy, and how does it affect the gendering of work?
6 What factors affect the gendered wage gap?

Suggested Readings

1 Guinier, Lani *The Tyranny of the Majority: Fundamental Fairness in Representative Democracy*. New York: Free Press, 1994.
2 Hartmann, Heidi. "The Unhappy Marriage of Marxism and Feminism: Towards a More Progressive Union." *Feminist Theory: A Reader*, 4th ed. Eds. Wendy Kolmar and Frances Bartkowski. New York: McGraw-Hill, 2013: 307–316.
3 Murray, Pauli "The Liberation of Black Women." *Feminist Theory: A Reader*, 4th ed. Eds. Wendy Kolmar and Frances Bartkowski. New York: McGraw-Hill, 2013: 200–207.
4 Rubin, Gayle "The Traffic in Women: Notes on the 'Political Economy' of Sex." *Feminist Theory: A Reader*, 4th ed. Eds. Wendy Kolmar and Frances Bartkowski. New York: McGraw-Hill, 2013: 240–253.
5 Weeks, Kathi *The Problem with Work: Feminism, Marxism, Antiwork Politics and Postwork Imaginaries*. Durham, NC: Duke University Press 2011.

Notes

1 Though we talk a lot about social mobility across classes as a U.S. norm, data indicate that American society involves lower social mobility than societies with more equal education systems. In the U.S., where education funding is tied to local property taxes, poor children do not receive the same educational opportunities that students in middle-class and wealthy school districts do, and as a result, they are not eligible for many jobs outside their class position at birth.
2 Per the Census Bureau, 36.2% of Whites, 22.5% of Blacks, 53.9% of Asians and 15.5% of Hispanics over 25 have Bachelor's degrees or higher.
3 Bias also blocks change, in many ways.
4 See also Ava DuVernay's film *13th.* A prison record affects the ability to work and (for felons) to vote, once out of jail.

References

Al Jazeera. "Who Got The Right to Vote When? A History of Voting Rights in America." 2016, accessed April 5, 2018. https://interactive.aljazeera.com/aje/2016/us-elections-2016-who-can-vote/index.html

Altintas, Evan and Oriel Sullivan. "Fifty Years of Change Updated: Cross-National Gender Convergence in Housework." *Demographic Research* 35, no. 16 (August 2016): 455–470. www.demographic-research.org/volumes/vol35/16/default.htm

Benner, Katie and Mike Isaac, "As Uber Leaders Step Aside, Arianna Huffington's Influence Grows," *New York Times*, June 17, 2017, accessed April 5, 2018. www.nytimes.com/2017/06/17/business/uber-arianna-huffington-board.html

Bennet, Jessica. "Ellen Pao Is Not Done Fighting," *New York Times*, September 8, 2017, accessed April 5, 2018. www.nytimes.com/2017/09/08/style/ellen-pao-gender-discrimination-silicon-valley-reset.html

Catalyst 2019, "Women in S&P 500 Companies," accessed February 28, 2019, www.catalyst.org/knowledge/women-sp-500-companies

Corbett, Christianne and Catherin Hill. "Graduating to a Pay Gap: The Earnings of Women and Men One Year after College Graduation," *AAUW*, October 2012, accessed April 5, 2018. www.aauw.org/files/2013/02/graduating-to-a-pay-gap-the-earnings-of-women-and-men-one-year-after-college-graduation.pdf

Goettner-Abendroth, Heide. *Matriarchal Societies: Studies on Indigenous Cultures across the Globe.* New York: Peter Lang, 2012.

Gregory, Elizabeth. *Ready: Why Women Are Embracing the New Later Motherhood.* 2nd edition. New York: Basic Books, 2012.

Guinier, Lani. *The Tyranny of the Majority: Fundamental Fairness in Representative Democracy.* New York: Free Press, 1995.

Hartmann, Heidi, Ariane Hegewisch, Barbara Gault, Gina Chirillo, and Jennifer Clark. "Five Ways to Win an Argument about the Gender Wage Gap," *Institute for Women's Policy Research*, September 2017, accessed April 5, 2018. https://iwpr.org/wp-content/uploads/2016/09/GWG-Talking-Points_2017.pdf

Hegewisch, Ariane and Emma Williams-Baron. "The Gender Wage Gap by Occupation 2016 and by Race and Ethnicity," *Institute for Women's Policy Research*, April 2017, accessed April 5, 2018. https://iwpr.org/wp-content/uploads/2017/04/C456.pdf

Kochhar, Rakesh and Anthony Cilluffo. "How Wealth Inequality Has Changed in the US since the Great Recession, by Race, Ethnicity, and Income," *Pew Research Center*, November 1, 2017, accessed April 3, 2019. www.pewresearch.org/fact-tank/2017/11/01/how-wealth-inequality-has-changed-in-the-u-s-since-the-great-recession-by-race-ethnicity-and-Income/.

Lee, Bruce. "Three New Studies Suggest Gender and Racial Bias In Medical Schools," *Forbes*, March 12, 2017, accessed April 5, 2017. www.forbes.com/sites/brucelee/2017/03/12/ three-new-studies-suggest-gender-and-racial-bias-in-medical-training/#72561c171930

Legal Momentum: The Women's Legal Defense and Education Fund, "Women and Poverty in America," accessed April 5, 2018. www.legalmomentum.org/women-and-poverty-america

NAACP, "Criminal Justice Fact Sheet," accessed April 5, 2018. www.naacp.org/criminal-justice-fact-sheet/

National Committee on Pay Equity, "The Wage Over Time: In Real Dollars, Women See a Continuing Gap," accessed April 5, 2018. www.pay-equity.org/info-time.html

Rutgers Eagleton Institute of Politics, Center for American Women and Politics, "Women in U.S. Congress 2017," accessed April 5, 2018. www.cawp.rutgers.edu/women-us-congress-2017

Schwartz, Pepper. *Peer Marriage: How Love Between Equals Really Works*. New York: Free Press, 1994.

U.S. Census Bureau. *Educational Attainment in the United States: 2015*, by Camille L. Ryan and Kurt Bauman. Washington, DC: Government Printing Office, 2016.

Weeks, Kathi. *The Problem with Work: Feminism, Marxism, Antiwork Politics, and Postwork Imaginaries*. Durham, NC: Duke University Press, 2011.

Zarya, Valentina. "Why There Are No Black Women Running Fortune 500 Companies," *Fortune Magazine*, January 16, 2017, accessed April 5, 2018. http://fortune.com/2017/01/16/black-women-fortune-500/

Part II

NEGOTIATING INEQUITABLE TERRAIN

GENDER SCHOLAR SPOTLIGHT: INTERVIEW WITH JEN JACK GIESEKING

Jen Jack Gieseking is an urban cultural geographer, feminist and queer theorist, environmental psychologist, and American Studies scholar. S/he is engaged in research on co-productions of space, justice, and gender and sexual identities in digital and material environments. Jack is working on his/her second book project, *Queer New York: Geographies of Lesbians, Dykes, and Queer Women,* and conducting research on trans people's use of Tumblr as a site of cultural production. S/he is Assistant Professor of Public Humanities in American Studies at Trinity College in Hartford, Connecticut. Jack identifies as a woman and uses both she/her/hers and he/him/his pronouns.

What led you to begin studying women's inequality?

The sharp distinction between the political, economic, and social affordances, material conditions, and geographical imaginations of the cisgender women (ciswomen) and gender non-conforming people (GNCP) that I have known, observed, and read about is stark. These contradictions often lead back to a sense of self-blame, doubt, or limitations in ciswomen and GNCP; I have never witnessed the same responses of ideas in cisgender men. In my earliest graduate classes, I noticed a great deal of work that observed and recorded gender injustice. I feel like I am part of the next generation of academics who, thanks to the Internet and social media, are able to increasingly bring this work to the public as a project of public humanities. The ability to intervene on behalf of justice in knowledge production is what keeps me studying women's and GNCP's inequality.

How have your lived experiences
shaped your research interests?

The experiences of the working middle-class White and Black women I went to high school with and the women in their families in the City of Baltimore stood in stark juxtaposition to the elite, New England, liberal arts, women's college which I attended for college. As I began my Ph.D., my devotion to the study of women's inequality was only further fueled by my own lesbianism and solidarity with other women. In my late 20s and 30s, I came out as transgender, being able to make sense of my masculine identity in a woman's body in new ways—many of which were fueled by the empathy, sympathy, and solidarity I have long held with, by, for, and about my research participants.

In your opinion, what scholarly works have been most
impactful in your research on women and inequality?

Every year I read and teach *This Bridge Called My Back*. I will be surprised and yet remain hopeful that I will live long enough to think that a text from the early 1980s is the most cutting-edge feminist work yet in print. The radical intersectionality and solidarity of its authors (Audre Lorde, Gloria Anzaldúa, Cherríe Moraga, Mitsumi Yamada, and on and on) galvanizes my own resolve to work first and foremost from the "personal as political" and encourage others to do the same. At the same time, it is the absences that have been equally impactful: George Chauncey's note in *Gay New York* that he could not study women because they were not arrested at the same rate as gay men through the turn of the 19th century; or Manuel Castells's note in *The City and the Grassroots* that lesbians did not have the "territorial aspirations" of gay men in San Francisco's and "relationships and . . . networks are ones of solidarity and affection."[1] Instead of reducing lesbian and queer history to some jokes about u-hauling and potluck (jokes I adore, by the way), what are the political economic structures that afford such a culture and what are the antiracist and anticapitalist interventions waiting to be learned from within?

What has been most challenging
about your field of work?

Geographies of sexualities are only in their third or fourth generation, so that much of the key, important work is still being done in this sub-field. In comparison, I recently found out that French geography never had the feminist revolution that remapped all of Western geography since the late 1980s. American Studies has been a devotedly feminist and queer field since the 1980s and 1990s, respectively. Finally, the digital humanities and social data sciences is deeply defined by feminism and queer work, while digital and computational studies, more broadly, barely touches on feminist and queer concerns. What is most challenging about my research is the effort and nuance to work across these disciplines, sub-disciplines, and their historic moments to keep each in conversation with the other.

Why is your work on women important?

Sometimes my own work on women feels too important: I am writing the first lesbian history of New York City. I was sitting in the Lesbian Herstory Archives in Brooklyn, New York, doing research. Suddenly, I couldn't recall the detailed minutiae of a small, poorly attended, but eventually wildly important protest in 1986—and I rose to go grab the lesbian history of New York City to check my dates. Then I realized I was writing that book and I fell back into my chair. When I tell people it's the first monograph—sitting in conversation with deeply gorgeous memoirs and fiction by activists the likes of Sarah Schulman and Amber Hollibaugh—people are stunned. That this is the state of the world stuns me as well and, each time, marks it as important.

Which scholar(s) (and why) has been most influential in developing your perspective?

Feminist, queer, and critical race geographies—along with the interdisciplinary field of environmental psychology—are my theoretical and methodological cornerstones, along with a spatial reading of feminist texts writ large. These scholars include Cindi Katz, Sallie Marston, Geraldine Pratt, Jan Monk, Susan Saegert, Lee Rivlin, Setha Low, Linda Peake, Katherine McKittrick, Ruthie Gilmore, and Melissa Wright, alongside Donna Haraway, Judith Butler, Michelle Fine, Adrienne Rich, and the women of *This Bridge Called My Back*, mentioned above. Marxist geographers the likes of David Harvey, Neil Smith, and Don Mitchell are also read through this lens. Geographers of sexualities are my comrades and constant companions of invigorating the long feminist Marxist geographic history through the lens of sexuality, race, and class, including Natalie Oswin, Kath Browne, Gavin Brown, Michael Brown, Larry Knopp, and Julie Podmore. As queer theory is descendant of the humanities and psychoanalytic theory, my use of it has required primarily drawing from trans, butch, gender non-conforming, and queer scholars of color who understand the pathologization within, namely Jack Halberstam, José Estaban Muñoz, Shaka McGlotten, David Eng, Siobhan B. Somerville, Juana Maria Rodriguez, Dean Spade, Kara Keeling, and Martin Manalansan. At the same time, LGBTQ historians and activists are those scholars who shape my understandings of queer time: George Chanucey, Liz Kennedy, Madelyn Davis, Christina Hanhardt, John D'Emilio, Maxine Wolfe, Joan Nestle, and Michael Bronski. It is Tara McPherson, Jessie Daniels, Mary Gray, Nancy Baym, and Lisa Nakamura in the digital humanities and social data sciences help me think carefully about the ethics, limitations, and possibilities of public humanities work by, for, about, and with publics. Finally, I am grateful for statistical analyses of census data, gender pay gap reports, archivists, and other materials collected and written by scholars who often go unnamed and unrecorded but form the evidence and the bridge between the qualitative and quantitative work that I do. Across these disciplines and sub-disciplines, scholars of American Studies exist among these groups and help me to bridge my thinking, writing, and activism.

What theoretical approach best guides your research?

I take a queer feminist trans approach to critical geography in the study of space and place, environment and landscape, time, history, and futures, including spacetimes material and digital, physical and imagined.

What pedagogical approaches have you found most effective when teaching on women and inequality?

The same commitment to queer feminist trans inquiry on behalf of social justice that propels my research also inspires my teaching. My pedagogical philosophy engages students with a practice-oriented approach to academic exploration. Inspired by the interdisciplinary, critical approaches central to American Studies, this method of teaching encourages students to apply theoretical concepts to everyday urban issues, cutting-edge technologies, and scholarly debates and papers in the actual *practice* of research. I have advanced my thinking about the roles in which writing and technology can function to foster collaboration and further understanding, as tools for learning rather than as answers in and of themselves. In the classroom, online, and in their everyday lives, my students learn to work individually and collaboratively to develop their technology and writing skills in order to become critically engaged citizens of the world.

In your opinion, what are the most pertinent issues facing the women in your area of research today?

My multidisciplinarity makes this a tough question to answer but, when I look across these fields, it is still a matter of numbers in many disciplines in regards to recognition and hiring in others (geography). Some disciplines or their interests are still often feminized (history), while others are regarded as labor usually worthy of postdocs to date (digital humanities). Most importantly, it is the vast absence of scholars of color, especially women and GNCP of color—in all disciplines with the exception of American Studies—that must be addressed. Without them, their concerns, voices, injustices, and work toward justice remains a tragic afterthought. If feminism cannot finally confront the racism within and without, it does not live its politics.

At the same time, it is important to recognize the increasing number of trans and gender non-conforming academics finally getting jobs—yet the lack of institutional support remains absolutely painful. These absences include a consideration of healthcare, support for surgeries and hormones, staff training, student training, colleague training, all-gender bathrooms, and so on. For real change to happen, reproducing the tokenism of having one or two trans people per campus and expecting them to educate others only perpetuates injustice.

Finally, there is still little if any lesbian studies work, and gay male stories, spaces, and lives often define "LGBTQ" to the masses. This must be interrupted.

Is there anything else you would like to add?

Thank you for including me. As a trans lesbian dyke queer who does this work, it means a great deal to me and to others like me to be counted among these scholars. And thank you for doing this work.

Note

1 Manuel Castells, "Cultural Identity, Sexual Liberation and Urban Structure: The Gay Community in San Francisco," in *The City and the Grassroots: A Cross-Cultural Theory of Urban Social Movements*. Berkeley, CA: University of California Press, 1983, 140.

4

UNFILTERED

Male Strangers' Sexist Behavior Towards Women

Melissa K. Ochoa Garza

Introduction

"I was in class waiting for my professor to arrive and start lecture in the afternoon. I overheard the group of students (White) behind me. A boy said, 'Hey why aren't you guys sitting next to us today?' The girl replied, 'Because we don't want to, Don't feel like it.' He did not like her tone and replied, 'Oh shit, ok, chill out. Stay there for all I care.' He then proceeded to say to his friend, 'Must be that time of month I guess, because shit—' It sounded like she turned around to face him, but didn't vocalize anything. No one around really said anything, and they stayed quiet the rest of the time. I found it very shocking that this male student actually said this and that no one said anything. I didn't say anything I guess, because it maybe wasn't my place, but I probably should have."

Latina, Female, 19 years old

Most women can probably recount a few instances in their lives where male strangers expressed sexist views or behavior directly to them. While the sexist behavior above is shocking and distressing, it has become normalized, in part because it is usually dangerous for women to confront male strangers. In the example, a 19-year-old Latina student recounts an incident she witnessed in a classroom among her classmates. A group of White women chose to not sit next to a group of White men, and when questioned by a male student, one female student responds, "Because we don't want to, don't feel like it." Instead of accepting their decision and letting this go, the male student insinuates that it was an out-of-control, irrational statement and attributes it to her menstrual cycle. The participant believes that the White woman gave him a dirty look, but no one said anything. The women did not defend themselves, the other men did not say anything, and the participant did not say anything, but indicates that she probably should have. Most importantly, the male student who made the comment does not apologize. In this instance, it was a small, populated public setting, so the women probably didn't feel physically in danger, but perhaps, they refrained from addressing his comment for fear of being gaslighted or otherwise verbally assaulted.

Gaslighting is a form of emotional manipulation, which strives to make the target feel as if his/her reaction is crazy and irrational (Abramson 2014). Like the woman who didn't want to sit next to her male classmate, most women have experienced being gaslighted by family, friends, and even strangers (Abramson 2014). Some research indicates women are more likely to be the targets of gaslighting, while men are more likely to be the perpetrators—a tactic that is used to maintain the gender hierarchy by making women doubt their own perceptions (Abramson 2014).

My research indicates that most men do not filter their sexist views or behavior in front of or to women, because not only do they not receive any negative repercussions from women or other men, but also because we do not have a widely accepted "political correctness" in regard to sexism that restrains the oppressor group from degrading the oppressed group publicly. Women are a vulnerable population, and according to my data, all women, regardless of race or class, report instances of experiencing sexism from male strangers. While U.S. racism is still rampant, most White groups will usually refrain from engaging in blatantly racist talk or overtly racist behavior in front of people of color (Picca and Feagin 2007). Men, on the other hand, can assert their gender dominance overtly, such as the male student in the above scenario. He felt rejected by a woman and reasserted his power by invalidating her choice to not sit by him as irrational. He reduced her to her biology and exclaimed out loud that she must be menstruating, because to him there was no good reason as to why she wouldn't want to sit next to him. It seems absurd, and yet, it is a common sexist scenario women experience. Many women can recount a memory of a man accusing them of being on their periods for just expressing firm statements. Men will assert their superiority to women in multiple ways, regardless of the context. Women experience similar types of sexism from male strangers as they do with male friends and relatives, which indicates that systemic sexism is still perpetuated openly in public settings.

Goffman's Frontstage and Systemic Sexism Theory

Renowned sociologist, Irving Goffman, investigated the roles people play in society and when they enact these roles. In his book, *The Presentation of Self in Everyday Life* (1959), he describes two different contexts: the "frontstage" and the "backstage." The "frontstage" is where people follow a socially acceptable script and present their best selves to others, or the strangers around them. They are spaces where there is diversity in gender, age, and race (Goffman 1959; Picca and Feagin 2007). On the flip side, the "backstage" is where people are more relaxed, because individuals are around people they know and trust. They don't have to be "politically correct" (Goffman 1959; Picca and Feagin 2007). I will be focusing on the "frontstage," because women are describing instances of sexism from male strangers, where arguably, these men should not be comfortable enough to behave that way. However, according to Feagin and Ducey (2017), men and women do engage in sexist behavior in frontstages, because not only is male-sexist framing embedded and normalized in our social structure, but also it is reproduced by the oppressors and the oppressed—that is, sexism is foundational and fully systemic.

There are four key points of systemic sexism: 1) The discrimination of women by men; 2) the gender hierarchy (men are unjustly at the top and benefit the most); 3) the maintenance and reproduction of gender inequalities, including women, and 4) the male-sexist frame that includes the many stereotypes, ideologies, emotions, prejudices, images, narratives, and interpretations that are essential to the everyday reproduction of sexism (Feagin and Ducey 2017). The dominant male-sexist frame perpetuates the notion that male supremacy and hetero-masculinity is the ideal, and the opposite (women and femininity) is inferior (Feagin and Ducey 2017). Both men and women, including those of lower socioeconomic status and people of color, participate in maintaining the systematically sexist structure of the United States by perpetuating everyday forms of sexist attitudes and behavior, including everyday discrimination of women.

Women experience male-sexist behavior in multiple ways, such as in occupational discrimination (Cohen and Huffman 2003; Correll et al. 2007; Stone 2008), economic wages (Cotter et al. 1997; Cohen and Huffman 2003; Correll et al. 2007; Stone 2008; Levanon et al. 2009), healthcare (Kristof and WuDunn 2009; Hudson et al. 2012), violence (Ronai et al. 1997; Kristof and WuDunn 2009; Allen et al. 2009; Hudson et al. 2012), legal justice (Crenshaw 1989; Crenshaw 1991; MacKinnon 2005), and political representation (Ronai et al. 1997; Kristof and WuDunn 2009; Hudson et al. 2012) just to name a few areas. These forms of sexism are systematically produced, but are reinforced at an individual-interactional level creating a perpetual cycle of sexism at micro and macro levels. Oftentimes, women's negative experiences with sexist behavior have come from male strangers. After describing the data and methods, I will discuss the themes that emerged from female participants.

Data and Methods

Recruitment and Sample

The study was conducted using undergraduate students from a large university in the South, as well as a large university in the North. In the Southern school, researchers received permission from instructors to recruit volunteers to be added to the Sociology study participation system; in the Northern school, participants were already registered in a study participation system. In both schools, there is representation of different majors and departments to increase diversity, and the target classes were those required by the universities. The sample size will eventually be a total of 240 participants. The sample is divided so that 120 participants are from the large university in the South and 120 participants are from the large university in the North. Each sample group will further be divided by gender and race equally, the breakdown is as follows: 20 Black men and 20 Black women; 20 White men and 20 White women; 20 Latinos and 20 Latinas. However, the study in this paper focuses on the experiences of 9 Latina women and 38 White women retrieved from both schools totaling 85 entries from Latina women and 187 entries from White women. The undergraduate students wrote journal entries over the course of six weeks with a minimum of 14 entries. The journals consist of detailed accounts, or stories, of daily events that were perceived forms of sexism by the participant. After all of the journal entries were submitted, participants received an online $20 Amazon gift card to make an online purchase at Amazon.com.

Analysis

After receiving the journal entries, I analyzed the 272 data entries using ATLAS.ti, a qualitative coding program that helped me code the themes and reveal patterns. I coded words or phrases that were repeated within the data. For the case of the paper, I focused on frontstage settings, in which male strangers were one of the main actors.

Results

In line with systemic sexism theory, the results indicate that the male-sexist frame shapes the conversations and actions men have with women in a way that reproduces gender inequality and perpetuates discrimination against women. I found that male strangers often made sexist remarks in the following ways: catcalling, objectifying women in conversation or in actions, claiming male superiority, and discrediting women's experiences of sexism. Each scenario described by the female participants is a frontstage setting, because it is in the presence of strangers, although it does not deter male strangers from engaging in male-sexist behavior. Whether the men are catcalling women, objectifying women in conversations or in actions, claiming male superiority, or discrediting women's experiences of sexism, we can see the key points of systemic sexism theory in these interactions. These men know that they are in positions of power and use sexist behavior to sustain themselves at the top of the gender hierarchy by using the male-sexist frame to discriminate against women. In the process, their remarks, behaviors, and actions reproduce our society's gendered norms that perpetuate inequality for women.

Catcalling

The images, stereotypes, narratives, and prejudices towards women promote the objectification of women by men. Catcallers operate in the male-sexist frame when they call out to women walking outside. Not only are they asserting their position in the gender hierarchy by objectifying women, but also they are only doing so to women. This behavior is an overt display of the reproduction and maintenance of gender inequality, because the perpetrators are men and the targets are women, insinuating male superiority. In the cases described below, all of the incidents were in public settings, indicating that the men did not feel the need to censor themselves. Both Latina and White women recalled instances of catcalling from groups of men, which suggests that the act of catcalling is tied to the performance of hetero-masculinity amongst male peers. One 18-year-old Latina describes a day, in which this happened more than once:

> After baking cupcakes with a group of friends, four of my friends and I went to the bus stop to wait for the bus. We were there for only about 2 or 3 minutes before a truck with a couple of guys drove by and whistled. We all laughed about it and kept talking. A few more minutes later, two more cars came by and whistled. It was pretty cold out so we were all wearing jackets and pants (so the "what were you wearing" excuse cannot be used here). I was amazed by how many guys felt the need to whistle at us while we were just minding our business.
>
> Latina, female, 18 years old

In the span of less than 15 minutes, this group of women was catcalled three different times by men in vehicles. The narrator makes it a point to state that "victim-blaming" could not be applied, because none of them were wearing revealing clothes. The notion that their clothing could have been a reasonable explanation to being catcalled is an example of how the male-sexist frame is also adopted and reproduced by women. According to the male-sexist frame, if women are objects for men, then what a woman *chooses* to wear is directly linked to her potential victimization, and therefore, her fault should an assault happen. Victim-blaming is perpetuated by both men and women when they believe that it is a woman's fault for acting or dressing a way that would result in an assault.

Two other women make a note of their clothing as well when they were catcalled. A 20-year-old White woman states:

I was walking down the street at about 2 p.m. when a pick-up truck full of men drove by me. As they drove by, the passenger (White male, ~22 years old) leaned out of the window and *screamed* at me as the car passed me. For the record, I was wearing a t-shirt and jeans. I don't think he said any words or maybe he was going too fast to hear, but I was scared out of my skin. The rest of the walk to class and several days afterwards I was paranoid about cars passing me.

White, female, 20 years old

Like the 18-year-old Latina, this woman is making a note that she did not dress a certain way to deserve to be catcalled. She describes her clothing to indicate that it was not a case of "victim-blaming" and so she truly was not at fault. Nevertheless, the event clearly affected her enough to be on high alert and not feel safe afterwards, because she was scared and paranoid about cars passing her for days after the incident. Another woman contemplates whether her workout attire makes her more "prone" to being catcalled, so she justifies her use of spandex to reaffirm that her clothing choice is not for the male gaze. She claims:

Some random stranger yells out of their car and makes an obscene comment. As I am a young adult who is 20, Mexican American, and a female, it sucks and is really gross for some random stranger to yell out of their car and make a comment. Now I am never able to really identify who the guy is, because they are in a car and I am not. It bugs me that if a guy is running outside most of the time, he does not get hit on or get catcalled. I also don't know if it's because I wear leggings, a shirt, and a hat while I run, which makes me "prone" or "deserving" of getting called on by a guy. But that is complete BS, I wear spandex because I hate when my legs rub together, so that is why I wear them.

Latina, female, 19 years old

Instead of claiming that it is BS for men to catcall her regardless of what she is wearing, she states a reason that points to the male-sexist frame, in which women are objectified by men. She recognizes that the catcallers may think that she is wearing spandex to arouse their attention rather than to make her workout more efficient. The catcallers probably believe that women dress for men to observe, as opposed to women wanting to look good or dress appropriately for the weather and activity.

Not only is the act of catcalling a way to target and objectify women, but it is also a way to promote hetero-masculinity amongst the catcallers. The catcalling is usually done by at least a couple of men, and often they do not refrain from catcalling a woman even when she is accompanied by a man. One 20-year-old White woman describes being scared after being catcalled by a group of men, and frustrated because her boyfriend thought it was funny:

My boyfriend (19-year-old Asian male) and I were walking to the mall around 4 p.m. I was wearing a cute dress with some makeup and feeling good. As we crossed the street, a group of guys in an SUV (unknown age/race) yelled out of the window, "Mmm girl I'd like that ass." My boyfriend thought it was funny. I was scared and wanted to go home. Why do men think that's an okay thing to do in public?

White, female, 20 years old

She asks why men, including her boyfriend, think it's okay to catcall a woman in public. Men are performing masculinity by degrading a woman with their group of friends, and feel no threat of receiving negative repercussions or punishment. In two cases described above, the women felt threatened even though the catcallers were in vehicles and the event was over in a matter of seconds. These experiences have a real emotional implication to the targeted women.

Another 19-year-old White woman describes being with a male friend who is "a little over 6 foot and is very intimidating at first glance." He was walking her home around 1:30 a.m. when *many* cars passed them and screamed comments like, "tap that ass!" In the situations in which other men are accompanying the women being catcalled, the men in the vehicles get a double boost of masculinity: one for degrading a woman, the other for doing so in front of a possible boyfriend without an altercation. They get to objectify someone else's "girl" and get away with it. Meanwhile, the group of men doing the catcall bonds over their masculinity performance, which may be particularly important in a college atmosphere, as is experienced by these female participants:

I got catcalled while walking by a fraternity. There were several males there, so I'm not sure which one did it, but two were Caucasian and one was African American. They all seemed to be in their early 20s . . . After they catcalled me, the guys were laughing and high-fiving each other.

White, female, 20 years old

Similarly, a 19-year-old White woman describes an incident while she was walking on campus:

It was in the late afternoon, and there was a gathering of males outside of the building. As I was briskly walking by, one of the

White male students scoffed under his breath and coughed the word "bitch" at me as I walked past them. His "friends" (also male students) all giggled and no other words were spoken. I didn't look at him or acknowledge them since that's probably what they were hoping for. I think it is sexist to call women names like that when you don't even know them or they haven't done anything specific to "earn" being called this. I was by myself when this happened and I did not know any of the males that were present.

White, female, 19 years old

In the incidents described above, the women were alone and did not know any of the men involved, but the men laughed and high-fived. They don't feel any fear of repercussion by catcalling these women, and may think that they are not doing any harm. However, as many women report, they are scared and are often affected after the incident. Even being with a male companion does not prevent the catcalling they receive.

One 19-year-old woman describes how she has experienced much more catcalling since attending the university, and how insulted she is when it happens to her. She states, "I am not being seen as a human being with a real personality, but rather a body that can be used for sex and only that . . . they don't focus on what I have to offer outside of the bedroom." These women understand that they are being objectified from male strangers whom they may never encounter again; however, women also experience this from male strangers they see on a regular basis. Catcalling is an interactional, micro-level behavior, but it is representative of macro-level sexism. Men discriminately target women to catcall, because of their male-sexist framing, while simultaneously reinforcing their top position in the gender hierarchy.

Objectifications of Women in Conversation or Actions

The catcallers objectify women in brief seconds as their vehicles drive by, but women also deal with being objectified in face-to-face conversation. Men don't have to censor themselves in front of women, because they are in positions of power, both in the gender hierarchy, and oftentimes, in the workplace. In the examples below, many are not just random strangers, but rather male strangers who vary from coworkers and classmates to preachers and professors. Women sometimes share these experiences with other women to deal with the cognitive labor. A 19-year-old White woman describes situations that were currently happening to her sister who is training to be an athletic trainer:

My sister was paired with another female student to work with a ~20–30-year-old male. While they were taking the job very seriously, he was making inappropriate comments. They had asked him what they should wear to the games so they would look professional and appropriate, but his response was "a thong and high heels." After this comment, he laughed and said it was a joke when the girls looked uncomfortable. Later during my sister's time with this man, he had to teach her a technique for constricting blood flow. She told me that he taught them a method that uses a baseball, which worked well for her and she liked using. When she told him that she liked that method, his response was to ask if she liked "to be choked in bed or something." Since this was her superior, this was a highly inappropriate situation for my sister to be in and he obviously has a blatant disregard for filtering his sexist comments.

White, female, 19 years old

For the participant's sister, these were not one-time incidents; the man was using his superiority to his advantage. The participant notes in other entries that athletic training is male-dominated, so her sister faces other challenges as well, which may be a reason why her sister and her female partner remain silent about these events. The male superior is using male-sexist framing, specifically the images and stereotypes that women are sex objects for men. When he states that his female coworkers should wear "a thong and high heels" or asks if they like "to be choked in bed," he is reproducing the notion that women are inferior to men, and he dismisses their uncomfortable responses. His sexist commentary is specific to women.

Men in superior positions, such as bosses, religious leaders, and professors, often go unscathed for their sexist and discriminatory actions. For example, a 20-year-old White woman describes her pastor addressing the congregation on a Sunday:

I was in church this last Sunday, and one of the pastors who is a White male in his 30s was addressing the congregation. He was talking about that no matter what you have done Jesus always loves you. He specifically said that even if you are a girl who has been used up by sex, you can still follow Christ. I thought this was sexist because he made no other specification of things that men may do. He only pointed out what girls do and he made it seem that no matter how much sex guys have, they are never seen as unclean.

White, female, 20 years old

She doesn't mention that anyone spoke up about the double-standard or showed any form of disapproval, but in this case, a religious leader felt comfortable enough to claim that some girls are "unclean" and "used." He described women's bodies as objects, higher in value if virginity is intact, although he still offers "salvation" for those women that have been "used." The pastor reproduces the madonna/whore dichotomy by only viewing women's bodies as either "clean and untouched" or "unclean and used." As the participant mentions, his comments are specific to women and does not include men. He used his position of power, both at the top of the gender hierarchy and as a religious leader, to reproduce male-sexist framing to a congregation comprised of men and women.

Male professors and teachers also tend to make sexist remarks, and because of their superiority and authority, female students may be less likely to confront them or report it. One 21-year-old White woman tells of a time that she had to present a proposal to the head of her department, a White male about 60 years old:

> I did research for the Communications Department, so I had to present a methods proposal to the head of the department. It was just me and the head in his office. When I was done presenting everything, the first thing the head of the department that I was doing research for said was, "well aren't you adorable!"
>
> White, female, 21 years old

The participant does not counter his comment, so we can presume that he then went on to critique her presentation and did not reflect on his gendered language. In this scenario, we can see the male-sexist framing take place—there is a connotation that women are inferior in the workplace and in society. Had a male student given the presentation, the head of the department probably wouldn't have called him "adorable" or any similar adjective.

Interestingly, out of the many entries citing male strangers' sexist remarks to women, the majority seems to be from older White men. One participant recalls being told by a ~60-year-old White male customer that she was "too pretty to work and should just marry rich and be a stay-at-home mom" after she told him about her career goals, as well as her lack of desire to be a stay-at-home mom. In another case, an older male stranger scoffed at a 19-year-old woman on her way to a workplace harassment training telling her, "we should get to have some fun at work." In both of those cases, the men disregarded what the women were choosing to do (pursuing a career or going to a harassment training for a job) and gave very "pro-male" replies implying that the women's choices were unnecessary. Male strangers, whether complete strangers or those that are interacted with occasionally, tend to speak degradingly to women without any thought to filter their comments. The men's comments are male-sexist framed in that these men feel superior to judge women on their appearance, as well as to make inappropriate sexist remarks to women, regardless of the context. The men insinuate male-superiority and female-inferiority, which extends to intelligence, physical capability, and general knowledge.

Male Superiority and Female Inferiority

The belief that men are superior to women has an extensive history that has been reinforced for centuries through macro-level systems such as religion, education, economic system, and the government (Mies 1986/1998; Morgan 2001; Holland 2006; Federici 2004/2014; Feagin and Ducey 2017). This male-sexist framing on a macro-level is reproduced at interactional levels, in which women are presumed to be incompetent or incapable compared to men. One common theme among the female participants was being told to refrain from some activities because the men presumed that they were physically stronger and more capable to do "male" tasks. The women explained how frustrating it was to experience condescending remarks from male strangers. One 20-year-old Latina woman who is part of a military program at her university states that a male stranger laughed her at when she volunteered to help carry some military training tools:

> Someone from the class across the hall came in the classroom and asked for volunteers to help bring in rubber ducks (fake rifles used to train) from someone's car parked outside. I stood up and the guy asking for volunteers kind of chuckled and said "it might be too heavy for you, we meant for guys to come help." I was immediately offended and walked past him to help. I go past the female max in push-ups for the Physical Training test to prove I am just as strong and fit as my male buddies. I helped bring in the ducks with just as much ease as the other volunteers, the only difference was I was in my skirt and pumps.
>
> Latina, female, 20 years old

The same woman describes another situation, in which an older male alumnus restricts her from carrying heavy items at a tailgate:

> I was at a tailgate for some alumni. We were helping them set up, me and two guy friends. The male alumni's truck pulled up with two coolers filled with ice and sodas obviously weighing it down. He, my friends and I approached the truck to unload it and he automatically handed me the napkins and said, "it might be best to let the boys get the heavy stuff." As if I'm incapable of carrying heavy things because I'm a girl.
>
> Latina, female, 20 years old

The fascinating aspect of her interactions, as well as those of other women who experienced similar situations, is the complete disregard of their decisions by men. Despite the women volunteering their help—an indication that they believe they will be capable of carrying the heavy items—the men take away their agency. To preserve their masculinity, men are told to take care of women and to be stronger, so if a woman would prove to not need a man and be equally capable of carrying heavy items, it would break norms disrupting the gender hierarchy. Also, in both scenarios, the male-sexist frame is hidden in gender-inclusive language and context, and is only revealed when she volunteers to help. In the first case, the male student asks for *volunteers*, a gender-neutral term, but when she offers to help, he clarifies, "we meant for *guys* to come help." In the second scenario, she was there with her friends to help set up for the tailgate, which presumably entails carrying and moving heavy items. As she approached the heavier items in the truck, the older man just hands her the lightest object, napkins, and tells her that it is better for the boys to carry the "heavy stuff." The men are reproducing gender inequality by taking away her agency in disregarding her choice to help, and discriminating against women. Any "guy" or "boy" seemed to be a better choice to assist than a woman.

Women in male-dominated fields may struggle to succeed, because they are a challenge to the male-sexist frame. One 19-year-old White woman shares her friend's story:

> She is Hispanic and an engineering student, like me. She plans on going into mechanical engineering. We were talking about our engineering class and the current assignment we were working on. She was ranting about one of her group members because he made a very rude and sexist comment to her. They were starting to code for the final project and she was struggling to fix the errors her code produced. The guy who was best at coding turned to help her fix the codes, but after he was finished he said that it was ok she couldn't code because she was pretty.
>
> White, female, 19 years old

In the case above, the male classmate not only reasserts his power by completing the "male" task, but then uses gendered language condescendingly. He implies that she may still be successful in other areas, because she is "pretty." The male classmate would probably not have made the same comment to another male classmate with the same coding issue. Similarly, another female student attempted to work with a group of male students on a math problem, but was ignored. The 18-year-old White woman states:

> I attempted to talk through problems with them, but they would either ignore me or argue that I was wrong. They rarely ever argued with one another, so it was odd to me that they were so quick to shut my ideas down without a thought. Later on, I was stuck on a problem so I asked them for some help. Without even looking at me, one of the boys sternly said, "It's literally on the

board, you don't need our help." Little did he know that I had already checked the board and did not understand it . . . I felt very offended that they felt that I wasn't on the same level as them.

White, female, 18 years old

It was common for female students to be ignored or given secretarial work in engineering group projects, because "they have nice handwriting." Women often reported feeling anxious to admit that they did not know an answer or felt silenced when they did know and tried to give their input. One participant said her lab partner insisted that he deal with the chemicals so frequently, that she finally thought it was just best to "let him be nice" to her in order to get the project done. Not only are women not treated as equals, but also their agency is taken away when their male classmates refuse to let them participate equally. Their male classmates were unjustly benefiting in male-dominated areas, simply because they were men and were presumed to be more competent. Women who go into male-dominated fields face backlash from instrumental male strangers—their peers, professors, and bosses. Their male classmates can more easily maintain relationships with these other male strangers—a manifestation of the "old boys club." Women in these situations often have to make the choice to concede and risk not learning as well as their male counterparts, or feel completely isolated in these fields. Other than male-dominated career choices, some mundane activities are presumed to be "masculine," such as pumping gas or driving, and women are not expected to be good at them. In the following incident, a 20-year-old Latina was at a gas station when a male stranger assumed she needed help:

Yesterday around 5 p.m. on my drive home, I had stopped to get gas. I got out of my car and looked at the machine confused because the numbers were scrapped off the gas buttons, I usually pump 87. Some older gentlemen maybe mid to early 30s came up to me and said, "do you need help, darling? Pumping gas should be done by your boyfriend." I politely told him no and that I could take care of it myself.

Latina, female, 20 years old

She later mentions that she felt it was sexist in two ways: first, the assumption that she had or wanted a boyfriend, and that she was heterosexual. Second, that she was incapable of pumping gas on her own. In these cases, the male strangers acted in ways that reinforced the belief that men are superior physically, intellectually, and in basic tasks. The women were attempting to participate equally or show equal capability, and men disregarded them because of their gender— imposing stereotypes and prejudices. The male-sexist frame is deeply embedded in our institutions and impacts our everyday interactions. The "pro-male" and "anti-female" worldview is not exclusive to male tasks or male-dominated areas, because the premise is that men are superior *always*. Thus, even when the topic is on women's issues, men still disregard women's experiences and science to make their own conclusions.

Men Discrediting Women's Experiences of Sexism

Women's experiences are often invalidated by men, but even when there is sufficient evidence to prove that women's experiences are not unique, but in fact, part of systemic sexism, some men will still deny its existence. One participant notes that a male classmate claimed that he had never witnessed any sexism in the university, but then proceeded to make sexist comments. The 19-year-old Latina recalls:

> I was sitting in my engineering class. Two male speakers had come in to give a presentation over sexism. We were given a question- naire by the presenters to fill out. It included questions about whether or not you had seen/experienced sexism in general, in the university, in the college of engineering, and in our particular engineering class. One of my tablemates seemed very confused. He stated that he had never witnessed sexism at the university. He then went on to tell a story implying that female engineers are incom- petent. He called the girls from one of his groups in a previous engineering class, "those chicks that didn't do anything." He then went on to say how on one of the activities one of the girls asked to help, yet she was unable, and started crying within 10 minutes of beginning. He also went on to talk about another girl that had sat and cried through an entire exam.
>
> Latina, female, 19 years old

The male student dismisses the male speakers discussing sexism, because he has never witnessed it, and yet he is a perpetrator of sexism in these engineering classes by labeling female engineers as incompetent. We can presume that the speakers might have given some data on its occurrence that the male student ignored, which is what happened in another inci- dent described by an 18-year-old Latina during a mixed-gender study group session:

> After reading a chapter in a study group, we were instructed to summarize the reading and discuss our thoughts in words. This chapter was on gender inequality and sexism. All of the students were either 18 or 19 and it was a very racially diverse group. One male said he didn't believe that women were treated unequally in the workforce, even though there were statistics, bar graphs, num- bers, personal statements, etc.; he still didn't want to understand.

This angered everyone in the group, especially the women, because there was nothing that we could say to get him to understand that women are treated as lesser in many places.

Latina, female, 18 years old

In both instances, it was male classmates that refused to believe sexism was happening regardless of the data published and the stories women told them. Both male classmates were under 21 years old, but participants also describe incidents in which older men exude the same behavior. While having a meal at a restaurant, a 21-year-old White woman overheard a ~30-year-old White man state that "poor women who had undesired pregnancies were too selfish and ignorant to avoid them." He did not give any role to the men that participated in the impregnation process or consider that poor women typically do not have access to healthcare or birth control—institutions controlled by majority men.

Men also interrupt women to "correct" them, even when they have less knowledge. In another case, a White woman was having a conversation with a woman whom she describes as "like her mom" about the sexism they have experienced and the rape cases that occur on campuses, in particular the Stanford rape case, in which the victim was unconscious and raped behind a dumpster until strangers intervened. The rapist was a top Stanford swimmer. While having this conversation, Steve, who is "like her dad" and his male friend (a stranger to her) interrupted stating that there really aren't any victims when alcohol is involved. She describes the situation:

Steve's friend so conveniently ignored the fact, which he obviously knew from the context of the conversation, that the victim in the case was unconscious at the time. When I pushed that fact on him, he persisted in saying that alcohol and "gender" was more to blame and that men regret "drunk" sex with women all the time, but you don't see them "crying" rape or acting like a victim.

White, female, older than 21 years old

The participant gives Steve and his male friend statistics on sexual violence against women, but they rejected the facts. Instead, the men told her she was biased because she was a woman. She states: "By asserting their dominance in the conversation, these individuals quickly overpowered me in the conversation. And unless my viewpoint aligned with theirs, my opinion mattered very little, despite my education, because I was a 'biased female.'"

Despite providing facts, having an education, and talking about their own experiences, these women were dismissed by men who believed themselves to be experts on women's rights issues. They dominated the conversation and would not be swayed to see the other perspective. Eventually, the women just gave up and changed topics. In this particular scenario, we can see the male-sexist frame being played out in two ways. First, it is apparent through the manner in which the men describe the Stanford rape victim and the rapist. They side with the rapist by stating that it was just drunk sex and by victim-blaming the woman for drinking too much alcohol. There was an assumption that she was asking for it and they denied or ignored her state of consciousness. Second, while downplaying the rape, they simultaneously disregard the women whom they interrupted. Despite their valid opinions, the men believe they are "biased" because they are women. Not for a second do they consider their own opinions to be biased because they are men. The assumption is that they have superior knowledge because they are more objective than women. Historically, women have been seen as too emotional or hysterical to engage in fruitful discussions with men, and those that proved to be capable were either disregarded completely or dealt with violently (Mies 1986/1998; Morgan 2001; Holland 2006; Federici 2004/2014; Feagin and Ducey 2017).

Conclusion

The male strangers in these micro-level interactions with women view women through the male-sexist frame, in which women are considered to be inferior. Their sexist attitudes, commentary, and behavior are representative of a larger system of oppression, or systemic sexism. They unjustly benefit from being at the top of the gender hierarchy and utilize that power to discriminate against women and reproduce notions of gender inequality. The macro-level sexism is embedded into our society's institutions, in which men are still dominant (Feagin and Ducey 2017). Men, White men in particular, continue to remain at the top of the social hierarchy, in which they are in the highest positions of power enabling them to continue to reproduce systemic sexism at a macro-level, while also affecting micro-level interactions.

While poor people and people of color face systemic classism and racism, respectively, systemic sexism is unique. Individuals of different races and socioeconomic statuses are typically segregated in housing, workplaces, healthcare, schools, and in social groups. However, women are integrated with men in all races, classes, and aspects of society. In social groups, such as family and friends, or the workplace, women have to interact with the oppressors, men. Women face sexism in the home, and they may excuse sexist behavior because of their reliance and personal relationships with their families. However, by not countering these events, the silencing of women extends to beyond the home and into everyday life. For women, there is no avoiding male strangers' sexist behavior and commentary.

In every situation, one of the main actors was a male stranger, which made all the settings frontstage. When studying racism, Picca and Feagin (2007) found that fewer blatantly racist remarks were made in racially diverse frontstage settings, than in backstage settings among just White family and friends. In studying sexism, however, we find that men do not censor their sexist commentary, regardless of who is in their presence. The foundation of each incident is the male-sexist frame, or the view that male supremacy and masculinity is better than the opposite, and we can see the four key points of systemic sexism in every category.

In the cases of women being catcalled, we see that women were the main targets from men, which is not only a reproduction of gender inequality, but also a reminder of the gender hierarchy. Only those in power (men) could publicly degrade others (women). When women experienced face-to-face objectification through conversation, it often led to being discriminated against whether at work, school, or church. The sexist commentaries were "anti-women" and viewed women as objects for men. Women were silenced, ignored, or dismissed when they tried to show equal capability, but were stereotyped as incapable by other men. In this realm, women were trying to break gender norms in male-dominated areas and perform "male" tasks. However, sexism is not exclusively experienced in male-dominated fields. Even in situations in which women were the main topic, men still disregarded women's opinions as "biased" even when they provided scientific evidence to support their arguments.

The data indicates that women are constantly receiving blatant and subtle connotations that women are inferior in some way, even when they do not seek the information. When women are "minding their own business," they are objectified, dismissed, and silenced, or not given the chance to show they are equally capable physically and intellectually. What women experience in male-dominated fields, all women experience in everyday life. Regardless of whether women are on a run outside, at the grocery store, at work, or in school, or even choosing a seat in a classroom, every day sexist interactions remind women they are living in a male-dominated society.

Discussion Questions

1 Do you think the race and gender of the men who are being sexist towards these women is relevant? Why or why not? Why do you think that these men so freely behaved in a sexist manner?

2 How do these forms of sexism in conversation between men and women compare to forms of racism in conversation between White people and people of color?

3 In these accounts, women often shared these experiences with other women. What role do you think recounting these experiences with other women have in terms of resistance?

4 The men in these accounts were strangers to the participants. Do you think that their male friends and relatives would be as unfiltered? Why or why not?

Suggested Readings

1 Lerner, Gerda. 1987. *The Creation of Patriarchy.* New York: Oxford University Press.
2 Holland, Jack. 2006. *A Brief History of Misogyny: The World's Oldest Prejudice.* London: Constable and Robinson, Ltd.
3 Picca, Leslie Houts and Joe Feagin. 2007. *Two-Faced Racism: Whites in the Backstage and Frontstage.* New York: Routledge.
4 Feagin, Joe, and Kimberley Ducey. 2017. *Elite White Men Ruling: Who, What, When, Where, and How.* New York: Routledge.
5 Goffman, Erving. 1959. *The Presentation of Self in Everyday Life.* Garden City, NY: Anchor Books.

Suggested Media

1 *Miss Representation*
2 *Tough Guise 2*
3 *The Hunting Ground*

References

Abramson, Kate. 2014. "Turning Up the Lights on Gaslighting." *Philosophical Perspectives* 28(1): 1–30.
Allen, Christopher T., Suzanne C. Swan, and Chitra Raghavan. 2009. "Gender Symmetry, Sexism, and Intimate Partner Violence." *Journal of Interpersonal Violence* 24(11): 1816–1834
Cohen, Philip N., and Matt L. Huffman. 2003. "Individuals Jobs and Labor Markets: The Devaluation of Women's Work." *American Sociological Review* 68(3): 443–463.
Correll, Shelley J., Sarah Thébaud, and Stephen Bernard. 2007. "An Introduction To The Social Psychology of Gender." *Social Psychology of Gender* 24: 1–18.
Cotter, David A., JoAnn DeFiore, Joan M. Hermsen, Brenda Marstellar Kowalewski and Reeve Vanneman. 1997. "All Women Benefit: The Macro-Level Effect of Occupational Integration on Gender Earnings Equality." *American Sociological Review* 62(5): 714–734.
Crenshaw, Kimberlé Williams. 1989. "Demarginalizing the Intersection of Race and Sex: A Black Feminist Critique of Antidiscrimination Doctrine, Feminist Theory, and Antiracist Politics." *University of Chicago Legal Forum* 1989: 139–167.
Crenshaw, Kimberlé Williams. 1991. "Mapping the Margins: Intersectionality, Identity Politics, and Violence against Women of Color," *Stanford Law Review* 43(6): 1241–1299.
Feagin, Joe, and Kimberley Ducey. 2017. *Elite White Men Ruling: Who, What, When, Where, and How.* New York: Routledge.
Federici, Silvia. 2004/2014. *Caliban and the Witch: Women, the Body, and Primitive Accumulation.* Brooklyn, NY: Autonomedia.

Goffman, Erving. 1959. *The Presentation of Self in Everyday Life.* Garden City, NY: Anchor Books.

Holland, Jack. 2006. *A Brief History of Misogyny: The World's Oldest Prejudice.* London: Constable and Robinson, Ltd.

Hudson, Valerie M., Bonnie Ballif-Spanvill, Mary Caprioli, and Chad F. Emmett. 2012. *Sex and World Peace.* New York: Columbia University Press.

Kristof, Nicholas D., and Sheryl WuDunn. 2009. *Half the Sky: Turning Oppression into Opportunity for Women Worldwide.* New York: Vintage Books.

Levanon, Asaf, Paula England, and Paul Allison. 2009. "Occupational Feminization and Pay: Assessing Causal Dynamics Using 1950–2000 U.S. Census Data." *Social Forces* 88(2): 865–892.

MacKinnon, Catharine A. 2005. *Women's Lives, Men's Laws.* Cambridge, MA: The Belknap Press of Harvard University Press.

Mies, Maria. 1986/1998. *Patriarchy and Accumulation on a World Scale: Women in the International Division of Labor.* London and New York: Zed Books, Ltd.

Morgan, Robin. 2001. *The Demon Lover: The Roots of Terrorism.* New York: Washington Square Press.

Picca, Leslie Houts, and Joe R. Feagin. 2007. *Two-Faced Racism: Whites in the Backstage and Frontstage.* New York: Routledge Taylor & Francis Group.

Ronai, Carol Rambo, Barbara A. Zsembik, and Joe R. Feagin. 1997. *Everyday Sexism in the Third Millennium.* New York: Routledge Press.

Stone, Pamela. 2008. *Opting out? Why Women Really Quit Careers and Head Home.* Berkeley, CA: University of California Press.

5

I AM AMERICAN!

Taiwanese Immigrant Women Battling Everyday Racism

Chien-Juh Gu

Introduction

For non-White immigrants, the change of their status from being a racial majority in the sending country to a visible minority in the host society requires tremendous adjustment, even for those who are privileged with their social class. Unlike native-born minorities who live in racially strati-fied societies their entire lives, many foreign-born minorities experience race for the first time only after immigration. Without prior knowledge and "preparation" to face racial inequality, non-White immigrants have to handle prejudice and discrimination on their own. How do they per-ceive their race? How do they interact with other racial groups? How do they handle situations in which they experience racial prejudice and dis-crimination? Based on 45 life-history interviews, this chapter documents encounters of everyday racism in Taiwanese immigrant women's lives, their accounts of these encounters, and their responses.

I begin with a brief review of sociological studies of Asian Americans' racialized ethnic experiences, followed by an introduction of the meth-ods and data used in this study. Next, I describe various encounters of racial prejudice in Taiwanese immigrant women's everyday lives. Please note that all subjects in this study lived in predominantly White sub-urban areas, and professionals worked in primarily White workplaces. Subjects had very limited experience with non-White groups, such as Blacks, Latinos, and other Asians (except Chinese immigrants). Thus, all racial encounters chronicled in this chapter are interactions between Taiwanese immigrant women and Whites. Based on subjects' interpre-tations and responses of these experiences, I discuss how citizenship constitutes a significant structural factor in shaping the women's reac-tions to everyday racism and their negotiation of American identity in racialized U.S. society.

Asian American Experience of Everyday Racism

Asian immigrants and their offspring have a more than 150-year-long history of racial oppression in the United States. From the "yellow peril" over a century ago to the 1922 Ozawa case when the U.S. Supreme Court justified denying their naturalization by ruling that "Asian immigrants were not White," historically, Asian immigrants have been perceived as an "alien race." In contemporary U.S. society, the significant increase of the Asian American population since the 1960s and many Asian Americans' economic successes have not prevented them from experiencing racial hostility and discrimination. Quite the contrary, Asian Americans continue to be viewed as foreign, submissive, and non-native speaking—even for native-born Asian Americans who speak perfect English (Tuan 2003). Asian Americans are also stereotyped as high achievers and model minorities, while their actual accomplishments are often discounted as being done by "nerds" who are socially awkward (Chou and Feagin 2010). Applying Chou and Feagin's concept, Asian Americans are considered a "racial other" by a White-imposed racial frame in the United States. Their "othered" status echoes what Tuan (2003) calls "forever foreigners" and what Lowe (1996) terms the "foreigner-within."

Regardless of the persistent racial hostility and inequality Asian Americans face, their experiences with everyday racism are largely invisible in social research. Among the few studies of Asian Americans' racialized experience, it is often the second or third generation, not the first generation, who are the focus of the research (e.g., Dhingra 2007; Kibria 2002; Tuan 2003). Further, gender is rarely an emphasis of scholarly discussion on racialized experiences (for exceptions, see Gu 2015; Murti 2012). Moreover, Asian immigrant housewives' experience with racism is simply non-existent in major publications that provide overviews of the literature on gender and immigration (see Donato and Gabaccia 2015; Gabaccia 1992; Hondagneu-Sotelo 1999; Pearce et al. 2011). To fill these gaps, I document encounters of everyday racism experienced by first-generation Taiwanese immigrant women, both professionals and housewives.

Methods and Data

Data presented in this article are part of a larger project based on 45 life-history interviews with Taiwanese immigrant women (33 professionals and 12 middle-class housewives) in a Midwest urban area. These women ranged in age from 30 to 62. Except for one permanent resident, all were U.S. citizens at the time of the interviews. They immigrated to the United States between 1968 and 2006. Professional subjects worked in a range of fields, including computer science, accounting, pharmaceuticals, and academia. All these professionals had at least a bachelor's degree or higher.

Housewives were from middle-class backgrounds and lived in predominantly White suburban areas. These subjects were also highly educated—three had earned advanced degrees in the United States, six had bachelor's degrees, and three held professional diplomas in Taiwan (equivalent to 15 years of formal education).

I used the life-history approach laid out by Atkinson (1998) to design my interview schedule. I typically began by inquiring about their lives in Taiwan (childhood, schooling years, family relations, employment, career goals, etc.), why they decided to move to the United States, and how they adjusted to their new lives in the United States. Ranging from two to twelve hours, these interviews were conducted in either Taiwanese or Mandarin Chinese. All interviews were transcribed verbatim and analyzed based on the inductive approach and principles outlined in Grounded Theory (Glaser and Strauss 1967). The interview questions covered a wide range of topics, including gender relations, familial relations, parenting, work experiences, social networks, adaptation, distress, and community involvement. This chapter is based on the women's narratives concerning their radicalized experiences in their everyday lives after migrating to the United States. All names used in this chapter are pseudonyms.

Everyday Racism in Immigrant Women's Lives

Moore (2008: 447) argues that, "Everyday racism is not about racists, but about racist practice, meaning racism as common societal behavior." According to Bonilla-Silva (2017), racism refers to a dominant racial ideology that frames, produces, and reinforces the status quo—it serves the powerful and is used by Whites in various ways to justify racial inequality. Tuan (2003) uses the Ito-D'Amato incident in the O.J. Simpson trial to illustrate how a well-accomplished, well-respected Los Angeles judge who was a third-generation Japanese American was racially ridiculed by a White senator—a third-generation immigrant himself. By mocking and complaining about Judge Ito's "accent," Senator D'Amato revealed his attitude towards Ito as an inferior foreigner whom he did not respect, rather than a fellow American citizen who had a career-long record of outstanding achievements (ibid.). During the 2016 presidential campaign, Americans witnessed déjà vu: a federal judge, Gonzalo Curiel, was attacked for his Mexican heritage despite the fact that he is a native-born citizen. Although Judge Curiel is not Asian American, the same White-imposed racial frame is evident because such racial ridicules, devaluations, and othering happens only to non-Whites.

In *The Myth of the Model Minority*, Chou and Feagin (2010) discuss the racial prejudice and racist treatment Asian Americans receive in various contexts, including workplaces, schools, and public places. Instances of this everyday racism include, but are not limited to, White strangers throwing racial slurs and beating up a young second-generation Asian American at a bar, a first-generation Asian American receiving an unusually high finance rate from a local car dealer, and many Asian American kids being mocked for their lunch items. Unlike African Americans who have had a long history of fighting racial oppression since the slavery era, Asian Americans do not have a collective memory of racism, nor do they have much social support for open confrontation with discriminatory Whites. As a result, the emotional costs of enduring everyday racism are enormous (ibid.).

In their everyday lives, visible racial minorities carry their "racial marker"—skin color—that explicitly reveals their non-White status. Foreign-born non-White immigrants often add another type of status marker to their social interactions with others the minute they speak with a foreign accent. These two status markers place non-White immigrants in a vulnerable position that makes them prone to receiving racial prejudice and being treated as foreigners (a "non-us" or "othered" status). Moreover, immigrant women inherit an additional layer of disadvantage because of their gender. Their non-White, non-male, and non-native-speaking status constructs multiple structural inequalities, even for those who are advantaged in their socioeconomic status.

The two groups of women in my study—housewives and professionals—experience similar racial prejudice in their everyday lives regardless of their higher education and middle-class backgrounds. What is different between them is the vocabulary they used to describe their racialized experiences. Professionals directly identified and used the word "racism" in their narratives, whereas housewives told their stories of everyday racism more indirectly when describing "unfair treatment" by Whites. When asked what was the major cause of such unfair treatment, housewives identified both race and their lack of fluency in English as main factors, while race was the sole factor in professionals' interpretations. In responding to racial prejudice, professionals and most housewives took a confrontational approach and a few housewives used the silent treatment as resistance. Such progressive reactions to everyday racism contradict stereotypes of Asian women as being passive, submissive, and quiet.

Many housewives described encounters in their daily lives that they perceived as "unfair treatment due to their race" (racial prejudice). The following are some examples of these experiences. A former nurse in Taiwan, Linda was a 53-year-old housewife who lived in a middle-class White neighborhood. She volunteered at her children's school three to four days a week when they were young. She described how other volunteers treated her at school:

Most teachers were very nice to me, although I spoke poor English. I think they appreciated my help. But, there were a few [White female] parents who were very rude to me. We volunteered in the school library and worked together three days a week, but they never talked to me. There was a mother who was especially rude. When I said "Hi" to her, she always turned her head away and pretended that she didn't see me. After a few times, I stopped saying "Hi" to her.

Another college-educated housewife, Sophia, reported a similar experience:

One of our neighbors is very unfriendly. We see each other very often because they live just behind us, and our children go to the same school. But, every time I said "Hi," she just turned her head away. I don't know what her problem is . . . Is it because I'm Asian? I don't know, but she is very unfriendly.

Gina, who held a Master's degree from a U.S. university, described an unpleasant encounter at a grocery store:

Several years ago, one day, when I went grocery shopping with my two kids, my one-year-old daughter was cranky. She was crying and running around while I was paying for the groceries. I was so distracted that I misspoke something in my conversation with the cashier. It was something like . . . I said "one" instead of "a" or the other way around . . .

The cashier corrected me and said: "You know, English is very difficult. You've got to work harder on your English so that you don't make a mistake like this." I feel very angry every time I think about this incident. Yes, I misspoke one word, but she [the cashier] treated me with this disrespectful, dismissive attitude . . . it was like, she assumed that I was uneducated or illiterate. Even if I were uneducated or poor, I am a customer at the store. You cannot treat me like that! It's racism!

I asked Gina if she did something in responding to this incident. She explained:

I wanted to complain to the store manager, but at that moment, my two children were arguing and pushing each other. They were so cranky that, at that moment, my focus was to calm them down and take them home. I regret it that I did not do something right away. If it happened again, I would definitely go to the manager. They can't do this [to me]. I am American, although I look Asian.

When I asked what could cause such prejudiced treatment, Gina generalized that usually people with little education or those from the lower class tend to hold racial prejudice. Sophia explained that both her race and immigrant status shape people's assumptions about her and attitudes toward her. She said:

> Before they [Whites] get to know you, they have already assumed that you don't speak English and that you are uneducated, just because you are an immigrant homemaker. But, in fact, I have good education and speak decent English. We live in this nice middle-class neighborhood, which indicates that we are a good family. But, I guess some people just don't like foreigners [immigrants]. I feel that some Whites just don't want to have anything to do with you, even when you are neighbors.

Immigrant women who are professionals and fluent in English are not exempt from the racial prejudice their housewife counterparts encountered. Tiffany was a retired computer programmer who held a Master's degree from a U.S. university. She described an unpleasant experience at a bookstore:

> One day, as I was walking into a bookstore, I saw a [White] gentleman, who appeared to be in his early 60s, also coming toward the bookstore from the other end of the street. I held the door wide open to let him go inside before me. As he walked by, he looked at me and said: "Do you know you must be able to read to come here?" I wondered, would I be asked the same question if I were White? No, of course not! This is racism! When they [Whites] see you [an Asian woman], they just assume that you must be uneducated.

Ann, a 41-year-old scientist at a pharmaceutical company, insightfully explained why everyday racism occurs in middle-class immigrant women's lives. She used her own experience to illustrate her perspective:

> At work, people know that I am a scientist with a Ph.D., so I get the respect that I deserve. But, when I leave my workplace, it's a totally different story. Because I look Asian, people just assume that I don't speak English and that I am uneducated. In fact, my education might be higher than most [White] people that I encounter in my daily life.
>
> One time, I was at a grocery store. As I was paying for my groceries, I asked the casher if they had tic tacks. The cashier didn't know what I meant, so I repeated "tic tacks" a few times. Finally, she got it and found a pack for me. Then, she mocked my accent

and laughed with another cashier. I said to them: "Well, I know I speak English with an accent. That's probably because I speak four languages, so sometimes I don't pronounce every word precisely. How many languages do you speak, by the way? The two cashiers looked embarrassed and stopped laughing. Gosh, you should see their faces! If they did not look so embarrassed, I would go to their manager and complain about it. This is racism!

Like Ann, most professional subjects used the terms "racism" or "racial prejudice" to conclude their experiences of prejudice. Elena was a director at a public service institute in downtown Chicago. She described her experience of racial stereotypes and prejudice:

> I am so tired of being asked "Where are you from?" At work, I am the boss and people [co-workers] know that. Outside of my office, I am just an Asian woman. Like, for example, once I went to the salon on the second floor to get a haircut. The hairdresser asked me: "Where are you from?" and I said "from upstairs!" [laugh] They would not ask this question if I were White. They just assume that you must be from elsewhere. I am American, ok?! So, every time people ask me where I come from, I always say "I'm from Chicago" [smile].

Beth, a researcher for a pharmaceutical company, similarly pointed out others' assumptions of her being a foreigner.

> Once, when I walked into an elevator in a business building, a [White] lady said to me: "Where you are from must be very warm." I was, like, "What?" "What did you just say?" you know, I did not even open my mouth. I could have been a native-born Asian American, but she just assumed that I must be a foreigner. Another time, when I went to pick up a prescription at a pharmacy inside of a grocery store, the pharmacist asked what my last name was, and I said "Liou." She didn't understand me and asked to spell it. I did. She appeared that she still didn't get what I said and asked to see my card. So, I gave her my insurance card and then she found my prescription. As she was giving me my prescription, she mocked my accent and imitated the way I spoke in a teasing tone: "You were saying L—ou—on?" I was so angry! It's not just insulting and offensive, it is racial prejudice!! I went to the manager and filed a complaint right away.

Jamie, a college professor in her 40s, described a scene she and her son encountered at a cafeteria:

A year ago, my family took a trip to a national park. My son and I went to the cafeteria to get something to eat. We were waiting in line to get our food, and then, a [White] guy came up to us out of nowhere and shouted: "Do you understand English?" I stared at him and said, "Of course, I am a college professor and have a Ph.D.!" Then, he walked away.

That was a weird encounter, but it was not the first time that people made racist comments or acted upon racial prejudice to me or my son. I have had numerous conversations with my son, explaining what behaviors reflect racial prejudice and why, and how we should not let others define who we are just because we look different [from Whites]. I told him he was born in the U.S. and that he is American, and that he should never let others tell him otherwise or respect him less.

Like Jamie, many mothers took the responsibility of teaching their children how to deal with everyday racism. One mother, Carol, talked about how she helped her son accept and appreciate his differences from his White peers and resist prejudice. She said:

I made mostly Asian food for my children's lunch when they were in elementary school. One day, my son came home crying. He told me a [White] girl made fun of his sushi lunch. In front of other kids, the girl said: 'Yuck! That looks disgusting!' He was very sad. So, I told him: "Well, too bad, I don't think she has tried it before. Maybe you should tell her you have no idea what you're missing!" The next day, the same girl teased him again. He responded: "Oh, you don't know what you are missing. This is the best thing ever! Oh, my goodness, it's so yummy! Yum . . . yum!" That girl has never said anything afterwards.

Carol turned this incident into a teachable moment to help her children understand why people say negative things about others and how to handle similar situations in the future. Mindy, a clerk at an importing company, described one situation:

One day, I was shopping with my 8-year-old son at a department store. When we walked by two female [White] store employees, we overheard them talking about Asians in a disrespectful way loudly. My son asked me: "Mommy, why do they talk about Asians that way? Did we do anything wrong to make them mad?" I went to the manager to report this incident. The manager apologized and promised to educate their employees about racial diversity issues. I had a long talk with my son that night about race. It was not an easy topic for an 8-year-old, and honestly, I'm not sure if he totally understood. I'm hoping that the incident did not leave a scar. He may encounter more difficult situations when he grows up. We must prepare him for that.

Whites' insensitivities to racial diversity and unawareness of their racial prejudice were often mentioned in the interviews. For instance, Kelly, an adjunct professor at a community college, recalled an encounter with a staff in the school district office when her family first moved to a predominantly White neighborhood. She said:

When we first moved here, we went to the school district office to ask about the schools in the area. The [White] staff who greeted us was very friendly. After an informative introduction, she said to us: "This is a very nice area. We have very few racial minorities here, so it's very safe." I was furious and responded: "What do you mean? We are a racial minority." She then apologized. I think she meant Blacks, not Asians, but that's not okay, no matter which racial minority she referred to.

Frances, a 50-year-old housewife, told a similar story. She described:

One day, I was talking with some other parents about an academically gifted program in our school district while waiting for my son outside of his school. A teenager was there with her mom. We talked about some kids we knew who qualified for the program because they scored very high on the SAT. That girl said to her mom [in front of us]: "Do you know Tina Chen also qualified for the advanced ELA program? English is not even her language!" I was shocked by this comment, because Tina is second-generation Taiwanese who was born here [the United States]. English IS her first language! But, Tina's White peer still considered her a foreigner!

Frances continued:

When my son was in sixth grade, he told me a girl at school asked him where he was from. He was confused by the question because he was born and raised here, just like that girl. Another kid lifted his eyes up with fingers and made fun of my son's "Chinese look." I had to explain to my son how people often mistake Asian Americans as foreigners, but it's incorrect. Besides, we are Taiwanese Americans, not Chinese or Chinese Americans. I also taught him that everyone looks different. It's *not* okay to tease people about their looks. I had a long talk with him about his cultural heritage and race in America. I told him that he *is* American, period.

Teaching the next generation about racial prejudice is a major challenge that immigrant mothers face. These mothers not only stand for themselves when encountering everyday racism, but they also take it seriously when their children are involved. They usually did not initiate the "race talk" until their children asked questions about race, or when racial prejudice occurred in their interactions with others. Among all the mothers, Lisa was particularly proactive in advocating awareness of racial diversity and inclusion. She was a computer programmer at a large IT company that practiced extensive employee training on affirmative action policies and racial diversity issues. One day, her second-grade daughter came home crying because some kids at school called her names and made fun of her Asian looks. Lisa went to the principal the next day to discuss this matter. She recalled:

> I asked the principal if the school had resources to train teachers about affirmative action and cultural diversity issues. He said no. He said that it's [the] parents' responsibility, not the school's, to teach their children how to interact with racial minorities. I disagreed.
>
> I told him about how my company provided employees with resources and training to increase their awareness and sensitivity around racial minorities. I believed that schools can and should do the same. So, I discussed this matter with my boss and asked what we could do. My company began to provide consultation and resources to local schools and helped train teachers about diversity issues. We also organized a parents' network to provide input and support.

Lisa's initiation and active involvement promoted public education on racial diversity issues in the local schools and the community. Many White parents joined the network and worked alongside minority families to advocate respect and appreciation of cultural diversity. The network later extended its efforts to promote diversity among teachers and to help recruit teachers of color for public schools. Although Lisa began learning about diversity issues in middle age, she successfully applied what she learned from her workplace to the larger community.

Discussion and Conclusion

Growing up in a single-race society, Taiwanese immigrant women did not need to deal with race-related issues until they moved to the United States. Appearing as a visible racial minority, they encounter prejudice and mistreatment in their daily lives regardless of their higher education and high socioeconomic status. Moreover, professionals who are respected in their workplaces for their education, management authority, and professional knowledge and abilities appear the same as their housewife counterparts—they simply look

Asian within the larger society. Compared to their male counterparts who are often stereotyped as IT professionals, immigrant women tend to be perceived as being uneducated and unemployed. Moreover, immigrant women bear another layer of disadvantage than native-born Asian Americans—they speak English with a foreign accent. Therefore, they face multiple inequalities as being non-White, non-male, and non-native speaking, which make them prone to receive prejudice and multiple layers of oppression shaped by race, gender, and nationality.

In "Who Benefits from the White Coat? Gender Differences in Occupational Citizenship among Asian-Indian Doctors," Murti (2012) documents incidents of racism that Asian Indian physicians encounter in their daily lives. She argues that Asian doctors' honorary membership in middle-class America is accepted only when others recognize their occupation. Nevertheless, female Asian Indian physicians receive less respect than do their male counterparts because the public perceives their non-White femininity as incompatible with scientific competence, which is associated with White masculinity (ibid.).

Professional subjects in my study do not have the "white coats" that Asian Indian physicians use to reveal their occupational citizenship and earn social acceptance, as illustrated in Murti's study. Although respected in their workplaces for their education, management authority, and professional knowledge and skills, Taiwanese American women simply "look Asian" and speak with a foreign accent in public. Professionals and housewives alike experience similar racialized ethnic interactions within the larger society. In this chapter, I document many instances of everyday racism that these women encounter at grocery stores, at their children's schools, and in their own neighborhoods. They are often treated with disrespect, and excluded from the mainstream social circles because of their skin color and foreign accent. Moreover, their native-born children are also assumed foreign and considered an "other" by peers and their parents.

Interestingly, regardless of subjects' multiple structural disadvantages and lack of experience with racism prior to immigration, most act confrontationally to challenge prejudiced attitudes and treatment, including the housewives who speak little English. Their behaviors contradict prevalent social stereotypes of Asian women as passive, quiet, and submissive—characteristics of Asian femininity that are also highly valued in their society of origin.

What contributes to these women's progressive acts? As revealed in the women's narratives, their good understanding of racism shows a certain degree of acculturation. Their American identity further empowers them with a sense of entitlement to assert themselves and act upon what they consider the "American spirit"—protecting one's own rights and speaking up against injustice. For example, Ann, Gina, Elena, and Beth all said "I am American. They can't treat me like that. It's racism!" Carol, Frances, Jamie, and Lisa told their kids that "You are American. Don't let others tell you otherwise or respect you less." In fact, these perceptions and statements largely depart from the prominent cultural values in subjects' society of origin, a patriarchal Asian society in which conformity, respect for hierarchical social positions, and relational harmony are norms for social interactions. The women's fearless contests against everyday racism exemplify their agentic resistance to racial-power imposition. As Foucault argues, "there are no relations of power without resistances" (Foucault 1980: 142). Although racist practice continues, the women's American identity shaped by citizenship equips them with a toolkit and vocabulary to unapologetically negotiate their equal stance in U.S. society.

Discussion Questions

1   Why do people assume that immigrant women are uneducated and cannot speak English? Where does this assumption come from? What are major social factors that shape this assumption? What can we do to change this stereotype?

2   Why do some people avoid interacting with immigrant women, even when they are neighbors? In this chapter, these women live in middle-class suburban areas, and their children go to the same schools that their White neighbors attend. Why do some neighbors continue to ignore immigrant women, even when they work side by side at their children's schools?

3   Why are Asian accents ridiculed, while European accents are considered "cute" in U.S. society? What are major social factors that shape these different perceptions? What do these ideas tell us about the larger social structure?

4   Why do young children tease their non-White peers? Where do they learn about the concept of race and the vocabulary of mocking non-Whites at a young age? What are the social consequences of such behaviors? What should parents do to prevent their children from developing racial prejudice? How should teachers handle racial bias and implicit prejudice at school?

5   In everyday life, when we witness instances in which non-White individuals encounter racial prejudice or discrimination, what should we do to advocate social justice, rather than being bystanders?

6   Have you ever felt you were treated unequally because of your race, gender, sexuality, religion, or accent? Describe your experience and how you felt at that moment. How did you respond? Would you respond differently if it happens to you again? Why? In your opinion, what is the best way to combat prejudice?

Suggested Readings

1   Bonilla-Silva, Eduardo. 2017. *Racism without racists: Color-blind racism and the persistence of racial inequality in America*. 5th edition. Lanham, MD: Rowman & Littlefield.
2   Chou, Rosalind S. and Joe R. Feagin. 2010. *The myth of the model minority: Asian Americans facing racism*. Boulder, CO: Paradigm.
3   Feagin, Joe R. 2013. *The white racial frame: Centuries of racial framing and counter-framing*. 2nd edition. New York: Routledge.
4   Gu, Chien-Juh. 2017. *The resilient self: Gender, immigration, and Taiwanese Americans*. New Brunswick, NJ: Rutgers University Press.
5   Schwalbe, Michael. 2014. *Rigging the game: How inequality is reproduced in everyday life*. 2nd edition. London: Oxford University Press.
6   Tuan, Mia. 2003. *Forever foreigners or honorary whites? The Asian ethnic experience today*. New Brunswick, NJ: Rutgers University Press.
7   Yuen, Nancy Wang. 2016. *Reel inequality: Hollywood actors and racism*. New Brunswick, NJ: Rutgers University Press.

Suggested Social Media

1   "A Conversation with Asian-Americans on Race" New York Times. 2016. Op-Docs:Season5.www.nytimes.com/video/opinion/100000004308529/a-conversation-with-asians-on-race.html
2   "Race in America." New York Times. #thisis2016: Asian-Americans Respond. www.nytimes.com/video/us/100000004706646/thisis2016-asian-americans-respond.html

References

Atkinson, Robert. 1998. *The life history interview*. New York: Sage.

Bonilla-Silva, Eduardo. 2017. *Racism without racists: Color-blind racism and the persistence of racial inequality in America*, 5th edition. Lanham, MD: Rowman & Littlefield.

Chou, Rosalind S. and Joe R. Feagin. 2010. *The myth of the model minority: Asian Americans facing racism*. Boulder, CO: Paradigm.

Donato, Katharine M. and Donna Gabaccia. 2015. *Gender and international migration: From the slavery era to the global age*. New York: Russell Sage Foundation.

Dhingra, Pawan. 2007. *Managing multicultural lives: Asian American professionals and the challenge of multiple identities*. Stanford, CA: Stanford University Press.

Foucault, Michel. 1980. *Power/knowledge: Selected interviews and other writings 1972–1977*. London: Vintage.

Gabaccia, Donna (Ed.). 1992. *Seeking common ground: Multidisciplinary studies of immigrant women in the United States*. Santa Barbara, CA: Praeger.

Glaser, Barney G. and Anselm L. Strauss. 1967. *The discovery of grounded theory: Strategies for qualitative research*. New York: Aldine De Gruyter.

Gu, Chien-Juh. 2005. "Racial Glass Ceilings, Gendered Responses: Taiwanese American Professionals' Experiences of Otherness." *Sociological Focus* 48: 126–149.

Hondagneu-Sotelo, Pierrette (Ed.). 1999. *Gender and U.S. immigration: Contemporary trends.* Berkeley, CA: University of California Press.

Kibria, Nazli. 2002. *Becoming Asian Americans: Second-generation Chinese and Korean American identities.* Baltimore, MD: Johns Hopkins University Press.

Lowe, Lisa. 1996. *Immigrant acts.* Durham, NC: Duke University Press.

Moore, John Hartwell. 2008. "Everyday racism." In *Encyclopedia of race and racism*, edited by Angela Doolin. Detroit, MI: Macmillan Reference USA.

Murti, Lata. 2012. "Who benefits from the white coat? Gender differences in occupational citizenship among Asian-India doctors." *Ethnic and Racial Studies* 35: 2035–2053.

Pearce, Susan C., Elizabeth J. Clifford, and Reena Tandon 2011. *Immigration and women: Understanding the American experience.* New York: New York University Press.

Tuan, Mia. 2003. *Forever foreigners or honorary whites? The Asian ethnic experience today.* New Brunswick, NJ: Rutgers University Press.

6

QUEER FACES, UNSAFE SPACES

Everyday Discrimination Experiences of Lesbian and
Gender Non-Conforming Women

Dresden N. Lackey and Rosalind S. Chou

Despite the intention and imagery of a progressive, egalitarian country, overt hate crimes against LGBTQs in the U.S. have continued to increase each year (Hansen-Weaver 2009). From the years-long controversy of which bathrooms trans people are permitted to use, to the recent ban on trans persons serving in the military by Donald Trump, show that discrimination can take place in many legal, publicly supported ways. Moreover, as the myth of equality for all gains popularity, veiled forms of heterosexism are used as discriminatory tools against queer populations to maintain the heteronormative status quo. For gender non-conforming and lesbian women, encounters with discrimination begin early in life and occur daily in both overt and covert ways, in the forms of blatant heterosexism, expectations of emphasized femininity, and the perpetual endorsement of heteronormative behavior.

Sue (2010) claims that while 40% of gay men report being the victim of violence or property crimes, 12–13% of lesbian women report the same issues. Rather than suggesting women are less often the victims of anti-queer discrimination, consider how often queer women experience harmful covert prejudices. Swim et al. (2007) note the importance of understanding subtle, everyday forms of homonegativity, as they are less likely to gain media attention than overt hate crimes, yet the frequency with which they occur has lasting and negative impacts (Sue 2010; Nadal et al. 2010). As these disguised assaults are less obvious, seemingly innocuous, and thus difficult to identify, the repercussions for the perpetrators are slim to none, allowing such attacks to be utilized against the victim frequently and without consequence. Both the hidden insult and the blatant prejudice experienced by gender non-conforming and lesbian women push to portray gender-normative behaviors and can manifest easily in common daily settings, most notably within the family home, school, and work.

Everyday Discrimination

Gender non-conforming and lesbian women experience everyday discrimination in a variety of ways. Antigay legislation, physical and sexual violence or threats, and hate speech are all common examples of overt daily harassment faced by queer women. Trans women are especially at risk of violent and deadly assaults, implemented by men who feel "deceived" while media coverage perpetuates the framework that trans women are deceptive men in disguise (Schilt and Westbrook 2009). Sue (2010) further points to several actions that perpetuate invisible heterosexism alongside these more obvious forms of prejudice, including heterosexist language/terminology, the assumption of abnormality, and the endorsement of heteronormative culture and behaviors. While heterosexist language may be openly derogatory (such as "*dyke*," "*butch*," or the intentional misgendering of someone), the everyday messages conveyed in its subtler usage reflects a worldview of heteronormativity that alienates and others queer women's behavior. The assumption that a woman's status as queer is a phase or identity crisis, for example, suggests their identity development is abnormal, immature, or incomplete.

Further, discrimination is not only maintained by the actions and beliefs of people themselves; queer women must navigate a heteronormative culture that fails to nourish and support their statuses as gender non-conforming or lesbian, where the expectation is such that women are supposed to be straight, feminine, and have a gender presentation that matches their gender assigned at birth – any deviation from even one of these heteronormative expectations is considered abnormal. Societal tolerance about violence against LGBTQs further prevents many sexual minorities from seeking support out of fear it may lead to further victimization, and institutional factors such as inadequate training for educators and other adults who work with youth further contribute to the pervasiveness of bullying (Mishna et al. 2009). When faced with repeated daily discrimination in these ways, often by close friends, family, or the inescapable environments of home, school, or work, the detrimental impact of such assaults on queer and gender non-conforming women are lasting, including internalized sexual stigmas, identity development and disruption, poor academic performance, substance abuse, homelessness, and psychological distress (Sue 2010; Mishna et al. 2009).

Family and Home

For many queer and gender non-conforming women, queer discrimination begins in the home. Blatant heterosexist comments and beliefs from family members communicate at an early age that queerness is not tolerated, while subtle discrimination in the home often takes form in gender-conforming rules regarding clothing, toys, and behaviors.

This imposition sets heteronormativity and gender conformity as the accepted standard in the home.

When queer youth recognize their own deviations from this standard, attempts to remain closeted or risk familial ostracism are psychologically harmful. In their study examining White and Latinx queer youth, Ryan and colleagues (2009) found that respondents who reported greater family rejection during adolescence had poorer health outcomes in young adulthood, including an increased risk of suicide attempts, depression, illegal drug use, and unprotected sex, when compared to families with little or no levels of family rejection.

School

School is a common, often mandatory, experience for queer and cis-het youth alike. As Wyss (2004) points out, children are rarely able to choose which school they attend, or whether they will attend school at all. However, while 9% of straight youth report experiencing violence at school, most queer youth must attend schools that expose them to harassment, bullying, and assault on a daily basis; despite the underreporting of bullying, 84% of queer youth report verbal harassment and approximately 25% of queer youth report physical violence, and 70% of queer youth report issues in school due to sexual orientation discrimination alone (Friend 1993; Mishna et al. 2009). In her study examining the high school experiences of gender non-conforming youth, Wyss (2004) found daily incidents of harassment ranging from verbal threats to physical violence to sexual assault and rape. Her respondents believed these attacks were specifically due to their refusal to conform to gender norms, and often remained silent after the attacks. Toomey and colleagues (2010) further found that victimization due to LGBTQ status was significantly associated with negative psychosocial adjustment for queer youth in schools, the effects of which last for years beyond the average age of grade school attendance.

Evidence suggests that homophobic bullying starts early, and is pervasive in elementary school, high school, and at university (Mishna et al. 2009). Unfortunately, little protections are in place for queer youth, as many teachers and school administrators display a tolerance of such bullying, and fail to intervene when violence and harassment of students perceived to be queer was witnessed; the missed opportunity to intervene further sends the message that harassment of queer students is accepted (Mishna et al. 2009). For trans and queer youth facing daily abuse from peers, school is rarely a place of learning, rather than a place of survival.

Work

Full-time employed adults spend almost 25% of their time at work every year (Hollis and McCalla 2013). Like school, work may often be a place of harassment or bullying for queer women, as workplace discrimination and bullying occurs disproportionately for LGBTQs (Hollis and McCalla 2013). In a review of previous research, Croteau (1996) found that data from several studies revealed evidence of formal and informal discrimination in the workplace against queer women, including refusing to hire or advance someone due to their sexual orientation, verbal harassment, and property violence. Further, research suggests that queer women frequently reported a fear of discrimination in the workplace if their sexual orientation was revealed on the job (Croteau 1996). The impact of heterosexist bullying in the workplace is dire; Hollis (2012) found that 24% of their queer respondents left a job specifically to escape a bully. Further impacts include depression, anxiety, lowered employee morale, and poor organizational effectiveness (Hollis and McCalla 2013).

At the time of this writing, sexual orientation is not protected against workplace harassment and discrimination in every U.S. state, sending a nation-wide message that heterosexism and bullying is tolerated. Sexual orientation is often ignored as a diversity issue in many workplace organizations, and anti-discrimination policies and workshops largely exclude queer-focused antibullying training (Pichler et al. 2010). While some organizations have made attempts at being inclusive of their queer employees through domestic partner coverage and LGBTQ support groups, Hollis and McCalla (2013) argue that these policies do not adequately cover bullying.

Method

Sample

Individual in-depth interviews were conducted with eleven students at a southern, metropolitan university. Of those eleven, eight identified as women, gender fluid, or as trans femme. The sample consisted of two individuals who identify as lesbian, three individuals who identify as bisexual, one individual who identifies as asexual,[1] and two individuals who identify their sexual orientation as queer. Half of the sample identified their race as White, while a quarter identified as Asian/Asian American, one respondent was Black, and one respondent was Latina. The pronouns used throughout are specific to the pronouns each respondent identified as their own. For that reason, pronouns including *she* and *they* are used depending on respondent.[2]

Recruitment & Procedure

Data was collected during the 2016–17 academic school year. To be included, respondents must have first completed a separate online survey regarding on-campus experiences at a southern, metropolitan university and opted in to the optional in-person interview at the end of the online survey. Thus, all respondents were students. Interviews were conducted in a private office in the Sociology department of the southern university by two researchers. Respondents were given contact information upon interview collection in the event that they may further share follow-up comments or experiences not identified during the interview.

Interviews lasted between 45 and 90 minutes. The interview questions began with childhood experiences including family and school experiences, and progressed to life as a student, and as a resident of a southern metropolitan city. All respondents were asked about familial expectations regarding their gender and sexual orientation.

Data Analysis

Researchers sought to examine the types of harassment experienced by queer and gender non-conforming women. Specifically, how types of violence from family and peers differed depending on sexual orientation and gender of respondents. In addition, researchers sought to reveal dimensions of familial approval and disapproval in respondents' identities as queer women and their experiences of gender-conforming expectations. Coding began after all interviews were completed. Elements of both Grounded Theory and Thematic Analysis[3] were used. Interviews were transcribed and initially examined without coding to familiarize the researchers with the content of each interview. Codes included "Bullied, Othered, or Picked on," with child nodes of physical violence, emotional abuse, and transphobic or heterosexist verbal remarks; "Family Influence," with child nodes of family disapproval, family approval, gender socialization, emotional abuse, and heterosexism or transphobia; "Gender or Hetero Conforming Expectations"; "Gender or Hetero Non-Conforming Behaviors"; "Mention of Friends/Acquaintances"; "Public Spaces," with child nodes of school and work; "Religion Mention"; and "Self-Identity," with child nodes of certain self-identity and uncertain self-identity, with further grandchild nodes of desire to be someone or something else, and hiding true self from others.

The most prominent codes throughout the four interviews included transphobic or heterosexist verbal remarks, familial heterosexism and transphobia, family disapproval, and hiding true self from others. Several matrix queries were produced to compare case attributes with experiences. The matrices produced include Gender vs. Family Influence (and all child nodes), Gender vs. Bullied, Picked On, or Othered (and all child nodes), Sexual Orientation vs. Bullied, Picked On, or Othered (and all child nodes), Gender vs. Heteronormative Expectations and Gender Non-Conforming Behaviors (run as a single matrix).

Results

Family and Home

Findings indicated that cisgender respondents experienced less aggressive homophobic messages from family members. Specifically, cisgender respondents reported no instances of physical violence and fewer instances of emotional abuse and heteronormative/transphobic verbal remarks compared to their trans counterparts. Still, elements of prejudice existed across all family types. Io, a White, queer trans femme who was raised as a boy in a highly religious family, recalls members of their family repeatedly equating even the slightest gender non-conforming appearance to "being a weirdo":

> My grandpa used to always make comments that I was a "weirdo," which he meant as like, a sissy basically, because I had long hair, it was kind of like, similarly styled to how I have it now but it was really long and shaggy and it was not what boys were supposed to have and I would dye my hair blonde and he would always make comments about that or I would mention I want a piercing and he would be like, "don't do that, you shouldn't be a weirdo."

Transphobic verbal remarks were typically aggressive in nature, and were directed at both the respondent as well as other people perceived to be LGBTQ *to* the respondent. Other verbal remarks were less aggressive, but still portrayed heteronormative and othering messages about queer populations. Daniella, a Latina undergraduate lesbian, remembered hearing her family name-calling gender non-conforming strangers:

Daniella: Just generally speaking they're like, they'll have, names like, they'll say for girls, just kind of like, a little tomboyish, I can't remember the name or the word, but they would say, oh she's, ah—*marimacha*. I have no idea what the translation is, but basically saying she's a girl but she's also kind of (pause)—

Interviewer: Masculine.

Daniella: Masculine, yeah. So they weren't saying anything yet about her sexuality, but they were saying she has these traits and they are kind of weird, if you want to say it like that. And for the guys it was just like, if he liked this or that, or maybe he wasn't even exactly gay but maybe he was a little bit more feminine if you want to say that, they would say oh he might be a girl, he might be this or that, but nothing explicit, like it's totally wrong, you can't do things like that. It was just kind of like, mean names.

Cis and trans women alike experienced gender-conforming and heteronor-mative expectations from family members in childhood. Though there were higher reports of gender-conforming expectations by family for trans respondents, the number of incidents per individual was relatively similar. Gender-conforming expectations from family were portrayed both verbally and in behaviors, including comments about a future heterosexual marriage, or the insistence of certain gendered toys, dress, or extracurricular activities. Lauren, a White, queer trans woman raised as a boy, recalled a story her mother shared about her abusive father imposing gendered standards as early as six months old:

'You know when your dad, when you were a baby and you were just six months old, you were playing with a Barbie and your dad just like, turns to me and asks me, he was just like, "*is he gay? He's playing with a Barbie!*"'

Lauren goes on to describe the detrimental impact of being pressured into masculine hobbies when her gender expression differed greatly from the expectations of her family:

So it's just like this constant process of trying to push me into sports and trying to push me into these other things which only increased the feelings of like, isolation and alienation because all my friends were girls, I was perceived as very feminine, so I was just bullied kind of from day 1, and like, very much putting me in these mas-culine and like male-only social groups was actively detrimental.

For gender non-conforming and lesbian women, these detrimental impacts of a lack of familial support ranged from isolation and social withdrawal to physical self-harm. Io recalls how they reacted to the transphobic abuse from their father after he learned they identified as gay at age 14:

I started drinking at that point and smoking cigarettes and cutting myself and yeah, so it's like, that was like the biggest thing I guess, it's just, (pause) like the way he reacted and, like he threatened to ship me out to live elsewhere, or would just make comments about how disgusting I was, or like he and my mom would fight and he would blame me even though it was his fault and so, yeah, I started doing all of those things; I would like, write poetry about being depressed or ending my life, and yeah.

Coding for family approval and support indicated an acceptance or encour-agement of respondents in direct relation to their identity as queer or gender non-conforming. Cisgender respondents reported higher instances of family approval and support and fewer instances of overall family disapproval, while trans respondents, like Io and Lauren's accounts above, exposed between 1.5 and 2.5 times more instances of family disapproval and abuse than cisgender counterparts and from 0–1 single instance of familial approval and support. As family is often, if not exclusively, the first relationships people of all genders learn to form and navigate, familial disapproval of one's self-expression can be consequential for children both in childhood and throughout the life course.

School and Work

Respondents reported both school and workplace as settings of heterosexist abuse, riddled with both overt and covert discrimination from coworkers, peers, and administration alike. Due to the nature of the interview setting, respondents' discrimination in school was more salient than workplace discrimination for respondents. Bullying at school by peers was largely verbal and heterosexist in nature, though physical violence was also present. When administration and staff noticed bullying against queer students, little, if any, effort was put forward to dispel the abuse. Lauren reported physical violence at school to such an extent that she suffered broken bones from the abuse. The punishment for the perpetrator was two days of lunch detention, though Lauren was confined to a splint for several months. She further recalls an incident in which another student was physically violent toward her in front of apathetic staff:

> I never threw a punch. All I did was walked away. I tried to walk away so many times, I tried to go closer to where the coaches were, and when I finally got to the coaches and they were like, hitting me and stuff, and I explained what was happening, and I ended up getting suspended from school. And I think I actually got suspended more than the main guy who was hitting me. So it's just kind of like these examples of like, the coaches could clearly see what was going on. They knew me, they could clearly see what was going on, and they just chose to do nothing. And (pause), a lot of harassment in class, teachers would just look away. [. . .] And I feel like my femininity was almost like, enough to justify that in their minds. Because they either wouldn't defend me, or, and it's very interesting because, you know if a boy was saying these things or like hitting a cis girl, they would have been all over that, but since I was trans, in a way they were just like, "I didn't see it!"

Though Lauren tried to walk away from the abuse, staff punished her as if she had instigated and participated willingly in the fight. Staff and administration's indifference to the violence committed against her further exposed school as a transphobic and unsafe place.

Respondents further discussed discrimination they experienced beyond grade-school age and well into higher education. Janae, a Black Ace undergraduate, described living with a cisgender straight suitemate in on-campus housing that often questioned and othered Janae's sexuality, repeatedly expecting Janae to educate her on all queer information and issues. When the suitemate saw her Ace flag after a PRIDE parade:

> She immediately asked, "does that mean you're like, gay or something?" and I was like, did you not read the description? I eventually just turned around and I was like alright, and eventually I just laid it all out and, oh my God, so, she was asking all these questions and I was like, alright, okay (laughs) and you know, "oh, so are you comfortable with the way you dress?" and whatnot I was like, what's that mean? I picked out these clothes specifically (laughs). Like did you expect me to be more masculine? Because that's not my personality. Just all kinds of other questions she would preface with, "this is probably a stupid question." Well then don't waste my time.

Janae's experience seems to be common among respondents. Microaggressive verbal remarks are easily disguised as well-intentioned questions, yet only serve to isolate queer women in covert and frustrating ways. To avoid harassment from peers, several respondents reported altering their behaviors to appear more gender conforming, straight, or cisgender. For example, both trans respondents reported dating women in high school to appear straight, and one trans respondent reported using fake girl names for romantic crushes at school that were on boys, to appear straight. Trans respondents reported several instances of heteronormative/transphobic verbal remarks and physical violence, as well as higher instances of emotional abuse from peers. The fact that almost all respondents felt the need to hide their true selves at school indicate the lack of safety school settings offer for open gender and sexuality expression. Both trans and cis respondents reported several comments from peers in school settings that denied or questioned their gender expression or sexual orientation. Rather than school facilitating an education, it instead became yet another setting of inescapable queer discrimination from peers and administration alike.

For queer respondents, workplace discrimination often began as early as the job interview. Io recalls having a difficult time getting past the interview step of several potential service-industry jobs in the southern metropolitan city: "I've had shitty experience finding work here. Like the first place I walked into I think when I had an interview, the whole staff turned around and laughed, as in, right when I walked in the door."

Io further reported obtaining jobs and quitting shortly after, due to transphobic verbal harassment from coworkers. To date, less than half of all U.S. states protect against employment discrimination for LGBTQs, yet seemingly innocuous tactics are still used to prevent safe, mobile employ-ment for queer women. Thus, not only are heterosexist and transphobic perpetrators affecting the psychological well-being of queer recipients, but further affecting the immediate income, financial security, and future employment opportunities for queer people as well.

Everyday Discrimination

Discriminatory incidents at home and in school portray only two settings where abusive heteronormativity occurs. Respondents further remarked on several other daily, common situations and circumstances where they have been the victims of discrimination due to their gender expression or sexual orientation, revealing how inescapable queer prejudice is. Microaggressions that portray any gender non-conforming behavior as deviant perpetuate the idea that lesbian and non-feminine women are not "normal people." Io, a queer trans femme, remarks on these comments that suggest they are being deceiving:

> People just make microaggressive comments I guess, I get asked a lot, is that your real name, when I tell them my name, they think I'm a performer and I'm giving them my drag name or something and, what else, people tell me that my being non-binary is just a millennial thing.

Seeing sexuality or gender expression as a generational phenomenon or a trendy phase was also mentioned by both cis and trans respondents. Instances of verbal harassment from peers further buttressed this idea as they mocked non-binary and non-hetero labels, and refused to use pronouns. Amy, a White cisgender bisexual recalled how she internalized the importance of labels, yet sometimes felt lost without one:

> There were days where I just didn't feel good about myself, which was weird. That never really happened to me before. So yeah just kind of that sense of not belonging especially growing up, like I guess I was millennial; got to label everything and then not having a label was a bit disconcerting. And then realizing there are some people who just don't have labels, that doesn't mean it's wrong. Especially if you can't control it, so once I accepted that, that was kind of like, okay I don't need to do this to myself, I just accept it.

Gender non-conforming behaviors were coded as behaviors that do not align with the societal norms of the respondents' gender-assigned-at-birth. These behaviors included instances of personal style (hair, clothing, body jewelry), and primarily befriending peers of the opposite gender-assigned-at-birth. Trans respondents reported more instances of gender non-conforming behaviors in childhood than their cis counterparts. Lauren recalled the majority of her childhood friends being girls, much to the confusion of the adults around her:

> I would like, play with girls and stuff like that, and I would keep wondering why did they treat me differently and things like that. And then just those subtle pushes of like, "why are you hanging out with girls all the time?" or assuming that because I'm hanging out with girls that I was attracted to them. It's kind of like hetero-normative reading of like, "oh you're a boy and you're hanging out with these girls so you must be attracted to them," even though I was four.

Lauren's account notes the heteronormativity that was imposed on her, even at the age of four. Her preference to play with girl peers was interpreted by adults as a romantic attraction rather than a platonic interest. Lauren, who identifies as queer, notes that even in adulthood she is not attracted to women. This misreading of gender non-conforming behaviors in childhood further pushed her to the isolation we saw in previous sections:

> I didn't really know how to place the feeling, I was more . . . it was kind of just like, why are they treating me differently, or why are they treating me like this, and I kind of like, didn't understand or like, why other people would react these certain ways if I would behave this way or whatever, and then it kind of just became more of this like . . . alienation.

The reality of everyday discrimination is that very few settings are safe for queer women. Seemingly everyday tasks, such as running errands or visiting a restaurant, always create the risk of microaggressions or more overt verbal harassment from strangers or peers alike. Several respondents noted feeling unsafe even in gay neighborhoods of the area, due to racism and transphobia within cis, White queer circles, exposing the need for education about queer and trans populations in all communities.

Discussion

The largest limitation to this study is the extremely narrow sample size. Due to this, generalizations about race, sexual orientation, and gender outside of these eight cases cannot be made. Race matrices were conducted in terms of familial influence and bullying. It is important to note that both trans respondents were also White, and thus, race cannot be implied as a unique individual factor generalizable to trans people of color, who face a unique burden of discrimination. A larger sample size that includes both trans and cis respondents from all racial backgrounds being examined is needed to understand racial influence on queer discrimination more fully.

Further, future coding may include more specific types of discrimination, including overt and covert discrimination from peers and family. In the present analysis, all discrimination was included under "Bullied, Othered, or Picked On," with child nodes to identify physical, verbal, or emotional harassment. However, these child nodes can be further broken down to consider microaggressive behaviors and hate crimes.

The results expose the realities of bullying, heteronormative expectations, and transphobia that exists for gender non-conforming and queer women, especially for those who identify as trans. Results indicate that not only do trans respondents suffer from more bullying of all types, but also from more familial abuse than cis counterparts. Responses show that neither public nor private settings provide a safe space for full expression of gender identity. The lack of intervention and inclusive training communicates the notion that queer women should accept being harassed in everyday settings. Lauren notes how she saw this acceptance as mandatory for a long time:

> I feel like for a long time I kind of just internalized it and I didn't really think about it, I kind of just internalized it as, well this is what I gotta deal with. Or even like, said, oh this is just the price I pay for being trans. And I don't think that that's what it should be about, like I don't think that we should just expect people to sacrifice their time, their safety, and like mental and emotional being, and even physical well-being just to participate in higher education, especially when so many trans women face harassment and trans people in general or specifically trans women of color are facing a lot of harassment and dropping out of schools in huge numbers because of these issues that would, in some cases, be fairly simple to fix.

These results highlight the importance of inclusive, thorough training for teachers and school administrators on queer bullying, as well as a more thorough understanding of at-home abuse for queer youth. Vanessa, a Filipina lesbian studying queer women in her graduate program, highlights the importance of visibility for herself and other sexual minorities:

> What motivates me [. . .] to be out, and to have my work reflect a lot of the unspoken or unknown is, there is so much invisibility as a young person; that here I am as an adult, and I am almost trying to make up for all that. I didn't have access or there were no resources for me or I didn't know how to articulate the need for resources. That motivates me to do those things, and to make those things, and to work with other folks, too, so that other folks don't have to suffer in silence.

In this light, further limitations include the dearth of research specifically examining gender non-conforming and queer women. A review of the literature found that much of the queer research conducted to date examines LGBTQ populations in their entirety, without specific, individual attention on cis and trans women per se. Thus, many findings apply to men and women alike, often without individual comparisons of women-identifying populations. Additional research is needed to examine the unique experiences of queer women, without being compared to queer men.

Discussion Questions

1 In what ways has everyday discrimination against queer populations changed in your lifetime? Consider your immediate circle, such as with peers, family, and school, as well as institutional ways, such as policy and law.
2 Discuss ways in which everyday discrimination for queer and gender non-conforming women may differ based on race, class, or setting?
3 Do "safe spaces" truly exist for queer populations? Discuss some spaces that are marketed as "safe" but may not be, and which spaces may be truly safe for queer women of all types.

Suggested Readings

1 Halberstam, Judith. 1998. *Female Masculinity*. Durham, NC: Duke University Press.
2 Butler, Judith. 2006. *Gender Trouble: Feminism and the Subversion of Identity*. New York: Routledge.
3 Foucault, Michel. 1978. *The History of Sexuality, Vol. 1: An Introduction*. New York: Vintage press

Notes

1 Asexuality will be further referred to as "ace."
2 We have lightly edited the interview quotes for grammar, stutter words ("you know"), and clarity. Pseudonyms are given to all respondents to conceal their identity, and some details have been omitted or disguised in the quotes from interviews to increase the anonymity of participants.
3 Charmaz, K. 2014. *Constructing Grounded Theory*. Los Angeles, CA: Sage.

References

Croteau, James M. 1996. "Research on the Work Experiences of Lesbian, Gay, and Bisexual People: An Integrative Review of Methodology and Findings." *Journal of Vocational Behavior* 48: 195–209.
Friend, Richard A. 1993. "Choices, Not Closets: Heterosexism and Homophobia in Schools." In *Beyond Silenced Voices: Class, Race, and Gender in US Schools*, edited by L. Weis and M. Fine. Albany NY: SUNY Press, pp. 209–235.

Hansen-Weaver, Jessica. 2009. *Behind the Wave of Anti-Gay Hate Crimes.* Socialistworker.org. Retrieved October 31, 2017 from https://socialistworker. org/2009/01/19/anti-gay-hate-crimes

Hollis, Leah P., and Scott A McCalla. 2013. "Bullied Back in the Closet: Disengagement of the LGBT Employees Facing Workplace Bullying." *Journal of Psychological Issues in Organizational Culture* 4(2): 6–16.

Hollis, Leah P. 2012. *Bullying in the Ivory Tower: How Aggression and Incivility Erode American Higher Education.* Wilmington, DE: Patricia Berkly LLC.

Mishna, Faye, Peter A. Newman, Andrea Daley, and Steven Solomon. 2009. "Bullying of Lesbian and Gay Youth: A Qualitative Investigation." *British Journal of Social Work* 39: 1598–1614.

Nadal, Kevin L., David P. Rivera, and Melissa J. H. Corpus. 2010. "Sexual Orientation and Transgender Microaggressions: Implications for Mental Health and Counseling." In *Microaggressions and Marginality: Manifestation, Dynamics, and Impact,* edited by D. W. Sue. Hoboken, NJ: John Wiley & Sons, pp. 217–240.

Pichler, Shaun, Arup Varma, and Tamara Bruce. 2010. "Heterosexism in Employment Decisions: The Role of Job Misfit." *Journal of Applied Social Psychology* 40(10): 2527–2555.

Ryan, Caitlin, David Huebner, Rafael M. Diaz, and Jorge Sanchez. 2009. "Family Rejection as a Predictor of Negative Health Outcomes in White and Latino Lesbian, Gay, and Bisexual Young Adults." *Pediatrics* 123(1): 346–352.

Schilt, Kristen, and Laurel Westbrook. 2009. "Doing Gender, Doing Heteronormativity: "Gender Normals," Transgender People, and the Social Maintenance of Heterosexuality." *Gender & Society* 23(4): 440–464.

Sue, Derald W. 2010. *Microaggressions in Everyday Life: Race, Gender, and Sexual Orientation.* Hoboken, NJ: John Wiley & Sons, Inc.

Swim, Janet K., Nicolas B. Pearson, and Kristen E. Johnston. 2007. "Daily Encounters with Heterosexism: A Week in the Life of Lesbian, Gay, and Bisexual Individuals." *Journal of Homosexuality* 53(4): 31–48.

Toomey, Russell B., Caitlin Ryan, Rafael M. Diaz, Noel A. Card, and Stephen T. Russell. 2010. "Gender-Nonconforming Lesbian, Gay, Bisexual, and Transgender Youth: School Victimization and Young Adult Psychosocial Adjustment." *Developmental Psychology* 46(6): 1580–1589.

Wyss, Shannon E. 2004. "This Was My Hell The Violence Experienced by Gender Non-Conforming Youth in US High Schools." *International Journal of Qualitative Studies in Education* 17(5): 709–730.

7

BUT I'M THE LUCKY ONE

A Narrative

Dean Ohmsford

In spite of everything, I've been incredibly lucky. I can say that on account of how I'm still alive. A staggering 46% of trans men attempt suicide. I'm one of them, but it never took. Things might have been different had I been bullied, harassed, verbally attacked by my family, or had I experienced more frequent or more severe discrimination. But I was already an adult when I started consciously questioning my gender. I had supportive friends and spouse, my family checked out of my life rather than attacking, and my stealth game was strong. Also no one tried to murder me. Like I said: lucky. As my identity evolved, I was faced with new and difficult challenges, but I learned to avoid the ones I could and adapt to the ones I could not. I was seldom able to predict them ahead of time, however, and several times found myself in unfortunate circumstances. As an autistic person, I already had difficulty navigating institutional settings. Unspoken rules of conduct and unconscious social norms were particularly challenging, but I learned from my mistakes. I learned to conceal my authentic identity from institutions, and when that became unbearable, I learned to choose my battles and thicken my skin. Too many others do not share my privilege and luck; thus, it is critical to examine the ways in which institutions systemically attempt to regulate our bodies and identities, so we might mitigate the deleterious effects on less fortunate marginalized individuals.

The first major episode of institutional discrimination I faced came when I was an administrative assistant for the IT department at a major shipping company. The entire department was contracted, and I was therefore subject to the contracted company's authority. I enjoyed this job immensely, as it gave me the opportunity to utilize both my logistics and data entry skills. The other technicians were all cisgender males, and while I had not yet begun to transition, I had always felt more comfortable as "one of the guys" and thus enjoyed the camaraderie—and the dirty jokes. After I'd been employed for about a year, however, things went south. I had gained a good deal of weight, and also begun dressing in less feminine ways.

One afternoon, my supervisor came to my desk and asked me if I was wearing a bra. I was a bit bemused, because it was quite obvious that I was not, but I couldn't imagine why he would ask such a thing. He informed me that this was a violation of the dress code, and that someone from the shipping company had complained. I didn't see how this was possible, as our department was in an isolated basement room and I had not been upstairs that day except for a brief trip to the cafeteria. Besides, even if somebody had noticed, I couldn't imagine any of the other employees complaining. However, salespeople came in from the field frequently, and it was possible that someone who did not know me had seen me in the cafeteria. I was mortified. I didn't think that there was anything wrong with the way I looked, but just imagining someone staring at my chest that way made me sick to my stomach. My supervisor informed me that I would be sent home without pay, as this was my fault for violating the dress code. I went home, shaking with humiliation and uncertain whether to be angry or to blame myself. I came back the next morning wearing an extremely uncomfortable bra underneath a too-large official polo, ready for my disciplinary meeting with my supervisor and the regional manager. They both appeared to be extremely uncomfortable, unsurprising given they were two middle-aged men talking to—for all intents and purposes—a young female in a subordinate position about a topic that was at least peripherally sexual. They tried to convince me to sign a written warning sheet, but I read the fine print and refused when I saw that if I signed it would remove my right to legal recourse. I'm sure this disturbed them greatly, and almost certainly led to what happened next. I was contacted by a company HR representative, who assured me that no discrimination had taken place because the dress code clearly stated I had been in violation. However, I had a copy of both the shipping company's and the contractor's dress codes. Neither one said anything about wearing a bra. The HR representative stumbled a bit, but finally concluded that the appropriate undergarments clause spiritually, if not directly, indicated a bra was required. In the course of the conversation, I learned something else: no one from the shipping company had complained. The person to complain had been my supervisor. Funnily enough, he never complained when I weighed less and looked more feminine. Feeling like one of the guys had just become a nightmare. I continued to work at the job for another week. By the end of the week, I was called to a meeting in which my employment was terminated. I was assured that this was completely unrelated to the bra incident, even though their supposed reason was bogus and I had never been in trouble for any reason before this.

It was a further humiliation, and also an outrage, but mostly it was a relief, despite the financial implications for my family. My final week of employment had been a living hell. Every moment I was in the office, I felt tense and sick, wondering who was staring at my body and how I would be shamed next. Lacking the self-confidence I now possess, I nonetheless undertook to correct the wrong I felt had been done me. I first contacted the ACLU, only to be informed that they did not work with individual cases. They recommended I contact the EEOC. I did this, and explained my situation. The woman speaking to me, in a tone of mingled disgust and incredulity, told me in no uncertain terms that she would write down what I had said, but I really should have been wearing a bra to work. Embarrassed once again, angry, but now despairing, I decided there was nothing I could do but file for unemployment. Fortunately, while the company tried to fight it, the government agreed that I had been fired as retaliation rather than for cause. My husband and I would not lose our apartment, but what little self-esteem I had had been crippled. I had never before been subjected to such rigid gender role enforcement, nor made to feel so ashamed of my body.

Traditionally, our society highly prizes strict adherence to stereotypical gender norms. Even today, violation of these norms is not universally accepted, and can result in serious consequences. Our society's overarching, hegemonic views of what constitutes masculinity and femininity are both institutionally and socially enforced (Lindsey 2011). Women and gender non-conforming (GNC) individuals who were assigned the female gender at birth (AFAB) are subjected to a unique form of prejudiced treatment that rewards strict conformity to the hegemonic feminine ideal while severely punishing any deviance from it (Glick and Fiske 2011). This ambivalent sexism is comprised of two parts: the first, benevolent sexism, includes seemingly positive attitudes (women are nurturing, loving, caregivers who should be cherished) and behaviors (chivalry, opening doors, paying for meals) to which many women would not object (Glick and Fiske 2011). However, these benevolently sexist (BS) thoughts and acts are intrinsically linked to their negative counterparts in hostile sexism (women are weak and emotional, they should get back in the kitchen, sexual harassment is perfectly acceptable); hostile sexism always accompanies BS—that is, benevolent sexism (Glick and Fiske 2011).

In few places is this sexist dichotomy so apparent as in corporate America; there is still an underrepresentation of women, and those who reach upper management face the double standard of needing to act like their male counterparts to succeed, and then being seen as less feminine for having done so: a cold, aggressive bitch (Hochschild and Machung 2015). At my low place on the corporate totem pole, I had no interest in "success," and while I was not yet actively questioning my gender, I had no interest in being seen as feminine, either. My "one of the guys" attitude was accepted (with some amusement) by my coworkers. My desire to dress like them was not.

We are constantly engaged in the act of "doing gender": looking, dressing, talking, and acting in a way that signals to those observing us what we would like them to think about our gender identity (Lindsey 2011; West and

Zimmerman 1987). Our outward presentation certainly does not have to match our identity—both are socially constructed, and neither is necessarily stable over time—but if we publicly claim an identity that our presentation seems not to match, we risk censure for violation of traditional gender norms (Lindsey 2011; West and Zimmerman 1987). Gender non-conforming people are, of course, quite out of luck in this regard. Binary trans people who do not "pass" successfully as their identified gender face even more censure, as being trans is seen as the ultimate gender transgression.

By not wearing a bra, I was unconsciously doing gender in a way that did not fit societal norms. My stated identity at the time (cis woman) meant that my body was subject to certain institutional regulations (a dress code) that would have been different or absent had I been a cis man. The institution wanted me to take certain steps to regulate my appearance in a particular way that was heavily rooted in traditional, sexist gender norms. By failing to do so, I was "doing gender" incorrectly. This led to me being humiliated by my supervisor and in the end cost me my job. Had their dress code been more explicit, the same gender transgression would have cost me my unemployment benefits as well.

It is important to note that this institutional regulation was based on my body—my ascribed identity, assigned to be by society based on the approximate shape of my outer genitalia at birth (Haggerty and Ericson 2000; Lindsey 2011). Had I been out as a trans man at the time, I would likely have been subject to the same regulation—my breast size meant I would be classified as female no matter how I identified, and my only options would have been a bra or a chest binder. My natural body with its assigned, ascribed gender was "inappropriate" for unregulated public viewing, unless I used an uncomfortable undergarment to force it into a more socially acceptable shape.

Another troubling gendered arena, airport security, is problematic for literally everyone who chooses to fly. The intensely intimate surveillance of our bodies in situations in which we are often stressed at best and frantically late at worst is unpleasant and untimely. However, transgender air travelers face a particularly questionable form of scrutiny by the TSA. Anyone who looks at all differently than the stereotypical representation gleaned from their birth name or gender presentation are singled out as suspicious. During the first phase of my transition, I was certainly feeling more and more masculine, but I had kept all of my old stereotypically feminine clothing. I already knew that it would be hopeless—or at least prohibitively difficult—to expect anyone in the airport to respect my name and pronouns when I already had to deal with an ID and a ticket that both identified me by my deadname and gender assigned at birth. I also knew that I would be forced to step through a body scanner, and were I wearing a chest binder and a prosthetic penis, the surveillance equipment would quickly see through to what airport security would consider my "real body" (Lyon

2002; Browne 2015). The advanced imaging machines used in modern airports generate "a three-dimensional image of the passenger's nude body, including breasts, genitals, buttocks, prosthetics, binding materials and any objects on the person's body, in an attempt to identify contraband" (NCTE 2014). This could be seen as an attempted disguise, and after 9/11 it would be a dangerous gamble that could lead not only to me missing my flight but also several hours of unpleasant probing and interrogation. Therefore, I pulled out my old clothing each and every time I was forced to board a plane during these years, and tried to convince myself that the push-up bra, makeup, and sexy dress were in fact a clever disguise rather than an intensely dysphoric invalidation of my personhood. I was never stopped in security wearing these clothes, and in fact several times I did not even have to remove my shoes or step through the body scanner, as most non-feminine-presenting passengers did.

Clearly this oversight, while dubiously beneficial to me personally, was representative of benevolent sexism (Glick and Fiske 2011). And since BS doesn't exist without its counterpart, hostile sexism, things would not have gone well for me if on those occasions I had presented myself authentically, as I would have been violating gender norms again. Ambivalent sexism goes hand in hand with transphobia, in this case. Trans women in particular, even when dressed in very similar outfits to the ones I wore at the time, are much more likely to be hassled, delayed, and interrogated in airport security, thanks in part to a general distaste for trans women as the antithesis of masculinity (Lindsey 2011; Hughto et al. 2015), and in part to a statement by the Department of Homeland Security that "terrorists will employ novel methods to artfully conceal suicide devices. Male bombers may dress as females in order to discourage scrutiny" (Sjoberg 2015). However, any trans or GNC individuals forced through a security scanner are subject to humiliation as well as invasion of privacy by being subjected to identification threat: "a struggle over control of one's body as well as the definition of social membership" (Currah and Mulqueen 2011: 561). The TSA helpfully suggests that, regardless of how they feel about it, trans and GNC people should present as their gender assigned at birth, use their deadname, and use pronouns that match their assigned gender whenever they are traveling (Sjoberg 2015).

Airport security falls into one of the more insidious realms of identity control through biometric surveillance—a realm that problematizes and others anyone who does not conform to certain normative standards. Trans and GNC people are particularly vulnerable to invasive surveillance practices: since their achieved identity is often only superficially embodied through their outward gender presentation, their ascribed identity can be easily determined and revealed by biometric devices. The revealing of deeply personal, private information, such as one's gender assigned at birth, can be traumatic as well as intrusive: by "producing a truth about . . . one's identity (or identities) despite the subject's claims," the use of biometrics is inherently alienating (Browne 2015: 110). This is an issue of both personal privacy and social justice, since surveillance of this kind is used to sort people phenetically ("classification based on measurable similarities and differences"), into categories that may place them at severe disadvantages (Lyon 2002: 5). Knowledge about one's body allows authority to make discriminatory decisions; the government could not enforce a same-sex marriage ban, for example, if they didn't "confirm" the sex of the people applying for a marriage license (Currah and Mulqueen 2011). In the case of the TSA, any oddity with regards to a person's gender necessitates treating that person as a potential threat, leading to "humiliating interrogations, sexually assaultive pat downs, outing to colleagues, even denial of travel" (Currah and Mulqueen 2011: 562). Some trans and GNC people are so distressed by these experiences that they no longer attempt air travel; a clinical psychologist on the board of directors for the World Professional Association for Transgender Health reported having trans patients with "increased anxiety and even panic attacks just contemplating the possibilities. Those prone to depression went deeper into depression as their option to travel was taken away" (Currah and Mulqueen 2011: 565).

By spring of 2016, I identified fully as male and began taking steps toward full social transition. I was also ready to begin medically transitioning, and decided with my newly acquired health insurance to ask my primary care doctor to refer me to an endocrinologist for hormone replacement therapy. However, the innumerable religious posters decorating my doctor's office building, as well as its location in White suburban Kansas, made me extremely nervous about coming out. I decided to simply ask for the referral without explaining the reason. My husband accompanied me to the doctor's office, where as usual I bore constant misgendering and deadnaming in nervous silence. When I spoke to the doctor about a referral to an endocrinologist, he insisted that he know the reason. I told him I was concerned about my hormone levels—not an untruth. Unfortunately, I was ill-prepared for overcoming a transitional gatekeeper at this time. I don't know for certain if the doctor suspected something, but when I mentioned hormones, he informed me that he would happily refer me to an OB/GYN for—and he stressed this—*female hormones*. I accepted the referral, and simply left the office, trying not to despair. This was the last time I would see this doctor, because while he remained the primary on my insurance, I was simply too intimidated to visit the office again, even for non-trans-related health problems.

I would eventually go to Planned Parenthood for my hormones, but since then, at every doctor's office I have had to deal with being misgendered and deadnamed as I fight for a legal name and gender marker change; even the offices that are the most considerate must keep my legal name front and center in their system for insurance purposes, and many have no way to insert a preferred name in a place where anyone will see it. The worst institutional invalidation of my identity that I experienced ironically happened when I checked into the hospital for suicidal ideation (in part caused by tensions between myself and my heterosexual husband, who was struggling with my transition). The best hospital in my area for inpatient mental health treatment was an Adventist organization, and in past ER visits, my trans identity had remained closeted. At this time in my life, however, I knew that my already precarious mental health could not tolerate pretending to be someone I was not, for a visit that was likely to last at least three days. Participating in group activities, individual doctor consultations, and interactions multiple times a day with various nursing staff while constantly being called "miss" or "ma'am" or my deadname would have been unbearable under normal circumstances, let alone in a scenario in which I was already quite fragile.

In many ways, again, I was still quite lucky. I could have been held longer, against my will, simply for my trans identity. I could have been insulted or abused. I could have been subjected to conversion therapy, or had all my problems blamed on my hormones or my gender identity. In fact, most of the staff was quite courteous. Some required more correction than others, and even on my last day I still had to correct people as to my name and pronouns. But at least they were trying. My initial admissions experience was much less fortunate, however. Already in a state of utter despondency, and after having spent many hours in the emergency room, at night I was taken to the mental health residency floor. My partners were not allowed to come with me once admitted, so I went alone with a nurse to the ward where I would be staying. I was taken into an examination room and told that I had to take off all my clothes. I immediately felt nauseous. Wasn't I already miserable enough? The nurse left, to be replaced by an aide whose job it was to check me for injuries. The aide tried to be reassuring, but her constant use of "ma'am" when instructing me, and her frequent use of "she" and "her" when calling out of the room to speak about me to other aides, all while I stood there naked, exposing parts of my body that I took immense pains to hide and pretend did not exist, made me feel subhuman. Worse than just humiliation at the invalidation of my identity, I felt like a freak and a monster, on display for the amusement of others. And I could not complain, or I risked being labeled as combative and held against my will. I had heard horror stories of what happened to other trans people in mental health institutions.

Thankfully, none of the worst came true. I endured the examination, and it was the last such event I had to experience. But the discomfort of having to constantly correct people, while being unable to assert my gender identity in any other way than verbally, stayed with me. I could not bring my chest binder as it was considered dangerously restricting, nor could I wear any clothing that required a belt or drawstring. Thus even when clothed, there was nothing I could do to hide my body, to hide my sex assigned at birth, from the dozens of people with which I had to interact during my stay.

Their constant ability to see my body in ways I did not want made it virtually impossible for most of them to stay mindful of my gender identity. The only control I had of how much could be seen was to fold my arms uncomfortably over my chest while holding something like a folder, and to sit in equally uncomfortable positions during groups. This did not stop the misgendering from happening, but I felt compulsively unable to simply walk or sit comfortably knowing how prominently my chest stood out. My discomfort was a constant distraction from my recovery process, and in the end I did not stay as long as perhaps I should have, nor did I go home in as positive a frame of mind as I might otherwise have done.

Nonetheless, I still consider myself fortunate when I compare my experiences to that of other trans and GNC people. Access to affordable, quality healthcare, and to gender-related care specifically, is more challenging for non-cisgender individuals, whether due to employment discrimination that keeps them from getting the sorts of jobs that provide good health benefits, to marginalizing practices in doctors' offices, or to a lack of insurance coverage for transition-related health services (Hughto et al. 2015). Those wishing to medically transition must frequently jump through hoops and appease gatekeepers in order to be allowed to align their bodies with their identities, but even those individuals who simply wish for their healthcare providers to treat their identity with respect may be disappointed (Hughto et al. 2015). These restrictive and othering practices that label transgender people as non-normative and restrict their life chances are representative of structural stigma that acts as a form of symbolic violence "in which structures . . . perpetrate violence through the laws, policies, and community mores that restrict and forcibly reshape transgender individuals in ways that ultimately serve to maintain the power and privilege of the cisgender" majority (Hughto et al. 2015: 224). One manifestation of this structural stigma is the "medicalization of gender nonconformity"; while this medicalization led to such "treatments" as hormone replacement therapy and gender affirmation surgery, it also serves to reinforce societal views of trans and GNC individuals as "deviant" (Hughto et al. 2015: 224).

Structural stigma also explains institutional discrimination that makes healthcare problematic for transgender people. A large study of transgender individuals in 2011 showed that nearly one-fifth of the respondents were refused healthcare due to their gender identity, more than one-fourth postponed healthcare that they needed for illness or injury, and one-third did not seek preventative care because of gender-based discrimination they had experienced (Lambda Legal 2016). Another national survey reported that 70% of transgender respondents had experienced direct discrimination from healthcare professionals, including physical abuse or being blamed for their health status; 27% stated they had been denied care for being transgender (Lambda Legal 2016). Respondents from this survey spoke of being laughed at, taunted, and subjected to slurs; having their HIPAA confidentiality violated; being misgendered and deadnamed; being forced to wait longer than other patients; having their restroom use challenged or forbidden, and being subjected to inappropriate questions and examinations, "including needless viewing of genitals", such as I experienced (Lambda Legal 2016: 3). Even more problematic is blatantly transphobic violence such as conversion therapy, involuntary hospitalization, and outright abuse; fortunately, these abhorrent practices are no longer common in the United States.

The days in which patently vicious official treatment of transgender and gender non-conforming individuals is the norm are, thankfully, passing—at least in the United States. Nonetheless, my own relatively minor experiences with systemic regulation of body and identity illustrate the difficult path still faced by non-cisgender people in our society. Control through discriminatory practices, surveillance, and restrictive access continues on an institutional level. In addition to more obvious hate crimes and physical violence, the symbolic violence of institutional discrimination poses a serious threat to the well-being of trans and GNC individuals. In many cases, simple changes of institutional policy and employee education—whether in business, airport security, healthcare, or any other field—are all that is necessary to improve the quality of life of this marginalized population. Unfortunately, these changes cannot be instituted without the understanding, and ultimately caring, of the responsible parties.

Works Cited

Browne, Simone. 2015. *Dark Matters: On the Surveillance of Blackness*. Durham, NC: Duke University Press.

Currah, Paisley and Tara Mulqueen. 2011. "Securitizing Gender: Identity, Biometrics, and Transgender Bodies at the Airport." *Social Research: An International Quarterly* 78(2): 557–582.

Glick, Peter and Susan T. Fiske. 2011. "Ambivalent Sexism Revisited." *Psychology of Women Quarterly* 35(3): 530–535.

Hochschild, Arlie Russell and Anne Machung. 2015. *The Second Shift: Working Families and the Revolution at Home*. New York: Penguin Books.

Haggerty, Kevin D. and Richard V. Ericson. 2000. "The Surveillant Assemblage." *British Journal of Sociology* 51(4): 605–622.

Hughto, Jaclyn M. White, Sari L. Reisner, and John E. Pachankis. 2015. "Transgender Stigma and Health: A Critical Review of Stigma Determinants, Mechanisms, and Interventions." *Social Science & Medicine* 147: 222–231.

Lambda Legal. 2016. "Creating Equal Access to Quality Health Care for Transgender Patients: Transgender-Affirming Hospital Policies." *Lambda Legal*. Retrieved November 23, 2017, www.lambdalegal.org/publications/fs_transgender-affirming-hospital-policies

Lindsey, Linda L. 2011. *Gender Roles: A Sociological Perspective*. 5th ed. Boston, MA: Prentice Hall.

Lyon, David. 2002. *Surveillance as Social Sorting: Privacy, Risk, and Digital Discrimination*. London: Routledge.

NCTE (National Center for Transgender Equality). 2014. "Airport Security." *National Center for Transgender Equality*. Retrieved November 22, 2017, https://transequality.org/know-your-rights/airport-security

Sjoberg, Laura. 2015. "(S)He Shall Not Be Moved: Gender, Bodies and Travel Rights in the Post-9/11 Era." *Security Journal* 28(2): 198–215.

West, Candace and Don H. Zimmerman. 1987. "Doing Gender." *Gender & Society* 1(2): 125–151.

8

ACTORS OF DISCOURSE

Gender Performativity in Women's Leadership

Daniella Graves and Martin J. Leahy

My daughter did not come into this world knowing she had to like the color pink. I recently gave birth to my first child: a healthy baby girl. I remember clearly the first couple of days after my daughter was born. As expected, we had plenty of visitors. Many of them brought gifts: pink items and frilly bows. Although I appreciated the gestures, I could not help but notice how we, as a society, impose gender norms on a person from the moment of birth. It was as if we could not leave this infant without a proper gender label, when there was no difference, other than physiological, between my baby girl and the baby boy in the hospital room next to me. In the first few hours and days of life, their only concern is to receive adequate care, nourishment, and to survive. Yet, others occupied themselves with the limits for the kinds of gifts my daughter could and could not receive. As I witnessed this enforcement of gender norms, I could tell that this was something much larger than I had realized. A topic that had been the object of some passion and scholarly curiosity for nearly two years all of a sudden held more urgency. I know that this is only the beginning, and as I watch my daughter grow into a leader of her own, I hope social norms and mechanisms of control do not impede her authentic trajectory in life. Yet I know that gender rules dominate the scripts society supplies for roles that are predetermined.

Playing the Part with Dramaturgical Discipline

As social creatures, human beings adapt to socially constructed situations by presenting images of ourselves that are congruent with our desired interactional outcomes.[1] And it is at work where outcomes matter most for many. The boss will assess performance, reward and recognize, and promote. Early in our careers, we become aware that how we present ourselves will impact how performance is measured, how *we* are judged. Those who aspire to leadership at work pay special attention to the impressions they make and as they rise up in the organization, image seems to count even more. Goffman[2] stated that individuals control their image throughout social interactions. People make purposeful attempts to manage self-presentation in an effort to procure a favorable image; this is known as impression management.[3]

So, in order to manage impressions effectively, it is important to know the leader's role, what the organization expects of its leaders, what counts as stellar performance. It is important to understand the social rewards available for certain leadership behaviors or characteristics and how the rewards vary by gender.[4] When it comes to leadership, organizations prefer masculine characteristics. Today's leaders receive rewards for traditional masculine traits, such as assertiveness, competitiveness, and persuasive communication skills.[5] Individuals who may not have strong innate competencies in traditionally masculine areas may project such traits through their presentation of self.[6] The preference for masculine leadership characteristics presents an issue for women leaders who constantly battle an atmosphere of inequality, while inadvertently feeding into the cycle by taking on masculine traits.[7] Ironically, leaders' dependence on masculine, competitive, or assertive presentation of self-techniques constantly reinforces the social construction of gender in order to present an image of success.[8]

Many factors contribute to leaders' felt need to control their impressions, among them, living in a highly competitive and fast-moving employment environment.[9] Others include: the patriarchal norms of our current society, the social benefits available to characteristically masculine leaders, and the social rewards available for managing the perceptions that leaders present to others.[10] A woman leader must exercise what Goffman called "*dramaturgical discipline.*"[11] She must remember her part and be wary of unintended gestures or mistakes in performing it. She must exercise discretion, cultivate presence of mind, possess the kind of self-control that enables personal emotions to be suppressed—all in service of playing the assigned role, while supporting other players and roles to deliver their lines and the overall performance as designed. While thoroughly immersed in the performance, she must observe her actions and the responses of others in order to be both faithful to the performance as designed and mindful of the way she would like to present herself.

However, this performance exacts costs on individual women and organizations. Women, of course, continue to experience barriers to progress and inequality in the workplace. As long as gender discrepancies exist in leadership expectations, organizations will suffer from unbalanced and non-comprehensive masculine leadership influence.[12] Other costs include: limited perspectives on management, lack of balanced gender representation, and minimized paths of equal gender development.[13] Overall, this perpetuates a narrowly defined conception of successful leadership. Reducing this problem will expand expectations and representations of effective leadership in today's highly diverse workforce. Such an endeavor begins with an assessment of leadership as a social construction.[14]

Relevant Literature

Early leadership studies generally concluded that a leader is the passive recipient of the role, given the possession of certain traits.[15] However, such early studies failed to explain the social negotiation and agency that occurs in leadership.[16] Similarly, early studies did not separate the leader role from the notion of hegemonic masculinity.[17] Therefore, the belief that one is a leader given innate, concrete, and predominantly masculine traits or characteristics is not only questionable, but problematic. Progressive contemporary studies ameliorate this critical flaw in the literature by suggesting that individuals are not passive, but rather active players in the co-construction of the social perception of gender and leadership.[18]

The tendency to promote masculine tendencies among leadership expectations is making it difficult for women to prove that they are able to lead effectively.[19] Women are finding it difficult to manage the two roles that they face in leadership: that of a leader and that of a woman.[20] This is partly because women are considered the nicer, kinder gender and therefore are expected to maintain social relations; yet, they experience challenges due to their lack of the more masculine, aggressive traits.[21] In such masculine environments, it seems that women stereotypes are not congruent with that of a leader and even women leaders with superior qualifications may have to overcome the preconceptions that precede them.[22] However, since women leaders are expected to encounter gender stereotypes in leadership, those that do reach a high level of leadership success may be perceived as highly competent leaders due to the fact that they were able to surpass the double standard.[23]

Women are up against a challenge when trying to step and uphold a leadership position. In leadership, "men's voices predominate in shaping discourses and practices."[24] However, allowing individuals a choice in presenting themselves and taking agency over their image inflates the boundaries of leadership. The stories become a vehicle for their "presentation of self."[25] In such identity communications, individuals cling to the binary gender socialization: the feminine, the masculine, or the unknown (androgynous). The leader is performing gender based on attributes they believe are appropriate and are "psycho-biological" in nature.[26] Therefore, both discourse and visual costumes aid the leader in performing a gendered conception of leadership.

Although individuals are not passive recipients of their persona and are instead actively engaged in the construction and articulation of their identities, there are nevertheless strong collective symbolisms that affect an individual's sense of self.[27] Leadership emerges from symbolic actions.[28] Such interaction with gender norms opens a space of negotiation, where boundaries are stretched in an intricate interplay between social expectations based on stereotypes, and individual decision-making.[29] The body becomes a tool for gender negotiation and construction, and style of dress becomes an avenue for self-presentation and formation.[30] As leaders negotiate their physical presence, they become an object and subject to themselves.

Leadership is a generative and iterative process of identification and social reinforcement. The dynamic nature of leadership identity work starts with the individual, strengthens through social engagement, and secures itself through the collective agreement of leadership.[31] Therefore, leadership itself is a social construction. Behaviors do not constrain individual leaders, but their social forces influence them. Leaders must be aware of the discourse they hope to engage in. As such, they are involved in the production and reproduction of leadership performance norms. On the one hand, leaders display agency in their performance and creation of leadership, and on the other, a larger-spanning sense of social regulation guides their behavior. This highlights the significance of a social setting to the creation and performance of leadership.

Conceptualizing leadership as a binary result of gender reinforces gender stereotypes and sets limits on how leadership can be socially constructed and accepted.[32] It is difficult for individuals to fit neatly into their gendered label, let alone their gender-sanctioned leadership role.[33] However, realizing that gender and leadership are not concrete realities, but rather social constructions, individuals become no longer bound by stark and limiting vestiges of cultural, political, and historical inequalities.[34] The dichotomous division that individuals attach to their identities, both as a product of their individual efforts and their social influences, simplifies expectations of leadership in the sense of making gender black-or-white. Leadership and gender are much too convoluted and dynamic to be constrained by such simple binary expectations.[35] Theorizing leadership and gender as fluid social constructions allows for increased performativity, boundary negotiation, and expanded notions of success.[36]

The Study and Methods

While we know that women, like all leaders, engage in impression management, it is not known how individual women leaders' use of impression-management techniques impact their actual or perceived success rates, or performance, or what gendered meaning they derive from their leadership performance. Without proper knowledge of leadership dependence on impression management, there is no basis for anticipating leaders' role agency and social incentives, regarding their image performances.[37] Thus, the research questions for this study were: How do societal gender expectations inform organization leaders' self-presentation and impression management strategies, and what meaning do individual leaders derive from such leadership performances?

Using Charmaz's[38] approach to constructivist grounded theory to build a theory "'grounded' in data from participants who have experienced the process,"[39] this study examined the presentation of self by women who had succeeded at sustaining leadership tenure (at least a year, any leadership position, at any level). It drew upon semi-structured interviews with twenty women leaders who identified as leaders engaging in impression management. Specifically, participants included leaders who answered affirmatively to the question, "Do you occasionally undergo purposeful, goal-oriented behavior, meant to project an image of successful leadership?" Therefore, the researcher collected data and recruited respondents using the purposive sampling technique. By asking respondents about their projected image, the researcher operationalized "impression management" in line with Goffman's[40] description of impression management as an image of oneself presented in social situations. This study included only those individuals who indicated their pursuit of impression-management expression. The collection of respondents depended on random sample through virtual professional networks, such as LinkedIn.

In-depth interviews were used to explore the experiences of those leaders who acknowledged employment of impression management. All interviews were conducted face-to-face, either in person or via Skype or other form of videophone, and lasted between thirty to sixty minutes. A recording device was used to capture the interview sessions; pseudonyms were assigned to protect the respondents' identities and insure confidentiality. A transcriptionist was hired to transcribe audiotapes of interview conversations into texts for analysis.

Coding and memo writing were critical aspects of the development of the emerging theory.[41] Data analysis began with immersion in the interview transcripts, choosing meaningful words or phrases, coding them by creating codes to begin building analytic categories, and comparing coding categories across interview transcripts. From this, recurring and dominant codes categories ensued. Using Charmaz's[42] techniques, the data was coded based on content topics, starting with open coding, and ending with axial coding. After initial coding with the data, a working theory emerged for how and why leaders used impression-management techniques and the role played by gender norms.

During initial data collection and analysis, theoretical ideas were recorded and formulated in analytical memos; this was coupled with constantly returning to the field to check or expand the emerging theory. To substantiate the budding theory, there was a return to the field and more data collection with an eye to the emerging theory (for theory expansion, adding cases, or finding nuances of the theory). Therefore, there was a "simultaneous involvement in data collection and analysis."[43] Data collection prompted the reflexive study of the emerging theory. These categories became separate components presented below in the theory section.

Charmaz[44] rejected an external reality and data as objective representation of that reality. Instead, grounded theory captures a social reality that is constructed by the research participants, and the researcher. This co-constructed reality emerges from the process of interpretation and dialectic interaction.[45] Therefore, the "reality" presented is a relative construction that is created through interaction, informed by interpretation and deemed fit for the immediate social surrounding. Both researcher and participants contributed heavily to the theory that follows.

The Theory

The major themes presented here help understand the nuanced ways through which women leaders present their sense of self and manage their impressions as informed by societal gender expectations. It provides a gateway to their meaning-making processes and helps understand the feelings, motivations, and challenges of women leaders. The theory contains three major constructs. Women start with *awareness of both roles*, the parts they are to play, as woman and leader, and the *scripts or social norms* associated with each role.

The Roles and the Scripts

Female leaders are thought to face more obstacles than their male counterparts when it comes to maintaining a position of power.[46] This is partly because men are believed to be task-oriented and autocratic, as well as "aggressive, enterprising, independent, self-sufficient, dominant, competent, or rational,"[47] while maintaining a sense of emotional detachment and analytical rationality to their work.[48] In this sense, the conventional leadership role is scripted based on hegemonic masculinity. Women do not always fit the leadership expectation because they are believed to display nurturing and communal characteristics, as well as generosity, sensitivity, affection, and compassion.[49] Clearly, gender norms permeate behavioral expectations, leading to the entanglement of assessment of women's leadership abilities and gendered stereotypes.[50] The literature on gender in leadership clarifies a need to disassociate with gender norms and evaluate leaders individually.[51] However, given the tight enmeshment of gender norms with leadership expectations, it may be difficult to untie the two.

The women leaders who were interviewed in this study acknowledged the fact that women are believed to be more relational and nurturing, that the script they received is one of maintaining relationships. In other words, they have been socialized to take on specific roles in their leadership position, such as being relational or communal.[52] For instance, Rebecca stated "women tend to be more nurturing . . . " and Janice echoed this belief by stating "I think women naturally are more nurturing and wanting to be able to help people." Lastly, Katrina claimed that "females are more nurturing than the males are." Women's relational leadership role largely draws from their compassionate and nurturing persona.

Moving beyond understanding of the script, women leaders enacted such relational and communal expectations in their positions. For instance, Kate conveys that fostering personal relationships among the team is a main focus of her leadership:

By being relational, I focused on relating to my employees and getting to know them. What their spouses did for a living, how their kids are doing in school. Being a woman, in those situations, really helped me in connecting with people . . . women don't just worry about getting tasks done. They worry about the working relationships among the group and between them and their staff.

Kate engages with her team at a deep level. She concerns herself with their personal lives in an attempt to forge relationships with them. Kate exemplifies the compassionate and nurturing qualities that many associate with femininity.[53] Kate believes that being a woman leader is more than accomplishing tasks; it also concerns upholding tight relationships within the team. As such, she exemplifies the communal feminine characteristics of fostering relationships associated with women leaders. Caroline agrees that women are prone to be more relational:

in terms of being a leader, I think women . . . are able to emotionally connect with people, so their leadership role, you know whether it's just in terms of like being a boss or a mentor or anything like that, you can connect to them . . . deeper . . . .

Caroline sets up the tone of her leadership by first assuring relationships among her team. She supports the notion that women tend to promote interpersonal relationships.[54]

Similar to Kate and Caroline, Cindy believes that women are naturally relational. For example, she said, "if we put women in charge of things because we're relational, because we have compassion, I think we do better." Rebecca added that being relational makes her job more pleasant: "the personal relationships I was able to develop. I mean it just makes your job nicer." Therefore, not only do personal relationships help promote effective leadership, they actually create an environment of satisfaction and enjoyment in one's work.

Enacting the Roles

Experiencing a Double Bind in Enacting the Roles

The women interviewed often had experiences that made the pursuit of leadership success seem formidable. If women leaders demonstrated a strong personality that somehow fell outside the realm of socially acceptable norms for women, they experienced the repercussions of social stigma, often through the use of negative labels. They worked hard to prove themselves in the face of scrutiny, and worked hard to find their authority. The experience they reported is consistent with the literature.

Gender interacts with leadership behavior and cultural expectations.[55] When women present behavior that deviates from their gender norm, such as presenting stereotypically male behavior, their leadership role is evaluated poorly and they are on the receiving end of derogatory labels.[56] If women leaders succeed at traditionally male-gendered work, not only are they less liked at a personal level, but their competence is questioned.[57] For instance, Madison stated that "for a woman, anything that you're strongly endorsing or trying to advocate for looks more like you're emotionally connected to it . . . if a woman did that, it would be misconstrued to where she is being bitchy." Madison's statement suggests that women are not expected to strongly advocate anything in their position. This goes back to gender norms, which suggest that women should be more quiet and accepting in their behavior.[58] Madison added:

if a woman is expressing frustration or critique, it can be termed as bitchy . . . There's just a certain level of maybe project urgency behind what I'm saying and so I cannot, I'm not as flexible. I think that's another thing—women are expected to be a lot more flexible than men as leaders.

Madison suggested that women are to be agreeable and flexible, and if they do not fall in line with such social expectations, they experienced social stigma in the form of demeaning labels. This is another way of exerting social control on gender norms and expectations. Others had similar experiences. Consider the following examples:

If you're too direct, you're a bitch. If you're too demanding, you're bossy. If you're too nice, you're a pushover. It's always that you want to be direct and demanding and nice, but apparently there's a line and women aren't supposed to cross that line without getting labeled as something derogatory.—Kate

Women get labeled as a bitch if they are even remotely assertive. I know that I can both be aggressive and assertive and I've got a mouth on me. And I can say some really cutting things, but I can only be labeled or perceived in that ugly language of you know, strong woman has to be a bitch . . . but actually, I'm not a bitch. I just am assertive and sometimes I'm really clear about what's needed or not needed. And I'm really clear about a direction we need to take.—Cindy

Both Kate and Cindy experienced similar situations as Madison, whereby any attempt to deliver a strong message automatically elicited deprecating language and titles for women. Again, this shows the consequences of transgressing gender norms insofar as women are expected to be passive and docile while looking for social harmony at all costs.[59] The previous examples resulted in a "bitch" label for women, yet this is only one repercussion. Other attempts resulted in women being accused of attempting to reclaim the opposite gender label.

Some women leaders experience comparisons to men in their attempts to demonstrate their leadership. For instance, below are some examples of labeling women leaders as more masculine in their approach:

> If you're like an alpha woman, then you're going to be more like a man because I've seen that too. I'm a strong, "you're going to do it my way" type of woman.—Rebecca
> I want to seem tough and more dominant. I do want to be seen as strong leader. By doing so, I think I try to seem more like the men.—Emily

Rebecca and Emily took on the belief themselves that in order to be a strong alpha leader, women needed to be more like men. This suggests that displaying strength in leadership or demeanor points to naturally masculine behavior. Again, gender norms informed perceptions of how these women leaders should behave, and if they did not fall in line with the expectations of being a woman, they could take on the label of the opposite gender.

The issue stems from the perceived incongruence between the feminine social role and the leader social role. Traditionally, leadership and managerial roles have been gendered as masculine, meaning that the characteristics that are believed to be necessary to succeed in such a role are more likely to be associated with men.[60] This creates a two-part problem. On the one hand, the leadership role requires certain attributes, which align with masculine meaning; and on the other hand, if women do hold the characteristics needed to succeed as a leader, they lose esteem and act in disagreement with their gender prescription. Women leaders suffer from displaying behaviors or demeanors that transgress social norms. Once again, this points to deeply instilled gender norms wherein women are expected to be relational and collegiate.[61]

Given such deeply held gender norms, women often feel that they must prove themselves as leaders. The internalization of such gender and leadership expectations by the women themselves is striking. There seems to be a double bind in terms of knowing what is required in order to succeed as leaders and not wanting to reinforce limiting gendered beliefs. The way women negotiate this double bind is through individual agency and the construction of their presentation of self.

Constructing a Presentation of Self

Women leaders are well aware of their image or appearance and read their situation in order to properly present the desired impressions on others.

In order to properly manage such impressions and present themselves strategically, women leaders look outside of themselves and instead look at their social audience for guidance. The women leaders interviewed in the study were sensitive to the ways in which they came across. When reflecting on their presentation of self, they were aware of their image on two levels: first, they assessed their own appearance, and second, they made assessments by taking on the perspective of their audience and attempting to make judgments from their viewpoint. These women leaders put in a conscious effort into molding the way they present themselves to maintain a level of control over their image.

Some women opted to manage others' impressions by actively controlling the way they dress. As Janice stated, "we always have to present a certain . . . appearance that shows that we're professional." In this case, she is aware that her way of dressing affects her professional image. As a woman leader, she chooses to manage her impression through her style of dress. In such cases, dressing professionally in business attire conveys a level of proficiency in one's leadership position. This, in turn, will lead to increased social acclaim and professional interactions as others judge women leaders' appearances. For, as Rebecca suggests, "I think it just makes you more credible . . . higher up people will listen more if you're dressed more professionally." Rebecca aligns with the assessment that others make judgments on one's style of dress and afford respect and professional esteem if one's image displays credibility and professionalism, but what is professional attire?

The women leaders were in agreement that their appearance was responsible for conveying professionalism and respect, and they had specific examples of what consists of professional attire:

> dressing professionally . . . translates to slacks and a nice shirt or blouse. You know like a pencil skirt or whatnot. I'll wear cardigans or sleeved shirts when I'm interacting with anyone that I consider important . . . I'm more conscious to not give people a chance to you know, see a flaw whether it's wardrobe or my speech or you know, other forms of appearance like hairstyles.—Samantha
>
> I have been dressing for the role of college president since, for 15 years. And very intentionally almost aging myself dressing for a more mature look so that I could be taken more credibly than who I am and what age I'm at. So suited up, polished, you know . . . a little bit mature, not too sassy and kind of stick with neutral palate tone, colors.—Cindy
>
> I find women that just dress professionally, that tone down the makeup, are kind of benign . . . There's nothing specifically flashy about them. They're not masculine; they're not overly feminine . . . If you stay neutral when you're going in, you divert the attention to what you can bring rather than having it directed at you . . . Stick to your navy, your beige, and your black and be

modest in the amount of jewelry that you wear. You don't want people looking at you personally, you just have to remember to be more conscientious about deflecting their attention to what you can bring instead.—Natalie

There's got to be less of an emphasis on fashion, if you want to be in the kind of role that I'm in . . . conservative means powerful and conservative means you're doing what you need to be doing and you're on top of your job.—Michelle

The women mentioned above all have a strong understanding of how they must present themselves as leaders. For instance, Samantha wore specific items like slacks, pencil skirts, and cardigans when meeting with "important people," which suggests that she believed these items of clothing would procure social acceptance and deter anyone from interpreting her attire as an indicator of her flaws. Cindy also understood that her appearance sent out a message. She purposely attempted to dress to appear more "mature" so that others took note of her leadership skills, rather than her age. Additionally, Cindy was attracted to business suits. She took great pride in her suits and attempted to bridge the gap between wearing neutral suits and looking "feminine." Her attire, then, is an active negotiation on her part to look professional, yet womanly in her role.

Like Cindy, Natalie believed in the power of neutral accessories and colors. To Natalie, appearing neutral meant diminishing any kind of ostentatious attention onto oneself. She thought this helped promote a benign and gentle appearance in leadership. Natalie believed that by deflecting others' attention from a showy wardrobe, a leader would be able to showcase her abilities and skills instead. This aligned with Cindy's comment that she tried to dress maturely to detract attention from her age and lead it to her capability as a leader. Additionally, Michelle agreed with Natalie that fashionable, or flashy clothing, did not promote a favorable image for women leaders. Michelle believed opting for a more conservative style of dress is key, as it suggests that a leader takes her job seriously.

Aside from one's appearance, women leaders described adjusting their communication style in order to develop a favorable social image. For example, consider the following interview quotes:

take a good amount of time to sit back and observe the dynamics before you speak. You become a leader because you're outspoken, but I think that when you become a leader, it's good to take two steps back . . . and observe the dynamics of how people interact or how they interact with different roles or positions, or genders so you have a good transition into the conversation.—Nicole

One thing I do is sometimes mirroring others . . . I observe what other people are saying and the way in which they're saying it, the terms the use ... you want to mirror others so that they feel comfortable. That's one thing in adjusting my communication style. I've learned to be just more slow in how I communicate things and trying to be really, really mindful of the words that I'm using.—Madison

Nicole and Madison presented different techniques that they use to help promote positive social interactions. Nicole believed that taking a moment to observe situational dynamics before strategically joining the conversation would help arm her with a calculated advantage. Madison agreed with the power of observation. She believed that mirroring others would help create a feeling of comfort and connection in the interaction. Madison also attempted to slow down her dialect and purposely choose the words she uses in an effort to increase the smoothness and favorability of the social interaction. Nicole and Madison tried to control the impressions they set through their communication.

Another way leaders manage their self-presentation is through the elimination of traces of emotion in their communication. For example, Cindy stated:

years ago, I was prone to tears . . . I was going to bite my tongue. I was going to swallow hard but I was not going to let myself get to the point where a tear came out. I was going to fight it back. And I have. And so I think that is a vulnerability that it's better if I don't show that . . . Sometimes when I get really upset or I'm really stressed and I know it's going to be a heated meeting, and there's a likelihood that I could be upset, or . . . emotional, I have my bottle of water with me. And I will drink water when I pause, when I think I'm going to start to get choked. So it's a technique.

Cindy saw that some individuals might interpret crying in conversations as a weakness or vulnerability and purposely attempted to prevent tearing-up. She resorted to such techniques as sipping water when she thought tears are coming, in order to hold them at bay. This eliminated any trace of vulnerability or emotionality, and puts herself in control of how she appeared. Additionally, Susan said:

when I speak, I'm very cautious of the words that I choose, and I'm cautious of my demeanor. In other settings, if I was excited I might clap my hands or I'm kind of an ebullient person . . . I would never do that in the boardroom largely because the men . . . in that setting I'm also very aware of gender difference and stylistic behaviors and you dial up and dial down.

Susan acknowledged that at times she could be emotionally demonstrative in dialogue. She reported being careful to tone down her excitement depending on her audience, paying particular attention to gender, in an attempt to gain their social approval. These women leaders were aware of the expressive power of their performances, and as such, they chose to present themselves in a concerted and conscious manner.

One last way through which these leaders controlled their self-presentation in discourse was the tone chosen for a conversation. For instance, Samantha stated:

> I was giving a talk at one point and I was approached later by a faculty member; A female faculty member, telling me that my voice is too high-pitched and that it's something that a lot of females suffer from, but that I should work on that because it doesn't make me seem as professional or experienced . . . I try to, when I speak try to be sort of loud and to the point, succinct . . . I do think I try to avoid the stereotypical woman voice, you know being really [high], especially towards the end of, their speech like trailing off. And never finishing sentences and having trouble coming up with the word . . . I'm very aware of that. And I try to avoid that.

Samantha, in an attempt to appear more professional and experienced, deliberately focused her attention on eliminating her high-pitched tone, while speaking in a manner that is loud, succinct, and not trailing off. As a result, Samantha attempted to present an image of professional success. Once again, one can see the power of transformation that occurs when consciously and intentionally controlling one's presentation of self.

For the women interviewed, leadership identities are not fixed; they are continuously changing and give rise to ambivalences and contradictions within individuals. Leadership agency allows leaders to create an image of success.[62] Through the use of storytelling, dress, and leadership characteristics, women leaders have the option of creating the self they want to project. However, each of these areas have been infused with cultural notion of gender, which separate masculine and feminine expectations.[63] Due to the fact that gender continues to permeate leadership expectations, women leaders will continue to struggle against gender-based assessments of success.

Discussion

This study explored and examined the relationship between leadership identity construction and societal gender norms. Each woman leader's experiences and perspectives were unique, yet the process of presentation of self and gender socialization were present, albeit nuanced, in their responses. Presentation of self and impression-management efforts were explored at an individual and societal level, while the concept of gender continued to infuse and inform the dynamics, as the women expressed a deep

ACTORS OF DISCOURSE

understanding of social gender expectations. They described their experiences with typecasting, obstacles, and their own beliefs about innate gender differences. In an attempt to present a favorable leadership image, the women leaders described their impression management through dress and communication—indicating the social construction and gendered performance of leadership today.

The findings indicate that women leaders' presentation of self and impression management was influenced by ideas and preconceptions of favored leadership behaviors and gender expectations. The data showed the obstacles and challenges that women faced when trying to bridge leadership expectations, gender norms, and self-presentation efforts. Yet, individual women in this study took leadership performances into their own hands. They displayed agency and choice when presenting themselves as leaders in the way they dressed, spoke, and interacted with others. These performances, however, derived from the leadership expectations enmeshed in larger societal gender norms.

This study presents an analytic understanding of women leaders' attitudes, beliefs, and behaviors about their leadership image. Considering one's leadership role as a social construction that connects gender and identity helps explain how one's presentation of self is a mindful creation as individual leaders take an active role in the construction and projection of their self-conception. Women strive to be competitive, assertive, and dominant, breaking through gender categories and adopting inter-gender duality. In other words, the women leaders worked with and acknowledged their woman identity, yet also pushed to present characteristics that were once thought to be masculine. This study demonstrates the importance and necessity of breaking through narrowly defined gender categories to value leadership capacity free from the chains of gender expectations.

Conclusion

As indicated by the women leaders in this study, women leaders are well aware of their expectations as women and as leaders. They take agency over presenting a favored and viable image to sustain positive social interactions and acclaim. Therefore, in an attempt to perform and present one's self, individuals compound the social construction of femininity and leadership. In the trajectory for success, individual actors are creators and projectors of social norms. They are caught in a self-fulfilling prophecy of internalizing, projecting, and strengthening social outlooks and expectations. These valuable conclusions help free leadership from the constraints of limiting gender stereotypes and suggest that individuals are creators and performers in the course of their social pursuits. In this sense, they become active designers of their roles rather than passive recipients of them. To answer the research questions directly, societal gender expectations proved to greatly inform organization leaders' presentation of self and impression-management strategies, as the leaders imbued their performances with purposeful and gendered social meaning. The reduction of gender-specified leadership roles makes for highly constricted gendered leadership roles and aspirations in today's workplace. However, this study suggests that gender and leadership are not tangible certainties. Instead, they are subjective social constructions. The binary social partition that individuals ascribe to their identities, both as a product of their individual agency and their socialization, reduces the expectations of leadership whereby it is believed to fit perfectly into one of two dualistic categories. Both gender and leadership are complex social constructs, not meant to suffer from the constraint of binary social categories.[64] Therefore, the underlying thematic influence discovered in this study supports the idea that leadership and gender are dynamic constructions, which in turn frees women leaders to strive for performativity, category and label negotiation, as well as a more substantive and encompassing sense of success and acceptability.

In order to promote a more equal and gender-free notion of leadership, individuals must work to redefine the way leadership is constructed and accepted. Releasing leaders of the confines of gender not only separates individual leaders from the dichotomous divisions in their identities, it also frees the notion of leadership from narrow and confined hegemonic perspectives. Therefore, if leaders are to succeed in breaking societal expectations and gender norms, society must stop placing limits on their definition and acceptance of leaders. Women leaders currently find themselves at a threshold, and their success requires the collaboration of social and individual forces to emancipate leadership and gender from the confines of the past. Promoting tolerance for differences and praise for women's contributions is a first step. This is followed by promotion of performativity and boundary negotiation for the expansion of leaders' reach and impact on society. Women leaders may use this study to better understand the micro social dynamics behind their leadership expectations, efforts, and challenges while also focusing on macro issues, such as limitations in their surrounding social systems at the societal and organizational level.

Although the findings of this research study present an innovative take on leaders' presentation of self as a pivotal link between identity, image, and gender expectations, there are possible limitations. Since the researcher conducted twenty interviews in geographic proximity, the research findings are not transferrable to all contexts. For example, issues of race, class, and culture were not taken into consideration. The findings represent the subjective recounting of a select and limited group of women leaders. Additionally, some women leaders may have chosen to actively engage in impression management during the interviews themselves. Such self-censoring might have inhibited some women from being completely forthcoming about their actual opinions and actions. In the event that researchers attempt to replicate this study, it would be valuable to consider how men leaders engage in presentation of self or impression-management techniques. If gender is such an influential part of leadership presentation, it seems imperative to see how the other gender engages with societal expectations. This will provide a full spectrum of analysis when studying the role of gender in leadership behavior.

Discussion Questions

1 How do the media help perpetuate binary gender expectations and standards?
2 How do you think we all contribute to the social construction of leadership? How can we change such expectations to be more expansive and inclusive of differences?
3 Why do you think there are relatively few women in top leadership positions? List both micro and macro forces.
4 Traditional gender norms suggest that women are judged on their appearance far more likely than men. How do you see this play out in today's leadership positions?

Suggested Readings

1 Coleman, R. (2008) The becoming of bodies—Girls, media effects, and body image. *Feminist Media Studies* 8(2): 163–179.
2 Kelan, E.K. (2008) The discursive construction of gender in contemporary management literature. *Journal of Business Ethics* 18(2): 427–445.
3 Kelan, E.K. (2013) The becoming of business bodies: Gender, appearance, and leadership development. *Sage* 44(1): 45–61.
4 Liu, H., Cutcher, L., and Grant, D. (2015). Doing authenticity: The gendered construction of authentic leadership. *Gender, Work & Organization* 22(3): 237–255.

Suggested Media

1 Sheryl Sandberg TED Talk: https://www.youtube.com/watch?v=18uDutylDa4
2 Eleanor Tabi Haller-Jordan TED Talk: https://www.youtube.com/watch?v=9ZFNsJ0-aco

Notes

1 Herbert Blumer, *Symbolic Interactionism: Perspective and Method* (Los Angeles, CA: University of California Press, 1969).
2 Erving Goffman, *The Presentation of Self in Everyday Life* (New York: The Overlook Press, 1973).

3 Ibid.
4 Robin Ely, Herminia Ibarra, and Deborah Kolb, "Taking Gender into Account: Theory and Design for Women's Leadership Development Programs," *Academy of Management Learning & Education* 10, no. 3 (2011).
5 Beatriz Arbaizar and Javier Llorca, "Leadership and Sexual Behavior," *Psiquiatria* 15, no. 19 (2011); Robin Ely, Herminia Ibarra, and Deborah Kolb, "Taking Gender into Account."
6 Ibid.
7 Alice Eagly and Mary Johannesen-Schmidt, "The Leadership Styles of Women and Men," *Journal of Social Issues* 57, (2001).
8 Robin Ely, Herminia Ibarra, and Deborah Kolb, "Taking Gender into Account."
9 Stephen Robbins and Timothy Judge, *Leadership: Essentials of organizational behavior* (10th ed.) (Boston, MA: Prentice Hall, 2010).
10 Robin Ely, Herminia Ibarra, and Deborah Kolb, "Taking Gender into Account."
11 Erving Goffman, *The Presentation of Self in Everyday Life.*
12 Robin Ely, Herminia Ibarra, and Deborah Kolb, "Taking Gender into Account."
13 Beatriz Arbaizar and Javier Llorca, "Leadership and Sexual Behavior."; Robin Ely, Herminia Ibarra, and Deborah Kolb, "Taking Gender into Account."
14 Keith Grint and Brad Jackson, "Toward 'Socially Constructive' Social Constructions of Leadership," *Management Communication Quarterly*, 24, no. 2 (2010).
15 Mark Bolino et al., "A Multi-Level Review of Impression Management Motives and Behaviors," *Journal of Management* 34 (2008); Sandy Wayne et al., "The Role of Upward Influence Tactics in Human Resource Decisions," *Personnel Psychology* 50 (1997): 979–1006; Timothy Judge, and Robert Bretz, "Political Influence Behavior and Career Success," *Journal of Management* 20, (1994); Charlotte Gerstner and David Day, "Meta-Analytic Review of Leader–Member Exchange Theory: Correlates and Construct Issues," *Journal of Applied Psychology* 82, no. 6 (1997); Stephen Robbins and Timothy Judge, *Leadership: Essentials of organizational behavior*; Scott DeRue, et al., "Trait and Behavioral Theories of Leadership: An Integration and Meta-Analytic Test of their Relative Validity," *Personnel Psychology* 64, (2011).
16 Scott DeRue and Susan Ashford, "Who Will Lead and Who Will Follow?"; Kevin Barge and Gail Fairhurst, "Living Leadership: A Systemic Constructionist Approach," *Leadership* 4, no. 3 (2008); Edward Peck et al., "Performing Leadership: Towards a New Research Agenda in Leadership Studies?" *Leadership* 4, (2009).
17 Isabel Cuadrado et al., "Gender Differences in Leadership Styles as a Function of Leader and Subordinates' Sex and Type of Organization," *Journal of Applied Social Psychology* 42, no. 12 (2012); Marloes Van Engen and Tineke Willemsen, "Sex and Leadership Styles: A Meta-Analysis of Research Published in the 1990s," *Psychological Reports* 94 (2004); Alice Eagly and Mary Johannesen-Schmidt, "The Leadership Styles of Women and Men"; Yvonne Billing and Mats Alvesson, "Questioning the Notion of Feminine Leadership: A Critical Perspective on the Gender Labeling of Leadership," *Gender, Work and Organization* 7, no. 3 (2000).
18 Judith Butler, *Undoing Gender* (New York: Routledge, 2004); Dana Christman and Rhonda McClellan, "Discovering Middle Space: Distinctions of Sex and Gender in Resilient Leadership," *Journal of Higher Education* 83, no. 5 (2012); Scott DeRue and Susan Ashford, "Who Will Lead and Who Will Follow?; Kevin Barge, and Gail Fairhurst, "Living Leadership."
19 Anne Koenig et al., "Are Leader Stereotypes Masculine? A Meta-Analysis of Three Research Paradigms," *Psychological Bulletin* 137, no. 4 (2011).
20 Ibid.
21 Ibid.

22 Isabel Cuadrado et al., "Gender Differences in Leadership Styles as a Function of Leader and Subordinates' Sex and Type of Organization,"; Robin Ely, Herminia Ibarra, and Deborah Kolb, "Taking Gender into Account."

23 Anne Koenig et al., "Are Leader Stereotypes Masculine?"

24 Judi Marshall, "En-Gendering Notions of Leadership for Sustainability," *Gender, Work & Organizations* 18, no. 3 (2011): 274.

25 Erving Goffman, *The Presentation of Self in Everyday Life.*

26 Niels Van Doorn, Lisbet Van Zoonen, and Sally Wyatt, "Writing from Experience: Presentations of Gender Identity on Weblogs," *European Journal of Women's Studies* 14, no. 2 (2007).

27 George Mead, "The Self and the Organism." In *Self and Society: From the Standpoint of a Social Behaviorist,* 135–143, edited by Morris, Charles (Chicago, IL: University of Chicago Press, 1934).

28 Kevin Barge and Gail Fairhurst, "Living Leadership."; Gail Fairhurst and David Grant, "The Social Construction of Leadership: A Sailing Guide," *Management Communication Quarterly* 24, no. 2 (2010).

29 Dana Christman and Rhonda McClellan, "Discovering Middle Space."

30 Judith Butler, *Gender Trouble: Feminism and the Subversion of Identity* (New York: Routledge, 1990).

31 Scott DeRue and Susan Ashford, "Who Will Lead and Who Will Follow?"; Kevin Barge and Gail Fairhurst, "Living Leadership."; Gail Fairhurst and David Grant, "The Social Construction of Leadership."

32 Roya Ayman and Karen Korabik. "Leadership: Why Gender and Culture Matter." *American Psychologist* 65, no. 3 (2011); Robin Ely, Herminia Ibarra, and Deborah Kolb, "Taking Gender into Account."

33 Dana Christman and Rhonda McClellan, "Discovering Middle Space."

34 Judith Butler, *Undoing Gender;* Dana Christman and Rhonda McClellan, "Discovering Middle Space; Scott DeRue and Susan Ashford, "Who Will Lead and Who Will Follow?"; Kevin Barge and Gail Fairhurst, "Living Leadership."

35 Dana Christman and Rhonda McClellan, "Discovering Middle Space."

36 Keith Grint and Brad Jackson, "Toward 'Socially Constructive' Social Constructions of Leadership."

37 Mark Bolino et al., "A Multi-Level Review of Impression Management Motives and Behaviors"; Robin Ely, Herminia Ibarra, and Deborah Kolb, "Taking Gender into Account."

38 Kathy Charmaz, "Grounded Theory" In *Qualitative Psychology: A Practical Guide to Research Methods,* 81–110, Edited by Johnathan A. Smith (London, Sage, 2007).

39 John Creswell, *Qualitative Inquiry and Research Design: Choosing Among Five Approaches,* 3rd ed. (Thousand Oaks, CA: Sage, 2013): 83.

40 Erving Goffman, *The Presentation of Self in Everyday Life.*

41 Kathy Charmaz, "Grounded Theory."; John Creswell, *Qualitative Inquiry and Research Design.*

42 Kathy Charmaz, "Grounded Theory."

43 Ibid.

44 Kathy Charmaz, "Grounded Theory."; Kathy Charmaz and Karen Henwood, "Grounded Theory." In *The SAGE Handbook of Qualitative Research in Psychology* (Thousand Oaks, CA, Sage, 2008).

45 Lise Allen, "A Critique of Four Grounded Theory Texts," *The Qualitative Report* 15, no. 6 (2010).

46 Isabel Cuadrado et al., "Gender Differences in Leadership Styles as a Function of Leader and Subordinates' Sex and Type of Organization,"; Roya Ayman and Karen Korabik. "Leadership"; Robin Ely, Herminia Ibarra, and Deborah Kolb, "Taking

Gender into Account"; Robert Fairlie and Alicia Robb, "Gender Differences in Business Performance: Evidence from the Characteristics of Business Owners Survey," *Small Business Economics* 33, (2009).

47 Isabel Cuadrado et al., "Gender Differences in Leadership Styles as a Function of Leader and Subordinates' Sex and Type of Organization."

48 Robert Fairlie and Alicia Robb, "Gender Differences in Business Performance."

49 Isabel Cuadrado et al., "Gender Differences in Leadership Styles as a Function of Leader and Subordinates' Sex and Type of Organization,"; Robert Fairlie and Alicia Robb, "Gender Differences in Business Performance."

50 Isabel Cuadrado et al., "Gender Differences in Leadership Styles as a Function of Leader and Subordinates' Sex and Type of Organization,"; Robert Fairlie and Alicia Robb, "Gender Differences in Business Performance."

51 Isabel Cuadrado et al., "Gender Differences in Leadership Styles as a Function of Leader and Subordinates' Sex and Type of Organization."

52 Isabel Cuadrado et al., "Gender Differences in Leadership Styles as a Function of Leader and Subordinates' Sex and Type of Organization."; Robert Fairlie and Alicia Robb, "Gender Differences in Business Performance."

53 Ibid.

54 Isabel Cuadrado et al., "Gender Differences in Leadership Styles as a Function of Leader and Subordinates' Sex and Type of Organization,"; Roya Ayman and Karen Korabik, "Leadership."; Robin Ely, Herminia Ibarra, and Deborah Kolb, "Taking Gender into Account."

55 Roya Ayman and Karen Korabik. "Leadership"; Robin Ely, Herminia Ibarra, and Deborah Kolb, "Taking Gender into Account."

56 Roya Ayman and Karen Korabik. "Leadership."

57 Robin Ely, Herminia Ibarra, and Deborah Kolb, "Taking Gender into Account."

58 Isabel Cuadrado et al., "Gender Differences in Leadership Styles as a Function of Leader and Subordinates' Sex and Type of Organization."; Robert Fairlie and Alicia Robb, "Gender Differences in Business Performance."

59 Ibid.

60 Robin Ely, Herminia Ibarra, and Deborah Kolb, "Taking Gender into Account."

61 Isabel Cuadrado et al., "Gender Differences in Leadership Styles as a Function of Leader and Subordinates' Sex and Type of Organization."; Robert Fairlie and Alicia Robb, "Gender Differences in Business Performance."

62 Jill Goodman, Greg Knotts, and Jeanne Jackson, "Doing Dress and the Construction of Women's Gender Identity" *Journal of Occupational Science* 14, no. 2 (2007); Francesca Granata, "Subverting Assumptions of Female Beauty: An Interview with Ann-Sofie Back," *Fashion Theory: The Journal of Dress, Body & Culture* 11, no. 4 (2007).

63 Isabel Cuadrado et al., "Gender Differences in Leadership Styles as a Function of Leader and Subordinates' Sex and Type of Organization."

64 Dana Christman and Rhonda McClellan, "Discovering Middle Space."

References

Allen, Lise. "A Critique of Four Grounded Theory Texts." *The Qualitative Report* 15, no. 6 (2010): 1606–1620.

Arbaizar, Beatriz, and Javier Llorca, "Leadership and Sexual Behavior." *Psiquiatria* 15, no. 19 (2011): 1–15.

Ayman, Roya, and Karen Korabik. "Leadership: Why Gender and Culture Matter." *American Psychologist* 65, no. 3 (2011): 157–170.

Barge, J. Kevin, and Gail Fairhurst. "Living Leadership: A Systemic Constructionist Approach." *Leadership* 4, no. 3 (2008): 227–251.

Berg, Bruce. *Qualitative Research Methods for the Social Sciences*. Boston, MA: Allyn & Bacon Publishers, 2007.

Billing, Yvonne and Mats Alvesson. "Questioning the Notion of Feminine Leadership: A Critical Perspective on the Gender Labeling of Leadership." *Gender, Work and Organization* 7, no. 3 (2000): 144–157.

Blumer, Herbert. *Symbolic Interactionism: Perspective and Method*. Los Angeles, CA: University of California Press, 1969.

Bolino, Mark, et al. "A Multi-Level Review of Impression Management Motives and Behaviors." *Journal of Management* 34 (2008): 1080–1104.

Butler, Judith. *Gender Trouble: Feminism and the Subversion of Identity*. New York: Routledge, 1990.

Butler, Judith. *Undoing Gender*. New York: Routledge, 2004.

Charmaz, Kathy." Grounded Theory." In *Qualitative Psychology: A Practical Guide to Research Methods*, pp. 81–110. Edited by Johnathan A. Smith. London: Sage, 2007.

Charmaz, Kathy, and Karen Henwood. (2008). "Grounded Theory." In *The SAGE Handbook of Qualitative Research in Psychology*, pp. 240–241, 259. Edited by Willig, Carla, and Wendy Stainton Rogers. Thousand Oaks, CA: Sage, 2008.

Christman, Dana, and Rhonda McClellan. "Discovering Middle Space: Distinctions of Sex and Gender in Resilient Leadership." *Journal of Higher Education* 83, no. 5 (2012): 648–670.

Compton, Michele. "Dress the Part." *Women in Business* 59, no. 1 (2007): 12–14.

Creswell, John. *Qualitative Inquiry and Research Design: Choosing Among Five Approaches*. 3rd ed. Thousand Oaks, CA: Sage, 2013.

Cuadrado, Isabel, et al. "Gender Differences in Leadership Styles as a Function of Leader and Subordinates' Sex and Type of Organization." *Journal of Applied Social Psychology* 42, no. 12 (2012): 3083–3113.

DeRue, D. Scott, and Susan Ashford. "Who Will Lead and Who Will Follow? A Social Process of Leadership Identity Construction in Organizations." *Academy of Management Review* 35, no. 4 (2012): 627–647.

DeRue, D. Scott, et al. "Trait and Behavioral Theories of Leadership: An Integration and Meta-Analytic Test of their Relative Validity." *Personnel Psychology* 64 (2011): 7–52.

Eagly, Alice. and Mary Johannesen-Schmidt. "The Leadership Styles of Women and Men." *Journal of Social Issues* 57 (2001): 781–797.

Ely, Robin, Herminia Ibarra, and Deborah Kolb. "Taking Gender into Account: Theory and Design for Women's Leadership Development Programs." *Academy of Management Learning & Education* 10, no. 3 (2011): 474–493.

Fairhurst, Gail, and David Grant. "The Social Construction of Leadership: A Sailing Guide." *Management Communication Quarterly* 24, no. 2 (2010): 171–210.

Fairlie, Robert, and Alicia Robb. "Gender Differences in Business Performance: Evidence from the Characteristics of Business Owners Survey." *Small Business Economics*, 33, (2009): 375–395.

Gerstner, Charlotte, and David Day. "Meta-Analytic Review of Leader–Member Exchange Theory: Correlates and Construct Issues." *Journal of Applied Psychology* 82, no. 6 (1997): 827–844.

Goffman, Erving. *The Presentation of Self in Everyday Life*. New York: The Overlook Press, 1973.

Goodman, Jill, Greg Knotts, and Jeanne Jackson. "Doing Dress and the Construction of Women's Gender Identity." *Journal of Occupational Science* 14, no. 2 (2007): 100–107.

Granata, Francesca. "Subverting Assumptions of Female Beauty: An Interview with Ann-Sofie Back." *Fashion Theory: The Journal of Dress, Body & Culture* 11, no. 4 (2007): 391–401.

Grint, Keith, and Brad Jackson. "Toward 'Socially Constructive' Social Constructions of Leadership." *Management Communication Quarterly*, 24, no. 2 (2010): 348–355.

Judge, Timothy, and Robert Bretz. "Political Influence Behavior and Career Success." *Journal of Management* 20 (1994): 43–65.

Koenig, Anne et al. "Are Leader Stereotypes Masculine? A Meta-Analysis of Three Research Paradigms." *Psychological Bulletin* 137, no. 4 (2011): 616–642.

Marshall, Judi. "En-Gendering Notions of Leadership for Sustainability." *Gender, Work & Organizations* 18, no. 3 (2011): 263–281.

Mead, George. "The Self and the Organism." In *Self and Society: From the Standpoint of a Social Behaviorist*, pp. 135–143. Edited by Charles Morris. Chicago, IL: University of Chicago Press, 1934.

Peck, Edward et al. "Performing Leadership: Towards a New Research Agenda in Leadership Studies?" *Leadership* 4, (2009): 25–40.

Robbins, Stephen, and Timothy Judge. (2010). *Leadership: Essentials of organizational behavior* (10th ed.). Boston, MA: Prentice Hall.

Van Doorn, Niels, Lisbet Van Zoonen, and Sally Wyatt. "Writing from Experience: Presentations of Gender Identity on Weblogs." *European Journal of Women's Studies* 14, no. 2 (2007): 143–158.

Van Engen, Marloes, and Tineke Willemsen. "Sex and Leadership Styles: A Meta-Analysis of Research Published in the 1990s." *Psychological Reports* 94 (2004): 3–18.

Wayne, Sandy, et al. "The Role of Upward Influence Tactics in Human Resource Decisions." *Personnel Psychology* 50 (1997): 979–1006.

9

THE CULTURAL NEGOTIATIONS OF GENDER THROUGH RELIGION AMONG KABYLE ALGERIAN IMMIGRANTS IN FRANCE

Susan Rasmussen

Introduction

In a predominantly-Kabyle immigrant church of new converts, refugees from Algeria in a small municipality bordering Paris, France, a male pastor gave a sermon in French, translated simultaneously into Kabyle by another church leader, for about an hour. Later in this service, as in others, there was lively hand-clapping by adherents standing on their feet much of the time. Suddenly, a few women in the back rows of the sanctuary ululated enthusiastically, less characteristic of these services. One of the leaders gave them a solemn, disapproving look. They stopped their ululating, smiling a bit sheepishly though not greatly embarrassed.

At a church coffee following another service, a woman adherent related how she felt nostalgia for the mountains of Kabylia, "our home region (in Algeria)," but added that nonetheless, she preferred France because she felt that "women in Algeria are not as free as here."

This chapter explores the complex uses of religion to negotiate gender constructs and relations between the sexes, as well as to cope with discriminatory experiences, in France among a group of diasporic North African Kabyle people, who speak a Berber (Amazigh) language and French.[1] Most are former Muslims who converted to Christianity, and fled from Algeria, where they have experienced ethnic and linguistic marginalization and political violence, but also promoted cultural revitalization, over the past few decades. In France, they face some economic and religious marginalization, but their predicament is complex and paradoxical, in effect, situated on the "edges" of Europe and Africa, between North African Islam, Protestant Evangelical and charismatic Christianity, and official French secularism.

I analyze the peregrinations of hinted matrilineal symbolism and other gendered cultural imagery, in particular relating to women and mothers—though also interacting socially with men—as transported from the "home" culture into the diaspora, expressed in selected church rituals and meetings, conversion testimonies, interviews, guided conversations, and informal sociability. The field sites for the present essay are a predominantly Kabyle-led church congregation just outside Paris and also social events outside church rituals with converts, preachers, and others in wider Kabyle community settings in their diaspora in France. The question explored is how the ethnic and gendered symbolic motifs—in particular, those deriving from Kabyle mythico-histories, both shape and are shaped by life in France, and how these processes are negotiated in ritual and sociability. Data are based primarily on this social-cultural anthropologist's field research among the Kabyle and other Berber immigrants and expatriates in France, with some added broader insights from my field research in Niger and Mali among the Tuareg, who are culturally and linguistically related to the Kabyle.

I argue that that the Kabyle immigrant converts, though now practicing Protestant Evangelical and charismatic Christianity, continue to draw on religious and cultural motifs from their home culture and previous religion in order to negotiate gender constructs and relations between the sexes in their new cultural setting, but do not exactly replicate or reproduce these gendered ideologies or practices. More broadly, the analysis contributes to understanding how cultural/ethnic identity, gender, and religious conversion are interwoven in cultural myth-making.

Relevant here are two widely disseminated mythico-historical motifs or themes: the so-called "Kabyle Myth" and the "Myth of the Kahina" (Goodman 2005; Hannoum 2001; Silverstein 2004). My concern is not whether these mythico-histories are "true" or "false"; rather, I analyze how they are powerful and meaningful symbols (Hale 1999; Lévi-Strauss 1962; Malkki 1995) shaping human classifications, albeit also resisted and modified in practice. My focus, moreover, is not primarily on a textual analysis of additional accounts of these mythico-histories; rather, I briefly review them here as a point of departure for analyzing Kabyle converts' referencing of them, both consciously and unconsciously, in their re-interpretations and negotiations of gender.

Religion, Myth, Gender, and Politics

The Mythico-Historical Legacy and Kabyle Cultural Constructions of Gender and Religion

The first motif, known as "the Kabyle Myth," arose in political ideology and colonial policies enacted by French colonial administrators, who viewed North Africa through a "Manichean lens" (Goodman 2005: 7; Silverstein 2004: 14). Despite a diverse populace comprised of various Arab and Berber descent groups, Turks, Andalusians (descended from Moors exiled from Spain during the Crusades), Kouloughils (offspring of Turkish men and North

African women), Black Africans (mostly slaves and former slaves from south of the Sahara), and Jews, the French classified the population in Algeria primarily as ethnic categories contrasting "Arab" and "Berber" (Lorcin 1995: 2).

A number of French military colonial governors contended that Kabyles were closer to French than to Algerian Arabs, and showed greater promise to be integrated into the French polity than their Arabic-speaking counterparts (Ageron 1960). This idea was driven by perceived sociological and religious differences between Arabs and Kabyle Berbers that French arranged into a rigid, ossified hierarchy. Because Kabyles were a sedentary, mountain-dwelling population living in small villages, they reminded the French colonizers of peasants living in France's own countryside, with romanticized qualities of industriousness and frugality(Goodman 2005: 7). In contrast, Arabs were caricatured as nomadic, tent-dwelling peoples lacking stability.

The French also viewed Kabyles as less "fanatical" in their Islamic practices than their Arab counterparts, and characterized their society as "matriarchal." French Catholic missionaries attempted to convert Kabyles to Christianity. Conversion was not widespread, however, until several decades after Algerian independence, when Protestant missionary efforts had some success (Graham 2008; Guion 2014; Kaoues 2014).

Also relevant here is the "Myth of the Kahina," adopted, transformed, and used by many ethnic and cultural groups in North Africa (Hannoum 2001). According to some variants, a character named Kahina died, along with her sons, in a last stand against Muslim invaders from Arabia. After her defeat, the Berbers became Muslims. Recently in Morocco, Berber nationalists began to name their daughters for her. Some there also associate the Kahina with Jewish roots, a reminder of bravery. Around 1988, a religious ideology inherited from the Salafist piety movement was adopted by some Arabic speakers in Algeria under a weakened regime there. This gave birth to an Islamist-reformist piety movement whose members became active preachers in schools and universities, which in the independent nation state's "Arabization" policies had been left to Arabophone teachers after independence, but less popular in Kabylia. After a military *coup d'état* against the pending legislative victory of the Islamist-reformists, civil war erupted, lasting throughout the 1990s. Around 2001, the Kabyle congregation community I focus on here was founded by an American Protestant missionary couple in France, after approximately twenty years of proselytizing in Kabylia, who later retired, turning over leadership to Kabyles. The first church members, an older generation who arrived in 2001 following state repression of Berber protests in Kabylia, later returned there, but new converts, predominantly youthful women and men in their twenties and thirties, many single, arrived over the next decade.

Importantly, it should be emphasized that most Islamist-reformist piety movements are not violent. Algeria's political violence has occurred on several fronts: post-independence conflicts between the independent (initially socialist and secular) central state, which opposed uses of Kabyle and other Berber languages and their cultural revitalization in policies favoring "Arabization"; and, throughout the 1990s, recurring armed conflicts between the state government of military rulers and the more militant Islamist-reformist factions following the cancellation of the latter's legislative victories.

Throughout these eras, the character of Kahina has metamorphosed across time and space (Hannoum 2001: xv), for example, changed from a Berber to a Jew, to a Christian, to a Byzantine, to an Arab. However, the description of the Kahina as a woman is the most stable, for example, she is sometimes described as a Berber heroine who fought against the Arabs, but later, because of the supremacy of Arab weaponry, she was defeated. Yet this identity, too, has been transformed in significance in differing ethnic, religious, and gendered contexts, for example, from a woman into a man, then into a eunuch, and even an androgyne. The Kahina legend is therefore relevant to some interpretations of North African ethnic, gendered, and religious culture and history, as this represents moments when North Africa changed, and also preoccupations with domination and resistance.

In my field research in France, I first heard "the Kahina" alluded to informally, rather than in full-length tales, by two women: a female Kabyle immigrant convert during an informal conversation with me at a church social event, and a secretary of Franco-Kabyle background. The woman at the church, Fatima (pseudonym) wore a pendant with a cross inside a Star of David. When I admired it and inquired about its meaning, she explained, "this symbolizes the [longstanding, traditional pattern] of religious mixing among us Kabyles, and also refers to the Kahina, our heroine of North Africa." This prompted other women present to also compliment each others' jewelry in gendered terms: for example, remembering them as gifts from mothers and husbands, and one lamented that one had been stolen from a desk drawer at her office. Fatima as a small child had heard a preacher on the radio back in Kabylia, and became converted to Christianity that way.

The secretary, whom I shall call Catherine, had relatives in Algeria around Kabylia and Tizi Ouzou. Her husband was also of similar cultural background, but was raised speaking French; whereas she was raised speaking Kabyle. In her experience, this caused people to classify her as "other" in France. She compared this to a "caste system." She insisted that, in North Africa, "Berbers were the first autochthonous inhabitants, and Kahina is important to us as an 'our ancient princess.'"

Although I do not systematically focus in this chapter on collected textual full-length tales, I introduce these motifs as points of departure for analyzing the re-formulations of gender in the Kabyle convert community in diaspora, as "mythico-histories" (Malkki 1995), conveying what is important to those who refer to them. They are important here because of the discourses and practices of the Kabyle converts in France alluded to this motif, either explicitly in conversations, obliquely in interpretations of religious dogma, or subtly in social practices.

Appropriations of what is conventionally called, in anthropology of gender, a "matrilineal mythology" (Bamberger, in Rosaldo and Lamphere 1974), became re-defined yet again in the context of Amazigh/Berber activists who rejected Arabism and Islamist reformist militancy. Myth as a vision of the world can shape a group's actions, though not determine them absolutely in every context. Myths can have a social function. I am interested in the subtle, less conscious, but nonetheless powerful forms these cultural legacies take among the Kabyle immigrant converts in negotiating relations between the sexes and in the "performance of gender" (Butler 1990) in ritual and sociability. In other words, rather than pursuing a textual analysis of these myths in their narrative forms as "folktales," I follow their motifs in their peregrinations, to use Bloch's concept (Bloch 1963: 41–57) throughout the discourses and practices of the converts as they navigate their new life in France. I trace the varied and changing mythico-historical, cultural, and gendered identities by which Kabyle women and men in France, recently converted to Christianity and first-generation immigrants, define themselves and relate to each other, as expressed in the context of religion.

Judith Butler (1990) argues that gender is reproduced through performative repetition. Yet there are disjunctive breaks, as hinted in the opening section of this chapter. What forms of control are exercised by women and men in the predicament of a group of Kabyle immigrant/refugee converts as they disseminate notions about cultural/ethnic identity that shape gendered constructs? How are symbols and images from local Berber/Amazigh mythico-histories interwoven into, and stand in tension with, Evangelical and charismatic Protestant theology in ritual, in local adherents' interpretations of dogma texts, and in social life in their diaspora in France?

Disjunctive moments occur when women's and men's performances deviate from the roles into which French colonizers, Berber nationalist activists, and church officials in their own ways have created competing pressures for them as they attempt to balance modernist gender ideology with village-based morality. In fact, I show that many women and men converts still care about village-based social mores, and retain close ties— psychological as well as literally travel-based—with their "home" villages. Church events, incidents, and symbols open new social imaginaries, however. Church sermons, rituals, prayer and praise meetings, and informal coffees both redress and reaffirm internalized gendered beliefs and practices

Both Fatima and Catherine, introduced earlier, spoke of multi-religious traditions: Jewish, Muslim, and Christian. Catherine added that "even St. Augustine was a Berber born in North Africa," and emphasized Amazigh-Christian links. Both women also deplored the violence in Algeria during the 1990s civil war between the central state government and the Islamist-reformist militants. Catherine continued: "While I was there visiting my family, I had to dye my hair and dress like an Arabic-speaking women [covering up more fully]. Several other women, new converts in the congregation I focus on here, indicated similar gendered motivations to leave Algeria and convert to their new religion, objecting to specific policies impacting women's public conduct promoted by the militant Islamists, but did not express any antagonism toward Muslims or Arabic speakers in general, only toward militants' agendas in Kabylia.

Another young woman, in her twenties, whom I'll call Amina, related to me in an interview that she converted to Christianity around 2011

> because I found too many restrictions and rules in Islam; these were hard, such as wearing the headscarf, and not moving around freely. Also, both the state government and the Islamist militants there [gesturing a bearded chin to convey the latter] oppress Kabyles there [limiting their local language use].

Yet conflicts should not be overdrawn along neat ethnic or religious lines. On further reflection, Amina added, "Actually, I was first prompted to convert on hearing beautiful praises and songs in my town's church and also, my neighbors were converts," thereby hinting that music, important in Berber cultural and aesthetic life, not solely fear of the militant reformist Islamists, had played an important role in this process.

A middle-aged male convert whom I'll call Amo, 35 years old, noted that it was a Muslim friend who first introduced him to Christianity by bringing him to Germany for work and education. There, he met Christians. He noted a change in his marital relationship since his converting: "before, I was nasty to my wife, but now I am more loving toward her."

The connections among gender, religion, culture/ethnicity, and politics are complex. The voices and gazes here are multiple and negotiated in contexts of both symbolism and power.

Recall that the French colonizers viewed Kabyles as "less fanatically attached to Islam" (Silverstein 2004: 53), and portrayed them as having "accepted the Qur'an, but not embraced it" (Daumas and Fabar 1847 I: 77). From their "worship" of "saints" and heteroprax marabouts (holy men), to their alleged failure to observe daily prayers, Ramadan fasts, and prohibitions on alcohol and pork, colonial observers asserted that "Kabyle people are far from the religious ideas of the Arab people" (Daumas and Fabar 1847 II: 55).

I found somewhat greater religious and social complexity than portrayed in either colonial tracts or post-colonial academic critiques of the "Kabyle Myth," and also some intriguing contradictions. A number of converts in the church setting felt that it was possible for a single family to include adherents to several different religions, for example, a few women indicated with pride rather than shame or disapproval that they had cousins who were Muslim, Jewish, and Christian. Although some Christian male converts hinted at political resistance to the state's Arabization as one motive for converting, and several women opposed the militant Islamist-reformists' policies, many converts celebrated cultural and religious differences. At a coffee following a church service, the male Kabyle pastor put it this way:

> Kabylia was especially selected by missionaries for conversions because there, we are religiously open and tolerant. For example, you can be a person adhering to different religions within a single family, and this is no problem . . . Also, another reason for this openness is that historically, diverse peoples entered Kabylia, such as Romans, Phoenicians, Arabs, and French.

A male drummer at the church during the Islamic month of Ramadan commented, "Although my elderly mother is also a Christian, she still fasts during the Ramadan fasting month." When I asked why, he explained, " Islam is part of our elders' culture, [is] deeply engrained in it." This drummer and another musician in the church said they were not fasting during Ramadan, but added, "mostly older people, especially women, do this , even if they have been converted to Christianity."

Hence the importance of age, gender, and culture across some diverse religious practices. Many converts in the Kabyle church community retained their Arabic/Qur'anic names. Reasons they gave emphasized their cultural identity, which, many insisted, "stays the same, even after conversion to this new religion."

Another man, Mohan (pseudonym) further elaborated on these issues. He converted from Islam around 2004 after he migrated from his home Kabylia region in Algeria to France to work and to escape political violence. His wife remained Muslim because, he explained, "this is rooted in her feminine Kabyle culture." Notably, this man's comments here contradicted some French colonial administrators' assumptions in "the Kabyle Myth," that all Kabyle were "lax" Muslims. Yet he subtly referred to "the Myth of the Kahina," using a maternal trope evoking the cultural importance of a female heroine/ancestor.

Mohan's wife followed Islamic religious food taboos because, the couple explained:

> these are really cultural, not religious, taboos, despite their nominal basis in Islam. For in Kabyle society, men, even Muslims, can hunt, cook, and eat wild pig or boar, even if this is considered pork in Islam, but women cannot. This is not just because of Islam, but because people frown on women eating wild pig [boar].

Thus wild pig is a masculine food in local cultural viewpoint, undomesticated (perhaps far from polluting urban garbage, and associated with the quintessential male cultural practice of hunting), even as pork (i.e., "pig" meat) is prohibited for both sexes on a religious basis in Islam. In other words, Mohan's wife's abstaining from eating pork had a gendered, not solely religious, cultural basis.

Different variants of the Kahina myth, not as a full tale, but as a trope subtly referenced in diaspora, reflect Berbers' long-term contradictory situations and their historical adaptation to them. Algerian feminists claimed Kahina as a model for women in opposition to the FLN Islamist-reformist piety party's political ideology. In some contexts, to say that one is a son or daughter of the Kahina is to say that one is a Berber, while in others, this motif is obliquely evoked to say that one is a Christian convert, but still Berber. Groups are never "set in stone," but vary internally, change over time, and travel.

Ethnographic and Historical Background and Their Contemporary Reverberations

The Kabyle Berbers in North Africa and in France

Kabyles speak a language (often called by the same term) that belongs to the Berber group within the larger Afro-Asiatic family. Other Berber languages and dialects spoken include Chaouia and Shlugh in Algeria; Tamazight in Morocco; Tamajaq, the language of the Tuareg and its various regional dialects in the central Sahara; Semitic languages, and ancient Egyptian. Most Kabyles living in France also speak French. Yet the term "Berber" is not of local origin. The local term for Berber today is either Tamazight or Imazighen, the former referring to the language, the latter to the people who use it (Brett and Fentress 1996: 5), though this terminology is not universally used by all Kabyles or by all Berber scholars. Goodman (2005: 11) found that most of her interlocutors referred to themselves as either Leqbayel or Berberes. My interlocutors in France tended to refer to themselves and each other as "Kabyle" or "Berberes," and to their region in Algeria as "Kabylia." Cultural revitalization leaders and activists sometimes use the term "Amazigh."

Historically in North Africa, Berber peoples encountered waves of Punic, Roman, Arab, and French rulers and settlers, all to varying degrees dominating and integrating into local society, prompting early migrations into the high mountains of the Kabylia region for defense. Arabs first encountered Berbers in Cyrenaica to the west of Egypt, and treated them as unbelievers, to procure both tribute in slaves and supplies of army recruits, who later went into Spain with the Arabs, but revolted in 740 CE in Tangier.

Later, under French colonialism, administrators sought to promote their perceptions of Kabyle as democratic, as well as secular (Hanoteau and Letourneux 1872–73). In the French colonial imagination, there was a primordial battle between Christians and Muslims, the Mediterranean and the Sahara, and Kabyles were viewed as potential allies to aid them in their colonial policies (Silverstein 2004: 52). Through laws and schooling, the French differentiated Kabyles from Arabs, and sought to assimilate Kabyles into the French polity and culture. French schools were built in Kabylia a generation earlier than elsewhere in Algeria (Ageron 1960; Lorcin 1995).

For the colonial powers, the alleged lack of religiosity of Kabyles was symbolized, above all, by the women. A far greater percentage of women in Kabylia completed high school and university than their counterparts in more Arabic-speaking communities (Brett and Fentress 1996: 244). Colonial observers generalized that Berber culture was originally "matriarchal," and that Islamic invasions from the seventh to eleventh centuries deposited "only a thin layer of patriarchy" on its surface (Silverstein 2004: 53). For colonial writers, these observations constituted evidence of a shared "kinship" with France, though stagnated in an earlier evolutionary stage Carette (1848: 60–70). Several post-colonial scholars (Chachoua 2001; Jansen 1987; Messaoudi and Schemla 1995) and Kabyle cultural revitalization leaders (Chakur 2001) later rejected colonial evolutionary ranking, but have argued, with some supporting data, that Kabyle women (particularly older women and grandmothers) manage the household, and that most women go about in public unveiled and interact freely with men. How do the immigrant/ refugee converts in France re-formulate these arguments?

Reconstructions of Gender and Religion in Church and in Wider Contexts

Here, I do not seek to "evaluate" how far these converts display "egalitarian" gender constructs according to Western feminist standards (which themselves are not in agreement) (Di Leonardo 1991); rather, I offer, as far as possible, local interlocutors' and research participants' viewpoints and actions, as encountered in my fieldwork. In their discourses, many Kabyle converts in France insisted that "we Kabyles hold women in high respect," without any prompting from myself. In social interactions and spatial orientations, as well as church rituals and meetings, I noticed general mutual respect. In a few conversion testimonies by men, there was some admission of being "nicer" to wives following their conversion, and at women's meetings I attended, thus far, only one instance of wife-beating was mentioned. In the converts' church community, the sexes do not sit apart either during the service, at coffees, other social events outside it, or at praise or prayer meetings. These latter are mixed-sex (though special women's meetings are not), and both women and men have voice in discussions interpreting Bible verses and offering advice to participants. However, higher church authorities tend to be male.

By contrast, there is a sharp sexual division of labor during the more informal sociability of church-related activities. Although men and women do not sit apart or on separate sides of the sanctuary during services (called *cultes*) (children tend to sit in an alcove to one side of the altar, instead), during church coffees and other social events and celebrations, the women prepare, set out, and serve coffee, tea, and food snacks, put away dishware, and clean the kitchen. Men do heavier work such as cleaning the church, moving furniture, etc. No women complained about this arrangement, or viewed it as indicative of hierarchy or inequality. Pastors giving sermons during formal services tend to be men. Recently, following several years of male leadership of prayer and praise meetings, a woman studying for her degree in theology became a leader of those groups, as well as women's meetings.

The foregoing patterns show the complex, dynamic meanings of gender, as reconstructed in context. They suggest that, as in Algerian Muslim communities (Goodman 2005: 10), the most salient contrasts in religion may not have been between Berbers and Arabs, but between men and women, in terms of a more orthodox or scriptural versus a more popular form of religious practice. For example, the diaspora religious arrangements in some respects recall the gendered differences between so-called "official" (organized) and so-called "unofficial/popular/para" religion. In Islam, whereas the mosque serves as a location for collective practice of Islam's five daily prayers and for assembling for Friday sermons or on Muslim holy days, small shrines and tombs, and some other informal assemblies and peripheral practices, are usually visited for guidance in personal matters.

In practice, the distinction between mosques and shrines articulates with gender divisions (though not gender hierarchies) in Arab and Kabyle communities, as in some other neighboring Berber Muslim communities (e.g., the Tuareg farther south): women are more likely to frequent shrines, while men tend to gather in mosques, although men also pay visits to shrines on special occasions, and this is not a rigid distinction. Also, dreams are highly significant in divination, and often take place at deceased marabouts' shrines and tombs. (Nicolaisen and Nicolaisen 1997; Rasmussen 2006, 2015).

The Kabyle converts, also, emphasize dreams in many of their conversion testimonies, by both men and women. Holy spaces are somewhat divided, as shown above, but both men and women traverse similar spaces in the important practice of testimonies (witnessing), relating conversion experiences. A number of testimonies that I collected relate encounters with Jesus Christ during a dream. Both women and men give these testimonies in public during church services, coming to the front of the altar area—like Islamic marabouts' shrines and tombs, a holy or sacred space—and standing before the congregations, thereby approximating, but also modifying in female and male participation patterns, the ritual dream divination experiences as found in Africa.

For example, one woman, approximately in her thirties, related: "First, I dreamed of a Bible verse, and then I dreamed that I arrived at a fork in a road, and asked for either Mohammed or Jesus to direct [guide] me. Jesus guided me, so I converted to Christianity."

Another woman's conversion occurred in conjunction with a dream prophecy and a miracle, as well. A hospital employee, she had been rejected by her mother, and loved by her father. But her father died, so she felt like an orphan. Her mother, too, died eventually. She then converted to Christianity. Later, in a dream, her mother (notably, not her father) appeared to her to reconcile with her. In that dream, her mother also warned her of an upcoming earthquake (which came to pass in Algeria). She ran and ran; and other converts insisted that she was protected by a wall of light.

The dream in this latter testimony has two main themes. One concerns the protective value of conversion and the foretelling of the future by the mother; here, as throughout many Berber communities, dreaming features divination with ancestors, which occurs in popular Islamic practices. This dream's other important theme—early rejection of a daughter by her mother followed by their later reconciliation—is striking in its compelling preoccupation with close and loving maternal kinship ties which, deviating from the ideal, were re-claimed.

In other contexts in the convert diaspora community, there is the evocation of the centralized female space in Berber architecture (Brett and Fentress 1996: 24), which has important symbolic and ritual significance. Each division of a room (whether a Tuareg nomadic tent or a Kabyle sedentarized house) has its own rituals, according to a balanced division between male and female spaces. The Berber household is traditionally managed by the wife or mother of the eldest male, considered the pillar of the Kabyle house: it is she who is entirely responsible for the household economy and behavior of younger women living with her (Brett and Fentress 1996: 242). It is the grandmother who is traditionally in charge of subsistence: for example, in Kabylia, she alone could open and close storage jars (Brett and Fentress 1996: 242).

In the Kabyle church community near Paris, I found that close contacts with older female relatives endured among many converts; for example, a female church leader prayed at meetings for her grandmother who was in a hospital in Algeria with diabetes complications, telephoned her relatives there regularly, and briefly visited them during this health crisis.

Goodman (2005: 79) shows how in the villages of Kabylia, houses are also the locus of social morality, situated in territorial map loosely organized on a patrilineal basis. The moral economy is organized by lineage, age, and gender in choices men and women make about mobility through village space (Mahe 2001). A young unmarried woman who travels alone outside her immediate group of households opens herself to scrutiny, risks being suspected of seeking a man, and being evaluated as lacking shame or modesty. At stake is *ihenna*, or respect that a household enjoys in the village. A good reputation is important; in particular, emigrant women must be careful while visiting their village in Kabylia to be seen as respectable. Men socialize in the public square. Women travel in pairs or groups to diffuse suspicion of sexual transgressions. If gossip of controversial actions of an emigrant living abroad reaches relatives in an Algerian village, one's reputation may suffer.

I found that both women and men converts conveyed fears of too much public scrutiny, though not solely on modesty and sexuality matters, but also on religious grounds. For example, a male convert with whom I met for coffees and extended interviewing in Paris's twentieth arrondissement wished to move to a different interview location in order to avoid being overheard by a café owner from near his hometown in Algeria, whom he had identified by his regional accent, and feared would resent his conversion.

Traditionally, the language of shame and modesty is widely used to explain why young women hesitate to walk alone outside a village section, why young women in principle should defer to their fathers and uncles, or why women refrain from smoking in front of families (Goodman 2005). Shyness or reserve (isethi) relationships of respect are expected in front of one's social superiors. Ideally, respectful attitudes and relations prevail, from the male perspective, between a man and his parents (father, mother, grandparents), a man and his siblings; a son-in-law and his parents-in-law, and more generally, any relationship between a man and all women except his wife in an intimate and private setting (Mahfoufi 1991: 53). From the female perspective, these attitudes and relations prevail between a woman and her father, brothers, uncles, and grandparents as well as her parents-in-law, and between a woman and all men outside her household. Relations of respect are relaxed when women are among themselves unless one of the above are present.

At church in the diaspora, subjects pertaining to shame, modesty, and respect often arise. For example, during one church service, the pastor announced the day's topic: unbridled passion. He encouraged everyone to overcome this, "because small things distract from big things. For example, the lure of cigarettes for youths, especially men." He focused on biblical references to passion's negative effects. He added, however, that "both men and women are equally vulnerable to passion." Notably, this conceptualization of modesty, shame, and respect, opposed as it is to passion and applicable to both sexes, differs from the Arabic *fitna* and *aur'ra*, related concepts that are applied more to women, not men, as well as some of Goodman's (2005) observations in Kabylia villages.

Yet convert women in diaspora do express some shame or reserve regarding topics to discuss in mixed-sex company. At women's group meetings, held each second Saturday of the month from 2:30 until 6 p.m., only women are present, according to participants, "because here, we can discuss problems we would prefer not to discuss with men present." In one meeting I attended, held after the men had moved furniture, cleaned the sanctuary, and left for home and jobs, the woman discussion leader read a selection from the Bible, Proverbs 5, addressing adultery. She commented on its meaning, analyzing its symbols (of the cistern/well/water=your neighbor's wife) and its interpretation (beware "drinking" from this), and also the seductress who uses words "like honey." In this text, a man warned his son about seductive married woman. In her commentary, the discussion leader gave several examples from her own female acquaintances, allegedly seduced by married men, for example, a girl whose parents opposed her marrying her cousin because of an old family feud, who subsequently stayed home and rejected all other suitors, wearing an unflattering headdress and continuing to "pine" for her cousin, who was now married to another woman, but whom she hoped he would divorce. A second example concerned a colleague who was harassed by a married man, and allegedly was tempted by his advances.

The discussion leader then asked for the group's comments. The prevalent viewpoint was that men and women can seduce or be seduced, and that both sexes share responsibility for enforcing sexual mores.

The leader then asked each of the women present to state her goal or wish. Another young (approximately in her twenties) woman convert, a mother of two, came to France from Kabylia in order to pursue higher education and work. Her special areas of interest were English and archeology, but lately, she had a growing interest in art history because, she explained, "archeology is just a lot of dates and numbers, and also, one must do archeology in the field, but since I am now a mother, this is difficult." In France, she had a year of *sabatique parentale* (maternity or parental leave), but hoped to resume her studies and work only after her children were older.

Thus motherhood had priority. This maternal theme reverberated throughout many church sermons, with such themes as Mary, mother of Jesus Christ, and family relationships. For example, in one church service, the pastor said:

all families have problems, but the holy family should inspire us, for Joseph respected and loved Mary, did not repudiate her even when he knew that she was pregnant and he was not the father. Her child was of God. Mary and Joseph traveled, and Jesus as boy disappeared to discuss matters with healers and priests. But Mary and Joseph, though upset at first because they could not find him, accepted Jesus' explanation of purpose (to discuss religion and meditate with specialists).

The pastor then focused on Mary's life. He said that after she lost Jesus, and later was widowed at around forty years of age, she then dedicated her life to the ministry of Jesus. She died when she was around seventy. Joseph's life is less well-known. But both parents should inspire contemporary people in our church to carry on the ministry, and to have harmonious family relationships.

Significant here is this Kabyle pastor's emphasis on Mary, mother of Jesus Christ, as a Kahina-like model of a "mother" of Berber people, the latter, recall, emphasized by some female adherents. The myth of the Kahina here was in effect submerged in the biblical myth of the Mother of Christ and the "virgin birth," as well as the French Mother's Day, the latter approaching at the time of the service. At its conclusion, the pastor asked children present to come to the altar, gave each a rose, and had each child then give the rose to a mother in the congregation. At a baptism of two newborn infants, a pastor commented that they were "woven in their mother's stomachs," without reference to the father. In these contexts, matrilineal attachment became re-worked symbolically into Christian theology and ritual.

In another church service, the pastor in his sermon read and commented on the texts of Paul 5, which addressed husband-wife relationships, and said that "a woman must submit [*soumettre*] to their husband," but interestingly, he went on to criticize this as having a negative connotation in French, so he re-translated this as "depend on" and "respect" the husband. He made a distinction between a literal translation and a dynamic translation, favoring the latter. He said "the husband must love his wife as he loves himself." Then he made an Lévi-Straussian structuralist double analogy: "the church: woman:: Christ: men." Christ and the Church love each other as they love themselves. Churches and spouses love each other as Christ and the Church love themselves (and each other). Hence the construction, in mythemes à la Lévi-Strauss here, in effect a structural transformation of the Kahina myth.

The same pastor also referred to the Kabyle ideal that "women are central to the home, men do not like to be in the kitchen, [chuckling], but men should help women in other ways." In other words, he did not reproach Kabyle men for this sexual division of spaces and work, but rather, introduced an alternative that would accommodate the needs of both wives and husbands. The pastor emphasized the complementary roles of the sexes and also, affection between both siblings and the generations. Sibling relationships in fact are central to many immigrant converts in France. Often, men attempt to obtain visas and other documents to enable a sister to come to France, while others try to bring a wife to France. This process takes much time, and many male converts at prayer meetings request others there to pray for success in their efforts.

Political violence against universities and national unemployment in Algeria have propelled many Kabyles to leave for France for education and work. Several converts in the church congregation I knew were married to, or had relatives married to, "native" French-born nationals, but even so, faced difficulties over obtaining immigration and residence documents. This, and also finding remunerative jobs and decent housing, was urgent for self-respect and social prestige for the young men. Although in contrast to some other immigrant groups in France, most persons in the group I focused on cannot be considered impoverished, and a few even had some university education, many nonetheless were marginalized since they faced economic difficulties at least indirectly caused by some discrimination toward immigrants, particularly the racialization of ethnicity, nationality, and religion in the tense atmosphere in and around Paris following attacks on a music venue, a café/restaurant, and a sports stadium. Many converts still held part-time jobs, with fluctuating income.

One man at a praise meeting sought advice on a new job offer; the group prayed, and suggested that he accept it "if it was not exploitative." Another worked as a security agent at a branch of a large French department store, with swing shift hours. In the case of young men, these difficulties challenged their sources of male gender-role pride. At one prayer and praise meeting, for example, a male convert related how he was trying to get his education degrees accredited in France, but was frustrated by the long process.

Another recurring men's complaint was the difficulty of marrying, dependent for many on jobs. Many young men during the time of my research had remained single longer than traditionally ideal. Several male converts, looking embarrassed and tense, appealed fervently, during prayer services, to other participants to pray for them to find a job and to marry.

Concluding Discussion

Thus there are different voices simultaneously speaking, and gazes viewing, the navigations of immigrant convert men and women in France: of African Kabyle and Muslim, of French and secular, and of American Protestant. These voices and gazes are selectively accommodated. The foregoing gendered concerns with religion, work, and marriage refer to mythico-historical voices, and gazes, as negotiated and re-worked in multiple religious and cultural encounters. These peregrinations and permutations of the Kabyle and Kahina mythico-histories, while not formally related as literal textual tales in these converts' narratives, re-negotiate gender in emergent multiple interpretations and representations. These re-negotiations of myth occur in encounters with wider political events and from personal subjective experience and memory, as well. More broadly, some meanings are continued in multiple encounters, though not as static forms of folklore or as imaginaries frozen in time, but through performing gender by juxtaposing and cross-application of not only texts, but also practices.

Discussion Questions

1   How do Kabyle converts in France draw on, but also modify, matrilineal motifs in myths surrounding their cultural/ethnic identity? What are some wider implications of these practices for gender?
2   What religious continuities, as well as discontinuities and ruptures, between Islam and Christianity emerge in Kabyle converts' narratives? What are the wider implications for the connections between religion, culture, and gender in this diasporic community?

3 What is the Kahina myth, and how powerful socially is the use of the Kahina myth as a symbol among Kabyle converts in their diaspora?

4 Explain the role and significance of gender in religious conversion for female and male Kabyle immigrants in this case study.

5 Discuss some connections between the history of the Berbers in North Africa and the religious conversion of some Kabyles.

Suggested Reading

1 Brett, Michael and Elizabeth Fentress. 1996. *The Berbers*. Oxford: Blackwell.

2 Goodman, Jane. 2005. *Berber Culture on the World Stage: From Village to Video*. Bloomington, IN: Indiana University Press.

3 Hannoum, Abdulmajid. 2001. *Colonial Histories, Postcolonial Memories*. Portsmouth, NH: Heinemann.

4 Silverstein, Paul. 2004. *Algeria in France*. Bloomington, IN: Indiana University Press.

Note

1 Although many converts in France alternate between speaking Kabyle and French, most tend to speak French more often. Our conversations and interviews were in French, though I also speak and understand another related Berber language, Tamajaq, spoken by the Tuareg in Niger and Mali. In particular, Kabyle is closely related to the Air dialect of Tamajaq in northern Niger where I have worked for approximately thirty years, in research projects on spirit possession, gender, aging and the life course, medico-ritual healing and specialists, rural and urban smith/artisans, verbal art performance, and youth cultures. In recent years, I have also conducted field research among Tuareg and other Berber expatriates and immigrants in France, including the Kabyle converts, particularly intensively in 2015, 2016, and 2017.

References

Ageron, Charles-Robert. 1960. La France a-t-elle eu une politique kabyle? *Revue historique* 1960 (April): 311–352.

Bloch, M. 1963. Reflexions d'un historien sur les fausses rumeurs de la guerre. In *Mélanges historiques*. Paris: Ecole Pratique des Hautes Etudes, vol. 1, pp. 41–57.

Brett, Michael and Elizabeth Fentress. 1996. *The Berbers*. Oxford, UK: Blackwell.

Butler, Judith. 1990. *Gender Trouble*. New York: Routledge.

Carette, Ernest. 1848. *Etudes sur la Kabilie proprement dite*. Paris: Imprimerie Nationale.

Chachoua, Kamel. 2001. *L'Islam Kabyle: Religion, etat et société en Algerie*. Paris: Maisonneuve et Larose.

Chakur, Salem. 2001. Mouloud Mammeri (1917–1989): Le berberisant. In *Hommes et femmes de Kabylie*, vol. 1, ed. S. Chaker, pp. 162–166. Aix-en-Provence, France: Edisud.

Daumas, General Eugene and M. Fabar. 1847. *La Grande-Kabyle: Etudes historiques*. Paris and Algiers: Hachette.

Di Leonardo, Micaela, 1991, *Gender at the Crossroads of Knowledge*. Berkeley, CA: University of California Press.

Goodman, Jane E. 2005. *Berber Culture on the World Stage: From Village to Video*. Bloomington, IN: Indiana University Press.

Graham, Don. 2008. Church Takes Root in Paris Apartment. *Baptist Press*, news service www.baptistpress.com, November 25, pp. 1–2.

Guion, Anne. 2014. Algerie: La pousse evangélique. In *l'Hebdomadaire la Vie*, June 5, p. 1.

Hale, Thomas. 1999. *Griots and Griottes*. Bloomington, IN: Indiana University Press.

Hannoum, Abdulmajid. 2001. *Colonial Histories, Postcolonial Memories*. Portsmouth, NH: Heinemann.

Hanoteau, Adolphe and Aristide Letourneux. 1872. *La Kabylie et les coutumes kabyles*. Paris: Imprimerie Nationale.

Jansen, Willy. 1987. *Women without Men: Gender and Marginality in an Algerian Town*. Leiden: E.J. Brill.

Kaoues, Fatiha (interviewed by Olivier Moos). 2014. Français: entretiens: Christianisme: l'Activité missionaire evangélique dans le monde musulman: entretien (Interview) avec Fatiha Kaoues. Interview by Olivier Moos in *Religioscope* May 29, 2014.

Lévi-Strauss, Claude. 1962. *Structural Anthropology*. Chicago, IL: University of Chicago Press.

Lorcin, Patricia. 1995. *Imperial Identities: Stereotyping, Prejudice, and Race in Colonial Africa*. London and New York: I.B. Tauris.

Maggi, Wynne. 2001. *Our Women Are Free: Gender and Ethnicity in Hindukush*. Ann Arbor, MI: University of Michigan Press

Mahe, Alain. 2001. *Histoire de la Grande Kabylie XIX–XX Siecles*. Paris: Bouchene.

Mahfoufi, Mehenna.1991. *Le répertoire musical d'un village berbere d'Algerie*. University de Paris X, Laboratoire "Etudes d'ethnomusicologie" (CNRS/UPR 165).

Malkki, Liisa. 1995. *Purity and Exile*. Berkeley, CA: University of California Press.

Messaoudi, Khalida and Elisabeth Schemla. 1995. *Unbowed: An Algerian Woman Confronts Islamic Fundamentalism*, trans. A.C. Vila. Philadelphia, PA: University of Pennsylvania Press.

Nicolaisen, Ida and Johannes. 1997. *The Pastoral Tuareg*. Copenhagen: Rhodos.

Rasmussen, Susan. 2006. *Those Who Touch: Tuareg Medicine Women in Anthropological Perspective*. DeKalb, IL: Northern Illinois University Press.

Rasmussen, Susan. 2015. An Ambiguous Spirit Dream and Tuareg-Kunta Relationships in rural Northern Mali. *Anthropological Quarterly* 88 (3): 635–664.

Rosaldo, Michelle and Louise Lamphere. 1974. *Women, Culture, and Society*. Stanford, CA: Stanford University Press.

Silverstein, Paul. 2004. *Algeria in France: Transpolitics, Race, and Nation*. Bloomington, IN: Indiana University Press.

Part III

PSYCHOSOCIAL EFFECTS OF INEQUALITY

GENDER SCHOLAR SPOTLIGHT: INTERVIEW WITH MARY BELTRÁN

Mary Beltrán is an associate professor with a focus on media studies, Latina/o studies, and gender studies at the University of Texas at Austin. She writes and teaches on Latina/o representation, on constructions of race, class, gender, and sexuality in film and television, and on racial diversity in the U.S. media industries. She is the author of *Latina/o Stars in U.S. Eyes* and co-editor of *Mixed Race Hollywood*. Her current project is the book *Bronzing the Box: Latina/o Images, Storytelling, and Advocacy in U.S. Television*.

What led you to begin studying women's inequality?

As a college student, the first women's studies course that I took really opened my eyes about the many ways in which our often-patriarchal culture maintains girls' and women's inequality. From my upbringing, I also was aware of how my relatives on my mother's side, who are Mexican, experienced clear disadvantages in terms of education and job opportunities in comparison to my relatives on my father's side, who are Anglo American. So my understanding of women's inequality also was always intersectional. Prior to getting my Ph.D., I also was a social worker, often working with working-class kids and families of color. My last social work job, in which I worked with teen parents in San Francisco, really made me think about how the entertainment media play a role in the intensely imbalanced playing field for girls and women of color. I wanted to go back to graduate school to learn more about that.

How have your lived experiences shaped your research interests?

As noted above, my experience growing up in a bicultural family really made a difference in allowing me to see how Americans of various ethnic backgrounds experience radically different treatment in the U.S. I think the risk that my parents took in choosing to marry and raise a family together also has instilled in me a strong belief that we can overcome personal and social biases such as sexism/misogyny and racism if we work hard enough and on many levels. My belief also in the importance of seeing ourselves in the media continues to fuel my desire to do research on Latina/Latino and mixed-race representation.

In your opinion, what scholarly works have had the most impact on your research on women and inequality?

Scholarship in Latina feminist film and media studies (e.g., Rosa Linda Fregoso, Angharad Valdivia, Michelle Habell-Pallan, and Isabel Molina Guzmán) and feminist film and television studies (Diane Negra, Julie D'Acci, Bonnie Dow, Elana Levine, etc.!) has been especially useful to my scholarship.

What has been most challenging about your field of work?

I love teaching. But I also have a hard time switching gears mentally while I'm teaching to focus on doing research and writing. So I suppose having the time to do the work and do it well is the hardest thing for me.

Why is your work on women important?

In subtle but important ways we are all influenced by media representation. I think it's vital to learn about how we've represented different groups historically and how images, storytelling, and advocacy affect us still today.

Which scholar(s) (and why) has been most influential in developing your perspective?

Scholarship that has acknowledged and helped to make sense of the prevalence of sexist and White and Western-centric media representation continued to inspire and help me make sense of the work that I'm trying to do. I have sought out and especially appreciate intersectional approaches to gender, race, class, and sexuality. Gloria Anzaldúa, Rosa Linda Fregoso, Richard Dyer, Ella Shohat and Robert Stam, Antonio Gramsci, and Stuart Hall have been particularly important to my thinking. Laura Mulvey's work on the male gaze also was incredibly important, even while I think there are a lot of problems with this theory.

What theoretical approach best guides your research?

I think of myself as a feminist critical and cultural studies scholar.

What pedagogical approaches have you found most effective when teaching on women and inequality?

I like to use a variety of approaches that allow my students to engage with the material that we're covering in a wide range of ways. This includes reading, journaling, small group discussions, structured debates, research for small group presentations in class, and the writing of research papers and creation of creative projects such as short videos.

10

HAIR STRESS

Physical and Mental Health Correlates of African
American Women's Hair Care Practices

Evelyn B. Winfield-Thomas and Arthur L. Whaley

Introduction

American culture has constructed a standard of beauty characterized by
an idealized depiction of European American physiognomy (i.e., straight
blonde hair, blue eyes, light skin tone), (Greene 1994, 1997; Hall 1995;
Hill-Collins 1991; Neal and Wilson 1989; Okazawa-Rey et al. 1987;
Robinson 1998; Sandler 1992). While only a few members of one segment
(i.e., European ancestry) of our multicultural society possess all of these
characteristics, they constitute the standard generally used to measure or
define attractiveness for the entire population. Consequently, individuals
from diverse cultural groups, especially females, feel pressure to conform to
these Eurocentric standards in order to be seen as "beautiful."

Women of color embrace such standards because physical attractiveness
represents an important form of social capital in American society. There is
a tendency to view those we consider attractive as more successful, intel-
ligent, and popular, as well as such individuals reporting higher levels of
self-esteem and feelings of worth (Cash 1981). Further, attractive persons
are discriminated against less and afforded more benefits, privileges, opportunities, class mobility, and prestige compared to those who are considered
less attractive (Jackson 1992; Neal and Wilson 1989; Rooks 1996; Russell
et al. 1992; Sandler 1992; Wade 1996). Individuals who are considered
physically unattractive may experience a poorer quality of life relative to
their attractive counterparts.

There is also substantial evidence from research on clinical and
nonclinical samples of men and women that personal perceptions of
unattractiveness or, in general, negative attitudes about personal physical
appearances (i.e., a negative body image) are associated with poor self-
esteem, social anxieties and inhibitions, sexual difficulties, and risks for
depression (e.g., Cash 1985; Cash et al. 1985, 1986; Eitel 2003; Lerner

et al. 1976; Noles et al. 1985; Rosen and Ross 1968). While both men and women evaluate their physical characteristics, and are judged against a European standard of beauty and attractiveness, the expectation for women to pay more attention to their appearance typically is greater (e.g., Cash and Pruzinsky 1990; Clark 1955; Grier and Cobbs 1968; Neal and Wilson 1989; Wade 1996, 2003). Moreover, the encouragement and effort to attain the characteristics associated with the ideal standard becomes an inherent part of the female socialization process.

Hair as a Symbol of Beauty

In American society, women's hair is one of the primary physical characteristics examined when determining their level of attractiveness or beauty regardless of ethnic or racial background. However, as pointed out by Rooks (1996), the socio-cultural experiences of African American women in relation to hair care plays a more significant and meaningful part of her identity development and satisfaction as a woman. African American women's hair care experiences are more complex and intense due to the meaning and significance in their history from the continent of Africa (Byrd and Tharps 2001; Morrow 1990). In many African civilizations, hair style served as a symbol or indicator of social status, one's mood or emotional state, or major transitions or events such as the pending death of a spouse or preparation for war (Byrd and Tharps 2001; Morrow 1990). During the period of enslavement, cultural oppression, and racism in the "New World," the significance of hair care remained for women of African descent (e.g., Boyd-Franklin 1989; Neal and Wilson 1989; Okazawa-Rey et al. 1987; Russell et al. 1992). However, during the process of enslavement, African women were prohibited from engaging in familiar self-care and grooming practices, yet were criticized and ridiculed for their appearance (Hall 1995; Martin 1964; Morrow 1990; Neal and Wilson 1989; Weathers 1991).

The lack of regard and appreciation for African cultural norms, practices, and diverse physical characteristics, along with the exposure to a Eurocentric standard of beauty, may be responsible for diminishing the collective sense of worth, esteem, and racial/ethnic pride and identity among African-descended people (Berg 1936; Greene et al. 2000; Hall 1995; Morrow 1990). Exposed to a socialization process of cultural oppression and racist propaganda including stereotypes that strongly promote and accentuate the Eurocentric standard of beauty, African-descended women were persuaded that African natural hair was unacceptable, unattractive, and undesirable. This set the stage for African American women to develop and internalize negative beliefs and feelings of rejection, shame, disdain, inferiority, and hatred toward tightly curled, thick, short-length, and coarsely textured hair (Ferrell 1996; Morrow 1990). Essentially, natural African hair became something to be rejected because it was associated with negative stereotypes and physical unattractiveness.

It is important to note that many European American women cannot fulfill the standard of beauty espoused by the dominant culture. Therefore, it should come as no surprise that this ideal is also unattainable for African American women (Greene 1994). Notwithstanding, many African American women are preoccupied with their hair and continue to base their notion of attractiveness and evaluate their physical attractiveness within a European cultural framework. There is a long history of Black women taking extreme measures in the hopes of achieving American society's standard of beauty in order to experience the benefits associated with it. But more importantly, whether done consciously or not, the underlying purpose of these efforts is to achieve the desired image and related positive self-esteem.

Hair care Practices' Economic and Health Costs

It is customary for women to spend billions of dollars annually on cosmetics and other beauty aids to reach a desired or perceived level of physical attractiveness. Approximately 11 million African American women spend nearly $5 billion annually visiting hair-styling salons every three to four weeks (Fletcher 2000; Rooks 1996; Williams 1996) and according to some reports this expenditure has risen (Ferrell 1996; Rooks 1996). From these economic indicators, it is apparent that a large proportion of the African American women are heavy consumers of hair care products reflecting the value they place on "getting their hair done."

In addition, African American women spend a considerable amount of time and energy attempting to create and maintain hair texture and length similar to images and models that emulate the European standard of beauty, which is virtually impossible for their natural hair (Rooks 1996). Typical hair-styling approaches to straighten and create length include mechanical (pressing) or chemical (permanent relaxing) processing and coloring (dyeing) to have the texture, and weaving or adding extensions of hair from other sources to achieve longer length. Some women use a combination of these hair-styling techniques simultaneously.

Hair Stress: A New Concept

The application of various mechanical treatments and absorption of chemicals may strip the hair of its natural moisture, and damage the hair follicle and root of the hair strand, resulting in dryness and breakage and a vulnerability to scalp disorders (Fletcher 2000; Ferrell 1996). Many women are unaware of, or fail to acknowledge, the relationship between certain hair and scalp conditions and persistent and improper hair care treatments. Existing conditions are often disregarded, so the traumatization of the hair and scalp continues with the potential for permanent hair damage and loss (Bulengo-Ransby and Bergfeld 1992; Earles 1986; Halder 1983; Kenney 1977). Dermatologists and other healthcare providers are limited in their awareness of the prevalence of these conditions among African American women (Bulengo-Ransby and Bergfeld 1992) as well as the psychological consequences produced by them. The cycle of repeated unnatural hair-styling practices may induce a combination of psychological and physical reactions called "hair stress." This is defined as the harmful physical (i.e., hair and scalp conditions) and psychological (e.g., symptoms of anxiety, depression, and low self-esteem) effects of hair-styling methods used to transform the hair from its natural state to achieve and maintain an unnatural texture and appearance.

Alopecia is a hair-loss condition for which people seek medical attention from dermatologists. There are certain types of alopecia that can be construed as a form of hair stress. Chemical alopecia is a condition that develops from repeated application and overuse of chemical hair care products to straighten/relax and dye one's hair. Traction alopecia is typically caused by the improper use of styling methods such as braiding, weaving/extensions, hot combing, blow drying, and using tight rollers. Both chemical and traction alopecia can overstress and traumatize the hair shaft and the hair itself (Bulengo-Ransby and Bergfield 1992). In a nationwide investigation of alopecia, 95% of a sample of predominantly African American women reported hair breakage, loss, and scalp injuries associated with the use of a hair-relaxing product (Swee et al. 2000). Ferrell (1993) indicated that 95% of her clients who have a history of applying chemicals to their hair suffer from some degree of hair and scalp damage and 20% have permanent hair loss or baldness. These effects can be very emotionally devastating for women; however, not enough is known about the psychological impact of these conditions on African American women. There is an absence of research specifically exploring the psychological impact of scalp irritation and hair loss due to women's hair care practices.

Most commonly, investigations have focused on the impact of Androgenetic Alopecia (AGA), a genetically predisposed hair-loss condition that affects men and women anytime after puberty. Overall, outcomes from these studies revealed that women with AGA experience more psychosocial problems due to hair loss than men (see review by Cash 1999). They reported higher levels of emotional distress and impairment (e.g., anxiety), and lower scores on measures of self-esteem, body image, psychological adjustment, and social adequacy and life satisfaction (Cash et al. 1993; Girman et al. 1999; Van der Donk et al. 1994; Van der Donk et al. 1991). Similar gender differences in adverse psychological correlates have been reported in studies of hair loss as side effects for patients receiving chemotherapy (Baxley et al. 1984; de Boer-Dennert et al. 1997; Kiebert et al. 1990; McGarvey et al. 2001). One can surmise from these findings that the greater impact on women might reflect more their concern about their attractiveness and physical appearance.

However, the studies cited above are based on samples of women who suffer from alopecia due to uncontrollable conditions and factors. Because AGA is an unexpected and unusual form of hair loss, it is an empirical question whether similar gender differences would emerge with self-induced hair loss from chemical or mechanical treatments. There is need for empirical investigations of women who have experienced hair and scalp problems from the use of chemical products and techniques used in straightening, lengthening, and dyeing their hair.

Empirical Study of Black Women's Hair Stress

With exception to gender, prior hair-loss studies have not clearly specified the psychosocial characteristics of the samples studied. We know that these conditions occur among African American women from dermatological studies (McMichael 2003; Swee et al. 2000) and hair stylists' reports of women seeking their services to address or remedy hair-loss conditions (Ferrell 1996). Thus research and anecdotal evidence indicate the harmful effects of hair loss on African American women's psychosocial functioning. Based on the positive relationship between a woman's physical appearance and her perceived attractiveness, hair damage (i.e., scalp irritation and hair loss) should be negatively associated with self-esteem among African American women. In other words, African American women's "hair stress" will be evident in the association between hair damage and self-esteem.

To our knowledge, empirical studies examining the relationship of hair care practices and resulting hair damage or loss to African American women's psychological well-being are not available in the current literature. This study aimed to develop and to evaluate a measure of hair and scalp problems due to hair care practices and its association with self-esteem in a sample of African American female college students, relative to their male counterparts. It was hypothesized that there would be a negative relationship between this measure of hair damage and self-esteem (i.e., hair stress) among women African American college students. It was also hypothesized that this association would not be mediated by general self-image problems.

Research Methodology

Participants

Participants were 106 African American female (n=89) and male (n=17) undergraduate students enrolled in psychology courses at a predominately African American university in a southern state. Ages ranged from

18 to 39 with the majority (85%) of the sample falling in the 18–21-year-old age group. The education level of the students in the sample was 2% (n=2) first year, 28% (n=30) second year, 29% (n=31) third year, 35% (n=37) fourth year and 6% (n=6) fifth year or more. Participation in the study was voluntary although it was offered as one of two comparable extra credit activities.

Measures

A 175-item survey comprised of multiple questionnaires was used to collect information about body image, self-esteem, lifestyle, and related health and demographic characteristics.

Multidimensional Body-Self Relations Questionnaire (MBSRQ)

The MBSRQ is a 69-item self-report inventory developed to assess attitudes about body image (Brown et al. 1990; Cash 2000). The instrument is comprised of the ten subscales. This includes seven "appearance evaluation" items (i.e., feelings of attractiveness or degree of satisfaction with one's looks), twelve "appearance orientation" items (i.e., degree of investment in one's appearance), three "fitness evaluation" items (i.e., feelings of being or value for being physically fit), thirteen "fitness orientation" items (i.e., extent of investment in being physically fit or athletic), six "health evaluation" items (i.e., feelings of physical health), eight "health orientation" items (i.e., extent of investment in a physically healthy lifestyle), five "illness orientation" items (i.e., extent of reactivity to being or becoming ill), nine "body areas satisfaction" items (i.e., extent of satisfaction with discrete aspects of appearance), four "overweight preoccupation" items (i.e., anxiety about gaining weight, dieting, eating) and two "self-classified weight" items (i.e., self-perception of weight). All the MBSRQ subscales had the 5-point Likert response option, ranging from (1) "definitely disagree" to (5) "definitely agree," except the "body areas satisfaction" subscale and one item, "I have tried to lose weight by fasting or going on crash diets," in the "overweight preoccupation" scale. The response options for the "body area satisfaction" items ranged from (1) "very dissatisfied" to (5) "very satisfied," and from (1) "never" to (5) "very often" for the "overweight preoccupation" item.

Additionally, "self-classified weight" was assessed by the items, "I think I am:" and "From looking at me, most other people would think I am:" with the response options (1) very underweight, (2) somewhat underweight, (3) normal weight, (4) somewhat overweight, and (5) very overweight. Each subscale score was obtained by summing item scores and dividing by the total number of items. Some items were scored in the reverse direction so that higher total scores reflected greater endorsement of a given subscale.

The internal consistency for the ten subscales are reported for the entire sample rather than separately by gender as there was no significant difference between the alpha coefficients across the subscales for the men and women in the sample. The Cronbach's alpha for the subscales were appearance evaluation = .84, appearance orientation = .75, fitness evaluation = .69, fitness orientation = .82, health evaluation = .70, health orientation = .74, illness orientation = .77, body area satisfaction = .85, overweight preoccupation = .73, and self-classified weight = .70.

Rosenberg Self-Esteem Scale

This ten-item scale developed by Rosenberg (1965) was used to measure global self-esteem (e.g., "On the whole, I am satisfied with myself"). The five-point response options ranged from (1) "strongly disagree" to (5) "strongly agree". The scale score was obtained by first reverse scoring indicated items, summing item scores and dividing by the total number of items. Higher scores reflect a higher level of self-esteem. The Cronbach's alpha for the current sample was .89.

Lifestyle and Health Survey

An 82-item survey was compiled to obtain information about health behavior and conditions. For this study, participants' responses to select items were used to measure hair damage and hair-related satisfaction and attitude.

A measure of "hair damage" was developed from the following two items: 1) Have you ever experienced scalp irritation or burns from using chemical relaxers or treatment? and 2) Have you ever experienced hair loss or damage from using chemical relaxers or treatment? Total scores ranged from 0 to 3 to denote the severity of the hair damage reported. The scoring values were (0) "no hair damage" indicating no scalp irritation or hair loss; (1) "mild hair damage" indicating scalp irritation but no hair loss: (2) "moderate hair damage" indicating hair loss but no scalp irritation; and (3) "severe hair damage" indicated both scalp irritation and hair loss.

An item selected from the MBSRQ body areas satisfaction subscale, a measure of the extent to which you are satisfied with certain areas of the body, was used to assess "hair satisfaction." Participants were asked to indicate, "How dissatisfied or satisfied are you with your hair (color, thickness, texture)?" on five-point scale from (1) "very dissatisfied" to (5) "very satisfied." Higher scores indicated greater hair satisfaction.

Another item, "liking natural hair," was developed to assess the extent to which participants like their non-chemically treated and/or non-relaxed hair. The response options for the question, "I like my natural hair" ranged from (1) "definitely disagree" to (5) "definitely agree," with higher scores indicating greater liking for natural hair.

Demographic Information

A 13-item measure obtained demographic information. The relevant variables for this study were age, gender, race/ethnicity, and education.

Procedures

The survey was administered by an African American female professor to her students during a class period. Number coding the surveys rather than collecting identifying information ensured the anonymity and confidentiality of the participants' responses. The length of time to complete the survey averaged about 30 minutes. The procedures for this study were approved by the Institutional Review Board of the University where it was conducted.

Research Findings

Assessment of Hair Stress

To test the validity of the construct of hair stress, a one-way ANOVA was conducted with self-esteem as the dependent variable and levels of hair

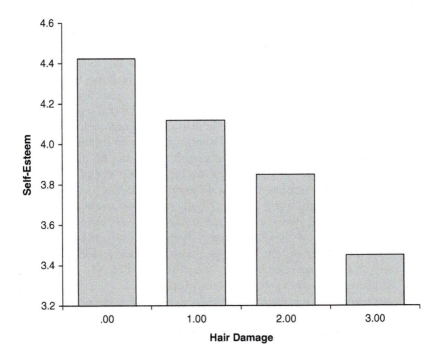

Figure 10.1 Relationship between severity of hair damage and self-esteem

damage as the independent variable. Univariate analyses showed a significant difference between levels of self-esteem as function of severity of hair damage, $F(1, 104) = 11.93$, $p < .001$. As depicted in Figure 10.1, hair damage is negatively correlated with self-esteem supporting the validity of the construct of hair stress.

A step-wise regression analysis was performed to examine the correlation between hair damage and self-esteem controlling for gender and self-image variables measured by the MBSRQ. Model 1 included hair damage only as the independent variable. Model 2 included hair damage and gender. Model 3 added the self-image variables including fitness evaluation, illness orientation, appearance orientation, health evaluation, health orientation, body area satisfaction, overweight preoccupation, fitness orientation, and self-classified weight. Model 1 was significant, $F(1,104) = 11.93$, $p < .001$ and accounted for 10% of the variance with hair damage ($\beta = -.25$, $t = -3.45$, $p < .001$) as a significant negative correlate of self-esteem. Model 2 added approximately 1% more to the variance, $F(2,103) = 6.07$, $p < .003$ and hair damage ($\beta = -.25$, $t = .-3.49$, $p < .001$) remained significant and negatively related to self-esteem. The inclusion of the self-image variables in Model 3 explained an additional 44% of the variance in self-esteem, $F(12.93) = 9.35$, $p < .001$. Hair damage remained a significant negative correlate ($\beta = -.14$, $t = -2.44$, $p < .02$). Body area satisfaction ($\beta = .34$, $t = .4.03$, $p < .001$), fitness evaluation ($\beta = .21$, $t = 2.65$, $p < .01$), health evaluation ($\beta = .25$, $t = 3.1$, $p < .001$), and illness orientation ($\beta = .13$, $t = .2.0$, $p < .05$) were also significant positive correlates of self-esteem. Overall, a total of 55% of the variance in self-esteem was explained by all the variables in the regression equation.

Gender Differences in Self-Image

Means and standard deviations for hair damage, liking natural hair, hair satisfaction, and each self-image variable by gender (female = 1, male = 2) are reported in Table 10.1. T-tests for independent samples were performed to examine gender differences across all variables. There were significant gender differences for liking natural hair, ($t = -4.75$, $p < .001$) hair satisfaction, $t = -2.52$, $p < .01$ and appearance orientation ($t = 2.65$, $P < .01$). Overall, the women in the study reported disliking their natural hair, dissatisfaction with their hair, and concern about their appearance more than the men. Pearson correlation analyses were conducted to examine the relationship among hair damage, liking natural hair, and hair satisfaction. A significant positive relationship between liking natural hair and hair satisfaction was evident ($r = .25$, $p < .02$), indicating that participants who like their natural hair tend to feel satisfied with their hair.

Because there were significant gender differences on these hair-related variables, a partial correlation of liking natural hair and hair satisfaction

Table 10.1 Means and standard deviations of hair-related and self-image variables by gender

Variables	Female		Male	
	M	SD	M	SD
Hair damage	.47	.92	.18	.73
Hair satisfaction	3.95	.99	4.59	.80
Liking natural hair	2.25	1.42	4.06	1.52
Appearance evaluation	4.99	.41	4.92	.43
Appearance orientation	3.87	.52	3.48	.70
Fitness evaluation	3.94	.84	3.84	.87
Fitness orientation	3.10	.75	3.21	.81
Health evaluation	3.57	.76	3.78	.54
Health orientation	3.22	.68	3.21	.61
Illness orientation	3.60	.89	3.19	.80
Body area satisfaction	3.55	.85	3.55	.72
Overweight preoccupation	2.54	.95	2.07	.90
Self-classified weight	3.31	.80	3.18	.78

controlling for gender was conducted. The non-significant partial correlation between liking natural hair and hair satisfaction suggests that the relationship between these two variables is mediated by gender ($r = .16$, $p > .05$). The gender differences are depicted in Figure 10.2. The pattern of correlations suggests that African American females report less satisfaction with natural hair. To determine whether participants' attitudes toward their hair reflected a desire to conform to dominant cultural standards of beauty, a supplemental analysis correlated the hair damage, liking natural hair, and hair satisfaction with the item from the overweight preoccupation scale on self-report of dieting to lose weight. Dieting variable was significantly associated with liking natural hair in the negative direction ($r = -.27$, $p < .01$). This finding suggests that participants who reported dieting to lose weight also tend to dislike their natural hair. This is consistent with the notion that disliking one's natural hair, as is dieting because of dissatisfaction with one's weight, reflects a desire to conform to dominant cultural standards of beauty.

A multivariate analysis of variance was conducted to further explore the relationship among the three hair-related items as dependent variables, and all the self-image variables and gender as independent variables. There were significant multivariate effects for appearance orientation, Wilks' Lambda = .91, $F(1, 88) = 2.94$, $p < .04$, health evaluation, Wilks' Lambda = .92, $F(1, 88) = 2.67$, $p < .05$, body areas satisfaction, Lambda = .87, $F(1, 88) = 2.67$, $p < .01$, and gender, Wilks' Lambda = .82, $F(1, 88) = 6.60$, $p < .001$. Univariate tests showed that appearance orientation had a marginal effect on hair damage,

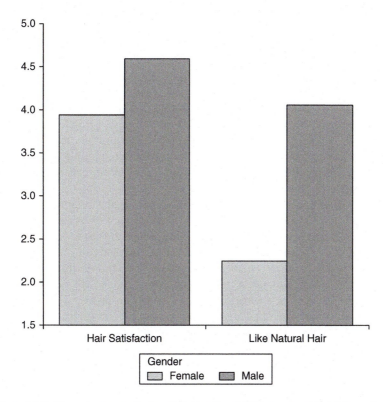

Figure 10.2 Mean scores on "hair satisfaction" and "liking natural hair" items by gender

F(1, 90) = 3.59, p <.06; health evaluation was significantly associated with hair damage, F(1, 90) = 4.52, p < .05; body areas satisfaction was significantly correlated with hair satisfaction F(1, 90) = 11.22, p < .001; and gender was significantly related to liking natural hair F(1, 90) = 13.82, p < .001 and hair satisfaction F(1, 90) = 6.05, p<.05. Parameter estimates revealed that women's experiences with their hair were less favorable for liking natural hair (β = -.65, t = -2.46, p < .05) and hair satisfaction (β = -1.54, t = -3.72, p < .001).

Summary and Conclusions

The present study tested the hypotheses that there would be a significant negative relationship between a measure of hair damage and self-esteem among African American college students and that this relationship would not be mediated by general self-image concerns. The first hypothesis was supported. Hair damage was inversely related to self-esteem, with greater severity of hair damage associated with lower levels of self-esteem. This finding supports the conceptualization and validity of "hair stress" as a construct, which defines the relationship between hair damage due to hair-styling practices and the resulting psychological impact.

It also is consistent with previous research that shows emotional distress and lower scores on measures of self-esteem as a reaction to hair loss among patients being treated for alopecia and cancer (e.g., Cash et al. 1993; McGarvey et al. 2001). More importantly, the findings provide evidence to support the idea that hair loss and scalp problems from the use of chemical products and techniques for straightening, lengthening, and dyeing have a similar impact on the psychological well-being of African Americans as other hair-loss conditions.

Because the existing literature reports psychological consequences of hair loss in addition to self-esteem (e.g., Girman et al. 1999; Van der Donk et al. 1994), future studies need to explore other correlates (e.g., anxiety) of hair loss and scalp irritation. Further, measurement and data collection procedures to obtain information from medical diagnostic tests or surveys used in dermatological research to assess hair damage will provide more extensive and accurate evaluations related to this problem. Given the relatively small sample size of college students in the current study, a replication of this study with a larger, more diverse sample of African Americans will help further test the reliability and validity of the "hair stress" construct and strengthen the methodology of future studies.

The second hypothesis that the relationship between hair damage and self-esteem would not be mediated by the self-image variables was also supported by the findings. Overall, the self-image variables accounted for nearly 45% of the variance in self-esteem independent from the effects of hair damage, and four self-image variables (i.e., body area satisfaction, fitness evaluation, health evaluation, and illness orientation) were significant positive correlates of self-esteem, suggesting that African American students' feelings about themselves are influenced by the extent to which they are satisfied with specific aspects of their appearance, perceive themselves to be physically fit, healthy, and free from physical illness, and attentive to symptoms of ill health.

In general, these findings are consistent with earlier research that indicates men's and women's perceptions of appearance and attractiveness are associated with self-esteem (e.g., Cash 1985; Eitel 2003). The finding that students' responsiveness to physical health symptoms or illness is correlated with self-esteem independent of hair-related problems raises the concern that these students, particularly the females in the study, may not view or acknowledge hair damage as a physical health condition deserving attention. Another explanation is the desire and benefits of emulating models of attractiveness outweigh the costs of harmful hair care. It will be important to clarify the relationship among these variables in order to establish relevant and effective approaches to raise awareness and change behaviors that result in hair damage and related health problems.

The significant gender differences between the African American male and female students among the hair-related and self-image variables are consistent with the literature and anecdotes of females reporting more negative beliefs, dissatisfaction, and problems associated with their appearance and physical characteristics (e.g., hair) than males (e.g., Neal and Wilson 1989; Ferrell 1996). This supports the literature that indicates societal expectations and pressures to emulate certain Eurocentric images and models of beauty tend to be higher for women than men (e.g., Neal and Wilson 1989; Wade 2003). Results from an additional analysis between liking natural hair and hair satisfaction revealed that students who like their natural hair reported feeling more satisfied with their hair, but gender was a mediator between these two variables. Generally, African American females demonstrate less satisfaction with their hair, in comparison to African American males.

As previously mentioned, the cultural socialization and experiences of African American females in relation to their hair care play a significant role in their identity development and feelings about their appearance (Rooks, 1996). Therefore, the extent to which females evaluate attractiveness within a European cultural framework will influence their ability to embrace and experience natural hair satisfaction. Unfortunately, it is not surprising that these women are vulnerable to physical and psychological health risks associated with hair care and styling practices to achieve and to maintain a virtually unattainable standard of beauty. This group of women definitely need more education and accurate information about the psychological and physical health conditions related to harmful hair care approaches, as well as the support to make healthier hair care choices.

The extent to which African Americans identify with the Eurocentric worldview plays a critical role in the beauty standards to which they conform. Size and weight are typical physical characteristics related to concerns about attractiveness among European American women (e.g., Cash and Pruzinsky 1990). The significant negative relationship between self-reports of dieting to lose weight and liking natural hair suggests conformity to Eurocentric cultural standards. In other words, the results from this study suggest that unfavorable feelings towards natural hair are influenced by mainstream standards of beauty. Thus the acceptance of their natural hair may be an indication of the degree to which African American women do not internalize values of the Eurocentric worldview in relation to physical attractiveness. In other words, African American women who like and wear natural hair styles may be less willing to conform to the European standard of attractiveness and less likely to experience "hair stress," leading to psychologically and physically healthier lives.

Obviously, more research is necessary to replicate and reinforce the findings from this initial investigation.

This study raises some important implications for consideration. One of the greatest challenges will involve addressing the effects of mainstream standards of beauty on the psychosocial, cultural, and identity development of members of the African American community, especially females. A cultural redefinition of what is acceptable by African American women is essential to reduce the pressure to emulate Eurocentric models of attractiveness. Counseling interventions, health education, and prevention approaches designed to proactively increase the understanding of the psychological and physical health consequences of using chemical-based hair-styling products and other hair-damaging techniques are necessary. Media campaigns and advertisements that create and promote alternative images of attractiveness such as depictions of African Americans modeling authentic hair styles presented with positive messages (e.g., beautiful, healthy, successful) are very important as well. Finally, it will be important for counselors and other healthcare professionals to provide recommendations or training in healthy approaches to the manageability and styling of natural hair, in order to support and affirm those who want to discontinue the use of unnatural hair care practices to prevent, or at least minimize, African American's experiences with "hair stress." Individuals interested in career counseling African American women around healthcare issues need to become familiar with these hair care practices.

The present study has several limitations not mentioned previously that should be addressed in future research. The small sample of college students, particularly African American males, does not allow for generalization to the broader Black community. All of the instruments were self-report, which could lead to reporting bias. There was no information on nature of hair care practices obtained from the participants. Finally, the data are correlational so no causal inference can be made about the direction of these associations. None of these problems are insurmountable. This preliminary investigation does indeed indicate that future research would be beneficial to the health and well-being of African American women.

Acknowledgments

We would like express appreciation to Dr. Lana N. Chambliss for her assistance with the data collection and the students who kindly volunteered to participate in this study. All correspondence regarding the article should be addressed to Evelyn B. Winfield-Thomas, Institutional Equity, 1220 Trimpe Building, Western Michigan University, Kalamazoo, Michigan 49800 5405, email: evelyn.winfield@wmich.edu.

Discussion Questions

1 What is hair stress among African American women?
2 Does the evolutionary perspective or socio-cultural perspective (internalized racial oppression) better explain the identity development and hair care and styling practices of African American women?
3 How might we prevent African American women from experiencing hair stress?
4 What are the short-term and long-term physical and psychological health benefits of natural hair-styling practices for African American women?
5 What are the implications of this study for psychological and medical healthcare professionals and providers in the service delivery to African American women?
6 What type of media campaigns might promote alternatives to the mainstream standard of beauty for African American women?

Suggested Readings

1 Bundles, A. (2002). *On her own ground: The life and times of Madam C.J. Walker.* New York: Scribner.
2 Byrd, A. D., and Tharps, L. L. (2001). *Hair story.* New York: St. Martin's Press.
3 Callender, V. D., McMichael, A. J., and Cohen, G. F. (2004). Medical and surgical therapies for alopecia in black women. *Dermatologic Therapy,* 17(2), 164–176. doi:10.1111/j.1396-0296.2004.04017.x
4 Morrow, W. L. (1990). *400 years without a comb: The untold story.* San Diego, CA: California Curl.
5 Russell, K., Wilson, M., and Hall, R. (1993). *Hair: The straight and nappy of it all. The color complex: The politics of skin color among African Americans* (pp. 81–93). New York: Harcourt Brace Jovanovich.
6 Smith, L. R., and Burlew, A. K. (1991). "Black consciousness, self-esteem, and satisfaction with physical appearance among African American female college students." *Journal of Black Studies,* 22(2), 269–283.

Suggested Media

1 Chenzira, A. (director) (1985). Hair piece: A film for nappy-headed people [DVD]. Available from http://www.wmm.com/filmcatalog/pages/c297.shtml

References

Baxley, K. O., Erdman, L. K., Henry, E. G., and Roof, B. J. (1984). Alopecia: Effect on cancer patients' body image. *Cancer Nursing,* 7(6), 499–503.

Berg, C. (1936). The unconscious significance of hair. *International Journal of Psychoanalysis*, 17, 73–88.

Boyd-Franklin, N. (1989). *Black families in therapy*. New York: Guilford.

Brown, T. A., Cash, T. F., and Mikulka, P. J. (1990). Attitudinal body image assessment: Factor analysis of the Body-Self Relations Questionnaire. *Journal of Personality Assessment*, 55, 135–144.

Byrd, A. D., and Tharps, L. L. (2001). *Hair story*. New York: St. Martin's Press.

Bulengo-Ransby, S. M., and Bergfeld, W. F. (1992). Chemical and traumatic alopecia from thioglycolate in a Black woman: A case report with unusual clinical and histologic findings. *Cutis*, 49, 99–103.

Cash, T. F. (1981). Physical attractiveness: An annotated bibliography of theory and research in the behavioral sciences (Ms. 2370). *Catalogue of Selected Documents in Psychology*, 11, 83.

Cash, T. F. (1985). Physical appearance and mental health. In J. A. Graham and A. Kligman (Eds.), *Psychology of cosmetic treatments* (pp.196–216). New York: Praeger Scientific.

Cash, T. F. (1999). The psychosocial consequences of androgenetic alopecia: A review of the research literature. *British Journal of Dermatology*, 141, 398–405.

Cash, T. F. (2000). *The multidimensional body-self relations questionnaire (MBSRQ) users' manual* (third revision).

Cash, T. F., Price, V., and Savin, R. (1993). The psychosocial effects of androgenetic alopecia among women: Comparisons with balding men and female controls. *Journal of the American Academy of Dermatology*, 29, 568–575.

Cash, T. F., and Pruzinsky, T. (Eds.). (1990). *Body images: Development, deviance, and change*. New York: Guilford Press.

Cash, T. F., Winstead, B., and Janda, L. (1985). Your body, yourself: A Psychology Today reader survey. *Psychology Today*, 19(7) 22–26.

Cash, T. F., Winstead, B., and Janda, L. (1986). The great American shape-up: Body-image survey report. *Psychology Today*, 20(4), 30–37.

Clark, K. B. (1955). *Prejudice and your child*. Boston, MA: Beacon.

de Boer-Dennert, M. de Wit, R., Schmitz, P. I., Djontono, J., v Beurden, V., Stoter, G., and Verweij, J. (1997). Patients perceptions of the side-effects of chemotherapy: The influence of 5HT3 antagonists. *British Journal of Cancer*, 76, 1055–1061.

Earles, M. R. (1986). Surgical correction of traumatic alopecia marginalis or traction alopecia in Black women. *Journal of Dermatology and Surgical Oncology*, 12(1), 78–82.

Eitel, B. J. (2003). Body image satisfaction, appearance importance, and self-esteem: A comparison of Caucasian and African-American women across the adult lifespan. *Dissertation Abstracts International*, 63, 11B. Retrieved February 10, 2008, from PsycINFO database.

Ferrell, P. (1996). *Let's talk hair: Every Black woman's personal consultation for healthy growing hair*. Washington, DC: Cornrows and Company.

Fletcher, B. (2000). *Why are Black women losing their hair?: The first complete guide to healthy hair*. Seat Pleasant, MD: Unity Publishers.

Girman, C. J., Hartmaier, S., Roberts, J., Bergfeld, W., and Waldstreicher, J. (1999). Patient-perceived importance of negative effects of androgenetic alopecia in women. *Journal of Women's Health and Gender-Based Medicine*, 8(8), 1091–1095.

Greene, B. (1994). African American women: Derivatives of racism and sexism in psychotherapy. In E. Toback and B. Rosoff (Eds.), *Genes and gender series: Vol. 7. Challenging racism and sexism: Alternatives to genetic explanations* (pp. 122–139). New York: Feminist Press.

Greene, B. (1997). Psychotherapy with African American women: Integrating feminist and psychodynamic models. *Journal of Smith College Studies in Social Work,* 67(3), 299–322.

Greene, B., White, J. C., and Whitten, L. (2000). Hair texture, length, and style as a metaphor in the African American mother-daughter relationship: Considerations in psychodynamic psychotherapy. In L. C. Jackson and B. Greene (Eds.), *Psychotherapy with African American women: Innovations in psychodynamic perspective and practice* (pp.166–193). New York: Guilford Press.

Grier, W. H., and Cobb, P. M. (1968). *Black rage.* New York: Basic Books.

Hall, R. (1995). The bleaching syndrome: African Americans' response to cultural domination vis-à-vis skin color. *Journal of Black Studies,* 26(2), 172–184.

Halder, R. M. (1983). Hair and scalp disorders in blacks. *Cutis,* 32, 378–380.

Hall, C. I. (1995). Beauty is in the soul of the beholder: Psychological implications of beauty and African American women. *Cultural Diversity & Mental Health,* 1(2), 125–137.

Hill-Collins, P. (1991). *Black feminist thought.* New York: Routledge.

Jackson, L. A. (1992). *Physical appearance and gender: Sociobiological and sociocultural perspectives.* Albany, NY: SUNY Press.

Kenney, J. A. (1977). Dermatoses common in Blacks. *Postgraduate Medicine,* 61, 122–127.

Kiebert, G. M., Hanneke, J., de Haes, C. J., Kievit, J., and van de Velde, C. J. (1990). Effect of peri-operative chemotherapy on the quality of life of patients with early breast cancer. *European Journal of Cancer,* 26(10), 1038–1042.

Lerner, R. M., Knapp, J. R., and Orlos, J. B. (1976). Physical attractiveness, physical effectiveness, and self-concept in late adolescents. *Adolescence,* 11(43), 313.

Martin, J. G. (1964). Racial ethnocentrism and judgment of beauty. *Journal of Social Psychology,* 63, 59–63.

McGarvey, E. L., Baum, L. D., Pinkerton, R. C., and Rogers, L. M. (2001). Psychological sequelae and alopecia among women with cancer. *Cancer Practice,* 9(6), 283–289.

McMichael, A. J. (2003). Ethnic hair update: Past and present. *Journal of American Academy of Dermatology,* 48(6), S127–S133.

Morrow, W. L. (1990). *400 years without a comb: The untold story.* San Diego, CA: California Curl.

Neal, A. M., and Wilson, M. L., (1989). The role of skin color and features in the Black community: Implications for Black women and therapy. *Clinical Psychology Review,* 9, 323–333.

Noles, S. W., Cash, T. F., and Winstead, B. A. (1985). Body image, physical attractiveness, and depression. *Journal of Consulting and Clinical Psychology,* 53, 88–94.

Okazawa-Rey, M., Robinson, T., and Ward, J. V. (1987). Black women and the politics of skin color and hair. *Women and Therapy,* 6, 89–102.

Robinson, L. C. (1998). Hair and beauty culture. In K. A. Appiah and H. L. Gates Jr. (Eds.), *Microsoft Encarta Africana: Comprehensive encyclopedia of Black history and culture* [CD-ROM]. Redmond, WA: Microsoft.

Rooks, N. M. (1996). *Hair raising: Beauty, culture, and African American women*. New Brunswick, NJ: Rutgers University Press.

Rosenberg, M. (1965). *Society and the adolescent self-image*. Princeton, NJ: Princeton University Press.

Rosen, G. M. and Ross, A. O. (1968). Relationship of body image to self-concept. *Journal of Consulting and Clinical Psychology*, 32, 100.

Russell, K., Wilson, M., and Hall, R. E. (1992). *The color complex*. New York: Harcourt Brace Jovanovich.

Sandler, K. (Producer). (1992). *A question of color* [Film]. San Francisco, CA: California Newsreel.

Swee, W., Klontz, K. C., and Lambert, L. A. (2000). A nationwide outbreak of alopecia associated with the use of a hair-relaxing formulation. *Archives of dermatology*, 136(9), 1104–1109.

Van der Donk, J., Hunfield, J. A. M., Passchier, J., Knegt-Junl, K. J., and Nieboer, C. (1994). Quality of life and maladjustment associated with hair loss in women with alopecia androgenetica. *Social Science Medicine*, 38, 159–163.

Van der Donk, J., Passchier, J., Knegt-Junk, C., Van der Wegen-Keijser, M. H., Nieboer, C., Stolz, E., and Verhage, F. (1991). Psychological characteristics of women with androgenetic alopecia: a controlled study. *British Journal of Dermatology*, 125, 248–252.

Wade, T. J. (1996). The relationships between skin color and self-perceived global, physical, and sexual attractiveness, and self-esteem for African Americans. *Journal of Black Psychology*, 22(3), 358–373.

Wade, T. J. (2003). Evolutionary theory and African American self-perception: Sex differences in body-esteem predictors of self-perceived physical and sexual attractiveness, and self-esteem. *Journal of Black Psychology*, 29(2), 123–141.

Weathers, N. R. (1991). Braided sculptures and smokin' combs: African American women's hair-culture. *Sage: A Scholarly Journal on Black Women*, 8(1), 58–61.

Williams, T. T. (1996, October 26). Black hair care is big business in Florida. *Bradenton Herald*. Retrieved November 17, 2000 from http://firstsearch.oclc.org

11

GENDER, ARTHRITIS, AND FEELINGS OF SEXUAL OBLIGATION IN OLDER WOMEN

Alexandra C. H. Nowakowski and J. E. Sumerau

Research exploring sexual health has proliferated in recent years. During this time, researchers have documented reciprocal relationships between medical practices, structures, and disparities on the one hand, and sexual practices, identities, and beliefs on the other in a wide variety of social contexts (see, e.g., Akers et al. 2011; Green 2008; Browning et al. 2008; Ueno 2010). However, many components of this relationship remain underexplored.

Considering the overall focus on the sexual health of youth and (to a lesser extent) people in middle age, scholars have overlooked the sexual health and aging of older adults (but see Slevin and Linneman 2010). Consequently, little is known about the ways older adults manage common health conditions *and* sexual experiences. Further, it is unclear what role medical diagnosis—especially in the case of serious illnesses such as arthritis, heart problems, or cancers—may play in the experience of later-life sexual health. In addition, little is known about variations in later-life sexual health due to people's differential positions within interlocking systems of oppression and privilege.

Feminist scholars have long noted the influence of pressure to have intercourse upon the lived experiences of women as well as large-scale patterns of gender inequality (see, e.g., Armstrong et al. 2006; Ezzell 2008; Martin 2005). In fact, recent research shows that expectations of sexual obligation—ranging from implicit pressure to engage in sexual activities to violent encounters of sexual assault—represents an ever-present influence in women's lives, and has become so common that many women perceive these pressures as a normal part of social life (Brownmiller 1993; Hlavka 2014). Further, researchers have found that organizations designed to combat and manage women's experiences of sexual obligation often rely upon gendered assumptions that ultimately reproduce women's victimization when they speak out, seek social and emotional support, and/or hold perpetrators accountable (Martin 1997).

While these studies have importantly revealed the powerful role women's perceived sexual obligation plays in the maintenance of gender inequalities, they have typically left women's perceptions of sexual obligation in later life unexplored. Gaps thus exist in current sociomedical literature on sexual health, especially with respect to intersectionality between gender, physical health, and sexual experiences. What is the prevalence of perceived sexual obligation in later life, how does it relate to chronic conditions frequently experienced by older individuals, and in what ways might these experiences vary in relation to different social and clinical locations?

Arthritis is a common later-life condition associated with changes in sexual functioning (Blake et al. 1988). Extant literature (see Abdel-Nasser and Ali 2006) does suggest that people with arthritis may experience sexuality differently in later life than people not affected by joint inflammation. Particularly striking differences may exist in females with and without arthritis (Yoshino and Uchida 1981). However, this literature focuses on physical determinants of sexual activity rather than psychological ones. It also does not address the potentially gendered context of motivation to engage in sexual activity among older adults with and without arthritis, nor does it capture relationships between late-life sexuality and other types of social disadvantage.

We thus examine these questions through cross-sectional analysis of Wave I of the National Social Life, Health, and Aging Project (NSHAP)—a nationally representative probability sample of older adults. Specifically, we investigate relationships between medical diagnosis, social location, and perceived obligation to engage in sexual activity. We explore the prevalence of perceived sexual obligation among older adults, whether or not diagnosis status predicts the frequency of engaging in sexual practice due to feelings of obligation, and how these patterns vary in relation to race, class, and gender. We conclude with implications for future research on perceptions of sexual obligation in later life, and how such inquiry may advance sociological understandings of gender and sexual inequalities.

Background

Previous research on social pressures surrounding sexual activity provides the foundation for the research questions analyzed in this study. By conceptualizing these pressures as a systemic social problem (Brownmiller 1993), scholars have suggested that feeling obligated to have sex may exert significant influence upon both individual lives (especially among women) and societal patterns of gender inequality. Further, this line of research reveals the ways such influences vary in relation to people's locations within interlocking systems of oppression and privilege. Taken together, this line of scholarship provides guidance for mapping the prevalence of perceived sexual obligation within older populations.

Pressure to Engage in Sex and the
Reproduction of Gender Inequalities

Over the last four decades, feminists have mapped the myriad of ways existing social practices and beliefs facilitate the ongoing subordination of women and other gender minorities (see, e.g., Connell 1987; Ridgeway 2013; West and Zimmerman 1987). In so doing, scholars have long noted societal expectations for women—especially White women—to signify femininity by adopting sexually passive and submissive roles. Similarly, scholars have noted the promotion of sexual aggressiveness and dominance as a hallmark of contemporary manhood. At the nexus of these interrelated ideals, researchers demonstrate a wide variety of ways males attempt to claim masculine status by aggressively pursuing, assaulting, objectifying, controlling, and otherwise treating females as obligated to share their bodies (see, e.g., Kimmel 2008; Schilt and Westbrook 2009; Schrock and Schwalbe 2009). Further, scholars have noted women's responses to and strategies for managing perceived sexual obligation in a wide variety of social settings and contexts (see Martin 2005 for a review). Rather than isolated phenomena, these pressures represent a systematic social problem rooted in the maintenance of gender inequalities.

Expanding upon these observations, some feminist scholars have conceptualized contemporary American society as a "rape culture," or a culture where pressuring others to have sex is normalized through shared understandings about sex, gender, and sexualities (Ezzell 2008). Beliefs about women's submission, devaluation, and lack of sexual drive, for example, facilitate and justify men's aggressive sexual behavior, interpretation of resistance as a normal aspect of sexual interaction, and community attempts to ignore or re-victimize victims (see Kimmel 2008). Further, media offerings that glorify sexual coercion, reduce women's value to their physical and sexual capabilities, and condition boys and men to view women as prizes to be won and objects to be collected present women's sexual obligation—as well as gender inequality—as a normative ideal and an example to be embraced. Considering the prevalence of these beliefs and images in contemporary American society, it would not be surprising if feelings of obligation surrounding sex represented an ever-present component of the life course for female-bodied people.

Despite the likelihood of experiencing pressure to engage in sexual activity throughout the life course, researchers have typically focused on the experiences of younger and middle-aged women. Even so, these studies provide guidelines for exploring perceived sexual obligation in later life. Examining experiences of younger and middle-aged people in various settings, for example, researchers find that gendered romantic (Hamilton and Armstrong 2006), interpersonal (Grazian 2007), and organizational (Williams et al. 1998) norms often reproduce the devaluation and submission of women's sexual desires, agency, and options. Similarly, research concerning middle-aged married women reveals that gendered and heterosexual marital norms often rely upon and reinforce the dismissal of women's concerns, the elevation of men's needs, and the submission of women's desires (see, e.g., Hochschild 1989; Pfeffer 2010). In fact, such studies also reveal pressures women face for maintaining sexual availability within the context of heterosexual marital norms (Hochschild 1989). We thus assess the potential presence of similar dynamics in social and sexual relationships during later portions of the life course.

Gendered and Sexual Health

In recent years, scholars have begun to devote more systematic attention to sexual and gendered health concerns. In relation to sexual health, for example, scholars demonstrate that societal ideals often invoke notions of physical prowess based on medical determination, and delineate between who can (e.g., younger and middle-aged) and who cannot (older) be considered sexual beings. On the other hand, researchers have found that many older people engage in sexual practice (Slevin and Linneman 2010), and often interpret later life as a time period free from many of the sexual constraints, responsibilities, and problems of younger and middle age (Dillaway 2005). Rather than halting at some point near the end of middle age, scholarship concerning sexual health reveals that sexuality often remains a focal point of social interest and experience in later life.

While sexuality remains salient throughout the life course, researchers have also uncovered gendered distinctions in later-life sexuality. Calasanti and Slevin (2001), for example, note that sexuality often gets stripped away from women as they age in ways that men do not experience. Whereas studies reveal women's pursuit of sexual pleasure throughout the life course, societal norms suggest that women's sexuality disappears somewhere around the end of middle age (Calasanti and Slevin 2001). Conversely, expectations of sexual behavior in later life often mirror early conceptualizations of women as "gatekeepers," and social institutions surrounding relationships—most notably traditional marriage—may intensify these pressures as women age (see also Rieker et al. 2010). Gendered beliefs thus strip women of sexual agency while continuing to require them to manage the sexual desires of others.

On the other hand, some medical studies suggest that chronic disease and resultant functional limitations can shape gendered sexual expectations in the opposite direction (Smith 2008; Iino 2011). For all groups together and for women specifically, disease and disability can diminish others' interpretations of particular individuals as sexual beings. As a result, people with chronic conditions—a common experience in later life—may experience less pressure to engage in sexual practices even in long-term relationships. In fact, older adults living with potentially disabling conditions may signify to others—intentionally or otherwise—that they are "growing out" of sexuality. As a result, one could simultaneously suspect that sexual obligation may remain constant, increase, and/or decrease in later life due to extant health concerns.

In this study, we thus incorporate medical diagnoses into our exploration of perceived sexual obligation among older adults. To this end, we focus on arthritis because it is one of the most prevalent conditions among older women and men, and is often considered a "usual" component of contemporary aging. Similar to physical disability of any type, arthritis may factor into social attitudes about sexual and gendered health and thus potentially exert influence on sexual obligation. In fact, older Americans with arthritis—and other chronic conditions—are frequently depicted as lacking the requisite physical health to engage in common social activities including but not limited to sexual practice. As such, we seek to uncover whether variations in perceived sexual obligation may be influenced by medical diagnoses.

Methods

In this study, we pose three main questions: 1) What is the overall prevalence of feeling obligated to have sex among older adults? 2) Does diagnosed arthritis predict differences in frequency of having sex due to feelings of obligation? 3) How do these patterns appear to vary along lines of race, class, and gender?

We explore these questions using data from Wave I of the National Social Life, Health, and Aging Project (NSHAP). Developed between 2005 and 2006, this biosocial dataset provides information on physical, mental, and social health among U.S. residents aged 57 to 85. The dataset includes 3,005 individual cases in total. Table 11.1 describes the number and aggregate characteristics of available cases for each included item.

NSHAP data documentation describes the study sample as "a nationally representative probability sample of community-dwelling individuals" (Waite et al. 2007). However, certain groups within the study population (African Americans, Latinos, men, and persons 75–85 years of age) are oversampled to boost statistical power (Waite et al. 2007). Data for the NSHAP are collected via a combination of questionnaires (administered during home visits), in-home interviews, and basic clinical techniques such as using cotton swabs to collect small amounts of saliva (performed during home visits).

We used the "In the past 12 months how often did you have sex primarily because you felt obligated or that it was your duty?" question to capture feelings of sexual obligation among respondents. This question allows respondents to indicate whether or not they have experienced this (response values "never" and "I have not had sex in the past 12 months") in the stated timeframe. We created and analyzed two different versions of our outcome variable: one that included people who had not had sex in

Table 11.1 Descriptions and Summary Statistics for Included Variables

Construct	Variable	Units	Cases	Mean	St. Dev.	Min.	Max.
Perceived sexual obligation	Frequency of sex due to feelings of obligation or duty in last 12 months (inclusive)	Points	2,345	0.43	0.91	0	4
	Frequency of sex due to feelings of obligation or duty in last 12 months (restricted)	Points	1,566	0.65	1.05	0	4
Arthritis	Diagnosed arthritis	Yes/No	3,005	0.53	0.50	0	1
Disability	ADL/IADL difficulty score	Count	2,635	1.21	1.87	0	9
Sex	Female	Yes/No	3,005	0.52	0.50	0	1
	Male			0.48	0.50		
Marital status	Married	Yes/No	3,005	0.60	0.49	0	1
	Not married			0.40	0.49		
Race	White	Yes/No	2,993	0.70	0.46	0	1
	Any minority			0.30	0.46		
Age	Years of age	Years	3,005	69.3	7.85	57	85
Socioeconomic status	Years of education	Years	2,971	12.48	4.10	0	32

the past year as never having sex because they felt obligated, and one that treated these individuals as missing cases. For study participants who have had sex because they felt obligated, the question also captures frequency. On an ascending scale, respondents can indicate how often (response values "rarely," "sometimes," "usually," and "always") they have experienced feelings of sexual obligation.

We measured sex using the NSHAP's binary "gender" question, which simply asks whether respondents are male or female. Neither this question nor any other accounts for intersex or transgender identity. This question also asks only about current sex, yielding no insight about sex at birth. People who have transitioned in sex identity may thus be represented in the sample, but are not differentiated from their peers. Likewise, no existing NSHAP questions capture information on gender identity or expression. However, all participants were at least 57 years old at Wave I, suggesting socialization in environments with little separation between sex and gender concepts. Because this indicator may provide substantial evidence of both sex and gender identity, we use the terms "females"/"males" and "women"/"men" to frame our findings.

To assess arthritis, we used NSHAP participants' self-reports of ever having been diagnosed with arthritis by a medical provider. Diagnosis with any type of arthritis (osteo, rheumatoid, polyinflammatory, etc.) constitutes a "yes" response. People with arthritis who had never made a medical office visit were ostensibly precluded from responding "yes." Incomplete capture of people with low financial and material resources thus presents a concern with this measure, especially because disadvantaged Americans show higher prevalence of arthritis across age groups. However, some affected but undiagnosed individuals may have given positive responses because of self-diagnosis, symptom history, laboratory test results, or other reasons.

We operationalized physical disability via activities of daily living and instrumental activities of daily living with which study participants experienced difficulty. We created a summative index by adding binary scores for each of the seven activities of daily living (walking one block, walking across a room, dressing, bathing, eating, getting in and out of bed, toileting) and two instrumental activities of daily living (driving in daytime, driving at night). This variable allowed us to model the potential mediating impact of functional impairment.

Several social structure variables allowed us to assess potential variations. Stratifying our aggregated models by sex enabled us to observe stark differences between male and female-identified participants. We also incorporated information on age, race, and socioeconomic status into expanded regressions of perceived obligation on diagnosed arthritis. We measured age in total years of life. Race was assessed as a binary variable to capture the different social constraints and pressures that Americans often experience if they are not White. Socioeconomic status was measured in years of formal

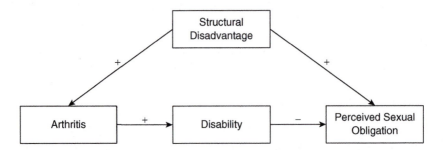

Figure 11.1 Preliminary Path Model of Relationships between Arthritis, Social
Structural Disadvantage, Disability, and Perceived Sexual Obligation

schooling. Previous research (see Nowakowski and Sumerau 2015) indicated that education could capture socioeconomic status more robustly than income for NSHAP participants due to their older age.

We developed a visual model (see Figure 11.1) outlining suspected relationships between our core study constructs. To develop this model, we performed basic path analysis using bivariate count and logistic regression techniques. We explored the net effects of diagnosed arthritis on feeling obligated to have intercourse, as well as mediation of these relationships by disability and additional inputs from social structure factors. We also assessed the ability of these same social structure factors to predict diagnosis with arthritis.

We checked included data for differential attrition (any loss of cases that introduces directional bias) on variables with substantial numbers of missing values. We used "summarize if" commands to summarize the data with missing values on each of these variables and compared to the data with real values on the same variables. Mean values and standard deviations on variables of interest for the missing cases were extremely similar to those for cases with complete sets of real values. Furthermore, we limited samples for nested models to exclude cases with missing values on any covariates used in the full models.

However, we did have concerns about completely excluding people who chose "I have not had sex in the past year" as a response option for the outcome question. Correlational analyses and bivariate regressions showed that females had 71% lower odds of engaging in sexual activity within the past 12 months than males. We thus not only stratified our analyses by sex, but also created two distinct case populations for modeling. The first population included only people who had engaged in sexual activity during the past 12 months; the second included everyone who contributed real data (including the "I have not had sex" response). We chose this approach because any given person who had not engaged in sex may have abstained despite feeling pressured to have intercourse, or because they did not want to deal with potential feelings of obligation. Comparing our findings for both case populations allowed us to gain more nuanced understanding of what the people in our sample may have experienced.

To assess net effects, we used diagnosed arthritis to predict feeling obligated to have sex. We generated a variety of different logistic and count regression models to reveal variation in the outcome according to diagnosis status. These models included all participants with real data on all covariates plus the appropriate version of the outcome variable. We computed aggregated models including data from both sex/gender groups, then stratified these regressions to reveal possible differences between males and females. After running raw models, we computed adjusted versions (using survey weights, clustering variables, or omnibus correctors). Finally, we ran postestimation diagnostics (Brant tests of parallel regression for ordinal logistic models, tests of equidispersion for count models) and sensitivity analyses (comparing predicted values to those generated by alternate frameworks) to ensure accurate specification of models.

Our initial modeling efforts and diagnostics revealed that count frameworks were most appropriate for overall modeling of the outcome data. We also noted that our outcome distribution was zero-inflated. We thus used both aggregated and zero-inflated regression techniques to generate our final models. First, we used negative binomial regression frameworks to assess the impact of arthritis on overall frequency of having sex due to perceived obligation for males and females. Second, we computed binary logistic regressions to assess whether or not being diagnosed with arthritis could predict males' and females' odds of ever having sex due to perceived obligation. Third, we computed negative binomial regressions to predict how often those who did feel obligated engaged in intercourse for this reason.

To assess mediating influences from disability, we used our summative index of functional limitation as an intervening variable in the above models. This enabled us to examine how arthritis may influence feelings about sexual activity in older adults. We also modeled the intervening role of disability between arthritis and feeling obligated to have sex, both independently and together with arthritis. This allowed us to assess the extent to which potential influences on perceived sexual obligation stemming from arthritis may operate via functional limitation and associated expectations. We used fit statistics (information criteria, component significance levels, and pseudo R-squared) to assess improvement when adding this suspected mediator.

To assess influences from marriage, we used marital status as a covariate. Specifically, we grouped participants into two categories: "married" and "not married." The latter category included anyone who was not currently married—respondents who were currently cohabitating, separated, divorced, widowed, and never married. We modeled the possible role of marriage in shaping attitudes toward sex and resultant behaviors. We also checked for statistical interactions between marital status and disability, as well as marriage and arthritis itself.

To assess variations, we used social structure variables as predictors of arthritis, disability, and sexual obligation. Our models examined age, racial minority identity, and socioeconomic status. We generated binary logistic models with arthritis as the outcome, and structural factors (both independently and collectively) as predictors. We generated count models with disability as the outcome, again using social factors as predictors both collectively and individually. Third, we modeled potential direct effects on sexual obligation from different social factors. We modeled independent and synergistic structural predictors of whether or not people had sex because they felt obligated to do so, as well as how often they engaged in sex due to these perceptions.

Results

Prevalence of sexual intercourse due to perceived obligation varied between 24 and 36% depending on the particular method used to calculate the outcome variable. When respondents who reported having no sex in the past year were excluded from estimation, about 36% of the remaining 1,566 respondents indicated having at least some intercourse due to perceived obligation. We then re-estimated prevalence including the 779 people who reported not having sex in the past year when answering the original question about perceived obligation. About 24% of the resulting 2,345 participants reported having at least some intercourse due to perceived obligation in the past 12 months.

We also found substantial evidence to suggest that diagnosed arthritis can impact whether or not older adults engage in sexual intercourse due to feelings of obligation. Specifically, we found consistent and significant negative associations between arthritis and two of our three measures of sexual obligation. On average, people with arthritis reported lower overall frequencies of sex due to feeling obligated. Diagnosed arthritis was also associated with significantly lower odds of having sex due to perceived obligation in the last 12 months. However, arthritis did not significantly predict frequency of sex due to perceived obligation among people who reported at least one instance of this outcome.

While arthritis consistently exerted a significant impact on intercourse due to perceived obligation for aggregated groups of participants, our stratified analyses revealed stark differences by gender. Specifically, arthritis exerted a significant negative impact on perceived sexual obligation for females, but no impact at all for males. We also found striking differences in how age and education shaped perceived sexual obligation in the two groups. Conversely, marriage and race exerted very similar impacts for men and women.

Table 11.2 shows results from modeling overall frequency of sex due to perceived obligation using inclusive measures capturing people who did not have intercourse during the last 12 months. (Parameter estimates

Table 11.2 Stratified Negative Binomial Regressions of Frequency of Sex Due to Perceived Obligation (Inclusive Measure)

Group	Variable	Model 1	Model 2	Model 3	Model 4	Model 5
Every one	Arthritis	−0.289**	−0.217*	−0.254**	−0.196*	−0.092
	Disability	–	−0.073*	–	–	−0.092**
	Married	–	–	+1.054***	–	+1.086***
	Race	–	–	–	+0.665***	+0.81***
	Age	–	–	–	−0.034***	−0.022**
	Education	–	–	–	−0.027*	−0.032*
Sample size		2,062	2,062	2,062	2,062	2,062
Prob > χ^2		0.0029	0.0005	0.0000	0.0000	0.000
Pseudo R-squared		0.0024	0.0041	0.0264	0.0249	0.0537

Group	Variable	Model 1	Model 2	Model 3	Model 4	Model 5
Females	Arthritis	−0.365*	−0.284†	−0.362**	−0.259†	−0.228
	Disability	–	−0.078†	–	–	−0.062
	Married	–	–	+1.876***	–	+1.82***
	Race	–	–	–	+0.366*	+0.586***
	Age	–	–	–	−0.055***	−0.034**
	Education	–	–	–	−0.007	−0.012
Sample size		1,001	1,001	1,001	1,001	1,001
Prob > χ^2		0.0131	0.0071	0.0000	0.0000	0.000
Pseudo R-squared		0.0036	0.0057	0.0813	0.0241	0.0989

(continued)

Table 11.2 (continued)

Group	Variable	Model 1	Model 2	Model 3	Model 4	Model 5
Males	Arthritis	-0.214	-0.159	-0.204	-0.138	-0.053
	Disability	–	-0.065	–	–	-0.095*
	Married	–	–	+0.268†	–	+0.389*
	Race	–	–	–	+0.884***	+0.939***
	Age	–	–	–	-0.016†	-0.011
	Education	–	–	–	-0.043**	-0.045**
Sample size		1,061	1,061	1,061	1,061	1,061
Prob > χ²		0.1037	0.0893	0.0648	0.000	0.000
Pseudo R-squared		0.0014	0.0025	0.0029	0.0379	0.0437

† p < 0.10, * p < 0.05, ** p < 0.01, *** p < 0.001

from negative binomial regressions are expressed as metric coefficients.) We found that arthritis significantly predicted lower average frequency when modeled independently. This association persisted for models incorporating disability, marriage, and social structure factors respectively. Disability also demonstrated ability to mediate the potential influence of arthritis on perceived sexual obligation partially, but not completely. The arthritis term became non-significant in fuller models incorporating disability, marriage, and social structure factors together as covariates. Models for females paralleled these overall findings for all terms except disability, which became non-significant in the full model. Other social factors may thus condition the mediating impact of disability.

Other social factors appeared to contribute independently to perceived sexual obligation. Marriage predicted increased frequency of sex due to feelings of duty more strongly than any other factor for the whole study population and even more strongly for females, but exerted only a marginally significant impact for males. Racial minority status predicted significantly higher frequency of sex due to perceived obligation among females, males, and both groups together. Age significantly predicted reduced frequency of sex due to perceived obligation for females and for both groups together, but did so weakly or not at all for males. By contrast, additional years of education significantly predicted reduced frequency of sex due to perceived obligation for males and for both groups together, but not for females.

Table 11.3 displays findings from repeating the above modeling frameworks with samples that did not include people who reported having no sex in the past 12 months. As these samples included dramatically fewer females, it proved unsurprising that the arthritis term became non-significant in most of the aggregated models. Likewise, this term remained either fully or marginally significant in models for females specifically. Findings otherwise paralleled those from our inclusive-sample models quite closely. These results suggest that including people who reported not having sex in the past 12 months in samples of individuals who "never" had intercourse due to perceived obligation during this time period may capture a substantial number of people who abstained from sexual activity by deliberate choice.

Table 11.4 shows results from modeling ever having sex due to perceived obligation using inclusive measures capturing people who did not have intercourse during the last 12 months. (Parameter estimates from logistic regressions are expressed as odds ratios.) We found that arthritis significantly predicted lower odds of ever having sex due to perceived obligation when modeled independently. However, this association was less consistent across models incorporating disability, marriage, and social structure factors for samples containing males and females together. Models for females showed a more consistent significant influence from arthritis, with diagnosed individuals having lower odds. Even among females, the arthritis term once again remained non-significant in fuller models incorporating disability, marriage,

189

Table 11.3 Stratified Negative Binomial Regressions of Frequency of Sex Due to Perceived Obligation (Restricted Measure)

Group	Variable	Model 1	Model 2	Model 3	Model 4	Model 5
Everyone	Arthritis	-0.149†	-0.118	-0.137	-0.096	-0.028
	Disability	-	-0.032	-	-	-0.063*
	Married	-	-	+0.477***	-	+0.570***
	Race	-	-	-	+0.657***	+0.740***
	Age	-	-	-	-0.013*	-0.007
	Education	-	-	-	-0.023†	-0.026*
Sample size		*1,419*	*1,419*	*1,419*	*1,419*	*1,419*
Prob > χ²		*0.0990*	*0.1320*	*0.0000*	*0.0000*	*0.0000*
Pseudo R-squared		*0.0009*	*0.0013*	*0.0063*	*0.0212*	*0.0309*

Group	Variable	Model 1	Model 2	Model 3	Model 4	Model 5
Females	Arthritis	-0.292*	-0.228†	-0.275*	-0.242†	-0.174
	Disability	-	-0.063†	-	-	-0.065†
	Married	-	-	+1.047***	-	+1.032***
	Race	-	-	-	+0.432**	+0.561***
	Age	-	-	-	-0.027**	-0.017†
	Education	-	-	-	+0.003	-0.008
Sample size		*570*	*570*	*570*	*570*	*570*
Prob > χ²		*0.0224*	*0.0153*	*0.0000*	*0.0001*	*0.0000*
Pseudo R-squared		*0.0037*	*0.0060*	*0.0334*	*0.0173*	*0.0495*

Group	Variable	Model 1	Model 2	Model 3	Model 4	Model 5
Males	Arthritis	-0.109	-0.098	-0.108	-0.056	-0.011
	Disability	–	-0.014	–	–	-0.054
	Married	–	–	+0.047	–	+0.230
	Race	–	–	–	+0.846***	+0.885***
	Age	–	–	–	+0.003	+0.005
	Education	–	–	–	-0.040*	-0.041**
Sample size		849	849	849	849	849
Prob > χ²		0.3878	0.6537	0.0659	0.0000	0.000
Pseudo R-squared		0.0004	0.0005	0.0005	0.0382	0.0404

† p < 0.10, * p < 0.05, ** p < 0.01, *** p < 0.001

Table 11.4 Stratified Logistic Regressions of Ever Having Sex Due to Perceived Obligation (Inclusive Measure)

Group	Variable	Model 1	Model 2	Model 3	Model 4	Model 5
Everyone	Arthritis	0.777*	0.857	0.821†	0.856	0.964
	Disability	-	0.892**	-	-	0.904**
	Married	-	-	3.897***	-	3.869***
	Race	-	-	-	1.658***	2.073***
	Age	-	-	-	0.952***	0.964***
	Education	-	-	-	1.006	0.998
Sample size		2,062	2,062	2,062	2,062	2,062
Prob > χ^2		0.0127	0.0001	0.0000	0.0000	0.0000
Pseudo R-squared		0.0027	0.0083	0.0567	0.0335	0.0877

Group	Variable	Model 1	Model 2	Model 3	Model 4	Model 5
Females	Arthritis	0.672**	0.741†	0.642**	0.758†	0.737†
	Disability	-	0.896*	-	-	0.950
	Married	-	-	9.10***	-	8.301***
	Race	-	-	-	1.094	1.593*
	Age	-	-	-	0.928***	0.948***
	Education	-	-	-	1.025	1.021
Sample size		1,001	1,001	1,001	1,001	1,001
Prob > χ^2		0.0081	0.0011	0.0000	0.0000	0.0000
Pseudo R-squared		0.0064	0.0124	0.1494	0.0559	0.1780

Group	Variable	Model 1	Model 2	Model 3	Model 4	Model 5
Males	Arthritis	0.916	0.995	0.932	0.989	1.083
	Disability	–	0.896*	–	–	0.883*
	Married	–	–	1.67**	–	1.829**
	Race	–	–	–	2.265***	2.481***
	Age	–	–	–	0.971**	0.978*
	Education	–	–	–	0.999	0.993
Sample size		1,061	1,061	1,061	1,061	1,061
Prob > χ^2		0.5350	0.0519	0.0099	0.0000	0.0000
Pseudo R-squared		0.0003	0.0048	0.0075	0.0316	0.0455

† p < 0.10, * p < 0.05, ** p < 0.01, *** p < 0.001

and social structure factors together. Disability again demonstrated ability to mediate the potential influence of arthritis on perceived sexual obligation.

As with models of overall frequency, other social factors appeared to contribute independently to perceived sexual obligation. Marriage predicted higher odds of sex due to feelings of duty more strongly than any other factor for the whole study population, and even more strongly for females. Here, the impact of marriage remained highly significant for males, but was much smaller in magnitude compared to females and both groups together. Racial minority status predicted significantly higher odds among females, males, and both groups together. Age predicted lower odds for females and for both groups together with a very high degree of significance, and for males with smaller magnitude and lower significance. In these models, additional years of education did not significantly predict odds in any group.

Table 11.5 displays findings from repeating the above modeling frameworks with samples that did not include people who reported having no sex in the past 12 months. Because these samples included dramatically fewer females, it again proved unsurprising that the arthritis term became non-significant in all of the aggregated models. Likewise, this term remained either fully or marginally significant in four out of five models for females specifically. Marriage exerted a strong and significant impact for females and both sexes together, but did not significantly predict males' odds of experiencing the outcome. Age was highly significant for females but not for males, whereas race was highly significant for males but not for females. Findings otherwise paralleled those from our inclusive-sample models. These results suggest that including people who reported not having sex in the past 12 months in samples of individuals who "never" had intercourse due to perceived obligation during this time period may capture a substantial number of people who abstained from sexual activity by deliberate choice.

Our negative binomial regressions of frequency of sex due to perceived obligation among people who reported at least one instance revealed no significant associations with arthritis. Single-predictor models for all participants, females, and males returned insignificant component and overall fit statistics. This may owe in part to smaller sample sizes: Estimation pools for each regression consisted of 521, 236, and 285 people respectively. Variation within these samples was also relatively limited. Of the 521 people who responded that they had engaged in sex due to feelings of obligation, more than half (270) indicated that this had occurred "rarely." The other three response categories had a total of 251 respondents, of whom 187 chose "sometimes." While this distribution was ideal for count modeling, the strong clustering of responses at the low end of the distribution may illuminate why the distinction of "ever" versus "never" proved more salient among participants.

We found mixed evidence concerning the ability of different social factors to predict diagnosis with arthritis. Neither marital status nor racial

Table 11.5 Stratified Logistic Regressions of Ever Having Sex Due to Perceived Obligation (Restricted Measure)

Group	Variable	Model 1	Model 2	Model 3	Model 4	Model 5
Everyone	Arthritis	0.926	0.981	0.952	0.982	1.064
	Disability	–	0.936†	–	–	0.931*
	Married	–	–	2.101***	–	2.213***
	Race	–	–	–	1.854***	2.134***
	Age	–	–	–	0.975**	0.983*
	Education	–	–	–	1.014	1.008
Sample size		1,419	1,419	1,419	1,419	1,419
Prob > χ^2		0.4871	0.1105	0.0000	0.0000	0.000
Pseudo R-squared		0.0003	0.0024	0.0156	0.0185	0.0373

Group	Variable	Model 1	Model 2	Model 3	Model 4	Model 5
Females	Arthritis	0.673*	0.744†	0.684*	0.727†	0.764
	Disability	–	0.900*	–	–	0.925
	Married	–	–	4.189***	–	3.83***
	Race	–	–	–	1.352	1.706*
	Age	–	–	–	0.950***	0.963**
	Education	–	–	–	1.041	1.028
Sample size		570	570	570	570	570
Prob > χ^2		0.0214	0.0055	0.0000	0.0000	0.0000
Pseudo R-squared		0.0068	0.0134	0.0673	0.0393	0.0913

(continued)

Table 11.5 (continued)

Group	Variable	Model 1	Model 2	Model 3	Model 4	Model 5
Males	Arthritis	1.064	1.099	1.070	1.116	1.183
	Disability	–	0.954	–	–	0.928
	Married	–	–	1.282	–	1.510*
	Race	–	–	–	2.369***	2.561***
	Age	–	–	–	0.995	0.999
	Education	–	–	–	1.006	1.003
Sample size		*849*	*849*	*849*	*849*	*849*
Prob > χ^2		*0.6757*	*0.5859*	*0.3817*	*0.0000*	*0.0000*
Pseudo R-squared		*0.0002*	*0.0010*	*0.0018*	*0.0249*	*0.0308*

† $p < 0.10$, * $p < 0.05$, ** $p < 0.01$, *** $p < 0.001$

background significantly predicted participants' odds of having an arthritis diagnosis. Education level did significantly predict diagnosis status; each additional year of schooling was associated with 4% lower odds of having arthritis. These results were relatively consistent between sex/gender groups, and also for both the expanded and reduced case samples.

We found stronger evidence concerning these same social factors' ability to predict limitations on physical functioning. Marriage significantly predicted lower average amounts of disability for both sexes and females, but not for males, in the larger study population. In the smaller study population, marriage did not significantly predict functional limitation. Racial minority status significantly predicted higher levels of disability for both sex groups and for females, but not for males. These findings were consistent across both study populations. Age significantly predicted higher disability levels for both sexes (independently and together) in both participant pools. Conversely, additional years of education predicted lower average levels of functional limitation for males and females in both analysis groups.

Discussion

Our findings indicate that people with diagnosed arthritis may experience changes in their identity concepts and relationship dynamics that alter expectations about sexual engagement and practice. Specifically, people with diagnosed arthritis appear to have less frequent sex due to feelings of perceived obligation, as well as lower odds of ever having sex due to such feelings. Previous research concerning physical health, functional disability, and sexual behavior supports this possibility, and recommends detailed exploration.

The differences we observed in whether or not arthritis could significantly predict particular measures of sexual obligation suggest that these relationships are nuanced, and likely influenced by multiple contextual factors. While we found that both overall frequency and odds of ever having sex due to perceived obligation were lower among individuals with arthritis, we did not find any significant relationship between arthritis and frequency among people who engaged in sex at least once because they felt it was their duty. These null findings for our third sexual obligation outcome may stem in part from social and emotional factors. Having sex because one feels pressured to do so can result in unpleasant feelings, including diminished desire for future sexual encounters. But more likely, the potential protective effect conferred by diagnosis with arthritis is binary in nature. Whether or not people experience this effect at all may be more important than the precise strength of the effect if one occurs.

The smaller and relatively homogeneous samples for frequency of sex due to perceived obligation among those who ever experienced it may also reflect deeper social dynamics. First, general norms associated with aging tend to prescribe relatively desexualized roles for older adults. Participants may thus feel less pressure to engage in sex for any reason than younger adults in otherwise comparable circumstances. Second, perception of frequency is subjective. The NSHAP questionnaire gives no absolute metrics (such as how many occurrences within a given time period constitutes a particular response level) by which to judge frequency. Taken together, these factors may create scenarios in which people do not frequently have sex due to feelings of duty because they both perceive lower levels of pressure and have sex less often.

Our findings also illuminate a number of variations. First and foremost, associations between diagnosed arthritis and perceived sexual obligation clearly and consistently differ for males and females. Females appear to derive a significant protective benefit from an arthritis diagnosis, whereas males exhibit no such potential effects. This pattern may owe in large part to the status of females as a subordinate group in contemporary American society (see also Schrock and Schwalbe 2009). Today, female U.S. residents often work in the same types of jobs and may earn salaries commensurate with or in excess of those of their male peers, especially at higher levels of education and in privileged ethno-racial groups. However, the hyper-sexualization of female-bodied people remains a persistent source of social disadvantage that cuts across other socio-demographic categories such as race and socioeconomic status (SES) (see Ridgeway 2013).

As a subordinate social group, heterosexual females are often expected to provide sexual satisfaction for their male partners, illustrating hegemonic perceptions of females as gatekeepers for sexual pleasure (Hochschild 1989). Consequently, older females are more likely than their male peers of comparable social position and health status to feel pressured to have sex even in later life. By contrast, people with diagnosed chronic conditions often experience fewer such pressures than their undiagnosed peers because they can use their condition as a cause for lack of sexual practice. Individuals possessing a formal diagnosis of arthritis (or any other chronic condition that impacts physical functioning) may thus experience less social and psychological pressure to engage in sexual activity.

Patterns observed for males may speak more to freedom from expectations of fulfilling others' sexual desires conferred by membership in the dominant gender group (Schrock and Schwalbe 2009). While individuals with conditions that impair physical functioning often become desexualized in broader social narratives, males may not experience as many changes in the psychological aspects of their intimate relationships because they are more likely to engage in sexual activity from a position of privilege. Males whose arthritis resulted in them feeling uncomfortable with the idea of having sex may have been selected out of the sample because they simply refused to have intercourse, or did not seek opportunities to engage in such intimacy. Females, by contrast, may have been more likely to allow partners to pressure them into sexual activity because of gendered expectations for behavior within relationships. These patterns may likewise illuminate variations observed across gender groups in effects for other socio-demographic characteristics related to privilege and status.

Membership in any minority ethno-racial group appears to increase males' frequency of feeling obligated to have sex. Race exhibited significant positive associations with perceived obligation for both sex groups, but the apparent effects were nearly twice as large for males, as well as more highly significant across models. Importantly, these findings suggest some racial minority males, seeking to compensate for their subordinate locations within existing gender and racial hierarchies, may feel pressured to use sexual activity to maintain their claim to a masculine self (see also Sumerau 2012). Similarly, if females experience more apparent benefit from a diagnosis of arthritis due to their subordinate group status, it follows that male members of other marginalized social groups could experience similar pressures from sources other than health status. People who are objectified by society in multiple contexts may experience similar feelings of subordination and obligation in intimate relationships (Grollman 2012), which in turn can translate to differences in sexual behavior and the experience of sexual coercion.

Similarly, educational attainment significantly predicts lower frequency of intercourse due to perceived obligation in males, but exerts no apparent effect for females. Just as membership in ethno-racial minority groups can confer subordinate social status, educational attainment can confer elevated status. Education has also traditionally been more salient in valuations of personal worth for men than women (see Kimmel 1996). Consequently, it makes theoretical sense that males might experience a significant protective effect from the social status conferred by additional years of education. Males with higher levels of education may also benefit from learned effectiveness (see Mirowsky and Ross 2003) in communicating with their partners about sexual activity, asserting their own needs and desires more clearly and actively than their female peers often feel comfortable doing. The dominant social position occupied by men may thus decrease the likelihood of sanctions for choosing not to engage in sexual congress.

While education appears to matter more for males than for females, the opposite is true of age. Yet similar mechanisms may explain the difference in apparent impact between these two characteristics. Age is often more salient in perceptions of the self as a sexual being for women than men (Calasanti and Slevin 2001). As females grow older, the extent to which others perceive them as sexual beings often declines sharply. By contrast, this effect is generally much milder for males, if it occurs at all. Whether or not men experience a similar decline in their status as sexual beings often depends on a variety of contextual factors related to social privilege, especially financial resources (see also Slevin and Linneman 2010). Consequently, women are likely to experience more dramatic differences in sexual obligation as they age. As female bodies grow older, the desexualization that frequently results can actually insulate people from pressure to have sex, though other negative psychosocial consequences may result from realizing that one is no longer regarded as a sexual being.

Finally, the structural context of sexual relationships themselves appears to matter strongly (see also Hochschild 1989). Marital status significantly predicts increased frequency and odds of sex due to perceived obligation among both older adults in general and females specifically, but not among males. Again, these observed differences likely owe to asymmetry in social scripts surrounding marriage for females versus males (Ridgeway 2013). Some U.S. states still have formal laws stipulating that marriages can be declared void if "consummation" does not occur with a certain frequency (Hochschild 1989). Even in states without such legislation, women may still face intense pressure to perform sexual acts as part of their spousal responsibilities. By contrast, males may face substantively different pressures that exert harm in other psychosocial domains—for example, the distinct but equally gendered expectation of earning significant amounts of money and providing materially for family members. Consequently, females may experience sharper declines in expectations of sexual engagement if they enter social roles that override the usual scripts of heterosexual marriage. Diagnosis with arthritis may thus disrupt existing expectations for female marital partners.

Conclusions

Our initial explorations of relationships between feelings of sexual obligation, gender, medical diagnosis, and varied social locations reveal many possibilities for understanding the psychosocial context of sexual health across the life course. Two key patterns demanding further understanding relate to the overall experience of pressure to have sex throughout women's lives and the relationship of these pressures in later life to gender inequalities. First is the strong likelihood that feeling obligated to have sex in later life may be common in many population samples scattered across the contemporary United States. Second is the recognition that social scripts about sexual duty are both continuous throughout the life course, and varied in relation to different race, class, gender, and medical statuses. In order to fully understand the normalization of sex without enthusiastic consent in American society (Hlavka 2014; Martin 2005; Armstrong et al. 2006), as well as possibilities for combating the sexual components of gender inequalities, we may need to expand our focus to the myriad of ways in which pressure to have sex influences women's lives—as well as those of subordinated groups of men and other gender minorities—from birth to death. In fact, such an understanding might shed light upon the intergenerational transmission—and thus the continued persistence (see Ridgeway 2013)—of these social problems.

To this end, our study incorporates a number of key strengths that may guide further investigation of sexual health in later life. First, we used social structure measures appropriate for an older American population. This enabled us to capture distinctions likely to be salient for these individuals without introducing noise into our statistical models. Second, we use nationally representative data to capture a realistic snapshot of perceived sexual obligation among older adults in America. The NSHAP allows sociomedical researchers to review tremendously rich information about study participants while simultaneously affording a reasonable degree of generalizability. Finally, we utilized the extensive knowledge researchers—and especially feminist scholars—have uncovered concerning sexual duty norms, gendered and sexual health, and the persistence of gender inequalities in American society to further demonstrate the wide-ranging consequences of both gender inequalities and feelings of sexual obligation. In so doing, we demonstrate the pervasive influence of pressures surrounding sexual activity throughout the life course, which may hopefully add even more weight to contemporary calls for gendered and sexual reform throughout American social structures, relationships, and cultural manifestations.

However, we also note several important limitations on our data and methodology. First, although this study lends support to the idea that arthritis can influence feelings of sexual obligation through and in concert with social mechanisms, it cannot hope to confirm causality. As noted above, this study constitutes a snapshot—it uses one wave of data to begin the process of mapping the experience of feeling obligated to have sex in later life, and demonstrate some ways other scholars may go about this process. Second, we only explore social structure at relatively macroscopic levels. For example, we do not examine subtle differences in outcomes between unmarried persons who are widowed, who have never been married, or those who have been denied marital rights. We seek only to illustrate that particular structural attributes may exert influence on feelings of obligation or duty in hopes of providing the foundation for more nuanced analyses of the multitude of ways these sexual and gendered patterns may play out within the context of people's lives and larger patterns of social experience.

We thus recommend several priorities for future research. First, we encourage others to replicate and extend these analyses using longitudinal frameworks and/or alternate sources of data. Second, we suggest that researchers who have large amounts of appropriate data examine more nuanced aspects of social structural influence on later-life sexual feelings and experiences. We also strongly recommend expanding these analyses to include data on gender identity as well as biological sex. Third, we recommend that qualitative researchers seek to capture in-depth information on older adults' motivations for engaging in sexual activity. In so doing, researchers may begin to fully map the contours of later-life sexual health and its relation to gender inequalities in hopes of transforming these patterns for future generations.

Discussion Questions

1   Discuss some ways people may feel and experience sexual obligation in their lives. Where do such feelings come from, and how might we combat them in our own lives and those of others?

2   In the article, women's health experiences are deeply tied both to perceived sexual obligations and other socio-demographic factors. Discuss some ways socio-demographic factors may influence a wide variety of women's health outcomes, and the ways health at different points in the life course may shape what it means to be a woman in contemporary societies, relationships, and other social settings.

3   Think about the messages about gender and health you have received throughout your life from families, media, schools, and other sources. How might these messages about gender and health influence your own later life sexual and relationship experiences?

Suggested Readings

1   Calasanti, Toni M. and Kathleen F. Slevin. 2001. *Gender, social inequalities, and aging.* Walnut Creek, CA: Altamira Press.

2   Martin, Patricia Yancey. 2005. *Rape work: Victims, gender and emotions in organizational and community context.* New York: Routledge.

3   Mirowsky, John and Catherine E. Ross. 2003. *Education, social status, and health.* New Brunswick, NJ: Transaction Publishers.

4   Ridgeway, Cecilia L. 2013. *Framed by gender: How gender inequality persists in the modern world.* London: Oxford University Press.

References

Abdel-Nasser, Ahmed M. and Essam I. Ali. 2006. "Determinants of sexual disability and dissatisfaction in female patients with rheumatoid arthritis." *Clinical Rheumatology* 25(6): 822–830.

Akers, Aletha Y., Melvin R. Muhammad, and Giselle Corbie-Smith. 2011. "'When you got nothing to do, you do somebody': A community's perceptions of neighborhood effects on adolescent sexual behaviors." *Social Science & Medicine* 72: 91.

Armstrong, Elizabeth A., Laura Hamilton, and Brian Sweeney. 2006. "Sexual assault on campus: A multilevel, integrative approach to party rape." *Social Problems* 53: 483–499.

Blake, D. J., R. Malsiak, A. Koplan, G. S. Alarcon, and S. Brown. 1988. "Sexual dysfunction among patients with arthritis." *Clinical Rheumatology* 7(1): 50–60.

Browning, Christopher R., Lori A. Burrington, Tama Leventhal, and Jeanne Brooks-Gunn. 2008. "Neighborhood structural inequality, collective efficacy, and sexual risk behavior among urban youth." *Journal of Health and Social Behavior* 49: 269–285.

Brownmiller, Susan. 1993. *Against our will: Men, women, and rape.* New York: Ballantine Books.

Calasanti, Toni M. and Kathleen F. Slevin. 2001. *Gender, social inequalities, and aging.* Walnut Creek, CA: Altamira Press.

Connell, R.W. 1987. *Gender and power.* Sydney, Australia: Allen and Unwin.

Dillaway, Heather E. 2005. "Menopause is the 'good old' women's thoughts about reproductive aging." *Gender & Society* 19: 398–417.

Ezzell, Matthew B. 2008. "Pornography, lad mags, video games, and boys: Reviving the canary in the cultural coal mine." In *The Sexualization of Childhood,* edited by S. Olfman. Westport, CT: Praeger.

Grazian, David. 2007. "The girl hunt: Urban nightlife and the performance of masculinity as collective activity." *Symbolic Interaction* 30: 221–233.

Green, Adam Isaiah. 2008. "Health and sexual status in an urban gay enclave: An application of the stress process model." *Journal of Health and Social Behavior* 49: 436–451.

Grollman, Eric Anthony. 2012. "Multiple forms of perceived discrimination and health among adolescents and young adults." *Journal of Health and Social Behavior* 53: 199–214.

Hamilton, Laura and Elizabeth A. Armstrong. 2006. "Gendered sexuality in young adulthood: Double binds and flawed options." *Gender & Society* 23(5): 589–616.

Hlavka, Heather R. 2014. "Normalizing sexual violence: Young women account for harassment and abuse." *Gender & Society* 28(3): 337–358.

Hochschild, Arlie Russell. 1989. *The second shift: Working parents and the revolution at home* (with Anne Machung). New York: Viking Penguin.

Iino, Yuriko. 2011. "On disabled access to the sexual realm: how does a feminist perspective contribute?" *Feminism & Psychology* 21: 536–541.

Kimmel, Michael. 1996. *Manhood in America: A cultural history.* New York: Free Press.

Kimmel, Michael. 2008. *Guyland: The perilous world where boys become men.* New York: Harper.

Martin, Patricia Yancey. 1997. "Gender, accounts, and rape processing work." *Social Problems* 44: 464–482.

Martin, Patricia Yancey. 2005. *Rape work: Victims, gender and emotions in organizational and community context.* New York: Routledge.

Mirowsky, John and Catherine E. Ross. 2003. *Education, social status, and health.* New Brunswick, NJ: Transaction Publishers.

Nowakowski, Alexandra C. H. and J. Edward Sumerau. 2015. "Swell foundations: Gender, fundamental social causes and chronic inflammation." *Sociological Spectrum* 35: 161–178.

Pfeffer, Carla. A. 2010. "'Women's work'? Women partners of transgender men doing housework and emotion work." *Journal of Marriage and Family* 72: 165–183.

Ridgeway, Cecilia L. 2013. *Framed by gender: How gender inequality persists in the modern world.* London: Oxford University Press.

Rieker, Patricia P., Chloe E. Bird, and M. E. Lang. 2010. "Understanding gender and health: Old patterns, new trends and future directions." In *Handbook of medical sociology.* Nashville, TN: Vanderbilt University Press.

Schilt, Kristen, and Laurel Westbrook. 2009. "Doing gender, doing heteronormativity: 'Gender normals,' transgender people, and the social maintenance of heterosexuality." *Gender & Society* 23: 440–464.

Schrock, Douglas P. and Michael Schwalbe. 2009. "Men, masculinity, and manhood acts." *Annual Review of Sociology* 35: 277–295.

Slevin, Kathleen F. and Thomas J. Linneman 2010. "Old gay men's bodies and masculinities." *Men and Masculinities* 12: 483–507.
Smith, Sarah. 2008. "Care and sexuality in disabled/nondisabled intimate relationships." In *22nd Hayes Graduate Research Forum*. Columbus, OH: Ohio State University.
Sumerau, J. Edward. 2012. "'That's what men are supposed to do': Compensatory manhood acts in an LGBT Christian church." *Gender & Society* 26: 461–487.
Ueno, Koji. 2010. "Same-sex experience and mental health during the transition between adolescence and young adulthood." *Sociological Quarterly* 51: 484–510.
West, Candace and Don Zimmerman. 1987. "Doing gender." *Gender & Society* 1: 125–151.
Waite, Linda J., Edward O. Laumann, Wendy Levinson, Stacy Tessler Lindau, Martha K. McClintock, Colm A. O'Muircheartaigh, and L. Philip Schumm. 2007. *National social life, health, and aging project (NSHAP)*. Documentation for dataset collected by researchers at the University of Chicago, Chicago, IL.
Williams, Christine, Patti Giuffre, and Kirsten Dellinger. 1998. "Sexuality in the workplace: Organizational control, sexual harassment, and the pursuit of pleasure." *Annual Review of Sociology* 25: 73–93.
Yoshino, S. and S. Uchida. 1981. "Sexual problems of women with rheumatoid arthritis." *Archives of Physical Medicine and Rehabilitation* 62(3): 122–123.

12

"I'M A SURVIVOR"

Reconsidering Identity, Stigma, and Institutions for Domestic Violence

Kesslyn Brade Stennis and Rasha Aly

Introduction

In the first decade of the 21st century, a song entitled "I'm a Survivor" emerged and was popularized by a girl-group named Destiny's Child. The lyrics of the song convey the group's identity as a survivor who defied the stigmas and stereotypes assigned to them as a result of a broken relationship. This message captivated the nation and became an anthem of empowerment for several groups, including those who had experienced domestic violence and intimate partner violence.

In syncopated rhythm, the song's chorus stressed the group's identity as a survivor, and suggests the process of surviving includes persistence, hard work and dedication to success. The lyrics also defied the identity, stigma, and victim-mentality often ascribed to women who are in relations that are discontinued either by choice or force.

Concepts, such as identity and stigma within the domestic violence community, are not only expressed in this song. They are also explored in scholarly writings. Several scholars have published on a cross-section of populations and subjects related to domestic and intimate partner violence (Balsam and Szymanski 2005; Hampton et al. 2003; Harter et al. 2005; Overstreet and Quinn, 2013; Overstreet et al. 2017). Through this chapter, the authors seek to add to the discourse by exploring specific challenges faced by domestic violence survivors including identity and stigma. Furthermore, the authors provide a framework for considering the concept of total institutions, and provide a recommendation of a type of total institution, which addresses identity and stigma, that can be used when providing care management for contemporary domestic violence survivors.

Exploring Identity

One challenge domestic violence victims face is the crisis they have with their identities. The abuse they endure beats them down, until they have no self-confidence or self-esteem (Walker 1979, 2017). Their abusers stripped away their identities—the identities they had before the abuse started. These identities are a vital part of their survival. Without their identities, they feel hopeless (Matheson et al. 2015; O'Doherty et al. 2016). One of the goals of a shelter is to build upon the women's stripped identities, and as a result, provide them with a stronger identity that would allow them to view themselves as survivors instead of victims.

According to Stets and Burke, "[a]n identity is a set of meanings that define who one is when one is an occupant of a particular role in society, a member of a particular group, or claims particular characteristics that identify him or her as a unique person" (2000: 3). For instance, a woman may have an identity of being a mother. The set of meanings included in this identity of being a mother is to take care of her children, make sure the children have all the food they need, and protect them, among other responsibilities. However, being a mother is not the only identity a person may have. A person can also have multiple identities as well. For instance, Lisa, who is a mom, can also be a sister, a nurse, or a daughter. These multiple identities are what tie an individual to a social situation (Burke and Stets 2009).

This idea that identities are based on the meanings attributed to different roles proposes that identities have three characteristics (Burke and Reitzes 1981). First, it suggests identities are socially constructed. This means identities are maintained through social processes. For instance, examine a situation where two individuals communicate with one another. As they communicate, they perform in front of one another. These performances activate signals which allow each person to know how to respond to the other; thus they are socially constructed (Goffman 1959).

The second characteristic is that each set of meanings, along with the role represented by that meaning, is organized in a hierarchical fashion to produce the self (Burke and Reitzes 1981; Stryker 1968). For instance, the role of being a mother, and the meanings that connect with that role, such as protecting the children, may be more important to Lisa than the role of being a daughter, nurse, or sister. In turn, Lisa may view being a daughter more important than being a nurse or sister. There is a hierarchical order to each meaning and the role that is attached to that meaning.

The third characteristic is that identities are symbolic and reflexive (Burke and Reitzes 1981; Stryker 1968; Goffman 1959). When individuals interact, they learn which actions represent certain roles. This learning process shows the symbolic and reflexive nature of identity. When Lisa responds to her daughter, who has gotten in trouble for stealing a cookie from the cookie jar, the response is a behavior which is appropriate to her role as a mother. She decides to punish her daughter by taking away her TV privileges for the day. However, Lisa (who is also a nurse) would not have the same response if a patient of hers at the hospital stole a cookie from the cafeteria.

However, when a woman endures abuse, these meanings that define who she is are taken away from her. O'Doherty et al. write, "[Intimate partner violence] produces fear and self-doubt; it threatens a person's life goals, safety and even survival; and it is associated with loss agency and ability to control the world" (2016: 227). She no longer has the self-esteem to fulfill the roles that she or society has given herself. In addition, there are scholars who argue the woman's *identity* is spoiled—a term first used by Erving Goffman in the 1960s. This spoiling can cause a person to cut herself off from society. The person sees herself as discredited. This notion of being discredited leads into our discussion of stigma (Goffman, 1963; Hague et al. 2003).

Stigma

When people maintain their identities, they try to display a façade of "normalcy" to the others they encounter (Goffman 1959, 1963). They do not want others to see any discrepancies. If discrepancies are seen, others may view them as "not normal," and as a result, they may be stigmatized. Goffman writes that a stigma occurs when

> an individual who might have been received easily in ordinary social intercourse possesses a trait that can obtrude itself upon attention and turn those of us whom he meets away from him, breaking the claim that his other attributes have on us. He possesses a stigma, an undesired differentness from what we had anticipated.
> (Goffman 1963: 2)

Domestic violence victims try to maintain this sense of normalcy. However, sometimes due to society's rules and regulations, the domestic victims feel, and in some cases are, stigmatized. Sometimes, the stigma is obvious, such as the bruises and black eyes that can be seen on the victim's face. Other times, the stigma may be felt inside, causing the domestic violence victim to ostracize herself from society on her own.

The problem, Goffman notes, is that stigma is something people avoid. People not only avoid having stigmas, but they also avoid being in the company of people who have stigma. As Goffman writes, "we believe the person with a stigma is not quite human" (1963: 3). As an example, Goffman notes that a person who has a long-shaped nose as a deformity will not be seen as human. Thus, people would avoid being around this person with this stigma.

Stigma and Domestic Violence

Society places a large stigma on domestic violence victims (Murray et al. 2016). Domestic violence survivors can feel stigmatized, because others do not understand the circumstances that surround a survivor's experiences. For instance, some people do not understand why a survivor stayed so long in an abusive relationship. Others may not understand how a survivor did not recognize the signs of an abuser when she first began the relationship. As a result, these other people may look down upon domestic violence survivors and cause these survivors to feel stigmatized.

Goffman identifies three types of stigma, each of which can be applied to domestic violence victims. The first type of stigma he discussed "are abominations of the body—the various physical deformities" (1969: 2). A number of domestic violence victims feel stigmatized under this category due to the injuries they've suffered as a result of their abusers. Research shows domestic violence is among the leading cause of injuries to women (Geary, Jr. and Wingate 1999; Goldsmith 2016). The National Coalition Against Domestic Violence website (2016) reports one in five women have been victims of severe physical violence due to abuse from an intimate partner, and one in three women have been victims of some form of physical violence with an intimate partner.

The next type of stigma Goffman mentions are the flaws individuals have in their personalities:

> Next there are blemishes of individual character perceived as weak will, domineering or unnatural passions, treacherous and rigid beliefs, and dishonesty, these being inferred from a known record of, for example, mental disorder, imprisonment, addiction, alcoholism, homosexuality, unemployment, suicidal attempts, and radical political behavior.
>
> (Goffman 1969: 2)

Domestic violence victims can be stigmatized under this category, because many believe a person is flawed if she stays in an abusive relationship (Walker 1989; Steiner 2009). However, leaving an abusive relationship is not an easy task, and there are many barriers to leaving. Studies show the most dangerous time for a woman is when she tries to leave her abuser (Walker 1989; Goodmark 2012; Stover 2014). Therefore, many victims are too scared to leave their abusers. Other women do not leave a relationship because they are worried about custody of their children. Some abusers threaten to take full custody of the children if the woman tries to leave the relationship and, as a result, women stay in the relationship (Jaffe et al. 2003). These are just some of the many examples why a woman stays in an abusive relationship. She has no flaws. Her thinking about staying in the relationship is based on rational thought (Walker 1989; Conner 2013).

According to Goffman, the third category of stigma encompasses "the tribal stigma of race, nation, and religion." These tribal stigmas are "stigma[s] that can be transmitted through lineages and equally contaminate all members of a family" (1969: 2). We suggest that tribal stigma could also be expanded to include ethnic and racial groups which transfer various cultural practices through socialization. Usually, most think of indigenous peoples, such as Native Americans, when they think of tribal stigma. However, tribal stigma can be expanded to race too—for instance, for many African American women whose religious beliefs and cultural practices emphasize the submission of women, the dominance of men, and the secrecy associated with racial loyalty. Often, the women in these types of relationships are overtly or covertly silent because of fears associated with the stigma of breaching cultural and social norms that require silence (Bent-Goodley 2005; Bent-Goodley and Fowler 2006; Brade and Bent-Goodley 2009; Bent-Goodley and Brade 2015). These examples show how these women feel stigmatized due to their "tribal" culture or heritage, and may choose to remain in the relationship for many reasons, including the avoidance of being stigmatized.

Making this issue of stigma more complex are some experts' suggestions that women may remain in a domestic violence relationship due to "learned helplessness"—a theory posited by Walker (1989), which suggests that a woman feels like her only choice is to stay in the relationship even though she has been shown a way out of the relationship. In this particular situation, the women may wrongly believe they cannot leave the relationship, because then they will be deported or shunned by those within their ethnic circle. Even though laws and programs exist which protect women, especially those who are victims of domestic violence by an American citizen and have the legal right to file for citizenship (Villalón 2010), the women still decide to remain in the relationship. More research needs to be done to explore the delineations and correlations between tribal stigma and learned helplessness.

Result of Stigmatized Domestic Violence Victims

Many in society may label domestic violence victims as the "black sheep of the family" (Villalón 2010). Others may discriminate against them or isolate them. Link and Phelan expand upon Goffman's idea of stigma and outline five components of stigmatization:

- A label is placed on differences between people. In this case, the label of being a domestic violence victim is placed on this specific population.
- These labels are associated with negative depictions. For instance, domestic violence victims are seen as weak and shameful.
- People then separate themselves from those with the label.
- As a result, those with the label have a diminished status. Thus, domestic violence victims have a diminished status.

- These same people are then denied access to "social, economic, and political power."

(Link and Phelan 2001: 367).

Many domestic violence victims develop a number of health and mental health issues including but not limited to depression and lower self-perception (Lacey et al. 2013). However, due to their dependence on their abusers, they do not have the resources to treat these health issues. In addition, many also do not have the power to reveal the abuse that is occurring, because they are concerned about the aforementioned consequences that may occur.

Institutions

While these women may not have a lot of resources, one place they go to for help is a domestic violence shelter. Shelters provide roofs over the heads of the women when they are in danger. While there is a lot of literature on domestic violence shelters, there is not a lot of literature on how domestic violence shelters influence the identities of the residents. One of the goals of this chapter is to show how institutions can influence the identities of the women who use the shelter.

Literature about total institutions shows that an individual's identity can be shaped by their affiliations with organizations, and that such organizations can affirm perceived identities (Loseke and Cavendish 2001; Reger 2002; Ward 2004). The first fundamental work showing how institutions can influence a person's identity is *Asylums* (1961) by Erving Goffman. In this study, Goffman shows the asylum environment can mold individuals into submissive clients, who become degraded human beings. He writes that the "inmates" who enter the asylum are stripped of all of their personal belongings and receive the institutional uniform they must wear (1961: 20–21). This starts the process where the "inmate" loses his identity: "At admission, loss of identity equipment can prevent the individual from presenting his usual image of himself to others" (1961: 21). Then, afterwards, these "inmates" are further degraded. In total institutions, they may be forced to take on certain postures or movements. For instance, Goffman says, "patients may be forced to eat all food with a spoon. In military prisons, inmates may be required to stand at attention whenever an officer enters the compound" (1961: 22). In some cases, the "inmates" may be forced to use call staff members as "sir" or "mam," further reinforcing the notion that they are subordinate to the staff or less than the staff (1961: 22). These activities causes the "inmates" to re-evaluate their identities. Their identities change once they enter through the door of the "total institution."

Goffman even writes that a person's identity is not only controlled by the individual, but it is also controlled by the individual's surroundings and those with whom the individual comes in contact with:

The self, then, can be seen as something that resides in the arrangements prevailing in a social system for its members. The self in this sense is not a property of the person to whom it is attributed, but dwells rather in the pattern of social control that is exerted in connexion with the person by himself and those around him. This special kind of institutional arrangement does not so much support the self as constitute it.

(1961: 168)

Therefore, it is interesting to find out what happens once a woman enters through the door of a shelter. However, it is important to point out that an asylum is an example of a total institution, where the residents who live inside the institution are unable to leave the building. Domestic violence shelters are not a total institution in that the residents have—for the most part—the freedom to enter and leave the shelter whenever they want.

While a domestic violence shelter is not a total institution, it is still a *type* of institution. Thus, it still can influence the residents' identities, but the change in identity should not be the same type of change inmates, who live in a total institution, undergo. Present research already shows that institutions, such as a domestic violence center, can influence the identities of the staff. In her research, Scott (2000) analyzed women's crisis centers by analyzing the policies these centers had in regards to racism and the meanings employees observed with these policies. She discovered centers, which used policies that included anti-racist messages, had employees who identified themselves as anti-racist individuals—even though at the time, most Americans had taken an anti-affirmative action stance (Scott 2000). The centers' pro-diversity policies caused the employees to embrace diversity more.

On the other hand, there is also research that shows the opposite. For instance, Kleinman (1996) researched the alternative organization, Renewal, which focused on using more democratic approaches to health care. To achieve this goal, Renewal administrators thought they needed to appear more like a legitimate organization rather than the alternative organization that the public perceived it to be. Thus, the administrators adopted more bureaucratic policies, like other "legitimate" organizations, which caused gender inequality within the company. This inequality within the organization was a direct contradiction to the company's democratic approach. This caused employees' self-concept to diminish, and many quit working at Renewal as a result of the organization's inconsistencies (Kleinman 1996).

Institutions, Domestic Violence, Identity, Stigma

Thus the question that remains is: How does the domestic violence shelter environment impact the residents who live within the shelter? Many of the residents already feel diminished and marginalized when they enter the shelter (O'Doherty 2016; Farrell 1996). Present literature does mention that shelters do help with identity construction. However, the research only concentrates on certain types of identity reconstruction, such as transforming the "battered woman" into the survivor (Loseke 1992).

Also, researchers have found that the construction of the woman's identity actually impacts the domestic violence shelter environment too. In her ethnography of "South Coast" shelters, Loseke found that shelters created and changed their rules and policies around the identities of the women who lived in the shelters. In addition, the women's identities also became the focal point for how the staff selected the residents who would live in the shelter (Loseke 1992). There have also been studies that show how certain residents are stereotyped with specific identities. For instance, domestic violence shelters, due to the stereotypes of certain residents who live in such places, may label some women with the identity of the "ideal mother," or other women may be seen as "problem residents" (Davies and Krane 2003; Peled and Dekel 2010).

Although not yet published, in her dissertation, Jessica Lynn Paull (2013) also studied identity construction and maintenance in domestic violence shelters. She discovered that some residents are able to establish a positive self-concept of themselves by using techniques identified by Snow and Anderson (1987). First, they either try to distance themselves from the shelter and the opportunities it provides, as a way of showing they are proud, deserving women who do not need help from the shelter (Snow and Anderson 1987). Or, they may embrace a "survivor status," which is an image that gives them a source of empowerment (Paull 2013; Snow and Anderson 1987). Others may engage in the method of storytelling, where the women will use stories of their past or fantasies about what they want their future to be to help reconstruct their identity (Paull 2013; Snow and Anderson 1987). These tactics helped the residents embrace a more strengthened identity. Itzhaky and Porat (2005) studied forty women to see how an Israeli shelter helped improve their self-confidence. Their studied showed small changes in the women's sense of empowerment (2005).

These studies show that domestic violence shelters do help residents in retrieving a more positive image of themselves. However, there are still research questions that need to be answered. What strategies do shelters use that help with this empowerment? What policies should be used? What prevents the residents from attaining such an image? Much more research is required.

Recommendations of Best Practices for a Domestic Violence Shelter

When considering institutions for domestic and intimate partner survivors, it is imperative to understand the impact of identity and stigma and to conceptualize and consider non-traditional alternatives. The question for practitioners and researchers to consider is: How do survivors and those who work with them develop such institutions that empower and facilitate holistic survival? This final segment of the chapter will provide the reader with recommendations for consideration.

First, it is imperative that researchers and practitioners recognize the existence and influence of formal and informal institutions in regards to domestic violence. Formal institutions like domestic violence organizations, domestic violence shelters, and even some faith communities have positively influenced and empowered domestic violence victim-survivors. While many seek to work with these formal institutions when seeking and providing resources for those in need, the informal institutions, which have less formal structure and hierarchy, are often unrecognized and underutilized. It is important to include informal institutions (i.e., family members, work acquaintances, friends, etc.) into the support equation when seeking, providing, and developing resources for victim-survivors. These informal institutions can sometimes have greater influence on survivors' perception of self and feelings associated with stigmas than the formal institutions.

Second, it is imperative that such support be provided from institutions in both direct and indirect forms. Remembering that domestic violence victims may not identify themselves as such, and that they may not display visible signs of victimization, institutions must provide direct support for those who identity as domestic violence victims, and indirect support for those who may be more covert with their struggles relating to self-esteem, depression, and isolation. Providing direct support like domestic violence groups or financial assistance may reach those victims who identify as such; however, institutions must strategize about how to provide support to those who carry less visible scars and are isolated due to the fears associated with stigma. In addition to the direct support like DV groups, classes and shelter care, we recommend that institutions include less direct domestic violence survivors' support by providing mentoring opportunities for everyone, authentic relationship-building opportunities, networking opportunities and even child care, which will supplement the aforementioned direct services and may reach the more isolated victim-survivors.

Third, it is imperative to consider how culture, race, ethnicity, and religion may impact one's self-perception and the stigma that they face. Institutions must also be aware of subcultures and norms within specific groups. This awareness can help institutions provide formal and informal supports that are culturally sensitive. For example, African American women of faith and Muslim women may perceive themselves differently, based on how they were socialized about relationships, than do members of other cultural, ethnic, and religious groups. Institutions that are effective may help de-stigmatize circumstances if they provide support in a manner that recognizes cultural norms and addresses them sensitively. Information about available supports and decision making may be impacted by such an awareness and sensitivity.

Fourth, institutions must listen to the victim-survivors' lived experiences and view the women as experts when developing supports that may be unorthodox or "outside the box." Whether in a total institution, as described by Goffman, or a transient institution, it is important that an institution has an identity that is malleable, based on the recommendation of the experts. Victim-survivors are well aware of the norms of institutions, cultures, and other structures that exist. If viewed as the expert, they could perhaps provide greater insight about best practices to operate both within and externally, to promote a healthy self-identity and minimize issues related to stigma. Existing institutions are encouraged to operate in a manner that empowers victim-survivors to express their experiential knowledge in a way that can shape institutions in a manner that is most beneficial to them—both victim-survivor and institution. This act alone can subconsciously enhance the self-perception of survivors.

Finally, additional work needs to be done which considers the relationship and impact of formal institutions, such as domestic violence shelters, on self-identity and stigma. Such research is crucial in developing new programs and providing the necessary legislative and fiscal resources associated with building and renovating current shelters. With such a shortage of domestic violence shelters, this information could provide data which validates the positive impact of shelters and validates the need for additional shelters and programs that are sensitive to self-identity and stigma.

Conclusion

While there may be several approaches that can be used to address identity and stigma for domestic violence survivors, the recommendations above can serve as the foundation for contemporary supports and interventions. Without consideration of challenges with self-identity and stigma, the fear is that victim-survivors will continue to be isolated from formal and informal institutions that can provide direct and indirect support. However, supports that consider cultural dynamics are based in developing authentic relationships through shared experiences and common interests, and valuing the voices of the victim-survivor, have a greater opportunity to meet the holistic needs of those who have experienced domestic and intimate partner violence.

Discussion Questions

1   Other than those recommended by the authors, how can survivors and those who work with them develop such institutions that empower and facilitate holistic survival?

2   What additional direct and indirect supports can be garnered to strengthen the identities of survivors?

3   How might cultural awareness and sensitivity impact information that is disseminated bout about available supports and decision making?

4   What are some ways that existing institutions can operate in a manner that empowers victim-survivors to express their experiential knowledge in a way that can shape institutions in a manner that is most beneficial to them- both victim-survivor and intuition?

5   What additional work needs to be done which considers the relationship and impact of formal institutions such as domestic violence shelters on self- identity and stigma?

6   What role can one take to move the work of domestic violence shelters forward?

Suggested Readings

1   Bent-Goodley, Tricia B. "Health disparities and violence against women: Why and how cultural and societal influences matter." *Trauma, Violence, & Abuse* 8.2 (2007): 90–104.

2   Stennis, Kesslyn Brade, et al. "The Development of a Culturally Competent Intimate Partner Violence Intervention-START©: Implications for Competency-Based Social Work Practice." *Social Work and Christianity* 42.1 (2015): 96.

3   Sokoloff, Natalie J. and Ida Dupont. "Domestic violence at the intersections of race, class, and gender: Challenges and contributions to understanding violence against marginalized women in diverse communities." *Violence Against Women* 11.1 (2005): 38–64.

4   Sullivan, Cris M. and Maureen H. Rumptz. "Adjustment and needs of African-American women who utilized a domestic violence shelter." *Violence and Victims* 9.3 (1994): 275.

Suggested Media

1   Power and Control: Domestic Violence in America www.powerandcontrolfilm.com/all%20videos/

2   The National Coalition Against Domestic Violence https://ncadv.org

3   Domestic Violence Shelter & Program Search Tool www.domesticshelters.org/search#?page=1

4   Excerpts for the case, Thurman v. City of Torrington https://cyber.harvard.edu/vaw00/thurmanexcerpt.html

5   TED Talk by author Leslie Morgan Steiner, Why Domestic Violence Victims Don't Leave www.youtube.com/watch?v=V1yW5IsnSjo

6   Futures Without Violence www.futureswithoutviolence.org

References

Balsam, K. F. and D. M. Szymanski, "Relationship quality and domestic violence in women's same-sex relationships: the role of minority stress," *Psychology of Women Quarterly*, vol. 29, no. 3, pp. 258–269, 2005.

Bent-Goodley, T. B. "Culture and domestic violence: Transforming knowledge development," *Journal of Interpersonal Violence*, vol. 20, pp. 195–203, 2005.

Bent-Goodley, T. B. and K. Brade, "Intimate partner violence within church communities of African ancestry," in Andy J. Johnson (ed.), *Religion and Men's Violence Against Women*, pp. 133–148. New York: Springer, 2015.

Bent-Goodley, T. B., and D. N. Fowler, "Spiritual and religious abuse: Expanding what is known about domestic violence," *Affilia*, vol. 21, no. 3, pp. 282–295, 2006.

Brade, K. and T. B. Bent-Goodley, "A refuge for my soul: Examining African American clergy's perceptions related to domestic violence awareness and engagement in faith community initiatives," *Social Work & Christianity*, vol. 36, pp. 430–448, 2009.

Burke, Peter J., and Donald C. Reitzes, "The link between identity and role performance," *Social Psychology Quarterly*, vol. 44, no. 2, pp. 83–92, 1981.

Conner, D. H., "Financial freedom: Women, money, and domestic abuse," *Wm. & Mary J. Women & L.*, vol. 20, p. 339, 2013.

Davies, L. and J. Krane, "Critical reflections on practice with battered women: Insights from Maya's story," *Atlantis: A Women's Studies Journal*, vol. 28, no. 1, pp. 63–71, 2003.

Farrell, M. L. "The sense of relationship in women who have encountered abuse," *Journal of the American Psychiatric Nurses Association*, vol. 2, no. 2, pp. 46–53, 1996.

Geary Jr., Franklyn H., and Cheryl B. Wingate, "Domestic violence and physical abuse of women: The Grady Memorial Hospital experience," *American Journal of Obstetrics and Gynecology*, vol. 181, no. 1, pp. S17–S21, 1999.

Goffman, E., "The moral career of the mental patient," *Psychiatry*, vol. 22, no. 2, pp. 123–142, 1959.

Goffman, E. *Asylums: Essays on the social situation of mental patients and other inmates*, Garden City, NY: Random House Inc., 1961.

Goffman, E. *Stigma: Notes on the management of spoiled identity*, New York: Touchstone, 1963.

Goffman, E., "The insanity of place," *Psychiatry*, vol. 32, no. 4, pp. 357–388, 1969.

Goldsmith, Emily, "Domestic and family violence and homelessness in New South Wales," *Parity*, vol. 29, no. 10, pp. 31, 2016.

Goodmark, L. *A troubled marriage: Domestic violence and the legal system*, New York: NYU Press, 2012.

Hague, G., A. Mullender and R. Aris, *Is anyone listening? Accountability and women survivors of domestic violence*, London and New York: Routledge: Taylor & Francis Group, 2003.

Hampton, R., W. Oliver and L. Magarian, "Domestic violence in the African American community: An analysis of social and structural factors," *Violence Against Women*, vol. 9, no. 5, pp. 533–337, 2003.

Harter, L. M., C. Berquist, B. Scott Titsworth, D. Novak and T. Brokaw, "The structuring of invisibility among the hidden homeless: the politics of space, stigma, and identity construction," *Journal of Applied Communication Research*, vol. 33, no. 4, pp. 305–327, 2005.

Itzhaky, H. and A. B. Porat, "Battered Women in Shelters: Internal Resources, Well-Being and Integration," *Affilia*, vol. 20, no. 1, 2005.

Jaffe, P. G., C. V. Crooks, and S. E. Poisson, "Common misconceptions in addressing domestic violence in child custody disputes," *Juvenile and Family Court Journal*, vol. 54, no. 4, pp. 57–67, 2003.

Kleinman, S. *Opposing Ambitions: Gender and identity in an alternative organization*, Chicago, IL: University of Chicago Press, 1996.

Lacey, K. K., M. D. McPherson, P. S. Samuel, S. K. Powell and D. Head, "The impact of different types of intimate partner violence on the mental and physical health of women in different ethnic groups," *Journal of Interpersonal Violence*, vol. 28, no. 2, pp. 359–385, 2013.

Link, B. G. and J. C. Phelan, "Conceptualizing stigma," *Annual Review of Sociology*, vol. 27, pp. 363–385, 2001.

Loseke, D. R. *The Battered Woman and Shelters: The social construction of wife abuse*, Albany, NY: State University of New York Press, 1992.

Loseke, D. R., and J. C. Cavendish, "Producing institutional selves: Rhetorically constructing the dignity of sexually marginalized Catholics," *Social Psychology Quarterly*, vol. 64, no. 4, p. 347, 2001.

Matheson, F., N. Daoud, S. Hamilton-Wright, H. Borenstein, C. Pedersen and P. O'Campo, "Where did she go? The transformation of self-esteem, self-identity, and mental well-being among women who have experienced intimate partner violence," *Women's Health Issues*, vol. 25, no. 5, pp. 561–569, 2015.

Murray, C., A. Crowe, and W. Akers, "How can we end the stigma surrounding domestic violence and sexual violence? A modified Delphi study with national advocacy leaders," *Journal of Family Violence*, vol. 31, no. 3, pp. 271–287, 2016.

O'Doherty, L. J., A. Taft, R. McNair and K. Hagarty, "Fractured identity in the context of intimate partner violence: Barriers to and opportunities for seeking help in health settings," *Violence Against Women*, vol. 22, no. 2, pp. 225–248, 2016.

Overstreet, N. M. and D. M. Quinn, "The intimate partner violence stigmatization model and barriers to help seeking," *Basic and Applied Social Psychology*, vol. 35, no. 1, pp. 109–122, 2013.

Overstreet, N. M., J. L. Gaskins, D. M. Quinn and M. K. Williams, "The moderating role of centrality on the association between internalized intimate partner violence-related stigma and concealment of physical IPV," *Journal of Social Issues*, vol. 73, no. 2, pp. 307–321, 2017.

Paull, J. L. *Identity Construction and Maintenance in Domestic Violence Shelters*, Kent, OH: Kent State University, 2013.

Peled, E. and R. Dekel, "Excusable deficiency: Staff perceptions of mothering at shelters for abused women," *Violence Against Women*, vol. 16, no. 11, pp. 1224–1241, 2010.

Reger, J., "More than one feminism: Organizational structure and the construction of collective identity," *Social Movements: Identity, Culture, and the State*, pp. 171–184, 2002.

Scott, E. K. "Creating Partnerships for change: Alliances and betrayals in the racial politics of two feminist organizations," *Gender & Society*, vol. 12, no. 4, pp. 785–818, 2000.

Snow, D. A. and L. Anderson, "Identity work among the homeless: The verbal construction and avowal of personal identities," *American Journal of Sociology*, vol. 92, no. 6, pp. 1336–1371, 1987.

Stets, J. E. and P. J. Burke, "Identity theory and social identity theory," *Social Psychology Quarterly*, pp. 224–237, 2000.

Stover, C. S. and K. Lent, "Training and certification for domestic violence service providers: The need for a national standard curriculum and training approach," *Psychology of Violence*, vol. 4, no. 2, p. 117, 2014.

Stryker, S., "Identity salience and role performance: The relevance of symbolic interaction theory for family research," *Journal of Marriage and the Family*, pp. 558–564, 1968.

Villalón, R., *Violence against Latina immigrants: Citizenship, inequality, and community*, New York: NYU Press, 2010.

Walker, L. E. *The Battered Woman*, New York: Harper & Row, Publishers Inc., 1979.

Walker, L. E., "Psychology and violence against women," *American Psychologist*, vol. 44, no. 4, p. 695, 1989.

Walker, L. E., *The Battered Woman Syndrome*, Fourth edition, New York: Springer Publishing Company, 2017.

Ward, T. and M. Brown, "The good lives model and conceptual issues in offender rehabilitation," *Psychology, Crime & Law*, vol. 10, no. 3, pp. 243–257, 2004.

Part IV

KEY DEBATES AROUND WOMEN'S INEQUALITY

GENDER SCHOLAR SPOTLIGHT: INTERVIEW WITH KAZUKO SUZUKI

Kazuko Suzuki (Princeton, Ph.D. Sociology) was born in Japan and was an assistant professor at Texas A&M University at the time of this interview (she is now an associate professor). After working for a Japanese company for several years, she came to the U.S. for her graduate education. She specializes in International Migration, Race and Ethnicity, Gender, and East Asian Studies. She has fieldwork experience in Japan and Russia, as well as in the U.S. She is the author of *Divided Fates: The State, Race, and Korean Immigrants' Adaptation in Japan and the United States* and co-editor of *Reconsidering Race: Social Science Perspectives on Racial Categories in the Age of Genomics*.

What led you to begin studying women's inequality?

I was born and raised in a very traditional, conservative family in patriarchal Japan. Ever since my childhood, I felt that even just "being a woman" itself has been a humiliating experience. Having been treated as a member of a putatively inferior sex through various daily rituals in my family and society for most of my life, it was almost inevitable that I got interested in the mechanisms that oppress women.

How have your lived experiences shaped your research interests?

When I was a child, around the age of 7 or 8, I had a Zainichi Korean friend. We spent a lot of time together after school. Because he was Zainichi

Korean (an ethnic minority group severely discriminated against in Japanese society), he was bullied by his classmates and teachers. Having him as a close friend, my classmates threw stones also at me (an ethnic Japanese) with a racial slur against Zainichi Koreans. I always wondered why we had to go through humiliating experiences on a daily basis just because of a single attribute: for me as a woman, for him as a Zainichi Korean. This childhood experience was so powerful, and I have always wanted to study about the oppression of social minorities.

In your opinion, what scholarly works have been most impactful in your research on women and inequality?

Simone de Beauvoir. 1949. *The Second Sex* (*Le Deuxiéme Sexe*). The phrase, "one is not born, but rather becomes, woman" is well-known and has changed the lives of many women in the world.

What has been most challenging about your field of work?

The censorship I faced at U.S. customs and the U.S. postal service especially after 9/11. When I was working on my first book project about the Korean diaspora, most of my research materials in the Russian language that I collected through my fieldwork were "confiscated" and never returned. Therefore, I had to give up my original plan to compare Koreans in the former Soviet Union and Japan. In my current project on Yaoi or Boys Love (a literary genre of male-male romance by and for heterosexual women), I have had similar experiences. I am examining the functions and contributions of Yaoi for Japanese women, which was invented by them in the late 1970s and I am collecting Yaoi novels as samples of my study. Because of the explicit nature of texts and images of Yaoi, many of them were confiscated at the U.S. customs. It took much time and money to collect more than eight hundred samples.

Why is your work on women important

In my discipline, sociology, not many scholars conduct systematic cross-national comparisons. This is especially so in the area of qualitative research. I am trying to make contributions to fill this intellectual vacuum. Another important aspect of my work is to focus on "invisible" social oppression against minority groups such as immigrants, racial minorities, and women. Mechanisms of oppressions and creating inequalities are becoming more "invisible" after overt legal discrimination against minorities is lifted. Studies of more subtle forms of discrimination and oppression that lead to inequalities are necessary.

Which scholar(s) (and why) has been most influential in developing your perspective?

There are so many great scholars in the world that I am indebted to intellectually, so that I cannot enumerate all of them here.

What theoretical approach best guides your research?

Since most of my research projects are interdisciplinary, while based on traditional sociology, I employ various theoretical approaches. Currently, I am very interested in an intersectionality approach.

What pedagogical approaches have you found most effective when teaching on women and inequality?

I have found that comparative and historical approaches (my forte) are quite effective in teaching. My students love to hear about my fieldwork experiences.

In your opinion, what are the most pertinent issues facing the women in your area of research today?

As a female researcher who frequently conducts fieldwork, I must be even more conscious about the fact that I am a woman in the field, for safety reasons. When I enter dangerous areas or deal with particular kinds of people such as Yakuza (the Japanese mafia), I, as a woman, feel very vulnerable. I felt particularly so when I was conducting research on human trafficking in Japan.

Is there anything else you would like to add?

Here is one of my personal experiences that surprise my students as an example of how technologies can impact women. As I mentioned earlier, I was brought up in a very conservative Japanese family. Dining was a part of ritual where the "inferior" status of women of my family was routinely displayed. For instance, my younger brother had a higher seating order than my grandmother, mother, my younger sister, and me. He was always entitled to eat fresh hot white rice just like my grandfather and father. I had to frequently eat left-over cold rice in front of them as a duty of being a woman, which was not only not tasty, but humiliating. When my mother purchased a microwave oven, I was ecstatic. Hot, steamy rice was a symbol of "not being inferior" and I felt that I finally fled from twice-daily ritual of public humiliation.

13

IS THERE LIBERATION FOR THE SINGLE, SAVED, AND SEXUALLY REPRESSED?

Jacqueline F. Ballou

There are a growing number of African American Christian women in the United States who have never been married and acknowledge that the possibility of such a union for them in their lifetime is merely a dream grounded in a reality of low probability. In 2014, the Bureau of Labor Statistics estimated that 50.2% of women declared that they were living without a spouse, up from 37.4% in 1976. In fact, in 2005, married couples became a minority of all American households for the first time in our history and, according to the U.S. Census Bureau in 2011, 45% of the population is single. Marriage rates among Black women in America remain statistically lower than any other ethnic group. Only about 30% of Black women are living with a spouse, according to the Census Bureau, compared with about 49% of Hispanic women, 55% of non-Hispanic White women and more than 60% of Asian women.[1] An even more interesting statistic is the increase in the number of both Black men and women who have never been married. Nearly 51% of Black men have never married and 48% of Black women have never married, according to the 2014 U.S. Census Bureau's American Community Survey. More to the point, it is the belief of an increasing number of Black women that they will never get married. The percentage of Black women who are married declined from 62% to 31% between 1950 and 2002, and in 2014, only 26% of African American women were married.[2] Not only are African Americans marrying at a lower rate, they are also marrying at a later age. The Joint Center for Political and Economic Studies reports that by the age of 30; 81% of White women and 77% of Hispanics and Asians will marry, but only 52% of Black women will marry by that age. Black women are also the least likely to re-marry following divorce. Only 32% of Black women will get married again within five years of divorce; that figure is 58% for White women and 44% for Hispanic women.[3]

African American women are uniquely challenged by a perceived shortage in the number of eligible men within their ethnic group due to the

economic, social, and political disparities that exists in America's historically racist society. In 2016, the unemployment rate of Black America was
disproportionably higher than White America, at 8.8% versus less than
4.9% for Whites, according to the Bureau of Labor Statistics. Drugs and
the systemic incarceration of a whole generation of young Black males have
distorted almost all institutions in Black America. Out of 10.4 million U.S.
Black adult males, nearly 1.5 million are in prisons and jails, with another
3.5 million more on probation or parole, or who have previously been on
probation or parole. Black males make up nearly 75% of the total prison
population, compared with 7.7% of Hispanic men and 2.6% of White men,
and due to either present or past incarceration, Black males comprise the
most socially disenfranchised group of American citizens in the country
today.[4] Add to this the ravages of the HIV/AIDS crisis where the leading
cause of HIV infection among African American men is sexual contact with
other men; then you will find that the pool of marriageable Black men
has been dramatically reduced for the African American woman desiring
marriage to an African American male. Interestingly enough, however, the
rate of children born to Black women outside of marriage has continued to
increase, as the rates of other ethnic groups have declined.[5]

The proportion of married people, especially among younger age groups,
has been declining for decades. Between 1950 and 2000, the share of women
age 15–24 who were married plummeted to 16%, from 42%. Among
25–34-year-olds, the proportion dropped to 58%, from 82%.[6] Overall, a larger
share of men are married and living with their spouse—about 53% compared
with 49% among women. According to Dr. Frey, a demographer with the
Brookings Institution, a research group in Washington, DC, "since women
continue to outlive men, they have reached the non-marital tipping point—
more non-married than married. This suggests that most girls growing up
today can look forward to spending more of their lives outside of a traditional
marriage."[7] Ms. Smock, a researcher at the University of Michigan Population
Studies Center added, "men also remarry more quickly than women after a
divorce, and both are increasingly likely to cohabit rather than remarry after a
divorce."[8] Several factors are driving the statistical shift. At one end of the age
spectrum, women are marrying later or living with unmarried partners more
often and for longer periods. At the other end, women are living longer as
widows and, after a divorce, are more likely than men to delay remarriage,
sometimes delighting in their newfound freedom. According to Dr. Frey:

> for better or worse, women are less dependent on men or the insti-
> tution of marriage. Younger women understand this better, and
> are preparing to live longer parts of their lives alone or with non-
> married partners. For many older boomer and senior women, the
> institution of marriage did not hold the promise they might had
> hoped for, growing up in an "Ozzie and Harriet" era.[9]

This is yet another of the inexorable signs that there is no going back to a world where we can assume that marriage is the main institution that organizes people's lives. Professor Stephanie Coontz, Director of Public Education for the Council on Contemporary Families, a nonprofit research group, suggests that "most women may marry, or have married; but on average, Americans now spend half their adult lives outside marriage."[10] As there is a decline in marriage, there is an increase in cohabitation, suggesting that more women are not waiting for marriage to have sex.

From the time of sexual maturation and in some cases even earlier in their childhood, Christian women have been instructed by the Church to abstain from all sexual relations until they are married. With the increasing improbability of marriage for many African American women, due to social and cultural shifts away from marriage in the U.S., they are beginning to question whether or not it is truly God's desire that they never engage in any sexual relations in their lifetime simply because no man has chosen to take their hand in marriage. And what if these women chose for themselves never to marry—does that mean they can never experience a sexual relationship with another human being? Is it God's will that Christian women live sexless lives if they never marry? Does the righteousness of God really require that of unmarried women as the Church has proclaimed?

I have selected 1 Thessalonians 4:1–8 as the primary periscope that I will explore for this biblical hermeneutic. The theological key seems to be verse 3 which reads "For this is the will of God, your sanctification: that you abstain from fornication." According to the *Interpreter's Dictionary of the Bible: An Illustrated Encyclopedia*, fornication in the New Testament of the Bible refers to every kind of sexual intercourse outside of marriage.[11] I will draw from Acts 15:28–29 as my secondary source. I am interested in these texts as they have been used by many churches to repress the sexual desires of mature unmarried individuals, particularly women in our society. It appears that the Apostle Paul's somewhat ascetic attitude captured in 1 Thessalonians may be arcane in today's times, and a fresh word is needed from the Church which has grown silent on the issue of female sexuality in the 21st century.

I posit that 1 Thessalonians 4:1–8 is not a condemnation of sexual relations outside of marriage, but simply instruction for those who would chose to live an ascetic life similar to the one Paul himself led: a life of sanctification and holiness which he believed God would find pleasing. I contend that God's desire for humanity is for individuals to engage in quality human relationships that are loving, committed, and nurturing; relationships that provide a safe environment for free expression which may include sexual intimacy between consenting adults who are not married. Humanity as designed by God has a great need for companionship and deep friendship in which time is invested, life shared and intimate moments spent together. God himself declares in the creation story that "it is not good that man should be alone" (Gen. 2:18). As such, the Church must reconsider its legalistic stance on human sexuality when it falls short of the solitary standard of marriage. As Bishop Spong suggests:

> The Church must give up its elevated stance of righteousness and enter with its people into the more difficult gray area of life to seek a basis for decision making on sexual issues that is life giving, not life destroying, and is appropriate to the age and circumstances of the people involved. It does open the possibility that the same activity that is pronounced good in one relationship or at one age can be destructive in another relationship or at another age. It does move us away from rigid rules into the freedom of relativity.[12]

In my attempt to analyze these texts, I will employ a combination of the historical critical method and reader-response criticism. Following the lead of René Descartes who posits that "nothing should be accepted as true simply because it is in the tradition,"[13] I will attempt to remove the mystery and authority that many African American Christian women place on these Scriptures and present a case which suggests that the prevailing interpretations of these historical narratives are probable but not indisputable truths. I will explore when, and by whom, and under what circumstances, these passages were written in an attempt to identify the original meaning and the context in which they were written. I will take a historical look at how societies, Christian and non-Christian, viewed sex in antiquity and how those views may have influenced our current cultural milieu. Imperative to this study is the exploration of how scriptural texts such as the ones chosen have been interpreted by the early Christian Church. The one thing that I will not do that the historical-critical method suggests: I will not engage the material without prejudice because I am interested in what these texts mean for today's African American Christian woman. I will employ a womanist canon to engage the Bible as a hermeneutic of suspicion and liberation. I will be true to Alice Walker's proclamation that the womanist is "committed to survival and wholeness of entire people, male and female."[14]

Historical Context of Primary Text: Thessalonians 4:1–8

The First Epistle to the Thessalonians is the first letter that Paul wrote to the Thessalonian congregation that he had established after fleeing Philippi. It is believed that Paul wrote this letter from Corinth around 50 CE, after being unsuccessful in returning to Thessalonica after repeated attempts. 1 Thessalonians is the oldest surviving Christian document preserving how the new religion was established in Gentile territory. Thessalonica was the capital of the Roman province of Macedonia and was a commercial and cultic center during the time of Paul. The letter to the Thessalonians presupposes conflict between those in the Church and other Thessalonians, because of the Christian glorification of Christ within communities that favorably disposed to the Roman government. The Christianity that Paul preached was considered subversive to the basic religious institutions of Gentile society, because he contended that no truly committed Gentile Christian could maintain any other cult memberships.[15] This is a letter of friendly encouragement and affectionate praise for the Thessalonians' steadfast hope and consistent behavior in light of the hostile conditions that existed resulting from the Christian believers' countercultural glorification of Christ. Many commentators believe that Paul's letters to the churches he established were designed to help those followers deal with the tensions of life that existed while they awaited the Parousia (the Second Coming of Christ).

Historical Context of Secondary Text: Acts 15:28–29

My secondary text is taken from Acts 15:28–29. The inaugural event of the second half of Acts is the concluding speech at the Jerusalem Council by James, the brother of Jesus. As the new leader of the Jerusalem Church, he is prepared to render a decision on the prevailing issue before the council that solidified the Gentile movement—the issue being whether the Gentile converts should be circumcised as a religious practice as required by the Torah. It was clear to James that the uncircumcised Gentiles indeed would share equally in the blessing of Israel's salvation. James moved on to another matter of great concern as captured in Acts 15:28–29. In this pastoral exhortation that was sent to the Antiochene congregation, James wanted to counter the potentially deleterious effects that Gentile converts may have on repentant Jews with whom they share congregational life in order that the "gentilizing" mission in the diaspora would not lead to the attenuation of the Church's Jewish legacy.[16]

1 Thessalonians 4 is filled with numerous imperatives that convey an exhortative tone and includes descriptions of what the sanctified life looks like in preparation of the coming Apocalypse. Paul understands sanctification or the ongoing life of holiness to be God's will and he is certain that the end of days—the Parousia—is to come during his lifetime.[17] It is apparent from the historical accounts of the life of the early Church that the Christians set themselves apart from the culture and persisted in the way of God even in the face of death; and they chose to live sanctified lives as they awaited God's imminent coming. As such, Paul opens 1 Thess. 4:1–2 with exhortations, and offers not so much new counsel to the Thessalonians, but an approving observation about how they have indeed learned by his very own example. Paul asks the Thessalonian house churches to continue living (literally: "in the way it is necessary for you to walk"—to pos dei humas peripatein) in ways that please God. According to Cain Hope Felder, Paul rehearses here his so-called "Indicative of Salvation" sounded in Galatians 5:25 (the Indicative is "we live by the spirit"; the Imperative

is "let us walk/conduct ourselves [*stoicheo*] by the spirit"); and the teaching that informs such living is explicit in 1 Corinthians 11:1 where the Apostle intones "Be imitators of me as I am of Christ."[18]

In 1 Thess. 4:3–8, Paul links a number of imperatives to apocalyptic descriptions of the end time, describing for the Church the distinctive life of love and holiness that they must live before others as they await with assurance for the Parousia.[19] According to Felder, for Paul, how a person manages his or her intimate relations is a crucial factor in establishing a life pleasing to God. In this view, the Christian vocation is one of striving for a new level of personal morality manifested in sexual "purity" which of course Felder contends must be understood against the background of unrestrained sexual liaisons that often prevailed in the ancient Hellenistic world.[20] We must remember that Paul is greatly influenced by Greek philosophy of the body being evil and inferior to the mind and something which is in need of being controlled. We find in Galatians 5:23, Paul establishing "self-control" as one of the fruits of the Spirit, and in 1 Corinthians 6:12, he declares that "all things are lawful for me, but I will not be brought under the power of any." Both Scriptures reinforce Paul's belief that the body is something to be controlled.

The theme of sanctification or holiness is the common thread that Paul weaves throughout these verses. Paul offers a general maxim on sanctification in 1 Thessalonians 3 and three specific injunctions about the holy life in vv. 4–6a. These injunctions identified certain improprieties as a way of defining the boundaries within his Christian community. In vv. 6b–8, he follows with three motivations for living the holy life. In v. 6, Paul speaks of the Lord as the avenger, removing any notion of self-vindication among those wronged. The community of Christians is not to judge or avenge the violators of these injunctions; that is left solely to God. Paul stresses in v. 8 that God has equipped believers with what they need to live the sanctified life, namely the Holy Spirit. Thus for Paul, rejection of the life of holiness is ultimately a rejection of the gift of God, the Holy Spirit.[21] The hallmark of Paul's emerging teachings on "sanctification" is that holiness is first and perhaps foremost a spiritual state that emerges from within as contrasted to measuring up to outward standards.[22] Felder refers to v. 8 as "Paul's Holy Sentence" and suggests the following:

> Whereas Jesus of Nazareth in Matthew 23:23 speaks of certain spiritual and moral issues (e.g., faith, justice and mercy) as "weightier matters of the Law"; Paul considers sexual decency as a virtual "weightier matter of Grace". This becomes for him what Ernst Kasemann once called "a holy sentence of Paul" that is a foundational teaching emanating from his own direct revelation from God, but given as if it is on the same level as the Jesus tradition which he received after his conversion.[23]

In summary, 1 Thess. 4:1–8 is a call to holiness which Paul contends should be the goal of the Church as they await the imminent return of Christ.

Establishing boundaries for the early Church is of paramount importance to Paul. It has been suggested by scholars that perhaps in Acts 15 we find the Jerusalem Council in anticipation of the Gentile resistance to Paul's denunciation of pagan practices, establishing some pastoral guidelines that he could use to ensure that Christian fellowship in the mixed congregations would nurture faith rather than contaminate it.[24] We find James, the brother of Jesus, in Acts 15:28–29 encouraging repentant Gentiles to abstain from four impurities that observant Jews associate with the pagan world: 1) idolatry, 2) sexual immorality (fornication), 3) eating either food with blood or 4) strangled food. James contends that abstaining from these necessary things seems good to the Holy Spirit whom God has given to believers to make the attainment of such quest achievable. James' denunciation of sexual immorality/fornication may not be interpreted to mean fornication as modern-day Christians have defined it. The *NIB* suggests that the references to fornication in this text most likely refer to temple prostitution because of the broad moral currency that such acts had in the Greco-Roman moral thought of this period. Thus, it is probable that James, in Acts 15:29, is not referencing what we consider to be fornication (sex outside of marriage between two mature consenting adults who are engaged in a loving and nurturing relationship), but he is referring to temple prostitution which was a pagan practice of the time.[25] If this is true, then it is probable that Paul in 1 Thess. 4:3 is also referring to temple prostitution when encouraging the Church to abstain from fornication as an act of sanctification.

It is difficult to fully comprehend what the biblical writers like Paul were referring to when they spoke of fornication in the New Testament Scriptures, in opposition to achieving a state of holiness. Some early Christian leaders used Matthew 5:27–28 to suggest that Jesus implied in His Sermon on the Mount that all infatuations by the married and the unmarried was in essence fornication. Some suggest that fornication is used in the Scriptures in reference to temple prostitution only, and others refer to it as the practice of sexual immorality and harlotry; hence a symbol of idolatry. In the Old Testament, it is equivalent to "playing the harlot" (Gen. 38:24; Deut. 22:21).[26] It is generally accepted today that in the New Testament, the word "fornication" is used to refer to every kind of sexual intercourse outside of marriage.[27] Whether that was the definition used by the biblical authors and translators we may never know, but what we do know is that the word "fornication" and its use in the New Testament has been used by the Church to construct a moral ethic for unmarried Christians that they are required to meet in order to live a life that is pleasing to God. Is the expression of human sexuality by unmarried Christians incommensurate with the teaching of Scripture?

When developing a hermeneutic of 1 Thess. 4:1–8, we must remember that Paul is writing in an eschatological framework; meaning that he was not anticipating an extended future for humanity on this earth. He expects the existing world order to come to an immediate and dramatic end to be replaced with the Kingdom of Heaven. This may well be the reason why Paul did not waste a lot of time on the regulation of sexual behavior and on family life in general, suggesting that humanity simply abstain from fornication until the Kingdom comes and if unable to do so for such a brief period, then individuals should simply marry as to not burn in their lust (1 Cor. 7:9). Paul's advice on sexual morality found in Thessalonians and Corinthians was motivated not by the belief that sex was bad, but by the conviction that the end was near. When interpreting the Pauline corpus, it is also necessary to remember that he is writing during a period where Gnosticism and ascetic principles are greatly influencing the Church and community. Most Gnostic teachings condemned all sexual expression among both the married and the unmarried. Modern-day scholars contend that many of Paul's sayings may have been taken out of context by the over-zealous celibates of early Christianity, who tried to prove that Paul's position on sex was the same as their own,[28] for example, in 1 Corinthians 7:1 where Paul writes "Now concerning the matters about which you wrote. It is good for a man not to touch a woman." Most interpreters of the early Church have just used the latter sentence to state Paul's view on sexual activity; while it is just as likely that Paul is simply restating the question that has been presented to him to which he is now going to respond. The early Christian fathers Tertullian and Jerome both used the latter sentence to establish Christian doctrine, suggesting that even marital sexual relations are bad.[29] However, the Scripture immediately following (1 Cor. 7:2–4) makes it clear that Paul is actually defending marital intercourse as both a right and a duty. It is in Corinthians more explicitly than anywhere else in the Bible that it is affirmed that partners are equally obligated to surrender their bodies to one another in mutual enjoyment, implying that sexual activity is neither evil nor condemned by God.

Although the Bible does speak plainly about sex, it is not easy to summarize the basic teachings in terms that apply to the conditions of the society in which we live today. We see Paul in 1 Thess. 4:1–8 establishing injunctions for Christians as fundamental to living a holy life which pleases God. The clearest of these injunctions is the general maxim on sanctification that Christians are to abstain from fornication. This is one of the Scriptures that has been used by the early Church in establishing Christian doctrine on sexual behavior. Mace believes that the primary reason the early Christians seem to have moved so far from what the Bible teaches on sex is mainly because, in following Paul's teachings, they expected the end of the world to soon come.[30] Christian leaders following Pauline thought had taught separation from the world until the coming of the Kingdom of God, which seemed indefinitely postponed, leaving Christians to devote themselves to hope in a spiritual world beyond death and the pursuit of individual salvation.[31]

According to French writer de Sales, "the whole moral outlook of the Western man was based on the fundamental precept that the purpose of life was to deserve a place in heaven and that earthly satisfactions were more of a handicap than an asset".[32] The dominant Christian thought regarding human sexuality emphasized it as something that Christians should strive to overcome in order to live a life pleasing to God.

Early Christianity

Early Christianity was greatly influenced by Greek thought that denigrated the body and fostered a profound split between the body and the spirit; this dualism was crafted by Platonic or Neoplatonic thought. It was into this Greco-Roman world of dualistic philosophical thought that Christianity emerged. As a result of this influence, many believe that the early Church adopted a sexual ethic that looks nothing like God's original intent for humanity.[33] The creation story declares that God made man, "male and female created He them" (Gen 1:27b); suggesting that He deliberately created humanity as sexual beings and declared that everything He made was very good. In Genesis, the book of beginnings, we find God declaring that it was not good for man to be alone and He also instructs man to be fruitful and multiply—i.e., have sex and have children (Gen. 35:11). There is no indicator in the Genesis account that God viewed sex or the body as something evil or shameful. It appears that in the early centuries of Christianity, sexual ideology among Christians began to shift to the opposite of what God had declared for the creation: ideals about sexual behavior and companionship turned from "be fruitful and multiply" to isolation, separation, and abstinence.[34]

The fourth and fifth centuries of early Christianity were dominated by monasticism, originating in Egypt, which emphasized asceticism and renunciation of the world. One of the most pervasive threats to monastic life was that of fornication. According to Byron, many monastic writings of the period are dedicated to counseling young men on how to manage the demon of fornication, which was seen as a human weakness to be overcome. Byron records the writing of a 5th-century monk expressing his position on fornication, "For no man can endure the assaults of the adversary, neither can any extinguish or restrain the fire that leaps in our nature, unless God's grace shall give its strength to human weakness."[35] According to Byron, the monks were known to engage in extreme measures to defend against the wiles of women, the cause of their fornication: "A monk once dipped his cloak into the putrefying flesh of a dead woman, so that the smell might banish thoughts of her."[36] Monks viewed the body as a problem that must be mastered and controlled because pleasures of the flesh resulted in a falling-away from a life devoted to God; they believed that "the act of intercourse was one of the many aspects of their lives that they could bring under control through good sense and breeding."[37]

Similar views were further reinforced by the great theologians of the Patristic period like St. Augustine, whom many consider the founder of Christian theology. Augustine, greatly influenced by Neoplatonism, thought the body to be evil and in need of control. As a result of this belief and his own recorded struggles with sexual desire, Augustine developed a Christian doctrine of celibacy as the best way to live a truly Christian life and viewed fornication as a mortal sin deserving of eternal death. Augustine viewed marriage as the only divine institution that could make sex licit and for those that turned to marriage as an outlet for their uncontrollable sexual impulses; they were guilty of only venial sin, which could be pardoned. Augustine's concept of marriage as a remedy for sin is an obvious distortion of Paul's recommendation that it is better to marry than to burn in lust.[38] Augustine viewed human sexuality as contaminated by lust with the fall of Adam. According to womanist theologian Kelly Brown Douglas:

> Prior to the Fall, Augustine argued that every part of Adam's body was perfectly good and obedient to the will of God; pre-fall sexual relations were not sinful because they were controlled acts to procreate. But after the Fall, Adam lost control of his will. A sign of this was a loss of control over his body and body parts, specifically his genitalia. The involuntary movements of sexual organs (such as male erections) were the first sign of this loss of control and, hence, disobedience to God. Thereafter sexual activity was no longer a controlled act of procreation, but, instead became a kind of spasm in which reason is completely overtaken by passion. Augustine describes sexual activity motivated by passion as an act where "at the crisis of excitement it practically paralyzes all power of deliberate thought."[39]

The Middle Ages

Augustine's views on sexuality were embraced and carried forward through the Middle Ages by one of the most famous and influential theologians of the period, Thomas Aquinas. Aquinas did not deviate from the Patristic thinking relative to the sinful nature of sex; he systemized those thoughts in his *Summa Theologiae*. Aquinas supported the Augustinian position and argued from the *bonum prolis*: in sexual intercourse, nature intends the pro-creation and education of children; but it is necessary that parents educate and instruct their children for a long time. Therefore the law of nature demands that the father and mother live together for a long time.[40] Aquinas declares sex outside the bounds of marriage (fornication) as a mortal sin, for he is convinced that it breaks the due order of parent to child which nature intends. For Aquinas, marriage is ordained by God to secure the future of the children produced from sexual relationships. Any sexual activity outside of marriage is in violation with God's intent for humanity, and thus a mortal sin. Thus, sex acts must be done for the right purpose (pro-creation), with the right person (spouse), and the right way (heterosexual genital intercourse).[41] Aquinas, like Augustine, stressed that celibacy is the Christian ideal recognizing that Christian life could be lived at two lev-els: the higher spiritual level of the unmarried and the lower, less spiritual level of the married. This thought carried forward to Catholic doctrine and Western Christian thought and was made official at the Council of Trent in the 16th century. The Council concluded that sexual pleasure is not compatible with spiritual life and that the state of celibacy was supe-rior to married life.[42] The Council made marriage a sacrament in an act to acknowledge that marriage had been ordained by God, blessed by Jesus, and used by Paul as a symbol of union between Christ and the Church. Mace contends that the Catholic Church "solved their problem [created by their view of marriage as a lesser spiritual state] by exalting marriage as an institution while discouraging it as an enterprise."[43]

The Protestant Reformation

We see no real positive doctrine on sexuality emerge from the Church, as sexuality remained predominately identified with lustful urges of the body. Both Luther and Calvin, the Protestant Reformers, took the view that celibacy is the desirable state for those who seek the highest spir-itual levels, but Calvin concluded that "most, confronted by this challenge, would be compelled to marry from necessity because they had not the gift of continence."[44] Luther believed that much of the Church's teaching on sexuality was so far removed from what he read in the Bible that he called for change. He challenged the Church's position on celibacy and went on to marry and encouraged other monks and priest to marry as well. After all, many priests were living with women, engaging in sex, and creating children. So, Luther encouraged them to marry in order to relieve them of their guilt: "Marriage for him was a necessity so as to allow for some controlled response to this libidinal urge."[45] Luther took the position that marriage offered opportunities to cultivate spiritual qualities equivalent to those available to the celibate, and he opposed marriage as a sacrament. Luther asserted that marriage was a "universal institution, practiced by hea-thens and Christians alike, and that its regulation was therefore a secular matter to be handed over to the civil powers."[46] Calvin took the position that even within marriage sexual acts needed to be constrained by the rigid bounds of "delicacy and propriety."[47]

Impact on Women

According to James Nelson, "the dualistic philosophies that governed the Church's tradition in terms of sexuality were intrinsically misogynistic and

reflect a patriarchal dualism."[48] This dualism is inherently sexist and discriminatory towards women, as men are viewed as creatures of reason while
women are seen as body, passion, and irrationality. This thought was crafted
by Aristotle, who identified women as "the mutilated male" and concluded
that male is by nature superior to female because the reason is greater in the
male. Thus, for Aristotelians, Eve symbolizes all women as evil protagonist.
Even the great theologian of the early Church, Tertullian, stated that women
were the "devil's gateway." Some 11th-century monks identified women as
the "bait of Satan," by product of paradise, poison in their food, source of sin,
temptress, whores of lust, sirens and chief witches.[49] Byron suggests that 4th-
and 5th-century monks in Egypt viewed Ethiopian women as "dangerous
sexual vices that challenged their piety and self-control."[50] She contends that
the monastic writers of early Christianity's negative depiction of the Ethiopian
women has great implications for the many contemporary stereotypes about
Black women. The Ethiopian women symbolized the sexual vices that distracted the desert monks and as such were seen as something that must be
overcome. According to Byron, the Black Ethiopian woman's value was
demeaned by the monks in early Christian history and the effects of that have
carried over to the treatment of Black woman in Western culture today. [51]

In the Old Testament Scriptures, women's roles are clearly seen as sub-
servient to men, with women's roles being relegated to child-bearer and
caregiver. Noted biblical scholar Renita Weems suggests that the prophets
of the Old Testament Scripture created a demonizing view of women in
antiquity by viewing their sexuality as "deviant, evil and dangerous."[52] The
other view of women that was presented in the spiritualistic dualism was
one of a chaste virgin: "The perfect woman was cast as a combination of
Mary—virginal, pure and submissive—and one willing to produce children
for her man."[53] By associating sexual activity with the passionate, irrational,
and satanic nature of women, the male-dominated Christian voices have in
effect provided a safe haven in Church doctrine for their acts of domination
and oppression over women. If the woman is viewed as evil, then she is an
affront to God that man is compelled to control. According to Wartenburg
in *The Forms of Power: From Domination to Transformation*:

It is possible for one group to dominate another group by means
of ideas, by getting that group to think about themselves in a manner that allows them to be subjugated. Such a form of domination
is able to succeed because the true nature of ideas by which it
occurs is concealed in a form of language that has the appearance of
objectivity. In analyzing the use of the term "good" it is intended
to demonstrate that, despite the appearance of objectivity, such a
term functions subjectively in that its use is only justified from a
certain perspective. Since this perspective aspect of judgment is
concealed, however, the subordinate group views the judgments as

valid independently of the perspective from which they are made. As a result, a group can come to think of itself (and behave) in terms created by the perspective of another group without realizing it. It is this particular mechanism that is the origin of domination.[54]

Significance for Today

Attempting to outlaw sex outside of marriage has failed miserably in Christian history. This legalistic approach of "don'ts" has been very ineffective in governing behavior thus far. As long as the Church continues to adopt an authoritarian role and pretends to know clearly what is right and wrong, it will alienate Christians and non-Christians alike, potentially destroying the relationships human beings struggle to have with each other and with God. God's work of sanctification begins on the inside, in the heart, and works its way out as evidenced in the individual's attitudes and behavior. The Church needs to be prepared to teach Christians how to develop a deeper, more meaningful relationship with God in order for them to develop a character that God will be pleased with, and that character will produce behaviors that will need no regulation. The Church needs to commit to teaching the foundational principles of the Gospel of Jesus "Thou shalt love the Lord thy God with all thy heart, and with all thy soul, and with all thy mind . . . Thou shalt love thy neighbor as thyself" (Matthew 22:37, 39). Jesus tended to take this position in His teaching, preferring to judge every issue according to whether it was an expression of love for God and neighbor. Mace contends that Jesus stressed that the decisive question was what a man thinks in his heart, that the inward motive matters more than the outward act, and that the well-being of people takes precedence over respect for institutions.[55]

The Church needs to develop a practical theology for single adults that can guide behaviors and attitudes, particularly today, when there is a considerably longer time span between physical maturation and marriage. A deeper understanding of God's sexual economy has the best possibility for developing concepts and models that guide single adults towards sexual wholeness. Historically, single people have been an ignored or neglected group within the Church; there is often very little offered by way of a theology of sexuality for the single person. More often than not the simple advice offered in the area of sexuality to Christians is "sex is for marriage," or "just abstain," with little explanation as to why. Because of this attitude adopted by the Church, immature behaviors and attitudes have evolved within the Christian single adult community. According to liberal theologian Harvey Cox:

> churchmen, by allowing the Gospel to deteriorate into folklore and fiat, have contributed to this fatal oversimplification. I do not believe that an evangelical ethic of premarital sex can be chopped down to a flat answer without impoverishing and distorting it.[56]

There is much to be enjoyed in the complex world of human interaction and relationship. The Church needs to be equipped to teach Christians the skills of noticing and enjoying persons without zooming in on erotic interaction. Society over-emphasizes erotic sexuality and often neglects nonsexual relational intimacy that can be soul-satisfying for both genders; this is an opportunity for the Church to lead with some new fresh thoughts.

A positive embrace of human sexuality is critical to accepting the fullness of God's desire and love for humanity. Human sexuality is a part of the human composition created by God. God made humans with deep desires for completion, affection, connection, nurture, protection, and hormonal erotic attraction. These desires are good and normal, and are to be directed properly within the confines of a loving relationship. Not embracing that part of one's being is a rejection of God and displays self-hatred for the being which God created.[57] According to Rev. Dr. John W. Kinney, Dean of the School Of Theology at Virginia Union University, "you do not repress your body to be holy because you are repressing the creation of God; you should actualize your body in accordance to God's design."[58] In order for humanity to move toward a place of wholeness, they must accept every aspect of their being as created by God and that includes their sexual nature. Sexuality is that dimension of humanity that urges relationship. Some scholars view sexuality as a gift from God that, if properly appreciated, helps men and women to become more fully human by entering into loving relationships. Douglas suggests that "sexuality thus expresses God's intention that we find our authentic humanness in relationship."[59]

The Church has evaded the challenge to re-examine its teaching on sex for so long that it now finds itself in state of silence which puts in jeopardy a highly important aspect of human life for Christians. The Church is challenged today like never before in history; it is being told that many of its doctrines, as traditionally stated, are irrelevant to life in the scientific and technological age. Psychology is challenging its teaching on sin and salvation; sociology is exposing its complacency in condoning injustice and its inadequate emphasis on social concerns; archeology is presenting questions on the origin and nature of humanity; cosmology is challenging explanations about creation and eschatology, and sexology is accusing the religion of love of making a mockery of human love by trying to suppress one of its most meaningful modes of expression.[60] Certainly, the time has come for the Church to give attention to the issue of sexuality in the 21st century; because the culture in which we exist today is extremely different from that which existed during the formative days of Christianity.

The Church may grapple with the definition and interpretative meaning of the term "fornication" and it may struggle with the variances in the construct of marriages today verses those of the New Testament era. But there is one thing the Church must do if it is to be a relevant voice for Christians in the area of human sexuality: they must determine how to apply the biblical texts to meet the concerns of 21st-century unmarried women. If one were to adhere to the proposition of Richard Hays in *The Moral Vision of the New Testament* in his chapter on homosexuality, he contends that it is prudent and necessary to let the univocal testimony of Scripture and Christian tradition order the life of the Church on matters of sexuality. According to Hays:

> we must affirm that the New Testament tells us the truth about ourselves as sinners and as God's sexual creatures: marriage between man and woman is the normative form for human sexual fulfillment, and homosexuality is one among many tragic signs that we are a broken people, alienated from God's loving purpose.[61]

In this discourse, Hays suggests that heterosexual sex outside of marriage is another sign of such brokenness, contending that "it is no more appropriate for homosexual Christians to persist in homosexual activity than it would be for heterosexual Christians to persist in fornication or adultery."[62] He goes further to imply that heterosexual Christians should either marry or seek to live a life of disciplined sexual abstinence as the Scriptures command. Hays proclaims that "despite the smooth illusions perpetrated by mass culture in the United States, sexual gratification is not a sacred right, and celibacy is not a fate worse than death."[63] He declares that:

> The Catholic tradition has something to teach those of us raised in the Protestant communities. While mandatory priestly celibacy is unbiblical, a life of sexual abstinence can promote "good order and unhindered devotion to the Lord" (1 Corn. 7:35). Surely it is a matter of some interest for Christian ethics that both Jesus and Paul lived without sexual relationships. It is also worth noting that 1 Corinthians 7:8–9, 25–40, commends celibacy as an option for everyone, not just for a special caste of ordained leaders. Within the Church, we should work diligently to recover the dignity and value of the single life . . . The community demands that its members pursue holiness, while it also sustains the challenging process of character formation that is necessary for Jesus' disciples. The Church must be a community whose life together provides true friendship, emotional support, and spiritual formation for everyone who comes within its circle of fellowship. The need for such support is perhaps particularly felt by unmarried people, regardless of their sexual orientation.[64]

Practical Solutions

Nationally, there are ten single Black women for every seven single Black men. The picture looks even worse if you subtract those Black men who are incarcerated and unemployed. So, what is the African American

Christian single woman to do, who has thrown herself on the altar week after week asking God to send her a husband in order that she might create a family life that is blessed by God and engage in the beauty of human sexual expression? Does the Church have an answer for her, other than the standard Scripture reference so often given: "seek ye first the kingdom of God, and his righteousness; and all these things shall be added unto you" (Matt. 6:33)? What will the Church say when this woman who started her "disciplined abstinence" journey at sexual maturation matures to 42 years old and has limited childbearing years remaining and yet no man has requested her hand in marriage? She has done all the things the Church has commanded and her love and reverence for God are unwavering. What does the Church have to offer this woman, whose faith in what the Church has told her about human sexuality is weakening as she watches her dreams of marriage and family dissipate? For many years, this woman has fought the good fight of faith, taken up the cross of sexual virtue and denied herself any kind of sexual pleasure whatsoever. She's been the bridesmaid and maid of honor in several of her Christian sisters' weddings who happened not to have followed the "disciplined abstinence" approach promoted by the Church. She has also witnessed several of those marriages end in divorce. What she does know for sure is that her desire for healthy human connection with a man has not diminished nor has it been replaced by the strong love she has for God, as some theologians have suggested to her it would.

The Church must seek to find a relevant word for the hundreds of thousands of African American Christian women that find themselves in this very predicament. Not all of these women have the call to celibacy and many are offended when the Church proclaims that those who are married have been blessed by God. Does that imply that single men and women have not been blessed by God? If so, is the Church prepared to tell them why not? Human sexuality is given to us at inception and the freedom to express that sexuality has been regulated consistently by the Church for many centuries. However, times have changed and marriage is no longer seen as a viable option for many Christians, due to some of the factors mentioned previously in this chapter. As a result of these drastically changing times, the Church is compelled to seek a fresh word on the matter of human sexuality and sexual expression to meet the growing demands of its congregants.

Certainly in the 21st century, there are some viable alternatives to sexual abstinence and marriage between a man and woman that the Church could find compatible with the Christian faith. There are no strict rules within the Church commanding that people marry within their ethnic or racial group, so perhaps an option the Church can immediately embrace would be to encourage single women to seek marriageable men outside their ethnic/racial group. This is certainly an option that needs further discussion and consideration for African American women who are challenged the most by the significant shortage of eligible Black men. Some have suggested that the Church's endorsement of homosexual relationships would help to solve the problem created by a lack of marriageable partners. I am not convinced that this solution provides a sexual ethic that would resolve the challenges faced by heterosexual men and women. I suppose this could be a viable option for those men and women who desire an intimate trusting loving relationship with another human being and are not partial to any particular sex. The homosexual Christian compatibility debate is one deserving of its own forum and will not be argued here.

The Word of God needs to be relevant to the times in which we live. The marriage dynamics of the 21st century requires the Church to engage in a discourse and determine what if any are the incompatibilities with the Christian faith of a non-married loving committed sexual relationship between a man and woman. If the Church is going to maintain its position that human sexuality can only be expressed in the marriage relationship, then perhaps the Church should consider requiring men of eligible age to marry. Yes: mandatory sanctioned marriage. The Church could investigate the cultural practices of countries like India who practice the custom of arranged marriages to gain a better understanding of how such arrangements work. Arranged marriages are very common in the Middle East and parts of Africa and Asia, and perhaps there is something the Christian Church can learn from them. Polygamy is another alternative worthy of exploration; not only would this provide marriage opportunities for more people, it may possibly lead to a reduction in the rate of infidelity in marriages. The promotion of self-pleasuring (masturbation, phone sex, pornography, etc.) could be another alternative the Church might want to consider. These are just some of the options that the Church may need to at least discuss as they look to engage in a discourse on human sexuality for Christians in the 21st century. Based upon the history of the Church, surely many of these options will be objectionable at first, but if the Church is to have a relevant voice on human sexuality in the 21st century it must begin to engage in a discourse where practical solutions can be found. These discussions are already taking place in the secular world; the Church needs to engage before it becomes completely irrelevant in the lives of its congregants when it comes to matters of human sexuality.

Conclusion

So, what is the single, saved, and disciplined abstinent African American woman to do in order to be authentic in her confession of her faith and authentic in her fulfillment of personhood? How does she make the Bible relevant for her circumstance? Does she follow the ethic of Hays, who suggests:

While Paul regarded celibacy as a charisma, he did not therefore suppose that those lacking the charisma were free to indulge their sexual desires outside marriage. Heterosexually oriented persons are also called to abstinence from sex unless they marry (1 Corin. 7:8–9) . . . The heterosexual who would like to marry but cannot find an appropriate partner (and there are many such) are summoned to a difficult, costly obedience, while "groaning" for the "redemption of their bodies" (Romans 8:23).[65]

Hays contends that much of the contemporary debate is due to those operating under a simplistic anthropology that assumes "whatever is must be good: they have a theology of creation, but no theology of sin and redemption."[66] He also challenges the realized eschatology that equates personal fulfillment with sexual fulfillment and expects sexual salvation now. Hays posits that

the Pauline portrayal of human beings as fallen creatures in bondage to sin and yet set free in Christ for the obedience of faith would suggest a different assessment of sexuality, looking to the future resurrection as the locus of bodily fulfillment.[67]

In the midst of a culture that is obsessed with sex and instant gratification, perhaps Christians need a deeper reflection on what it means to be in the world and not of the world. As Hays declares, we are a nation obsessed with self-gratification and he contends that the Church supports that by preaching about a "false Jesus who panders to our desires."[68] This leaves room for those who are courageous enough to speak a word on obedience and sacrifice that will remind Christians that God's power is made perfect in weakness and that it is possible to live the higher call of righteousness and abstain from sexual relations until marriage.

I contend that women and men need to be constantly reminded that they are made in the image of God, male and female created He them. All that God created is good, thus the body is good and not evil. God's embodied presence in Jesus affirms the testimony in Genesis that all God made was good, including the human body. God created humanity with a sexual nature that it need not be ashamed of but honor and treat with dignity and respect. There is a lot that can be learned from African spirituality in this regard, because for many Africans the human body and the entirety of the human being are viewed as part of the sacred, as part of the divine, including the human being as a sexual and relational being. Douglas contends that this is why many African cultures did not view sexual intercourse as bad or evil, but celebrated this sacred part of life.[69] When considering the interpretations of the biblical text, we must always be mindful of the social location of the interpreter:

Biased eyes often turn to the Biblical witness in support of the bias, particularly when communities attempt to justify their oppression of other human beings. The Bible then becomes a tool of oppression and is taken up as a weapon to censor the behavior and restrict the life possibilities of others.[70]

To the modern-day Christian, how the Platonic and Gnostic notions of the flesh being evil were ever adopted by Christians remains a mystery in light of our modern understanding of Jesus the incarnate one. The beauty of God is that as we seek understanding, He will provide new and fresh revelation. The Church needs to seek such revelation in the area of sexuality in modern society. I am not suggesting that the Church condone what has in the past been condemned; I am simply suggesting that we not accept as truth everything tradition has passed down to us without careful examination. Human sexuality needs to be subjected to a thorough analysis using Scripture, tradition, experience, and culture in light of Christian faith. And if having done so, the Church finds that human sexual expression is only sacred in marriage—as Hays suggests, "there are two possible ways for God's human sexual creatures to live well-ordered lives of faithful discipleship: heterosexual marriage and sexual abstinence"[71]—then we shall at least know why.

Certainly, the time has come for the Black Church to give attention to the issue of sexuality in the 21st century. The culture in which we exist today is extremely different from that which existed during the formative days of Christianity. There is an alternative to the ascetic lifestyle promoted by those dedicated to monastic life and the other Christian influencers who adopted and promoted celibacy as the ultimate calling of God. African Americans need to return to their African heritage that believes in the goodness of God and all of His creation; a heritage that values children and views sexual expression as a spiritual gift from God and not something evil needing to be suppressed. For Africans, as well as the Hebrews of antiquity, children outside of wedlock was not the great calamity: the calamity was barrenness.[72] If we take a look at slavery in this country, we notice that the enslaved populations did not harbor the same "hypocritical" condemnation of sexual activity prior to marriage or for children born outside of wedlock as did White society. How could they, when the access that White society had to Black bodies during the antebellum period mitigated against such a strict code of morality in relation to sexual matters?[73] And where were White societies' strict Christian morals when they were engaging in the sexual exploitation of Blacks? Where was the condemnation of the Christian Church when sex crimes were being committed against the enslaved?

Surely, the moral sin of fornication was overlooked when White society realized they could gain economic power from the impregnation and creation of as many slave children as possible. Where was the moral Christian Church when the perversities of White society was thrust upon the vulnerable enslaved Africans? Once freed, why did African Americans chose to adopt the very practices and traditions of the oppressor? Many of the African cultures from which the enslaved came from did not ostracize humanity for having engaged in premarital sexual activity, nor for having children outside of marriage. In some African cultures, premarital sex was institutionalized after the onset of puberty.[74] Sex seen as dirty is a European construct, not an African one as so eloquently stated by Douglas:

> Because Africans so highly valued children, they could neither conceive of the European concept of celibacy nor, like the European, regard sexual intercourse as dirty, evil, or sinful. Puberty rites in West Africa, for instance, were either preceded or followed by training of the young in their sexual responsibilities.[75]

It should be noted that while premarital sexual activity was acceptable in some African cultures, extramarital sex was generally forbidden. Most often, couples were bound together only by affection as was the case for a lot of enslaved Africans in this country. And as Robert Staples points out "These bonds were just as strong, even when there was no legal marriage."[76]

Historically in the U.S., church membership has played a regulatory role in sexual behavior. For Blacks, after joining the Church, the enslaved and former enslaved women were expected to refrain from premarital intercourse and were censured and castigated if they did not. The literature of the enslaved says very little about the expectations of the male's sexual behavior once he joined the Church, thus reflecting the gender bias that still exists today. Some scholars feel that the enslaved Africans adopted the strict sexual ethics of the White society in response to the stereotypes that suggested Black people were nothing but lascivious wanton creatures.[77] It is time for the Black Church to take a fresh look at sexuality with less emphasis on what White society says and place more emphasis on what God says through the love and compassion of Jesus Christ. In conclusion, I concur with Kelly Brown Douglas:

> The Black Church and community must engage in a sexual discourse of resistance that empowers Black women and men to celebrate and to love their Black embodied selves. Such a discourse would help Black people distinguish who they are from what White culture suggests of them. It would help them name the pain of White culture's racialized sexual humiliation so that they could move on to a place of healing and regard for their body-selves.[78]

As we consider a new hermeneutic for 1 Thess. 4:3—*"For this is the will of God, your sanctification: that you abstain from fornication"*—I am convinced that it is not God's intent that this Scripture be used to condemn sexual expression outside of marriage, but this is to serve as exhortation and instruction for those who freely chose to live an ascetic life. For we know from experience, Scripture, and tradition that God is not a God of condemnation, but He is a God of love and compassion.

Discussion Questions

1 Why has outlawing sex outside of marriage failed miserably in Christian history?
2 How do Christian and non-Christian views on sex in antiquity influence our current cultural milieu?
3 How do many Christian churches use biblical texts to repress the sexual desires of mature, unmarried individuals, particularly women in our society?
4 Why are African American women particularly impacted by Christian doctrine on sex outside of marriage?

Suggested Readings

1 Byron, Gay L., *Symbolic Blackness and Ethnic Difference in Early Christian Literature*, New York: Routledge, 2002.
2 Douglas, Kelly Brown, *Sexuality and the Black Church: A Womanist Perspective*, Maryknoll, NY: Orbis Books, 2004.
3 Spong, John Shelby, *Living in Sin: A Bishop Rethinks Human Sexuality*, San Francisco, CA: Harper & Row Publishers, 1988.

Notes

1 Roberts, Sam, "Most Women Now Live Without a Husband," *New York Times*, January 16, 2007, pp. 1–4.
2 Copen, Casey, Daniels, Kimberly, Vespa, Jonathan, and Mosher, William, "First Marriages in the United States: Data from the 2006–2010 National Survey of Family Growth", *National Health Statistics Reports*, Number 49, March 22, 2012, p. 5.
3 Kinnon, Joy Bennett, "The Shocking State of Black Marriage: Experts Say Many Will Never Get Married," *Ebony*, November 2003, p. 1.
4 Boothe, Demico, *Why Are So Many Black Men In Prison? A Comprehensive Account Of How And Why The Prison Industry Has Become A Predatory Entity In The Lives Of African-American Men*, Full Surface Publishing, February 8, 2007, Introduction.
5 Robinson, Fatimah H., "Marriage and Black America: A Crisis of Commitment," *BustedHalo.com*, June 13, 2006, p. 2.
6 Roberts, "Most Women Now Live Without a Husband."
7 Ibid., p. 3.
8 Ibid.
9 Ibid.
10 Ibid.

11 Butterick, George Arthur, *The Interpreter's Dictionary of the Bible: An Illustrated Encyclopedia Volume 2*, Nashville, TN: Abingdon Press, 1962, p. 321.

12 Spong, John Shelby, *Living in Sin: A Bishop Rethinks Human Sexuality*, San Francisco, CA: Harper & Row Publishers, 1988, p. 214.

13 Brown, Michael Joseph, *Blackening of the Bible: The Aims of African American Biblical Scholarship*, Harrisburg, PA: Trinity Press International, 2004, p. 3.

14 Douglas, Kelly Brown, *Sexuality and the Black Church: A Womanist Perspective*, Maryknoll, NY: Orbis Books, 2004, p. 128.

15 Smith, Abraham, "The First Letter to the Thessalonians," *The New Interpreter's Bible Volume XI*, Nashville, TN: Abingdon Press, 2000, pp. 677–678.

16 Wall, Robert W., "The Jerusalem Council: The Verdict of James," *The New Interpreter's Bible Volume X*, Nashville, TN: Abingdon Press, 2002, pp. 217–218.

17 Harris, Stephen L., *The New Testament: A Student's Introduction*, Sacramento, CA: McGraw Hill Companies, Inc., 2002, p. 316.

18 Felder, Cain Hope, "The African American New Testament Commentary: 1 and 2 Thessalonians," in Brian K. Blount et al. (eds.), *True to Our Native Land*, Philadelphia, PA: Fortress Press, 2007, p. 18.

19 Smith, "The First Letter to the Thessalonians," p. 716.

20 Felder, "The African American New Testament Commentary: 1 and 2 Thessalonians," p. 18.

21 Smith, "The First Letter to the Thessalonians," pp. 716–720.

22 Felder, "The African American New Testament Commentary: 1 and 2 Thessalonians," p. 18.

23 Ibid., pp. 18–19.

24 Wall, "The Jerusalem Council," p. 220.

25 Ibid.,

26 Boring, Eugene, M., "Life in the Eschatological Community: The Law," *The New Interpreter's Bible Volume VIII*, (Nashville: Abingdon Press, 1995), pp. 188–198.

27 Butterick, *The Interpreter's Dictionary of the Bible*, p. 321.

28 Phipps, William E., *Was Jesus Married: The Distortion of Sexuality in the Christian Tradition*, (New York: Harper & Row Publishers, 1970), p. 118.

29 Ibid.

30 Mace, David R., *The Christian Response to the Sexual Revolution*, Nashville, TN: Abingdon Press, 1970, pp. 18–20.

31 Ibid., p. 65.

32 Ibid.

33 Douglas, *Sexuality and the Black Church*, pp. 25–26.

34 Mace, *The Christian Response to the Sexual Revolution*, pp. 14–22.

35 Byron, Gay L., *Symbolic Blackness and Ethnic Difference in Early Christian Literature*, (New York: Routledge, 2002), p. 92.

36 Ibid., p. 94.

37 Ibid., p. 103.

38 Mace, *The Christian Response to the Sexual Revolution*, pp. 46–50.

39 Douglas, *Sexuality and the Black Church*, p. 26.

40 Dedek, John F., "Premarital Sex: The Theological Argument From Peter Lombard to Durand", *Theological Studies*, 41 D, 1980, p. 653.

41 Ibid., pp. 654–660.

42 Mace, *The Christian Response to the Sexual Revolution*, pp. 51–53.

43 Ibid., p. 53.

44 Ibid., p. 63.

45 Douglas, *Sexuality and the Black Church*, p. 26.

46 Mace, *The Christian Response to the Sexual Revolution*, p. 62.

47 Douglas, *Sexuality and the Black Church*, p. 27.

48 Nelson, James B., *Embodiment: An Approach to Sexuality and Christian Theology*, Minneapolis, MN: Augsburg Publishing House, 1978, p. 46.
49 Douglas, *Sexuality and the Black Church*, pp. 27–28.
50 Byron, *Symbolic Blackness and Ethnic Difference*, p. 78.
51 Ibid., pp. 85–103.
52 Douglas, *Sexuality and the Black Church*, p. 27.
53 Ibid., p. 28.
54 Wartenberg, Thomas E., Wilson, *The Forms of Power: From Domination to Transformation*, Philadelphia, PA: Temple Press, 1990, p. 132.
55 Mace, *The Christian Response to the Sexual Revolution*, p. 116.
56 Rosenau, Douglas E., "Single and Sexual: The Church's Neglected Dilemma", *Journal of Psychology and Theology*, 2002, Volume 30, No. 3, p. 188.
57 Spong, *Living in Sin*, pp. 210–218.
58 Kinney, John W., "An Answer for X," Howard University Andrew Rankin Memorial Chapel, February 11, 2007.
59 Douglas, *Sexuality and the Black Church*, p. 114.
60 Mace, *The Christian Response to the Sexual Revolution*, pp. 90–120.
61 Hays, Richard B., *The Moral Vision of the New Testament: Community, Cross, New Creation; A Contemporary Introduction to New Testament Ethics*, San Francisco, CA: Harper Collins, 1996, pp. 399–400.
62 Ibid., p. 401.
63 Ibid.
64 Ibid., pp. 401–402.
65 Hays, *The Moral Vision of the New Testament*, p. 402.
66 Ibid.
67 Ibid.
68 Ibid., p. 403.
69 Douglas, *Sexuality and the Black Church*, p. 84.
70 Ibid., pp. 90–91.
71 Hays, *The Moral Vision of the New Testament*, p. 402.
72 Ibid., p. 65.
73 Ibid., pp. 63–67.
74 Ibid. p. 65.
75 Ibid.
76 Ibid., p. 66.
77 Ibid., pp. 60–88.
78 Ibid., p. 75.

References

Boothe, Demico, *Why Are So Many Black Men In Prison? A Comprehensive Account Of How And Why The Prison Industry Has Become A Predatory Entity In The Lives Of African-American Men*, New York: Full Surface Publishing, February 8, 2007.

Boring, Eugene M., "Life in the Eschatological Community: The Law," *The New Interpreter's Bible Volume VIII*, Nashville, TN: Abingdon Press, 1995.

Brown, Michael Joseph, *Blackening of the Bible: The Aims of African American Biblical Scholarship*, Harrisburg, PA: Trinity Press International, 2004.

Butterick, George Arthur, *The Interpreter's Dictionary of the Bible: An Illustrated Encyclopedia Volume 2*, Nashville, TN: Abingdon Press, 1962.

Byron, Gay L., *Symbolic Blackness and Ethnic Difference in Early Christian Literature*, New York: Routledge, 2002.

Copen, Casey, Daniels, Kimberly, Vespa, Jonathan, and Mosher, William, "First Marriages in the United States: Data from the 2006–2010 National Survey of Family Growth," *National Health Statistics Reports*, Number 49, March 22, 2012.

Dedek, John F., "Premarital Sex: The Theological Argument From Peter Lombard to Durand," *Theological Studies*, 41 D, 1980.

Douglas, Kelly Brown, *Sexuality and the Black Church: A Womanist Perspective*, Maryknoll, NY: Orbis Books, 2004.

Felder, Cain Hope, *Troubling Biblical Waters: Race, Class, and Family*, Maryknoll, NY: Orbis Books, 1990.

Felder, Cain Hope, "The African American New Testament Commentary: 1 and 2 Thessalonians," in Brian K. Blount et al. (eds.), *True to Our Native Land*, Philadelphia, PA: Fortress Press, 2007.

Harris, Stephen L., *The New Testament: A Student's Introduction*, Sacramento, CA: McGraw Hill Companies, Inc., 2002.

Hays, Richard B., *The Moral Vision of the New Testament: Community, Cross, New Creation; A Contemporary Introduction to New Testament Ethics*, San Francisco, CA: Harper Collins, 1996.

Kinney, John W., "An Answer for X," Howard University Andrew Rankin Memorial Chapel, February 11, 2007.

Kinnon, Joy Bennett, "The Shocking State of Black Marriage: Experts Say Many Will Never Get Married," *Ebony*, November 2003.

Mace, David R., *The Christian Response to the Sexual Revolution*, Nashville, TN: Abingdon Press, 1970.

Nelson, James B., *Embodiment: An Approach to Sexuality and Christian Theology*, Minneapolis, MN: Augsburg Publishing House, 1978.

Phipps, William E., *Was Jesus Married: The Distortion of Sexuality in the Christian Tradition*, New York: Harper & Row Publishers, 1970.

Robinson, Fatimah H., "Marriage and Black America: A Crisis of Commitment," *BustedHalo.com*, June 13, 2006.

Roberts, Sam, "Most Women Now Live Without a Husband," *New York Times*, January 16, 2007.

Rosenau, Douglas E., "Single and Sexual: The Church's Neglected Dilemma," *Journal of Psychology and Theology*, 2002, Volume 30, No. 3, 185–194.

Smith, Abraham, "The First Letter to the Thessalonians," *The New Interpreter's Bible Volume XI*, Nashville, TN: Abingdon Press, 2000.

Spong, John Shelby, *Living in Sin: A Bishop Rethinks Human Sexuality*, San Francisco, CA: Harper & Row Publishers, 1988.

Wall, Robert W., "The Jerusalem Council: The Verdict of James," *The New Interpreter's Bible Volume X*, Nashville, TN: Abingdon Press, 2002.

Wartenberg, Thomas E., Wilson, *The Forms of Power: From Domination to Transformation*, Philadelphia, PA: Temple Press, 1990.

14

SEX WORK

Free and Equal?

Sarah V. Suiter

Introduction

"What's freedom for me? It's going back, reliving those deep dark secrets that I said that I was going to take to my grave. Freedom is letting somebody else know that they are not the only one who has done something, or has been in places that you told yourself that you never wanted to go . . . Freedom is allowing somebody to see the struggle that you went through, and allowing them not to be able to live in the pit of hell. Freedom is knowing that, when I have been wrong, God loves me anyway. That's what freedom is to me."

(Lydia, Magdalene Graduate)

". . . where freedom comes from and where it begins, I don't know . . . but freedom to me means freedom to make your own choices in the world . . . freedom to live how you want to live. Freedom from drugs, freedom from having to buy and sell your body, freedom from verbal or emotional abuse from *anybody* . . . you're free to walk away from it . . . free to walk toward whatever you want to walk toward. I think that includes, you know, freedom from oppression by authority—whether it's judicial authority or church authority or whatever—that hasn't served you well. You're free to walk away from that. But also freedom to *be* . . . to be who you are . . . who you were created to be . . . ."

(Becca, Founder of Magdalene House)

"I think you can be in a prison without being in a prison . . . without being in a physical prison, and . . . that's what I was. I was in my own prison. Isolation, and . . . you know, just living a lie. Freedom to me today is being able to get up every day and do things with no guilt . . . I am who I am today, and I'm proud of who I am today. And I'm proud of where I came from."

(Evelyn, Magdalene Graduate)

These words were spoken by women who live, work, and participate in Nashville's Magdalene House, a recovery community for women with criminal histories of drug abuse and prostitution. Since opening its doors in 1997, Magdalene has served over a hundred women by providing them with a place to live, rent-free, for two years, along with free health care, mental health care, recovery support, education, and job skills training. The rates of recovery for women who stay at Magdalene House far surpass the rates of other recovery programs, and the personal stories of healing and recovery that are told by women, staff, and volunteers alike are tremendous. If you ask members of the Magdalene community about the purposes of their work, "women's freedom" is sure to come at the top of the list.

Though this community is something of a local icon, their views on prostitution and approach to women's freedom do not go uncontested. The topic of prostitution is one that carries a considerable amount of force, and more than its fair share of clichés. Some proclaim that "prostitution is the oldest profession," and others note "nothing divides feminism like prostitution." Though both are, perhaps, overstatements, they convey the magnitude of the historical, economic, political, and ideological debates around the practice of trading sex for money. Sex work is a topic that garners considerable attention because it is, well, sexy, but also because it engages multiple other debates that persist as some of the great questions of personhood and society: questions of gender, sexuality, masculinity, and femininity, and how these constructs relate to questions of autonomy and freedom.

Although definitions and concrete understandings of "freedom" remain somewhat illusive to scholars and activists alike, most would agree that the oppression that occurs through hierarchies based on gender, race, class, and sexuality are particularly detrimental to the freedom of individuals and the families and communities that surround them. To the extent that these systems of oppression influence the distribution of material resources (Sen 1999), access to physical and psychological wellness and security (Nussbaum 2000), and power and control in personal relationships (Tronto 1993; Hirschmann 2003), they restrict individual freedom. This is not to say that individuals that are constrained by these hierarchies are necessarily and totally unfree (indeed, we are all constrained by such systems to some extent, and indeed, we are all complicit in them), but rather that the freedom to pursue the type of life that one might deem "worth living" is restricted (Hirschman 2003; Nussbaum 2000; Sen 1999). It is not difficult to recall groups of people that have historically experienced great degrees of unfreedom—slaves, prisoners, and people who have been denied basic rights based on certain qualities of their person (such as gender, race, sexuality, religious affiliation, nationality, to name a few). While it is popular to say that such people have been excluded or removed from society, upon careful examination, it seems more accurate to say that they are, in fact, integral to society, but suffer unfreedom because of the way they have been integrated (Hirschmann 2003). Using this approach, it is possible to extend the interrogation of unfreedom to others who occupy a somewhat restricted and precarious social position due to the nature of their life experiences. Such an interrogation serves to uncover the many forces that work to support and/or restrict human freedom, and has the potential to offer an understanding of freedom that is grounded in lived experience rather than immaterial ideals (Mills 2005). The purpose of this chapter is to explore current debates around sex work as they relate to sexuality, inequality, and freedom. The lenses of three feminist political theories of freedom are applied to attempt to understand the ways in which inequalities related to gender, race, class, and sexuality express and perpetuate themselves for women who trade sex for money.

Defining Prostitution

Sex work has been loosely defined to encompass multiple forms of erotic labor, ranging from phone sex workers to dancers to street-walking prostitutes to call girls. O'Neill (2001) cites Nicholson, who offers a typology of prostitution existing in large cities:

> call services, both agency and private individuals; female streetwalkers who work for themselves; female streetwalkers who work for pimps; amateur streetwalkers who hustle part-time for themselves or boyfriends or partners; boy street-hustlers; weekenders working for excitement or enough money to party for the weekend; professional hustlers between the ages of 19 and 22 who have been working for a couple of years and who may be involved in pornography; survivors under the age of 18, boys and girls who have run away or who have simply been 'pushed out,' who lack education, work skills, skills needed for independent living; survivors under the age of 14.
>
> (Nicholson, in O'Neill 2001: 100)

More recent definitions of sex work have included people who are trafficked in the sex trade, as well as more performance-based varieties of sex work including window dancing, stripping, and escort services (O'Neill 2001). These definitions have also been expanded to embrace the growing number of men involved in the trade; however, these men still represent a significant minority (Vanwesenbeeck 2001). In general, prostitution involves male clients paying female sex workers in exchange for sexual services. There are significant benefits to defining sex work in an inclusive enough fashion that we are able to see the connections between these somewhat different types of work. In terms of political organizing in particular, the ability to talk about sex work under one umbrella has important implications. The broad definition can also be a disadvantage, however. Notably, there are meaningful differences between vocalizing sexual scenarios over the phone to someone who cannot identify you nor do you ever have to see, and walking the streets, hoping to be picked up by some man who is willing to pay a few dollars for illicit sex in the back of his car. For the purposes of this chapter, I will use the terms "sex work" and "prostitution" interchangeably, knowing that there are political and social meanings attached to each, and focus mainly on a limited spectrum of sex work that involves women providing physical sexual services to men who pay them. Additionally, I will purposefully avoid the topic of trafficking, though I discuss sex-work advocacy in international contexts. Trafficking is, indeed, an important aspect of the debate around sex work and its practice. However, a responsibly nuanced treatment of trafficking is beyond the scope of this chapter, so I have opted to exclude it altogether.

Due to the transient nature of the sex-work population, sex-work's illegal status in many parts of the world, and the broad array of activities that fit under any definition of sex work, it is difficult to quantify the number of people who are involved. However, best estimates range from relatively small percentages of the female population (such as 0.1% in Denmark) to much larger percentages (such as 8.7% in Nigeria) (Vandepitteet al. 2006).

Debates About Sex Work: Choice and Freedom

Although some women disagree that "choice" and freedom are fruitful ideals around which to organize debates about sex work, most see freedom and choice as the crux of the argument (Chapkis 1997). The debates about sex work often turn around the axes of what constitutes "freedom" for women in the context of sexual relationships, in working arrangements, and in the processes of identity and representation. We would be hard-pressed to find any sane person willing to argue that involvement in sex work under conditions of overt coercion is legitimate. What is less clear, and more frequently disputed, however, are the far more prevalent situations in which "coercion" is embedded in overarching social, economic, and political inequalities that shape the contexts of our lives and influence our formations of selfhood.

With this in mind, it is important to recognize that debates about freedom that rely on ideal notions of "free" and "unfree" are not particularly useful because no one is ever truly and totally unrestrained, internally or externally. Indeed, multiple forms of oppression and domination are operating at all times and in multiple ways on the basis of race, class, and gender, on men as well as women, and on some women more than others. The more important questions, then, seem to be about what contexts allow people to be more or less free? What are the conditions of freedom? In order to explore these questions, I will outline some of the debates around sex work, emphasizing the questions of freedom raised by each. After discussing the debates around sex work, I will then turn to three different theories of freedom proposed by feminist scholars in order to better understand the concept of freedom, and the conditions that make it possible.

Freedom in the Context of Sexual Relationships

Scholars and activists who argue that sex work is exploitation generally argue from a radical feminist perspective that views heterosexual sex as a location of inequality between men and women (Chapkis 1997; Vanwesenbeeck 2001). Feminists who espouse this position often see all sex as exploitive, and prostitution as especially so. They see involvement in sex work a result of material conditions that have forced women to choose to sell their bodies for sex, and prostitution as a result of worldwide trends in sexist oppression that make the buying and selling of women a socially and culturally viable option (Pateman 1988). Feminists in this tradition are generally critical of other arrangements in which heterosexual sex plays a role in a woman's relationship with a male partner. In her book, *The Sexual Contract*, Pateman (1988) demonstrates the ways in which marriage limits women's freedom more so than men's based on the very nature of the arrangement. For Pateman, a marriage in which both partners are equally free is impossible because institutions that have been created by a society founded upon patriarchy always disadvantage women. Additionally, she sees prostitution as uniquely exploitative because it requires a person to sell his or her body, not just a service. This perspective recalls Audre Lorde who later claimed, "selling oneself—alienates the unalienable" (Lorde 1991: 153).

Lorde brings us to another anti-prostitution feminist perspective that advocates sex (within certain boundaries), however it requires that sex involve intimacy (or at the very least, pleasure) in order to be considered "sex" rather than "abuse." From this perspective, sex can be positive when it is an expression of love, intimacy, or pleasure for both (or multiple) parties. It is negative when it is violent, anonymous, or representative of objectification (Chapkis 1997). While there are many people other than sex-positive feminists who would agree with these qualifiers for positive and negative sex, they are of particular interest to feminists because in scenarios of negative sex, women are typically the recipients of violence and the objectified party. Central to these notions of positive sex is the idea of relational reciprocity, a practice that must be established through trust and sharing (Chapkis 1997). In this context, money and contract are markers of exploitation rather than mutual exchange.

In opposition to the view that sees sex work as exploitation, many others, both within the sex trade and outside it, view sex work as a legitimate expression of sexuality, and argue that it should be treated as such. Organizations such as COYOTE (standing for "Call Off Your Old Tired Ethics") claim that sex workers are skilled practitioners, exercising and enjoying their own sexuality and providing a service to willing customers. Some participants report feelings of accomplishment and acceptance as a result of their work in the sex trade, and note the differences between standards of beauty and behavior that are experienced as unattainable in mainstream society versus more fluid and affirming standards that exist in some sectors of the sex industry (Chapkis 1997; Nagle 1997). Perhaps most important, feminists in this tradition are opposed to the illegal status of sex work because they see it as yet another attempt for a patriarchal legal system to control women's sexuality (Chapkis 1997; Rubin 1984).

Other theorists advocate a view of sex and sexuality that emphasizes that sex is often both exchange-based and intimacy- or pleasure-based. Central to this perspective is the idea that there are many forms of sexual arrangements that are technically exchange-based but are sanctioned as intimate by the very social norms that work to condemn prostitution. A colleague recently recounted an interview in which she asked a college-aged male informant, "Have you ever exchanged money for sex?" to which he replied, "Does dinner and a movie count?"

Well-regarded feminists throughout history have drawn comparisons between marriage and prostitution, arguing that the two have more in common than not. Mary Wollstonecraft (1983) called marriage "legal prostitution" in 1790, and as Simone de Beauvoir so famously wrote:

> the wife is hired for life by one man; the prostitute has several clients who pay her by the piece. The one is protected by one male against all the others; the other is defended by all against the exclusive tyranny of each.
>
> (1974: 619)

It is important to emphasize that none of these women were arguing for prostitution as a just or desirable relationship for women so much as they were arguing against the idea of marriage as such—prostitution served used as a proxy for the exploitation of women. Additionally, the economic and political situation of women has changed considerably since the times of Mary Wollstonecraft and Simone de Beauvoir, and women (typically) have more economic and political power than they did at the turn of the 18th century. However, it does help us to see the ways in which society works to sanction some things and not others, even when such things are, according to some, quite similar.

Despite the theoretical speculation and thought experiments illustrating the connections between prostitution and other sexual practices, empirical research on the topic demonstrates that women themselves generally do draw differences. Women involved in prostitution make clear distinctions between "sex at work" and sex in which they engage for the purposes of intimacy and pleasure (Chapkis 1997; Nagle 1997). Furthermore, many sex workers report a great degree of effort that goes into developing physical and psychological strategies to maintain the separation between the two (Delacoste and Alexander 1998; Sterk et al. 2000). For example, indoor sex workers in a qualitative study conducted by Sanders and Campbell (2007) reported that they require their clients to wear condoms, but dissuade their romantic partners from doing so as a means of separating "work and pleasure." Researchers who suggest that this distinction is less clear report that the line is most blurry for women in the most need. Often, for women without income or shelter, every relationship represents an opportunity to make money or get off the streets (Mulia 2002).

Theorists who work on sexuality have demonstrated rather convincingly that sexuality is socially constructed and contextually dependent rather than relying on purely natural "drives." Others have extended this theory to show how hierarchies based on gender-based oppression and domination influence sexuality (Hartsock 1996), and how hierarchies of appropriate sexualities influence what is deemed "desirable" (Rubin 1984). According to pro-sex activist and scholar Gayle Rubin, there exists a "hierarchical system of sexual value" (1984: 279), in which sexual behaviors are arranged based on their social acceptability. At the top of the hierarchy are sexual behaviors and arrangements deemed "good," such as heterosexuality, monogamy, marriage, and procreation. In the middle of the hierarchy are "major areas of contest," such as promiscuous heterosexual sex, homosexual sex, and sex involving more than two partners. At the bottom of the hierarchy are sexual behaviors deemed "bad," "abnormal," or "unnatural," and include behaviors such as sadomasochism and sex for money. According to Rubin, the problem with the system of sexual value (as with any hierarchical system) is that people at the top are treated differently than people at the bottom. For example, she demonstrates how this hierarchy influences laws about the proper boundaries of sex, and how these laws in turn influence the ways in which individuals are treated in terms of mental health diagnoses, access to economic opportunities, and legal protection. While some would argue that exchanging sex for money is in fact "bad" sex, the notion of the hierarchy combined with knowledge about why some women enter sex work demonstrates that dominant beliefs held about sex workers generally work to push already marginalized people even more to the fringe.

Neither women who think sex work is exploitation nor women who think sex work is liberatory would concede that the current sexual order is a site of freedom and equality for women. Rather, what is emphasized in the debates about freedom in the context of sexual relationships is that, depending on beliefs about sexuality, some women see sex work as exploitation, and others see sex work as an act of subversion. These debates lead us to questions of freedom such as: What kinds of contexts support women's ability to make meaningful choices in the context of sexual relationships? What kinds of relationships and contexts allow women to maintain control over their own bodies and their own sexuality?

Freedom in the Context of Work

Despite their beliefs about the nature of sex work, women overwhelmingly report economic pressures as the reason they entered the sex trade (Chapkis 1997; Mulia 2002; Vanwesenbeeck 2001). Whether they are graduate students dancing at a strip club in order to earn money to supplement their living expenses, or women selling sex on the streets in order to support their families, women see erotic labor as an opportunity to earn fast and much-needed cash. Indeed, in some communities, engagement in prostitution is viewed as the most desperate response to dire economic situations, and symbolizes "how bad" things have become (Durr 2005).

Alternatively, many women indicate that sex work is the most interesting and viable employment option available (Petro 2007), and though it may be far from utopia, it is preferable to other opportunities such as cleaning houses (Chua et al. 2000) or performing secretarial work (Chapkis 1997). Still others take the position that sex work is not a desirable occupation; however, it is the work that is available to them, and as such, the fact that they are "working" should be respected. While people who report this experience are more likely to endorse their involvement in sex work as economically coerced, they are often resistant to the idea that they are without agency. For these women, sex work is a site of resistance (Chapkis 1997; Chua et al. 2000; Kempadoo and Doezma 1998) and is an active response to marginalizing economic structures.

Central to the argument that sex work is work is the emphasis on similarities between sex work and other forms of employment (Nussbaum 1999). Sex workers draw parallels between sex work and other types of work in which one's body is one's economic vehicle (professional athletes) or one's services are one's commodity (nursing, for example, or other types of care work). That these two conceptualizations of work are also gendered only helps to bolster this analysis, and sex workers argue that the same types of professional standards and protections that are used to guarantee the rights and safety of these workers should be extended to the field of sex work (Chapkis 1997; Nagle 1997). While this is a compelling argument, it relies on surrender to a capitalist world where economic exchange is the mark of all things "standard" or "normal." Others point out that, ideally, a more fruitful argument might be advocacy for a world in which fewer, rather than more, things are for sale (Singh and Hart 2007).

Of particular concern to activists on all sides of the debate are the substandard work environments that sex workers endure as part of their occupation. Multiple studies of sex workers in various locations around the world demonstrate that working conditions make women particularly vulnerable to physical and sexual violence on the job (Sanders and Campbell 2007). Researcher estimates report anywhere from 50% to 100% of street-based sex workers in their samples had experienced violence (Sanders and

Campbell 2007). In addition to physical and sexual abuse, the women also fall victim to what some have termed "economic abuse": being robbed, not being paid, or being paid less than the previously agreed upon price for services (Sanders and Campbell 2007). Ward et al. (1999) report that street-based sex workers in the U.K. are over ten times more likely to die from violence at work than other women their age, and Kinnell (2006) reported that 86 sex workers were murdered in the U.K. from 1995 to 2005. According to Goodyear and Cusick (2007: 52), "standardized mortality rates for sex workers are six times those seen in the general population . . . the highest for any group of women. Death and violence are but a part of a spectrum of physical and emotional morbidity endured." Theorists who believe that violence is inherent to sex work identify prostitution itself as the cause for such violence. Others point to stigma, poverty, general violence of the streets, and the clandestine nature of street-based sex work as the reasons that women are abused. Research on indoor sex work demonstrates that moving sex work indoors and into a regulated environment does make it safer; however, violence persists.

When it comes to sex work performed in brothels, experiences of violence are considerably less, though they still exist, depending largely on the venue and the methods of regulation practiced by venue owners and local governments (Sanders and Campbell 2007; Vanwesenbeeck 2001). More often than violent physical or sexual attacks, women in indoor venues reported "nuisances" such as clients attempting non-negotiated sex acts, removing or attempting to remove their condoms, and offensive language and rude behavior (Chapkis 1997; Sanders and Campbell 2007). Women in indoor venues report similar economic abuse to that experienced by women on the streets (Chapkis 1997); however, these incidents (particularly robbery) tend to be less frequent (Sanders and Campbell 2007). While some attribute the differences in violence experienced by street-based sex workers and brothel sex workers to differences in the type of client, most attribute differences to the more controlled environment of the brothels (Nagle 1997). Indoor venues have more options for surveillance such as security cameras, and many indoor sex workers say that their relationships with coworkers offer security. Sanders and Campbell (2007) found that collective commitment to safety was embedded in the "culture" of the brothel they studied. Theoretically, women who work in indoor venues have more legal recourse against potential perpetrators in places where sex work is illegal (Vanwesenbeeck 2001; Chapkis 1997); however, this often fails to be the case (Thukral 2005).

That the conditions surrounding sex work are often dangerous and abusive is not up for contention. Rather, ideas regarding the cause of these conditions and what should be done about them are. Women who see sex work as exploitation believe that there is no practice of sex work that is not abusive. While improving working conditions for sex work would somewhat improve the situations of women involved in prostitution, it would also sanction a practice that is believed to be abusive, exploitative, and inherently "bad" for women. For others, the conditions of sex work are created by the stigma and illegal nature of the practice, not by the practice itself. From this perspective, the correct approach to prostitution is one that ensures a safe working environment and workers' rights.

On the surface, this debate proposes questions of freedom that engage the ways in which one's work environment and legal recognition and protection of such environment provides a context in which workers are more or less free: free to be safe, free to practice their profession without incurring harm by others, free to choose the type of work they define as desirable. The debate also indicates that a clear component of freedom is an environment in which women are not coerced to choose sex work out of situations of economic desperation. Perhaps more interestingly, however, this debate illustrates the ways in which capitalism has permeated our beliefs about morality. While prostitution is certainly not a solely capitalist institution, it is clear that capitalism provides the tools in which activists work to justify or negate the moral acceptability of sex work. In turn, the link to morality demonstrates the ways in which beliefs about morality influence our ideas of who should and should not have access to freedom.

Freedom in the Context of Representation and Identity

Particularly confusing to scholarship in the field of sex work is the large degree of disparity among experiences of women who participate: For women who work in high-end venues, their work environment affords a considerable degree of control over their interactions with their clients (Nagle 1997). Depending on the terms of the establishment, women can theoretically refuse men that they deem undesirable, and require appropriate protection when interacting with men they do (Chapkis 1997; Nagle 1997). This is not the case, however, for women who are involved in street prostitution—theirs is typically a world of violence and abuse, in which they have little control over who they see or how they service them (Nadon et al. 1998; Surratt et al. 2004). It is worth questioning, therefore, whether or not the category of prostitution is not itself a problematic one—one which makes invisible the vast disparities based on income, race, status, and mental health that exist under the single trope of "prostitution."

Furthermore, it is worth asking what the advocacy of one group does for the plight of another. When well-educated, upper-class call girls write essays in published anthologies glorifying sex work as a liberatory practice, does it do damage to the legitimacy of the voice of a woman working on the streets who claims her life is hell? Likewise, when women make claims that sex work is always abusive and exploitative, does it make victims out of women who would not identify themselves as such? Does it stigmatize the hard work of women who are participating in an industry that they enjoy?

The debate over representation is pervasive throughout the battle over the legitimacy of sex work. Sex-work advocates vehemently oppose images of sex work as a result of child abuse, drug addiction, sexual deviance, or sexual exploitation (Delacoste and Alexander 1998; Nagle 1997; Vanwesenbeeck 2001). Similarly, women who have experienced sex work as sexual exploitation voice frustration over activism that promotes sex work as a desirable arrangement (O'Neill 2001). A sex worker interviewed by Wendy Chapkis (1997: 127) claimed, "Maybe what they [pro-sex-work activists] were doing was glamorous. But they acted like their experience spoke for us all. Well, for the people in my group, it was not glamour." The woman went on to say, however, that anti-prostitution activists also used sex workers as a trope to support their activism more than to help women who were being exploited:

There are others who say that prostitution is evil because it contributes to violence against women and they'll have their "Take Back the Night" marches right through the Red Light district without even dealing with the sex workers as other women . . . They just turn us into symbols.

(Chapkis 1997: 127)

Likewise, racialized representations influence beliefs about sexuality and therefore the identities of sex workers themselves. As discussed earlier, the more nuanced accounts of women's sexuality (and by extension, prostitution) emphasize that sexuality is not a unified or independent dimension of human existence. Like everything else, it contains contradictions, particularities, and influences and is influenced by multiple other factors (Gonzalez-Lopez 2005).

The hierarchy within sex work is attributable to more than indoor/outdoor distinctions and image management. Rather, it is indicative of long-existing racist and classist beliefs that are as pervasive as the patriarchy that women claim to be fighting. For example, images and expectations of women's sexuality differ greatly on the basis of race. White women are expected to be pure, submissive, and domestic (Collins 1991), while images of Black women require sexuality that is aggressive and permissive (Collins 1991; Roberts 2000). Referencing Patricia Hill Collins (1991) and Carolyn West (1996), Roberts (2000: 904) states, "Black women have been portrayed by four controlling images: mammy, matriarch, welfare mother, and jezebel. These images work to make racism, sexism, and poverty appear to be natural, normal, and an inevitable part of everyday life for African American women." Accounts of ethnic minority sex workers confirm this statement holds in the context of sex work. Women interviewed by Nagle (1997) reported that the men who sought services in the brothel in which they worked used race a deciding factor depending on what type of experience they were seeking. For example, they reported men often chose them when they were looking for someone "exotic" or "dirty," and chose White women when they were looking for someone "classy." Furthermore, indoor female sex workers of color described being paid less than White women for similar services, because the brothel owners claimed that White women were more desirable, and therefore generated more "demand" (Chapkis 1997).

These images do more than create inaccurate stereotypes—they influence women's own perceptions and boundaries of what they can do and be (Hirschmann 2003). These images—and the women they play a role in creating—are important to the field of sex work because it influences people's perceptions of women's involvement in the trade.

Research itself plays into images and representations of sex work and sex workers. According to pro-sex work activists, street prostitution is overstudied precisely because it fulfills our expectations of "prostitution." In other words, when people think of women involved in prostitution, they want to believe that all women experience the horrors of the streets, as opposed to believing that there are women in the world who exchange sex for money in safe, comfortable environments, and do it out of choice rather than desperation. While the argument that street prostitution is overstudied, or that the image of street prostitution is the prevailing image of women involved in sex work, is contested, there is growing consensus that the research conducted with women involved in street prostitution has worked to cast them as images rather than humans (Vanwesenbeeck 2001).

Mulia (2002) describes how research and programmatic emphasis on health concerns (particularly HIV) of drug-abusing women has resulted in essentializing these women as disease vectors and dangerous women. These misrepresentations are important for practical and ideological reasons: they influence the type of care (or punishment) the women incur, but also perpetuate deep-seated beliefs about the appropriate bounds of female sexuality and stand as justification for regulating it (Ringdal 1997). Beliefs about prostitutes as carriers of disease is not a new one, nor is the practice of developing regulatory guidelines based on gendered notions of sexuality and disease. History tells us that the concerns voiced by Mulia and others like her are not unfounded: in Great Britain during the 1800s, it was believed that only women could carry or transmit venereal diseases. As a result, women involved in prostitution could be picked up by law enforcement officials, forced to undergo medical examination, and institutionalized in the event that they were diagnosed. No such process existed for men who visited prostitutes (Pateman 1988; Ringdal 1997). While we now know that venereal disease can be and is carried and transmitted by men as well as women, mechanisms for preventing and controlling it continue to assign different expectations and responsibilities in terms of sexual practices (Pateman 1988).

Hirschmann's (2003) account of women's freedom requires us to pay attention to the very powerful role of language in constructing the material and political possibilities that exist for women's lives and choices. For Hirschmann, the way we talk about things constructs the available options for who women can be and how they can live. These ideas have tremendous importance for the field of sex work, because it helps us to see how activism and advocacy around a topic that has deep-seated historical meanings can play on existing images to silence other possibilities for the women involved (Brinson 2006). To be more specific, activities that work to promote solutions for women who wish to leave prostitution, or programs that support the physical and psychological needs of women who are engaged in prostitution may draw up long-standing images of women as people in need of protection and services, or women who have been duped into participating in their own exploitation. These images may work to silence or discredit the activism of women who have chosen sex work as their desired form of employment, and who resent images of victimhood or helplessness. Similarly, activism on the part of women who promote sex work as a viable and desirable choice for employment may work to silence the voices of women who have not chosen sex work, who have entered into it through dire circumstances, or who need and want assistance to leave. The questions of freedom posed by debates over identity and representation include ideas such as: How do representations of women work to limit their opportunities to create identities in which they are seen as humans as opposed to stereotypes? In an environment that often fails to recognize differences between women, how do women represent their own interests without silencing the interests of others? How do we create environments in which women are more free to voice their concerns without doing damage to other women? Similarly, in what ways do women participate in shaping the contexts of freedom?

Feminist Political Theories of Freedom

In light of the many questions of freedom presented by debates in the field of scholarship that has been produced about sex work and prostitution, it seems instructive to explore various theories of freedom in order to better understand its definitions and dimensions. Although there are countless political and philosophical theorists who have written about freedom, I have chosen three approaches that I find most helpful for understanding some of the issues involved in the debates around sex work.

Traditional political theorists have understood "freedom" as a decidedly individualistic concept requiring individual agents attempting to act and prevent or enable others from acting as well. Rooted in the philosophies of men such as Hobbes, Locke, Rousseau, and Mill, traditional theories of freedom have proven to be somewhat ineffective for engaging the lived realities of society's more marginalized peoples. In response, recent freedom theorists have instead understood freedom in a manner more acquainted with contexts and institutions as "agents" that can restrain or support freedom. Likewise, they have paid more attention to the ways in which informal regulations such as norms, beliefs, relationships, and cultural expectations limit available choices and an individual's ability to make them. For the purposes of this chapter, I discuss three theoretical approaches that explore institutions and social contexts and their relationships to freedom: 1) the capabilities approach, based on the work of Amartya Sen and Martha Nussbaum; 2) an account of freedom drawn from theories of discourse and social construction, based on Nancy Hirschmann, and 3) care ethics, based largely on the work of Joan Tronto and Eva Kittay. I have chosen these three approaches because they represent three different strands of feminism, highlight three different aspects of the often-ignored contexts of freedom, and propose three different understandings of the constitution of the choosing self.

Freedom and Capabilities

In her book *Women and Human Development: The Capabilities Approach*, Martha Nussbaum (2000) works to create a universal theory of justice based on human capabilities. Focused especially on women, Nussbaum asserts that there are injustices readily identifiable across cultures and traditions that require universal normative treatment. After working through various critiques of universal norms and values, Nussbaum establishes a list of "central human capabilities" that she argues should serve as the minimum for human quality of life.

The Central Human Capabilities are:

1 Life
2 Bodily Health
3 Bodily Integrity
4 Senses, Imagination, and Thought
5 Emotions
6 Practical Reason
7 Affiliation
8 Other Species
9 Play
10 Control over One's Environment (Political and Material).

(Nussbaum 2000: 78–80)

Nussbaum argues that similar to Rawls's list of primary goods, these capabilities can be used to form the moral basis of constitutional guarantees, and she assigns no hierarchical ordering to the capabilities because each are equally important and necessary. Additionally, all items on the list are separate (it is not appropriate to "trade" or increase one at the expense of another), but it is important to also acknowledge that the items are related and can work to influence one another.

Nussbaum identifies the items on the list as combined capabilities, drawing distinctions between basic capabilities ("the innate equipment of individuals that is the necessary basis for development more advanced capabilities"), internal capabilities ("developed states of the person herself that are, so far as the person herself is concerned, sufficient conditions for the exercise of requisite functions"), and combined capabilities (2000: 84). Combined capabilities include both internal capabilities and environmental conditions (referring to one's social, political, economic, and cultural surroundings) that promote the exercise of such internal capabilities and other functions. Identifying her capabilities as combined capabilities proves important for Nussbaum, both in establishing their importance as the foundation for providing individuals with choice and for discussing the way they inform human rights.

Nussbaum situates her capabilities approach between two "extreme" types of justice theories: welfarism and platonism. In particular, Nussbaum is interested in distinguishing her theory of capabilities from welfarism in order to demonstrate that capabilities are different than preferences or desires. Welfarism argues for justice based solely on the preferences of those involved. After giving a tour of various characters in the school of welfarist thought, Nussbaum argues that welfarism is insufficient because even the most deeply welfarist theorist acknowledges that culture and experience influence a person's preferences and can even influence what that person thinks possible for him or herself. More explicitly, Nussbaum argues that welfarist theories are indefensible because: 1) they rely on normative standards (which the welfarist position, in theory, opposes) to develop appropriate procedures for individuals to form and act on their preferences, 2) individual preferences are shaped by adaptation to the individual's environment, 3) individual preferences are shaped by social and political institutions (rather than the other way around), and 4) deprivation of human capabilities is something that should be addressed as important "whether or not the person minds it or complains about it" (2000: 145). Nussbaum is not arguing that preferences have no importance in the process of justice, but rather that they are not a good basis for its establishment. Preferences are easily shaped and manipulated, unstable, and therefore not consistently adaptive.

In *Sex and Social Justice* (1999), Nussbaum discusses the ways in which sex roles and social context work to create situations of justice and injustice for the women who occupy them. She draws parallels between sex workers and other women who sell services intimately related to their person professionally—the professor (who receives money for her thoughts), the massage therapist (who receives money for non-sexual bodily services that involve pleasure), and the factory worker (who sells physical labor to create something that is most likely used by someone unknown to her). Nussbaum goes on to state that the central, important difference between prostitution and these other professions is the stigma attached to prostitution. She locates the sources of the stigma in two places: violation of socially determined "appropriate" sex roles, and gender-based domination, and she links the marginalizing role of stigma with the dangerous conditions in which women involved in prostitution work (Nussbaum 1999).

Interestingly, in her discussion of domination, Nussbaum never addresses the fact that women are grossly over-represented in sex work, more so than any of the other professions. Nussbaum never directly proclaims whether or not she believes that sex work is a situation of injustice; however, she concludes her section on sex work by advocating that we focus our work more on women's cooperatives (which she sees as a symbol of women's empowerment) and less on prostitution. In other words, the reader gathers that she believes sex work to be no more or less exploitative than other professions in which women sell personal services, provided that they are given adequate support to practice their trade in ways that are safe and provide them with some degree of choice and control. From this perspective, it is not impossible to draw conclusions regarding the relationship between Nussbaum's theory of freedom and the practice of sex work.

Nussbaum helps us to see the importance of material and institutional contexts in women's abilities to make choices based on their own beliefs about what constitutes human flourishing. She supports an ethic that requires certain assurances for all people—assurances that she believes enable them to identify the type of life they want to live and take actions to achieve it. Whether or not one actually takes action is less the issue than whether or not a context exists to support said action if one decided to take it. Nussbaum's theory helps us to gain a deeper understanding of the problem with women who enter prostitution based on economic necessity. For Nussbaum, a woman who enters prostitution (or perhaps any other profession) because she needs the money and has no other employment options, or has not received the education necessary to choose alternatives, is not free—she has not chosen out of a context that supports her capabilities. Similarly, it is possible that the contexts created by involvement in prostitution results in further lack of freedom for women. For example, to the extent that a woman is unable to request that her client use condoms or receive services in a safe location, her freedom to health and safety is jeopardized because her ability to choose these things is restricted. Conversely, it seems that Nussbaum would support that a woman for whom the capabilities had been met, and who still chose to engage in prostitution was acting freely.

Freedom and Discourse

Quite different from Nussbaum, Hirschmann's central question addresses how the choosing self is constituted. For Hirschmann, the self is constructed through language and discourse that in turn affects the individual's beliefs about the world, the material conditions in which the individual lives and interacts, and the meanings ascribed to the self, the world, and relationships. The self is always at once agential and restricted, constructed and constructing. Desires, beliefs, and internal conflicts are always formed in and through the "external" world of material reality and discourse. Likewise, the choosing self-acts on material reality and discourse to shape it, which in turn acts back on the self and others.

Hirschmann's notion of freedom is concerned with the ways in which social construction operating through language works to shape and produce the subject of freedom and the context in which the "choosing self" acts. Hirschmann is committed to a theory of freedom that links language and discourse with material realities, social structures and institutions, and the relationships in which women find themselves. By placing the often excluded and invisible aspects of women's experiences at the center of her theory of freedom, Hirschmann allows the reader to see the ways in which contexts often taken as "natural" create situations of unfreedom for their inhabitants. Because her task is to create a feminist theory of freedom, Hirschmann's special interest is the ways in which patriarchy works to create situations of unfreedom for women.

According to Hirschmann, social construction happens on three levels, all of which interact and rely upon each other. The first level, which Hirschmann calls "the ideological representation of reality," is reminiscent of Marx, and points to the ways in which language works to create a version of reality that is distorted or incongruent with what is actually occurring. To illustrate this level, Hirschmann provides a litany of "caricatures" that are often used to represent women (the virgin, the whore, the asexual mother, the sexual temptress) and notes that the problem with these images is that they "fail to recognize women's humanity, their membership in society, their differences from each other, and not just from men, their individuality and their commonality" (Hirschmann 2003: 78). At the second level of social construction, which Hirschmann calls "materialization," the ideological representation of reality goes beyond distortion and begins to shape the world according to its images. Reality is actually produced by language.[1] At this level, Hirschmann says, "the construction of social behaviors and rules take on a life of its own, and becomes constitutive not only of what women are allowed to do, but of what they are allowed to be" (p. 79). Environments that constrain and limit women more so than men are created by the ideological beliefs that women should be more constrained for reasons of desert, protection, or inability. At the third level of social construction, meaning takes its root in language where it "establishes the parameters for understanding, defining, and communicating about reality, about who women are, what we are doing, what we desire" (p. 80). Important to Hirschmann's theory is her idea that everyone (men as well

263

as women) are always already constructed by systems of patriarchy. She rejects the idea of an essential self, and proposes that each of us are continually forming and being formed by the discourses that construct our reality. Unlike many theorists who rely heavily on discourse, however, Hirschmann's argument does not preclude the ability to consider material conditions or the physical body in her account of freedom. Clarifying her position on such, she states, "That we are socially constructed does not mean that what is constructed is not real" (p. 210). Rather, the interaction between Hirschmann's three levels of social construction allows her to marry the work of postmodern discourse theorists (such as Michel Foucault and Judith Butler) and more materialist theorists (such as Catherine MacKinnon), who are otherwise quite at odds with one another (Hekman 2006). Hirschman instructs that both material realities and discursive construction are essential to women's freedom.

In summary, Hirschmann's theory seems to suggest that, when it comes to the case of prostitution, women who are engaged in sex work (regardless of their belief about it), people who work with sex workers, men who frequent sex workers, and politicians who form and enforce policies about sex work are all influencing and influenced by social constructions of women, sexuality, work, and relationships, as well as claims of agency and freedom. The construction of these concepts takes place at three levels: first of all at the ideological level, second at the material level (at which ideas and approaches reproduce themselves), and third at the level of language itself. In addition to the material conditions that influence freedom, and the language and discourse that shape these conditions and the choosing subject herself, care theorists point to the role of relationships in supporting and restricting "individual" choices.

Freedom and Relationships of Care

By constructing a political ethic that emphasizes interdependency and relationship, care theorists challenge us to construct a concept of freedom in which relationship and the existence of others allows and supports freedom, even as it restricts it. According to care theorists, freedom requires relationship and grows out of personal obligation. Discussions about care and relationships of responsibility entered political theory discourse through discussions about moral theory. While care ethics are often positioned in relationship to theories of justice, the concepts of care ethics are important to a fully formed notion of freedom because they help us to see the role of relationships in supporting and enabling freedom. Furthermore, care theory also shows us how the very same relationships that make freedom possible for ourselves and others often restrict freedom even as they enable it. Lastly, care theory upholds the value of care and relationships while at the same time noting that responsibilities for care and the restrictions that come with those responsibilities are not distributed equally. Like other burdens, the burden of care is distributed unequally along the lines of gender, race, and class, often leading to less freedom for those who are assigned roles of care-giving.

Care theory in the United States was anticipated by early feminists such as Jane Addams, Lucia Ames Mead, and Marietta Keis (Rogers 2004), and the origins of contemporary care theory are most often attributed to Carol Gilligan and her response to Lawrence Kohlberg's work on moral development. In her book, *A Different Voice* (1984), Gilligan challenges Kohlberg's theory of moral development by demonstrating its reliance on justice as the sole measure of morality. Additionally, Gilligan critiques Kohlberg for developing his theory through research using a sample of all male, upper-middle-class participants, and posing hypothetical moral dilemmas. For this reason, Gilligan and the theorists who compose the field of care ethics are often described as developing "a women's ethic"; however, most of these women note that care and responsibility to others are not values naturally inherent to women's being, but rather values that grow out of socialization and need.

Care ethicists such as Joan Tronto and Eva Kittay furthered Gilligan's ideas. Tronto defines care as "a species activity that includes everything that we do to maintain, continue, and repair our 'world' so that we can live in it as well as possible" (1993: 103). Tronto goes on to say that our world includes "our bodies, our selves, and our environment, all of which we seek to interweave in a complex, life-sustaining web" (p. 103). Important to this definition is the idea that "care" can go beyond human interaction with others to include objects, animals, and the environment. Furthermore, care is not conceived of in a way that is exclusively dyadic or individualistic, but rather embraces the social and political functions of care in any environment. Care is likewise largely culturally defined and ongoing. Tronto describes care as existing in four main forms:

1) Caring about, which involves recognizing human (or other) need and the necessity of care;
2) Taking care of, which involves assuming some kind of responsibility for the recognized need;
3) Care-giving, which involves the direct provision of care for recognized need, and
4) Care-receiving, which recognizes the response of the care-recipient.

These dimensions of care allow us to recognize that the majority of life activities are activities of care; however, care remains marginalized as a practice, and its role in sustaining systems of power and privilege remains largely invisible.

In addition to being made invisible as described above, Tronto notes that care is also contained as an essential and valuable activity by being cast as "natural" to certain members of society—members who often fall near the bottom of raced, classed, and gendered hierarchies. Tronto calls this ideological strategy "care as disposition" (as opposed to "care as practice").

Other ideological strategies include relegating care to the realm of "private" activity,[2] and disdain for care-receivers. The latter strategy involves denial of or embarrassment about individual experiences of need, experiences that challenge our ideas (and ideals) about individuality, autonomy, and independence. In order to re-center moral politics, Tronto recommends starting from the assumption that humans are interdependent. This move, she proposes, challenges the myth of the independent individual, and makes care more visible and more valuable. In a move that is familiar to the work of many feminists, she also recommends challenging distinctions between public and private life in order to expose the ways that practices associated with women (like care) are removed from the public realm and therefore divorced from conversations about politics and power. Lastly, Tronto advocates challenging the dichotomy between care and justice. This recommendation goes beyond that claim that they are both valuable to demonstrate that they are both constitutive of and necessary to each other.

The work of Eva Kittay (1998, 1999; Feder and Kittay 2003) illustrates what it might look like to put Tronto's challenges into practice through her writings on disability, care-giving, and women and welfare. In her 1998 article "Welfare, Dependency, and a Public Ethics of Care," Kittay uses welfare reform to demonstrate the ways in which both liberal and conservative approaches to public policy rely on a masculine idea of the independent self, and conceal the care-giving activities of (mostly) women. While Kittay does not see care as an inherently female activity, she does operate out of the understanding that duties of care fall mostly to women. In her critique, she points out that welfare policy assumes a masculine (and mythical) image of a wage-earner that is independent of other responsibilities and commitments, such as caring for children or adult parents. This assumption therefore leads to policies that fail to provide the monetary resources, community and/or institutional support, and extra time that would allow women to maintain their duties of care, therefore administering a double burden of a world of care that does not stop at the bounds of employment, and a world of employment that fails to recognize the duties of care. In addition to failing to acknowledge duties of care beyond the workplace, the independent wage-earner myth also fails to recognize the support and care received by the wage-earner himself in order to make his professional life productive and possible. About these omissions she says, "Neither questions the conception of social cooperation that presumes, but does not credit, women's unpaid labor as caretaker" (1998: 124).

It is difficult to imagine a conceptualization of freedom that is complete without exploration of the role of relationships of care and their effects on the understandings and practices of freedom. This seems particularly true when thinking about freedom in the context of sex work, and perhaps in more ways than one might initially identify. On the most basic level, we might think of care-giving in the context of a sex worker-client relationship.

Although many women view the relationship between themselves and their clients as one of solely economic exchange, others view their relationship as one of offering care and pleasure. In these cases, we might ask why it is (almost) always women offering care, and (almost) always men receiving it, but this does not separate sex work from many other professions. On another level, we might think of the ways in which the burden of care (for example, mothers caring for their children) falls more heavily on women, and how this burden works to place women at a higher risk of participating in sex work out of economic necessity. Many women cite the need to support their families as a reason for participating in sex work, and the hours and flexibility provided by sex work as an incentive for staying in the profession. On yet a third level, we might consider the ways in which care-giving professions (largely dominated by women) are marginalized economically (in part because it is often considered "women's work"), and how this economic marginalization makes women more susceptible to multiple types of exploitation, within the field of sex work and without. For these reasons, it is imperative to explore political theories of care and their bearings on freedom. Theories that emphasize the importance of relationships and the responsibilities of care-giving while also demonstrating the inequalities and non-freedoms implicit in the practice are important lenses to develop when examining sex work.

Despite their differences, all three of these theorists use their theories to reconcile individual women's experiences with broader, universal notions of freedom. All of the theorists developed their feminist theories of freedom by grounding them in women's experiences, and offering practical (though perhaps difficult to attain) solutions to the problems of restricted freedom that are created by patriarchy. Lastly, all three theorists demonstrate that freedom is intricately related to power and hierarchy. Though Hirschman is the only theorist who explicitly gives an account of power and its workings in the creation of freedom, all three accounts emphasize that patriarchy, as well as hierarchies that depend on race, class, and sexuality, influence freedom. These hierarchies influence the resources (both material and institutional) that people have available to them, the ways in which the self is constructed (including internal desires and beliefs, as well as the contexts that shape those desires and beliefs), and the relationships of obligation in which women find themselves. Where these hierarchies intersect, we find particularly complex dilemmas of freedom, both because the intersections are often more than a sum of their parts (Crenshaw 1991), and because hierarchies themselves are multiple and dynamic (Gonzalez-Lopez 2005).

Bringing It All Together: Freedom, Activism and Debates Over Legality

The reality is that in most cases, sex work has multiple meanings and represents a range of experiences (Elias 2007), and therefore poses considerable dilemmas to how we approach and understand sex work ethically, eco-nomically, and especially, legally. Because our social and legal structures tend to assign sex to the bedroom (and is therefore "private") and work to the workplace (and is therefore "public")—divisions that are arbitrary and often inaccurate, but no less socially meaningful—its existence is difficult to accommodate. This difficulty is illustrated in the many approaches that people take to the "problem" of sex work. While the women involved and the communities that surround them often differ as to what the problem is, exactly—as earlier discussed, some identify the existence of prostitution as the problem, whereas others identify the conditions under which it is practiced, and still others identify the social norms and prejudices against such practice—there seems to be the consensus that women involved in sex work are a particularly marginalized subset of society.

In general, legal structures have been the targets of activism and advocacy for most players in the debate, regardless of their position. The battle over legality is in and of itself interesting. Like many other social issues, access to justice means recognition by the legal system. For the subject of prostitution, this vying for legal status is typically framed in the rhetoric of protection—that when pros-titution is legalized and regulated, the women within it will be protected and legitimated. In other words, the law has material implications—people hope that making something legal will make it safer—but also symbolic implications as well—inclusion in the legal system means inclusion in society—exclusion means invisibility and marginality.

Advocates for viewing prostitution as a legitimate form of work claim that efforts to make such work illegal are not only ineffective, they are yet more attempts by governments to regulate women's bodies and sexuality. While those who argue for legal sanctions against prostitution are also con-cerned about regulation, the blame is placed in different locations—people who argue that prostitution should be illegal generally tend to locate the problem in cultures that promote the use and abuse of women through, among other things, their sexuality. The focus is less on legal structures and more on social, economic, and cultural practices and ideologies. Activists who point out the use of legal structures to regulate women's sexuality echo arguments made by feminist political theorists who demonstrate that such regulation is neither new nor unusual (McClintock 1995). Additionally, the act of criminalizing prostitution where it is legal draws merited concern. For women who are employed selling sex, the prospect of losing their job is no less serious than for those involved in any other industry (Chapkis 1997).

Why sex work is such a contentious issue is not an uninteresting (or inconsequential) question. It is important on one hand because it engages real people and presents real problems. Though this would seem to be reason enough for attention and interest (or disgust), sex work is also a contentious topic because it engages, challenges, and acts upon deep-seated beliefs about gender, sexuality, and the nature of freedom.

Most activism around sex work starts from the perspective that prostitution is a gendered issue: the controversies around prostitution exist, in part, because while "everyone" agrees that women are constrained, there is considerable disagreement about the source and nature of this constraint. Pro-sex work activists argue that sex work is work and a potentially liberating expression of sexuality (Chapkis 1997; Nagle 1997), and that the constraining factors are stigma and social norms that require women to be "good girls" in order to be respected and treated as legitimate members of society. Anti-prostitution activists argue that patriarchal structures dominate women and reduce them to bodies that exist for men's pleasure, and that prostitution is the basest expression of this (Farley and Barkan 1998; Pateman 1998).

In both of these accounts, the conditions in which women practice sex work are identified as dangerous and/or less than desirable; however the origin of these conditions depends on one's perspective of "the problem" with sex work. For pro-sex work activists, prejudice against sex workers forces them to work in marginalized spaces—both physically and economically. For anti-prostitution activists, the dangerous contexts are reflective of prostitution as an act of exploitation and coercion, and the kinds of conditions that would lead one to be involved in prostitution in the first place.

Additionally, activists disagree about the role and existence of women's agency in these scenarios. Multiple scholars have expressed concern that accounts of sex work that focus solely on the exploitation that exists within sex work, and the coercion that occurs to "make" women enter, does even greater damage to women's equality because it robs them of their agency to act within and upon the structures that constrain them (Chua et al. 2000; Kempadoo and Doezma 1998; Sorisio 2003).

More nuanced arguments about sex work acknowledge the differences between women involved in sex work, including the experiences of women involved, the reasons for entering and the opportunities to leave, and the many social forces and personal choices and desires that influence these differences. Similar to theories that highlight the intersectional nature of women's lives—theories that emphasize that women's experiences of being "women" are mediated by class, race, ethnicity, and sexuality, just to name a few—this "diversity" perspective on sex work seems to be the most useful in understanding how different women can have radically different experiences with sex work (Nagel 1997).

These debates illustrate one of the many difficulties in using gender as a basis for social argument. Though there seems to be consensus that patriarchy exists in some form or fashion throughout history and across location, and has resulted in relative disadvantage for women when compared to men, recent scholarship on patriarchy has showed us that patriarchy is a complex and multi-faceted system that often works in multiple directions at once (Gonzalez-Lopez 2005). To say that "men oppress women" is overly simplistic and not particularly useful, because it doesn't tell us which men, which women, in which ways, in which locations, at what times, for what reasons, or through what mechanisms; nor does it tell us how to interpret situations where women aren't oppressed by men, or give us room to explore the idea that perhaps the assumption and creation of gender difference is the site of inequality in the first place (Risman 2004)

Thus, we are faced with a problem: on one hand, it is important to be able to talk about sex work as a gendered institution that relies on and creates both material and discursive realities for the women involved. Conversely, oversimplifying the role of gender leads us to ignore some of the very important differences within the field of sex work, and runs us the risk of reifying "woman" as a distinct gender category that is always the site of patriarchal oppression. It seems, then, that the best way to approach the field of sex work, and bring about changes advocated by the women involved, is to act "close to the ground"—to develop strategies that are responsive to the needs and desires of individual women in particular contexts.

With this in mind, the irony of the debate around the legalization of sex work is that people on all sides of the discussion have put an incredible amount of energy and resources into courting the support of national and international legal structures, rather than developing community-based responses that are supportive of local women's interests, and attentive to their particular situations. The diversity of women involved in sex work tells us that the sweeping nature of legislation is probably inadequate to accommodate the myriad experiences and realities included in this practice. Furthermore, the structures to which activists are appealing are, in general, notoriously gendered, and rarely advocate liberatory environments for women, even when the creation of such environments is the stated goal (O'Neill 2007; Scoular et al. 2007). This is not to say that challenging existing legal structures that are oppressive to women (or racial, ethnic, sexual or other minorities that have historically been marginalized by these structures) should not be an important aspect of activism and advocacy. Notably, legal structures can support or interfere with community-based work. Rather, it is to say that seeking legitimacy solely through the law may be misguided and ineffective. Research on approaches to sex work indicates a shift in support for sex workers away from community-based organizational responses that provide much needed material support (health care and education, drug counseling, relational networks) and towards international network-based organizing and advocacy (Elias 2007). Though these strategies may be important in increasing public knowledge about sex work, transforming conventionally held images of sex workers, and gaining employment rights, they also detract attention from material strategies that are equally important. It is essential that approaches to sex-work activism and advocacy are broad enough to account for the multiple perspectives and realities included in the term.

Conclusion

Perhaps unsurprisingly, the absence of recognition of and attention to community contexts and resources is mirrored in our feminist theories of freedom, pointing to a place where we might seek to expand the theories. Although incredibly useful in providing theories that illustrate different components of freedom, none of our theorists explore the ways in which the communities that surround individuals play into their experiences of freedom or unfreedom. Feminists often shy away from communitarian theory because community contexts are often rife with the same patriarchy that informs other social institutions (Kittay 2001). Still, communities of place and communities of interest are powerful mechanisms for mediating dominant discourses (Rappaport 1995, 2000), influencing the distribution of material resources (Campfens 1997), and providing the context for relationships and relational commitments. Furthermore, discourse, the distribution of resources, and legal and economic institutions shape the communities that provide the immediate contexts for individual experiences. Although communities are sometimes "the problem" when it comes to women's freedom, they also represent opportunities for liberation.

Because of the increasing amount of energy spent on activism in the area of sex work, and the amount of services aimed at helping individual women (who have been medicalized as subjects), there has been little emphasis in terms of research placed on the role of communities in encouraging or preventing women to participate in sex work, little research on the support they have once they are participating, and even less research on the communities that help them leave should they decide to do so. Understanding the role of community and its implications for women involved in sex work, as well as its implications for feminist theories of freedom is an essential but underdeveloped body of knowledge.

Discussion Questions

1   What are the conditions of freedom from a capabilities perspective? From a care-theory perspective? From the perspective of Hirschmann's social constructionism?

2   Write your own definition of "freedom." Now apply it to an empirical example about which you are knowledgeable (e.g., sex work, reproductive justice, mass incarceration, welfare reform, etc.). How does your empirical example illuminate the strengths of your definition? What shortcomings of your definition does it expose?

3   If you were to design a freedom-promoting intervention for street-based sex workers, what would it look like? What types of advocacy, services, or policy changes would you recommend?

Suggested Readings

1 Chapkis, W. (1997). *Live sex acts: women performing erotic labor.* New York: Routledge.
2 Hirschmann, N.J. (2003). *The subject of liberty: toward a feminist theory of freedom.* Princeton, NJ: Princeton University Press.
3 Roberts, D. (1998). *Killing the black body: race, representation, and the meaning of liberty.* New York, NY: Vintage Books.
4 Suiter, S. V. (2012). *Magdalene House: a place about mercy.* Nashville, TN: Vanderbilt University Press.

Suggested Media

1 http://www.thistlefarms.org
2 http://www.npr.org/2011/04/25/135633315/magdalene-program
3 http://www.npr.org/2011/04/26/135702065/relapse-and-recovery-a-tale-of-two-prostitutes

Notes

1 This idea is also borrowed from Marx who describes how capitalist ideology produces relationships of alienation between workers and other workers, workers and themselves, and workers and their labor.
2 To illustrate this, Tronto notes: "Care is supposed to be provided in the household. Only when the household fails to provide care in some way does public or market life enter . . . the idea that daycare should be private is a major resistance to the establishment of a more formal daycare policy in the U.S." (1993: 199)

References

Brinson, S. J. (2006). Contentious freedom: sex work and social construction. *Hypatia, 21*(4), 192–200.
Campfens, H. (1997). *Community development around the world.* Toronto: University of Toronto Press.
Chapkis, W. (1997). *Live sex acts: women performing erotic labor.* New York: Routledge.
Chua, P., Bhavnani, K. and Foran, J. (2000). Women, culture, development: a new paradigm for development studies? *Ethnic and Racial Studies, 23*(5), 820–841.
Collins, P. H. (1991). *Knowledge, consciousness, and the politics of empowerment.* London: Routledge.
Crenshaw, Kimberlé W. (1991). Mapping the margins: intersectionality, identity politics, and violence against women of color, *Stanford Law Review, 43*(6), 1241–1299.
de Beauvoir, S. (1974). *The second sex.* New York: Vintage Books.
Delacoste, F. and Alexander, P. (1998). *Sex work: writings by women in the sex industry.* San Francisco, CA: Cleis Press.

Durr, M. (2005). Sex, drugs, and HIV: sisters of laundromat. *Gender and Society, 19,* 721–728.

Elias, J. (2007). Sex worker union organizing: an international study. *Capital and Class, 93,* 273–276.

Farley, M. and Barkan, H. (1998). Prostitution, violence, and post traumatic stress disorder. *Women & Health, 27*(3), 37–49.

Feder, E. and Kittay, E. (2003). *The subject of care: feminist perspectives on dependency.* Totowa, NJ: Rowman and Littlefield.

Gilligan, Carol. (1982). *In a difference voice: psychological theory and women's development.* Boston, MA: Harvard University Press.

Gonzalez-Lopez, G. (2005). *Erotic journeys: Mexican immigrants and their sex lives.* Berkeley, CA: University of California Press.

Goodyear, M. and Cusick, L. (2007). Protection of sex workers. *British Medical Journal, 334,* 52–53.

Hartsock, N. (1996). Community/sexuality/gender: rethinking power. In Hirschmann, N.J. and DiStephano, C. (eds.). *Revisioning the political: feminist reconstructions of traditional concepts in Western political theory.* Boulder, CO: Westview Press, pp. 27–53.

Hekman, S. (2006). The subject of liberty: toward a feminist theory of freedom/ Claims of culture. *Hypatia, 21*(3), 190–194.

Hirschmann, N.J. (2003). *The subject of liberty: toward a feminist theory of freedom.* Princeton, NJ: Princeton University Press.

Kempadoo, K. and Doezma, J. (1998). *Global sex workers: rights, resistance and redefinition.* London: Routledge.

Kinnell, H. (2006). Demonizing clients: how not to promote sex workers' safety. In M. O'Neill and R. Campbell (eds.). *Sex work now.* Cullumpton: Willan Press.

Kittay, E. F. (1998). Welfare, dependency, and a public ethics of care. *Social Justice, 25*(1), 123–145.

Kittay, E. F. (1999). *Love's labor: essays on women, equality and dependency.* New York: Routledge.

Kittay, E. F. (2001). A feminist public ethic of care meets the new communitarian family policy. *Ethics, 111*(3), 523–547.

Lorde, A. (1991). Uses of the erotic—the erotic as power. In Barrington, J. (ed.) *Intimate wilderness.* Portland. OR: Eighth Mountain Press.

McClintock, A. (1995). *Imperial leather: race, gender and sexuality in the colonial states.* New York: Routledge.

Mills, C.W. (2005). "Ideal theory" as ideology. *Hypatia, 20*(3), 165–184.

Mulia, N. (2002). Ironies in the pursuit of well-being: the perspectives of low-income, substance-using women on service institutions. *Contemporary Drug Problems, 29*(4), 711–748.

Nadon, S. M., Koverola, C., and Schludermann, E. (1998). Antecedents to prostitution: childhood victimization. *Journal of Interpersonal Violence, 206*(16).

Nagle, J. (1997). *Whores and other feminists.* New York: Routledge.

Nussbaum, M. (2000). *Women and human development: the capabilities approach.* Cambridge: Cambridge University Press.

Nussbaum, M. (1999). *Sex and social justice.* Oxford: Oxford University Press.

O'Neill, M. (2001). *Prostitution and feminism: towards a politics of feeling.* Cambridge, UK: Polity Press.

O'Neill, M. (2007). Community, safety, rights and recognition: Towards a co-ordinated prostitution strategy? *Community Safety Journal, 6*(1), 45–52.

Pateman, C. (1988). *The sexual contract.* Stanford, CA: Stanford University Press.

Petro, M. (2007). "I did it . . . for the money": sex work as a means to socio-economic opportunity. *Research for Sex Work, 9.* Retrieved December 12, 2007 from www.nswp.org/.

Rappaport, J. (1995). Empowerment meets narrative: listening to stories and creating settings. *American Journal of Community Psychology, 23*(5), 795–808.

Rappaport, J. (2000). Community narratives: tales of terror and joy. *American Journal of Community Psychology, 28*(1), 1–24.

Ringdal, N.J. (1997). *Love for sale: a world history of prostitution.* New York: Grove Press.

Risman, B. J. (2004). Gender as social structure: theory wrestling with activism. *Gender and Society, 18*(4), 429–450.

Roberts, A. (2000). Revisiting the need for feminism and afrocentric theory when treating African-American female substance abusers. *Journal of Drug Issues, 30*(4), 901–918.

Rogers, D. (2004). Before "care": Marietta Kies, Lucia Ames Mead, and feminist political theory. *Hypatia, 19*(2), 105–117.

Rubin, G. (1984). Thinking sex: notes for a radical theory of the politics of sexuality. In Carole Vance (ed.), *Pleasure and danger.* Boston, MA: Routledge.

Sanders, T. and Campbell, R. (2007). Designing out vulnerability, building in respect: violence, safety and sex work policy. *British Journal of Sociology, 58*(1), 1–19.

Sen, A. (1999). *Development as freedom.* New York: First Anchor Books.

Scoular, J., Pitcher, J. and Campbell, R. (2007). What's anti-social about sex work? The changing representation about prostitution's incivility. *Community Safety Journal, 6*(1), 11–17.

Singh, J.P. and Hart, S.A. (2007). Sex workers and cultural policy: mapping the issues and actors in Thailand. *Review of Policy Research, 24*(2), 155–173.

Sorisio, C. (2003). A tale of two feminisms: power and victimization in contemporary feminist debate. In C. McCann and S. Kim (eds.). *Feminist theory reader: local and global perspectives.* New York: Routledge.

Sterk, C., Elifson, K. and German, D. (2000). Female crack users and their sexual relationships: the role of sex-for-crack exchanges. *Journal of Sex Research, 37*(4), 354–360.

Surratt, H., Inciardi, J., Kurtz, S. and Kiley, M. (2004) Sex work and drug use in a subculture of violence. *Crime and Delinquency 50*(1), 43–59.

Thukral, J. (2005). Behind closed doors: an analysis of indoor sex work in New York City. *SEICUS Report, 33*(2), 3–9.

Tronto, Joan. (1993). *Moral boundaries: a political argument for an ethic of care.* New York: Routledge, Chapman and Hall, Inc.

Vandepitte, J., Lyerla, R., Cabbe, F., and Alary, M. (2006). Estimates of the number of female sex workers in different regions of the world. *Sexually Transmitted Infections, 82*(3), 18–25.

Vanwesenbeeck, I. (2001). Another decade of social scientific sex work: a review of research 1900–2000. *Annual Review of Sex Research, 12*, 242–289.

Ward, H., Day, S., and Weber, J. (1999). Risky business: health and safety in the sex industry over a 9-year period. *Sexually Transmitted Infections, 7*, 340–343.

West, C. M. (1996). Mammy, sapphire, and jezebel: historical images of Black women and their implications for psychotherapy. *Psychotherapy, 32*, 458–456.

Wollstonecraft, M. (1983). A vindication of the rights of men. In Solomon, B. H. and Berggren, P. S. (eds.). *A Mary Wollstonecraft reader*. New York: New American Library.

15

RECLAIMING WOMEN'S RIGHTS TO FREEDOM OF RELIGION

An Assessment of the Political and Legal Complexities Affecting the Domestication of CEDAW and the AU Women's Protocol in Nigeria

Abiola Akiyode-Afolabi

Introduction

Nigeria is a diverse country and as such open to several religions which often conflict with the enjoyment of the rights of women and girls. The diversity of the country often creates unnecessary religious and ethnic tensions (Ibidapo-Obe 2000) which can pose a threat to full enjoyment of women rights (Ezeilo et al. 2003). Therefore, negotiating between the perceived tensions: environment that supposedly supports discrimination against women and the existing legal framework on women's rights "requires a multi-pronged approach" (Imam 2010: 4).

According to a UN Women report, there is a complex link between religion and gender, and this can manifest in different ways through cultural, social, economic, and political norms of the society. As a result, religious texts continue to interpret gender roles and status of women and men the way they have been codified by conservative or patriarchal orders of religion for centuries. Women have been subjugated by these conservative views which have controlled their relationship with religion, making them the major implementers, responsible for the embodiments of religious teachings and traditions (UN Women).

Research has shown how that patriarchal transnational religious network impacts the confines and latitudes of women's rights at the global level. The influence of this international alliance is often reflected in the framing of human rights texts in a manner that limits full expression of women's rights. The alliance between the Vatican and Muslims at the United Nations determines women's rights and formulates the boundaries of women's rights based on the conservative world-view of whatever is perceived suitable to their religions, as opposed to global feminism advocacy towards reframing and reclaiming women's rights (Chappell 2004). This conservative network influenced the drafting of most texts relating to gender equality and connived in frustrating efforts aimed at entrenching women's rights as a global standard for affirming human dignity (Otto 1996), particularly rights to physical and mental integrity, equality, religious freedom, and practice.

The Convention on the Elimination of all forms of Discrimination Against Women (CEDAW) was adopted on December 18, 1979, by the UN General Assembly, opened for signature on March 1, 1980, and entered into force on September 3, 1981. Nigeria ratified the CEDAW in 1985, with no reservation and further re-affirmed its commitment to gender equality, by depositing its instrument of ratification for the Protocol to the African Charter on Human and Peoples' Rights on the Rights of Women in Africa (AU Women's Protocol) in July 2004. According to Viljoen, ratification by states represents an expression of their consent to be bound, while it is an established principle that merely signing is not a definitive indication of a state party's intention to be bound, but "rather provides evidence of promise of future compliance" (Viljoen 2012: 22). Thus, the signatory state to international human rights treaties is obliged to take steps to ensure that the object and aim of the treaty is not undermined. Signature and ratification of treaties form part of a process for guaranteeing application of the norms at the municipal level, while it remains a matter of the country's constitution how an international treaty finds expressions at the domestic level.

Nigeria is a dualist state by virtue of Section 12 of the 1999 Constitution of the Federal Republic of Nigeria (CFRN). By implication therefore, mere signing and ratification of an international treaty does not make that treaty applicable in the domestic plane in Nigeria, until the National Assembly enacts it into law. CEDAW and the AU Women's Protocol are therefore classified by the Nigerian Constitution as a category of treaties, which require the ratification of the National Assembly and the approval of at least two-thirds of the State Houses of Assembly to come into effect.

Gender and religion intermingles in Nigeria in complex ways; thus, several attempts to bring CEDAW and the AU Women's Protocol into domestic laws have been met with stiff resistance, supposedly owing to religious considerations (Para-Mallam et al. 2011). The fact that the law does not allow for direct implementation of treaties after ratification further complicates the transformation processes of these gender-equality human rights norms into the country's laws. The failure to domesticate these instruments is a major setback for the advancement of women's rights in several ways. Specifically, negative impacts on the women include infringement on rights to property, freedom from harmful traditional practices, discriminatory practices to citizenship, sexual and reproductive rights, violence against women in various forms, restriction of women's rights to political participation and socioeconomic rights, among other discriminatory practices that women and girls contend with in Nigeria (Imam 2010). The strong misogynist attitude within the religious order has also exposed women to dangers, including criminal penalties based on prevailing patriarchal religious laws. Therefore, in an attempt to reclaim the rights to freedom of religion for women, there is a need for a deliberate alteration of the religious patriarchal system by a firm legal framework rooted in the Constitution. Failure to do this might leave women with limited options, that will negatively impact on freedom.

This chapter therefore examines the role of patriarchal dominance in determining the limits of women's rights to freedom of religion and other rights in Nigeria and how religion has constituted a drawback to domestication of CEDAW and the AU Women's protocol. The chapter seeks to identify the key issues in contention as well as the divergent and convergent views in the domestication of these instruments. The chapter proposes the need to deepen conversations around issues of women's rights and religion to engender more constructive engagements with major religious platforms.

The first part of this chapter provides background information as well as introductory notes to the subject-matter, while the second part focuses on gender identity, religion and international human rights law, with specific reference to freedom of religion within the human rights regime. The third part examines the way the debates around antagonistic views as well as the points of convergence on gender and religion have manifested at global and national levels, while the fourth part is the summary of issues arising from counter-narratives by pro-CEDAW movements. The concluding remarks approximate options available to stakeholders in deploying strategies to ensure prompt domestication of CEDAW and the AU Women's Protocol.

Gender, Religion, and International Human Rights Law

Raday (2007) has shown that culture and religion have contributed immensely to defining women's identity, since gender identity often results from the norms of behavior imposed on men and women by culture and religion; noting that the story of gender in traditionalist cultures and religions is that of the systematic domination of women by men, of women's exclusion from public power, and of their subjection to patriarchal power within the family (Mccolgan 2009).

Historically, the ethos of traditionalist cultures and the monotheistic religions developed long before the legal codification of women's human rights, with orthodox religion as the mainstay of patriarchal values and practices. Parson has argued that monotheistic religion is based on the subjection of the individual and the community to the will of God and on a transcendental morality. Under this order, women are seen as second class; monotheist religion's source books show that women are relegated to the background and in several ways, their rights were restricted, making it difficult to make choices about their lives, property, participation, family, and care of their children, to mention just a few areas. The aforesaid runs contrary to the world-view and perception of the concept of human rights as developed post-Magna Carta as a human-centric ideology, which focuses on persons and rationalism (Mccolgan 2009).

Frictions between religious beliefs and women's rights manifest in several restrictions, including women's right to abortion, the ordination of women to religious positions, and determining women's role in the home and in public, particularly in their private lives. Yet as women are more engaged and committed to religion, they are also protected. Research findings have shown that even when women seek liberation from some aspect of religion, they may not necessarily wish to escape religion or belief as a source of meaning, a call of conscience and a bond of community (Sheen 2004).

The measures with which religions, particularly Christianity and Islam, have impacted on women's rights vary. For example, Catholicism adopted and retains a prohibitive attitude towards abortion and contraception, while recent developments also shows that some other branches of Christianity—Lutheran, Episcopal, Protestant—and Judaism (Reform, Reconstructionist, and Conservative) are changing their rules and embracing active participation of women in religious activities, leading to women's emergence as religious leaders. Islam, on the other hand, continues with the propagation of sharia law, but there have been some fundamental developments, as is the case with Tunisia, for example, which recently adopted a more progressive stance on gender equality. In Tunisia in 2002, the family law code abolished divorce by *Talaq* and provided for the equal rights of men and women in filing for divorce, as well as raising the permitted age of marriage to 17 for women and 20 for men.

This is in sharp contrast with Nigeria, where Islamic law has become more stringent, extending from covering not just civil laws but also criminal laws. No fewer than twelve states in northern Nigeria have extended sharia law to criminal cases. The adoption had raised several legal and jurisprudential issues, particularly because Nigeria is a secular state by virtue of Section 10 of the 1999 Constitution of Nigeria. The adoption of sharia law was seen as unconstitutional because the country was not expected to have a state religion, considering Nigeria's multi-religious nature. Notwithstanding this secular nature, however, potent arguments show that the same Constitution also allows individual states the independence to make their own law, since Nigeria supposedly practices federalism and each state is expected to be independent of the central government. Thus, in states where sharia law was adopted, the plausible argument was that such action became necessary to regulate the lives of Muslims.

The adoption in some Nigerian states of sharia penal codes in 2000 brought to the fore several issues regarding its limitations to the rights of women. Two cases, for example, demonstrate the extent to which sharia law can affect women's fundamental rights. In the case of Safiya Husseini Tungar Tudu,

279

a divorcee was tried for adultery under sharia law for having a child outside marriage and sentenced to death by stoning by a sharia court in Sokoto State, in northern Nigeria. It took the combined efforts of feminists both within the country and internationally to build up a strong campaign for her freedom. Her sentence was later reversed and dismissed following an appeal (Friedrich Ebert Foundation 2003). Another case, which also attracted international attention, was that of Amina Lawal, another divorcee sentenced for the same crime in a sharia court in Katsina State (Ibrahim 2004). The sharia Court of Appeal in the same state eventually overturned Lawal's case in 2003.

Feminists in Nigeria have argued that the implementation of sharia penal codes in northern Nigeria is flawed in several respects, but more fundamental is the fact that sharia does not adequately protect the rights of women. Therefore, cases of abuse, violence, and discrimination against women go unpunished as they are wrongly considered to be socially acceptable. In addition, women's testimonies are devalued and treated as that of a minor or a person without necessary legal capacity (Akiyode-Afolabi 2003). Often, these biases and attitudes also influence the judges and judgments of the sharia courts. As a result, the implementation of sharia in Nigeria has placed some restrictions on the rights of women in northern Nigeria.

For example, this writer has argued that in Safiya Husseini Tungar Tudu's case for instance, the question of gender bias has been raised on the following grounds: her pregnancy constituted the main evidence against her, but no scientific efforts were made to establish or disprove the paternity of the child; the only evidence of adultery was just pregnancy; the man named in the case was allowed to go free after denying responsibility for the pregnancy. These facts reinforce the belief that sharia law and its supporters hold the presumption of guilt against the women with regards to "offences" of adultery or fornication (Akiyode-Afolabi 2003).

Several instances exist where religion has been used to denigrate women's rights in Nigeria. A female journalist was threatened with a fatwa for publishing a story that was perceived to be religiously insensitive (Astill and Bowcott 2002), while women preachers have been butchered for their beliefs. Several women were also murdered by Islamic fundamentalists in north-eastern Nigeria for belonging to a different religion or refusing to convert to Islam. The country has had several religiously motivated conflicts, which have resulted in many deaths, and the disappearance of an uncountable number of women and girls on account of professing their religion or living in a community identified with a particular religion (Sampson 2014).

According to a "Gender in Nigeria" report, 80.2 million women in Nigeria have significantly worse life chances than men and to counterparts in comparable societies due to several reasons, including violence against women, neglect, and discrimination of different forms (British Council 2012).

Nigeria operates a complex legal structure (customary, Islamic and English law) with the women bearing the brunt of this multiplicity of laws, which often puts them at a disadvantage. Women are discriminated against in customary and religious laws, ranging from the status of women offering evidence in legal matters, the restriction of some women from choosing to defend themselves based on non-religious law, unequal status in inheritance and marriage as provided by customary law, and restriction from custody of their children and the right to own property (Imam 2010).

As witnessed so far in Nigeria, religion has the potential of creating deep-seated conflicts and gender discrimination, being a pluralist society where people from multi-ethnic backgrounds and multi-religious persuasions coexist. As rightly noted by Ibidapo-Obe (2000), developments both past and present within the Nigerian polity in the handling of religious issues, indicate quite clearly to the discerning mind the possibility of a religious crisis if conscious efforts are not made to re-evaluate the state policy regarding religion.

Legal Regimes Protecting Women' Right to Freedom of Religion

Traditional human rights norms protect religious freedom and provide for citizens the liberty to manifest one's religion or beliefs and the fundamental rights and freedoms of others. Article 18 of the Universal Declaration of Human Rights (UDHR) establishes *the right to freedom of thought, conscience, and religion*. This right is further amplified in Articles 18 and 27 of the International Covenant on Civil and Political Rights (ICCPR). As observed by Boyle, the UDHR failed to adequately specify the full effect of freedom of religion or belief in international law, and as such provides justification for the expansion of this right in subsequent treaties, leading to the comprehensive approach adopted in the ICCPR and other treaties addressing freedom of religion (Boyle 2014).

The expansion in the ICCPR provides a wider world-view beyond guaranteeing the right of individual to have freedom of thoughts, ideas and beliefs, the treaty also provides for citizens to reject religious beliefs that are not in agreement with their conscience. Article 18 of the ICCPR further offers protection against indoctrination, allows for freedom to practice one's religion and this can only be curtailed subject to prescribed laws and when necessary to protect public order and safety or the rights being enjoyed by others.

The UN Human Rights Committee (HRC) has confirmed this broad understanding of the text of Article 18, as protecting "theistic, non-theistic and atheistic beliefs, as well as the right not to profess any religion or belief." The Committee further calls for a holistic understanding of the terms "belief" and "religion." The HRC therefore expands the application of Article 18 to "traditional religions or to religions and beliefs with institutional characteristics or practices analogous to those of traditional religions." The Committee therefore dissuades any inclination to discriminate against any religion or belief for any reason, be it a new religion or of minority leaning.

In relations to women's religious rights, Article 18 (3) of the ICCPR, by clear allusion, restrains women from being subject to any religion that could offend public order, part of which is democratic living, which allows for freedom of association, participation, and to leave and manifest one's beliefs without any cohesion from patriarchal beliefs arising from custom or culture and religion. According to Raday (2007), the Convention on the Elimination of Discrimination Against Women complements the rights guaranteed in the ICCPR and recognizes the need for protecting women's human rights. The implied reading of this article justifies an obligation on States Parties to impose these rights.

The links between the CEDAW and other bills of rights are well established in international human rights law. The AU Women's Protocol is put together to ensure that the rights of women in Africa are promoted, realized, and protected in order to enable them to enjoy fully all their human rights. The Protocol is therefore apt with the provision: "[T]he dominant cultures and religions in Africa often bear an element of inequality, when not being clearly unfavorable to women. Furthermore, neither the African Charter nor CEDAW provide sufficient guarantees to African women as regards their rights." Thus the AU Women's Protocol cover the gaps in the earlier instrument in addressing women's rights and seeks to vindicate the rights of women in Africa, having expanded international human rights to include those that are central to African women, including women's right to freedom of religion. Nevertheless, the extent to which the Protocol has achieved its set goals within the African region is very much in doubt.

The Nigerian Constitution of 1999 by its Section 38(1) states:

Every person shall be entitled to freedom of thought, conscience and religion, including freedom to change his religion or belief, and freedom (either alone or in community with others, and in public or in private) to manifest and propagate his religion or belief in worship, teaching, practice and observance.

It is based on the potency of this constitutional assumption that Ayoola Justice of the Supreme Court in *Medical and Dental Practitioners Disciplinary Tribunal vs. Okonkwo* (1997), stated that

the rights of freedom of thought, conscience and religion, implies a right not to be prevented without lawful justification, from choosing the course of one's life, fashioned on what one believes in, and a right not to be coerced into acting contrary to one's religious belief. The limits of these freedoms as in all cases, are when they impinge on the rights of others or where they put the welfare of society or public health in jeopardy.

As postulated by Tahzib-Lie, the expression of the right to religion from a gender perspective can manifest in two ways: internal and external freedom. She describes internal freedom as that which denotes the individual's inner, private domain, which allows people to believe in a religion of their own choice without any form of coercion, while external freedom denotes the outer, often public, domain and has been defined as an individual's freedom, either alone or in community with others and in public or private, to manifest his/her religion or belief in teaching, practice, worship, and observance (Tahzib-Lie 2000).

However, the extent to which women enjoy internal and external freedom in complex, multi-ethnic, and religious society remains uncertain even if the Constitution of such countries guarantee rights to freedom of religion. In most countries of the world, women's rights are apparently violated mostly on the basis of cultural and religious practices and beliefs. Female circumcision, early or forced child marriage, and other harmful traditional practices affecting the health of women and girls are justified based on these patriarchal beliefs. Some of these gender-based violations are also politically motivated or perpetuated to ensure that men are continually favored and projected to the disadvantage and exclusion of women. Legitimization of gender discrimination through patriarchal politics is a deliberate machination to perpetually demean women and cast them as dissenting in a male-dominated society where the female is expected to remain unseen and unheard. In Nigeria, in spite of overwhelming public condemnation, it took painstaking vigilance and robust resistance of feminists and civil society activists to stave off attempts at legislating in favor of child marriage through political manipulation.

Tahzib-Lie, in explaining internal freedom, further argued that the definition of coercion should not be limited to the use of physical force or penal sanctions to obstruct people's right to religion, it could also mean "restrictive policies and practices such as those that restrict access to education, medical care, employment, or the rights to vote or participate in the conduct of public affairs" (Tahzib-Lie 2000: 970). In the context of Nigeria, this may be further manifested in the following ways: restricted access to justice suffered by women, or legislations that are oppressive to women, most of which are still in existence; abduction of women and forcible conversion of women and girls to a particular religion, and women suffering different forms of violation on the basis of religion. While the state may not be directly responsible for these acts or violation, it remains culpable where it failed to take steps to stop or prevent human rights violation.

The CEDAW and the AU Protocol are useful instruments for addressing restrictions on women's human rights generally and can effectively strengthen women's rights to freedom of religion. Since the State is responsible for bringing its domestic law and practice into conformity with its obligation under international law to protect and promote women's human rights, it is therefore argued that the failure of the government of Nigeria to remove any enactment, whether formal or religious, that impedes women's right to freedom of religion makes that government culpable.

Antagonistic Views Around CEDAW and the AU Protocol Bills in Nigeria

The attempt to domesticate the CEDAW into Nigerian laws can be traced to activities led by civil society organizations and the Federal Ministry of Women Affairs, the gender ministry in Nigeria since the late 1980s, immediately after the country's ratification of the instrument (Atsenuwa 2008). Unfortunately, despite the consistency of this group and institutions, the treaty is yet to find expression in Nigerian law.

Several studies commissioned to review the status of domestication of the CEDAW show that religious forces, particularly Christian and Muslim, in Nigeria have actively contributed to the failed attempt of the CEDAW domestication (Para-Mallam et al. 2011). All the studies undertaken to assess efforts toward domestication agree that there is clear evidence of considerable diversity within religious groupings around women's rights; the most critical areas of contention from the standpoints of religious groups are well presented in the studies edited by Ayesha Imam and others.

The studies identified the following issues as critical areas of concern for the major religious groupings in Nigeria; for example, the report shows that reproductive rights issues were opposed mainly by Catholic and conservative Muslim; while the provisions relating to equality of rights of women and men within marriage were opposed by all three major religions in Nigeria—Christian, Muslim, and traditional. The provisions relating to rights, responsibilities, and duties regarding children were opposed mainly by Muslims and traditionalists. While equality before the law in witnessing was opposed predominantly by Muslims, all three religions were opposed to the definition of key terminologies—for example, "equality" and "equity." Issues around women as leaders and affirmative action were opposed by some sectors of Christianity and Islam, and regulating the permissible age of marriage was contentious for Muslims.

The studies also show that there are provisions in both the CEDAW and the AU Protocol that religious forces have no objections to; these areas of common grounds include nationality, rights to work, and equal pay and conditions.

Other areas where both Islam and Christianity had consensus in the report included eradication of violence against women, opposition to marital rape, and suppression of trafficking and exploitation through prostitution. Other areas of common consensus include elimination of harmful traditional practices, ownership, acquisition, management, political participation, administration, enjoyment and possession of property, equality of access, opportunity to education and resources for training, women's right to work for income, and to equal treatment in employment, taxation, social security, and the right to development

The opposition recently gathered momentum, with the recent re-presentation of the CEDAW domestication bill in Nigeria in 2016, when a strong section of the Senate opposed the bill on the issues relating to the rights of women to marriage and family life; the right of widows to inherit, and the rights of widows to gain custody of their children. This issue of widows' rights was opposed on the grounds that it runs against the tenets of Islam on inheritance, while the Christians opposed the bill as an abortion bill because of the rights provisions relating to sexual and reproductive rights of women in the CEDAW bill. Another aspect of the CEDAW bill which was opposed by some lawmakers was the aspect where provision is made for the modification of socio-cultural practices; the opposing views argue that the provision is directly in conflict with the Nigerian Constitution, which recognizes the role of religion and custom-ary practices for all Nigerians.

From the above, there seem to be a rather pervasive notion that granting women freedom will compromise patriarchy and weaken the societal value attached to the male. This view was further strengthened when a prominent Muslim leader visibly opposed the bill and warned Muslims not to support its passage (BBC News 2016).

Counter-narratives by Pro-CEDAW Movements

In response to opposition to CEDAW bill, the gender equality groups led by the National Coalition on Affirmative Action mounted a campaign to pro-vide a counter-narrative to the opposition by religious leaders (*Independent* 2017). The group claimed that the provisions of the CEDAW domestication bill are not in conflict with Nigeria's 1999 Constitution; rather, they amplify and support the provisions of the Constitution, particularly the aspect dealing with prohibition of sex discrimination (Section 42) and that which upholds the preservation of cultures that enhance human dignity and are consistent with freedom, equality, and justice. Accordingly, the pro-CEDAW move-ments argued that the bill reinforces complementary and non-competitive relations between men and women, and proposed that such can be achieved through equal opportunities, mutual respect, and common benefits to both.

The group posited further that the bill will not take away family headship from men, which was a major concern by antagonists to the CEDAW bill; rather, the bill enjoins shared roles and responsibilities for family life. The group argues that the bill is consistent *with the fundamen-tal objectives* in the Constitution (Nwankwo n.d.), and argues that the domestication of the CEDAW and the AU Women's Protocol would provide respite for women against existing legal frameworks under religious law that infringe rather than protect the rights of women to religion. The group further argued that it is a matter of expression of the rights to equity, justice, and freedom for a widow to have an equitable inheritance of her husband's estate, to have custody of her children, and to continue to live in the matrimonial home upon the death of her husband. Such fears are more rooted in African traditional cultures than in modern religion, cannot stand in the face of the law, and would therefore appear to have been misplaced, since the two dominant religions in Nigeria preach the core values of human dignity, justice, and equity. Unfortunately, the counter-narrative is yet to yield any result, and the bill is yet to scale through public hearing, despite all efforts by feminist organizations to persuade the National Assembly and to engage religious leaders.

Concluding Remarks

Marked differences exist in the ways religious groups interpret gender roles and this also implies that women's religious rights are largely determined by theological and doctrinal fixations which derive from the patriarchal nature of religion. It is evident from analyses offered in this chapter that women's rights are determined by the age-old passion of religious faith doctrines which relegate women, rather than being dictated by emerging realities of human rights in the contemporary world. It is therefore not unexpected that opposition to the affirmation of women's rights is founded on stereotypical religious and cultural views which are mostly inexact. Notwithstanding the opposition to the Gender and Equal Opportunities Bill, the proposed CEDAW/AU Protocol domestication bill, it is advised that gender-equality groups further advocacy efforts at platforms that are antagonistic, deepen conversations around issues of women's rights and religion to engender more constructive engagements with major issues that remain contentious in the bill, as well as in key areas that pose difficulties for arrival at common ground towards the domestication of the CEDAW and the AU Women's Protocol. There are huge opportunities for sustaining inter-religious interrogations and conversations of the rights of women and religion in Nigeria; the group should take advantage of this space.

Discussion Questions

1   Highlight the provisions of the Convention on the Elimination of all forms of Discrimination Against Women (CEDAW) and the AU Women Protocol that can guarantee protection of women 's rights against discriminatory religious practices and laws.
2   In what ways can feminists deal with continuous backlash due to strong opposing religious views in secular states?
3   What can be done to further guarantee women's right to freedom of religion?

4   What protection exist under international human rights norms to pro-
     tect women and girls from discriminatory religious practices?
5   Are there strategies that can promote women's rights to religion?
     If there are, identify five key strategies that can provide a counter-
     narrative for antagonist religious views that have relegated women to
     the background.
6   What are the factors affecting women's rights to full enjoyment of free-
     dom of religion in Nigeria?

Suggested Readings

1   African Union, "Protocol to the African Charter on Human and
     People's Rights on the Rights of Women in Africa," www.refworld.
     org/docid/3f4b139d4.html
2   Akiyode-Afolabi, Abiola. "Democracy, Women's Rights and Sharia Law
     in Nigeria," *Pambazuka News*, January 23, 2003, www.pambazuka.org/
     gender-minorities/democracy-womens-rights-and-sharia-law-nigeria
3   British Council. "Gender in Nigeria Report 2012: Improving the
     Lives of Girls and Women in Nigeria," www.britishcouncil.org/sites/
     default/files/british-council-gender-nigeria2012.pdf
4   Nwankwo, Oby. "Briefing on the Domestication of the Convention
     on the Elimination of all forms of Discrimination against Women
     (CEDAW)," www.aacoalition.org/domistic_cedaw.htm
5   Sampson, Isaac Terwase. "Religion and the Nigerian State; Situating
     the de facto and de jure Frontiers of State-Religion Relations and its
     Implication for National Security." *Oxford Journal of Law and Religion*
     32, no. 3 (2014): 311–339.

References

African Union, "Protocol to the African Charter on Human and People's Rights on
     the Rights of Women in Africa," accessed April 19, 2017, www.refworld.org/
     docid/3f4b139d4.html
Akiyode-Afolabi, Abiola. "Democracy, Women's Rights and Sharia Law in Nigeria,"
     Pambazuka News, January 23, 2003, accessed April 12, 2017, www.pambazuka.
     org/gender-minorities/democracy-womens-rights-and-sharia-law-nigeria
Astill, James and Owen Bowcott. "Fatwa is Issued on Nigerian Journalist,"
     Guardian, November 27, 2002, accessed April 12, 2017, www.theguardian.com/
     world/2002/nov/27/jamesastill.owenbowcott
Atsenuwa, Ayodele. "Study of National Legislations, Policies and Practices
     Congruent and Incompatible with the Provisions of the Convention on the
     Elimination of Forms of Discrimination (CEDAW) and the Protocol to the
     African Charter on Human and People's Rights on the Rights of Women in
     Africa." Unpublished report, funded by CIDA. Lagos: Legal Research and
     Resource Development Centre, 2008.

BBC News. "Nigeria Sultan of Sokoto Rejects Gender Equality Bill," *BBC News*, December 28, 2016, accessed April 19, 2017, www.bbc.com/news/world-africa-38449822

Boyle, Kevin. "Thought, Expression, Association and Assembly." In *International Human Rights Law*, edited by Daniel Moeckli, S. Shah, and D. Harris, 257–279. New York: Oxford University Press 2014.

British Council, "Gender in Nigeria Report 2012: Improving the Lives of Girls and Women in Nigeria," accessed April 6, 2017, www.britishcouncil.org/sites/default/files/british-council-gender-nigeria2012.pdf

Chappell, Louise. "Contesting Women's Rights: The Influence of Religious Forces in the United Nations," Presentation at the Australasian Political Studies Association Conference, Adelaide, Australia, September 29–October 1, 2004.

Ezeilo, Joy, Muhammed Tawfiq Ladan, and Abiola Akiyode-Afolabi. 2003. *Shari'a Implementation in Nigeria: Issues & Challenges on Women's Rights and Access to Justice*. Enugu: Women's Aid Collective (WACOL).

Friedrich, Ebert Stiftung. *Protection of Women's Right Under Sharia Law: Safiya Tugartudu Husseini: A Case Study*. Lagos: Frankad Publishers, 2002.

Ibrahim, Hauwa, "The Rule of Law Prevails in the Case of Amina Lawal." *Human Rights Brief* 11, no. 3 (2004): 39–41. Accessed April 7, 2017, http://digitalcommons.wcl.american.edu/hrbrief/vol11/iss3/11

Ibidapo-Obe, Akin. *Essays on Human Rights Law in Nigeria*. Lagos: Concept Law Press, 2000.

Imam, Ayesha. *Adopting Women's Human Rights Legislations in Nigeria- A Synthesis Analysis Report*. Lagos: Infovision, 2010.

Independent. "Creating A Better Understanding On Gender Advocacy." *Independent*, April 22, 2017, accessed May 17, 2017, http://independent.ng/creating-a-better-understanding-on-gender-advocacy

Mccolgan, Aileen. "Class Wars? Religion and (In) equality in the Workplace." *Industrial Law Journal* 38, no. 1 (2009): 1–29.

Nwankwo, Oby. (n.d.) "Briefing on the Domestication of the Convention on the Elimination of all forms of Discrimination against Women (CEDAW)," accessed April 6, 2018, www.aacoalition.org/domistic_cedaw.htm

Otto, Dianne. "Holding Up Half the Sky, But for Whose Benefit? A Critical Analysis of the Fourth World Conference on Women." *Australian Feminist Law Journal* 6, no. 1 (1996): 7–28.

Para-Mallam, O. J., Bolatito Lare-Abass, Fatima Adamu, and Adebayo Ajala. (2011) "Role of Religion in Women's Movements: The Campaign for the Domestication of CEDAW in Nigeria," University of Birmingham, 2011. Accessed March 7, 2018, www.birmingham.ac.uk/Documents/college-social-sciences/government-society/research/rad/working-papers/wp-59.pdf

Raday, Frances. "Culture, Religion and CEDAW Article 5" In *The Circle of Empowerment, Twenty-Five years of the UN Committee on the Elimination of Discrimination Against Women*, edited by Hanna Beate Schopp-Schillin, and Cees Flinterman, 68–85. New York: The Feminist Press at CUNY, 2007.

UN Women (n.d.) "Religion and Gender Equality." *UN Women*. Accessed April 7, 2018. www.partner-religiondevelopment.org/fileadmin/Dateien/Resources/Knowledge_Center/Religion_and_Gender_Equality_UNWOMEN.pdf

Sampson, Isaac Terwase. "Religion and the Nigerian State; Situating the de facto and de jure Frontiers of State-Religion Relations and its Implication for National Security." *Oxford Journal of Law and Religion* 32, no. 3 (2014): 311–339.

Sheen, Juliet. "Burdens on the Right of Women to Assert their Freedom of Religion or Belief." In *Facilitating Freedom of Religion or Belief; A Deskbook*, edited by Tore Lindholm, W. Cole Durham, Jr., and Bahia G. Tahzib-Lie, 513–522. Danvers, MA: Martinus Nijhoff, 2004.

Tahzib-Lie, Bahia. "Applying a Gender Perspective in the Area of the Right to Freedom of Religion or Belief," *BYU Law Review*, 13, no. 3 (2000): 967–988.

UN Human Rights Committee (HRC), "CCPR General Comment No. 22: Article 18 (Freedom of Thought, Conscience or Religion)," accessed April 20, 2017, www.refworld.org/docid/453883fb22.html

Viljoen, Frans. *International Human Rights Law in Africa*, 2nd edition. Oxford: Oxford University Press, 2012.

Part V

PUSHING BACK: ACTIVISM AND RESISTANCE

GENDER SCHOLAR SPOTLIGHT: INTERVIEW WITH MALACHI D. CRAWFORD

A native of Pasadena, California, Dr. Malachi D. Crawford is Assistant Director of African American Studies at the University of Houston. He received his doctorate in Twentieth Century U.S. History from the University of Missouri-Columbia, with a focus on examining the histories of race and law enforcement, religion and law, and Africana Womanist intellectual traditions within the African American experience. More broadly, Crawford's research takes a historical approach to understanding the legal, religious, intellectual, and literary attempts by African-descended peoples to challenge the cultural foundations of civil law and human rights in the Western Hemisphere. In January 2015, the *Critical Africana Studies Series* at Lexington Books, an imprint of Rowman and Littlefield Publishing Group, Inc., released his first published book-length manuscript entitled *Black Muslims and the Law: Civil Liberties from Elijah Muhammad to Muhammad Ali*. Intellectually located within the critical race scholarship of A. Leon Higginbotham's classic works on American slavery jurisprudence, this study examines the Nation of Islam's quest for civil rights as a direct and inaugural challenge to the suppression of African American religious freedom as a matter of law. More recently, Humanities Texas, the state affiliate of the National Endowment for the Humanities, approved a major media grant in support of his first digital humanities project, *One False Step: A Visual History of Muhammad Ali and the Struggle for Civil Rights in Houston, Texas*.

What led you to begin studying women's inequality?

I first began studying women's inequality as a result of a void in African-centered pedagogy on the campus of the University of Missouri-Columbia in the fall of 2001. As an incoming graduate student (U.S. History) with a background in Africana Studies, I naturally looked for faculty and courses that supported my research interests and reaffirmed my identity and traditions. At the time, the only full-time faculty member who I could identify as a scholar familiar with historic origins, theoretical assumptions, and epistemological foundations of Africana Studies at MU was Dr. Clenora Hudson-Weems, the founder of Africana Womanism. I quickly enrolled in Dr. Hudson-Weems's courses and found her to be a warm, authentic, and revolutionary intellectual on campus. Among other things, Dr. Hudson-Weems made me feel welcome within this critical discourse. Eventually, I became one of her graduate assistants through my appointment within the Department of Black Studies under Dr. Julius E. Thompson. I should also mention another instructive voice and influence on my decision to critically study women's inequality: Mrs. Waheedah Bilal, an African American Muslim and my graduate colleague in the Department of History at MU. In my study of the Black Nationalist activist-intellectual tradition, she forced me to sharpen my analysis of the influence and role that Africana women had made to identity and community formation.

How have your lived experiences shaped your research interests?

Historically, African American women have provided the most stable models of human *being*-ness (how to be human) in my life. These women, such as my mother, were nurturing and not domineering, so I learned to be sensitive toward the feelings of others in my social environment. At the same time, although I had studied and critiqued structural and ideological systems of sexism and domination through my work, I do not believe that these forces became real for me until various social encounters with my two daughters forced me to engage and confront them head-on. Lastly, I consider myself profoundly fortunate for having studied under and been mentored by Dr. Clenora Hudson-Weems.

In your opinion, what scholarly works have been most impactful on your research on women and inequality?

I'll begin by saying that my research background and scholarly approach within Black/Africana women's studies is interdisciplinary. I draw my insights from critical theorists and fiction/creative non-fiction writers alike. Still, if I had to briefly identify those works that have most significantly impacted my research, the following texts (in no particular order) would be included:

- Hudson-Weems, Clenora. *Africana Womanism: Reclaiming Ourselves* (Bedford Publishers: 1994)
- Hudson-Weems, Clenora. *Africana Womanist Literary Theory* (Africa World Press: 2004)
- Aldridge, Delores P. *Focusing: Black Male-Female Relationships* (Third World Press: 1991)
- Hurston, Zora N. *Their Eyes Were Watching God* (Harper Perennial Modern Classics; Reissue Edition: 2006)
- Collins, Patricia Hill. *Black Feminist Thought: Knowledge, Consciousness, and the Politics of Empowerment* (Routledge: 1991)
- Ngũgĩ, wa Thiong'o. *The River Between* (Heinemann: 1965)
- Somé, Sobonfu. *The Spirit of Intimacy: Ancient African Teachings in the Ways of Relationships* (Harper: 2002)
- Karenga, Maulana. *Selections from the Husia: Sacred Wisdom of Ancient Egypt* (University of Sankore Press: 1989)
- Jeffries, Bayyinah. *A Nation Can Rise No Higher Than Its Women: African American Muslim Women in the Movement for Black Self-Determination, 1950–1975* (Lexington Books: 2015)
- Gammage, Marquita M. *Representations of Black Women in the Media: The Damnation of Black Womanhood* (Routledge: 2015)

What has been most challenging about your field of work?

One of the most challenging issues that I face concerns student presuppositions about the relationship between what might be called "truth" with respect to the field of Black/Africana women's studies. Particularly as it concerns students who have only encountered the traditional canons within the discipline of women's studies, there appears to be little insight into the nature of discourse and an understanding of how power and knowledge interact. Indeed, those students who have never or rarely encountered theories and theorists whose works are generally marginalized within the discipline of women's studies might incorrectly assume that these works are rightly dismissed because they are somehow less critical, less legitimate, or less explanatory than more popular theorists and theories.

Why is your work on women important?

Among other matters, my work represents a collaborative, communal approach to the development of critical paradigms and discussions within the field of Black/Africana women's studies. I see myself in conversation with a community of scholar-activists who share a similar orientation toward and concerns about issues such as social justice, human rights, and communal empowerment. In so doing, I hope to be among those who provide an alternative space and framework for women whose experiences and perspectives might otherwise be marginalized within the narratives that dominate women's studies. Perhaps most significantly, as my work is rooted in Africana Womanist critical theory, I likewise seek to demonstrate that men must and can be involved in struggle to end sexism.

Which scholar(s) (and why) has been most influential in developing your perspective?

Dr. Clenora Hudson-Weems, Professor of English and Black Studies at the University of Missouri-Columbia, was, undoubtedly, the most influential scholar shaping my analysis within the field of Black/Africana women's studies. Although I took and read scholarship from different faculty who studied inequality and women, Dr. Hudson-Weems (in my opinion) seemed to be the only scholar on campus approaching the subject from a critical race, gender, and class analysis. As I reflect, she was quite accessible and held a commanding knowledge of the latest scholarship and major arguments in the field. Ultimately, I not only took her classes, but also went on to serve as her graduate assistant for several years.

What theoretical approach best guides your research?

At its core, my work is rooted in many of the cosmological, axiological, and epistemological assertions found within Africana Womanism, a theory and term created by Prof. Clenora Hudson-Weems. Africana Womanism is a family-centered paradigm for Africana women (African Americans and other women of African descent) that emerged within the field of Africana Studies. Among other observations, the theory argues that the shared experiences and cultural traditions of African American people provide the most authentic resource for interrogating the lived realities of African American women—realities that are qualitatively different than those of women from other racial and ethnic groups in American society.

What pedagogical approaches have you found most effective when teaching on women and inequality?

In all my courses, I attempt to create a space that is open and inclusive, encouraging and critical, accepting of difference, and respectful of new knowledge. That being said, I have often found that a mixed approach to the use of sources—blending the visual, oral, and literary evidence and expressions of Africana women's lived experiences—is most effective as a tool of pedagogy in my area of study. I should also mention that Dr. Hudson-Weems would also engage students' senses of taste and smell through demonstrations of her cooking. Although I am not there yet, I believe that such exposure is a very effective means of experiencing community, intimacy, sociability, and many of the concepts associated with Africana Womanism.

In your opinion, what are the most pertinent issues facing the women in your area of research today?

In my discussions with my peers and colleagues, it seems that the proliferation of new scholars who have little or no understanding of the historical foundations or intellectual antecedents associated with their respective theoretical traditions continues to be a major challenge confronting the field. At best, this circumstance creates confusion as to the significant themes and principal assertions that demarcate and distinguish one theory from another; at worst, it leads to the conscious or unconscious intellectual appropriation of ideas that are inherently foreign to the basic premises upon which a theory might have been built. Thus, there remains a need to ensure disciplinary and theoretical clarity as it pertains to the various nomenclatures in the field.

Is there anything else that you would like to add?

Thank you, kindly, for allowing me to be a part of this extraordinary work.

16

I'M GOING TO GET WHAT I WANT

Black Women's Sexual Agency as a Form of Resistance

Stephanie Campos and Ellen Benoit

Introduction

This chapter explores how a sample of low-income heterosexual Black women living in New York City resist the interlocking oppressions of race, class, and gender through expressions of sexual autonomy and pursuit of sexual enjoyment. An intersectional analysis contextualizes the experiences of participants who live at the center of interrelated inequalities. These disparities contribute to negative consequences for Black women's sexual health and imagery. We analyze how these women resist their oppression through participation in sexual activities that are typically considered to be in the male domain and that transgress cultural standards for appropriate sexual behavior in women.

Crenshaw (1989) coined the term "intersectionality" in describing how Black women's experiences are erased when race and gender are taken into consideration separately rather than simultaneously. Intersectionality understands systems of oppression such as gender, race, and class as interrelated, unconfined, and mutually constitutive. They function together in varying times and spaces at the micro and macro levels to shape our social hierarchy, one's particular location within it, and accompanying social relations. Collins (2000) contributed to this framework the concept of the matrix of domination. This is the distinctive way in which intersecting systems of oppression are organized and operate through four spheres of power: structural, disciplinary, hegemonic, and interpersonal. Collins notes that resistance is possible within each domain.

Black women have historically experienced inequalities in ways that highlight their unique positionality within the matrix of domination. Examples include forced sex and reproduction during slavery, income-earning opportunities after slavery that were limited to feminized and consequently unskilled labor such as domestic work, and attempts to restrict Black women's reproductive rights through forced contraception and cuts in government assistance to single mothers (Roberts 1997). The intersection of gender and race also impacts the sexual health of Black women.

For example, they have disproportionately high rates of sexually transmitted infections such as chlamydia and gonorrhea (Fisher Collins 2006; Telfair Sharpe et al. 2012). Rates of new HIV infections among Black women are higher than for white women and those of other ethnic/racial backgrounds (CDC 2015). Black women are also more likely than white and Hispanic women to be victims of intimate partner violence. For example, 29% of Black women have experienced domestic violence and they make up almost one-third of homicides by intimate partners (IDVAAC 2008). Sixty percent of Black women have been sexually assaulted before age 18 (Black Women's Blueprint 2012).

These pressing issues make intersectionality a valuable tool for understanding how gender, race, and class "structure social relationships in ways that produce differentials in health and disease" (Mullings and Schulz 2006:7) and for multidimensional analysis of how health disparities impact different populations, particularly those that are marginalized (Bowleg 2012; Griffith 2012). As a methodology, it has been applied in women's health studies at the research design, fieldwork, and data analysis stages (Hankivsky et al. 2010). Researchers increasingly understand gender and sex as more than just discrete units of analysis and explain how they interact with other systems of power to construct distinct health circumstances for men and women (Hankivsky 2012), including HIV vulnerability (Higgins et al. 2010). Multiple social factors interact with gender to shape risk and experiences of living with HIV, including race (Bredström 2006; Bowleg et al. 2013), ethnicity, mental illness (Collins et al. 2008) and immigration (Doyal 2009).

The powerlessness of low-income Black Americans at the structural level is played out in their sexual relationships and elevated risk for HIV and STIs/STDs. Racial discrimination contributes to disproportionate rates of incarceration, joblessness, and underemployment for Black men (Bowleg et al. 2013). This, along with greater rates of premature death, reduces the pool of available sex partners for Black women (Adimora and Schoenbach 2005; Andrasik et al. 2014). This gender imbalance fosters power differences in heterosexual relationships (Newsome and Airhihenbuwa 2013), in which men are encouraged to have multiple female partners (Wingood and DiClemente 2000) and women may suppress their autonomy, often tolerating risky relationships (Bowleg et al. 2004).

While much attention has been devoted to explicating the interlocking dimensions of oppression, less has been given to resistance and autonomy (Hankivsky 2012). Dworkin (2005) critiques the use of gender as a monolithic category and suggests an intersectional approach that recognizes diverse expressions of sexual behaviors and the erotic. An exploration of the different ways Black women express sexual agency responds to these concerns. Black female sexuality is intimately tied to the construction of race in the United States. As Hammonds (1997) notes: "racial difference was tied to sexual difference" during slavery in order to justify the enslavement of Black men and women. Stereotypes of Black women's uncontrollable lust and inherent immorality were developed in contrast to the imagery of pure White womanhood and further served the sexual exploitation of Black women in the Antebellum South. The end of slavery did not end this victimization (Collins 2004; Staples 2006) and Black women continued to be sexual objects available to white men through assaults and via their subordinate positions as domestic workers in white households (Staples 2006).

The politics of respectability was one form of resistance to this oppression after slavery and migration to Northern cities (Hammonds 1997; Collins 2004). Middle-class Black women (and those of the working class who aspired to upward mobility) enacted the mainstream standards of proper behavior and conduct. Resistance, however, is not unproblematic. The politics of respectability contributed to a silencing of Black female sexuality (Hammonds 1997), erasure of non-heterosexual expressions of Black sexuality (White 2010), and close surveillance of working-class Black women's bodies by both white-dominated institutions and the Black middle class (Carby 1992). McGruder (2006) argues that Black sexuality was further ostracized after the Civil Rights movement through social science research like the *Moynihan Report*. It explained the economic marginalization of Black families in large urban cities by faulting low-income Black women and their intimate relationships with men. "Images of working-class femininity all articulate with the social class system of the post-civil rights era" (Collins 2004: 137) and include foundational archetypes of Black women such as the Jezebel, Mammy, Matriarch, and Welfare Mother (Stephens and Phillips 2003). More recent representations, especially in popular culture, include the Freak, Gold Digger, Diva and Dyke, Baby Mama, Earth Mother, Bad Bitch, and Hoe (French 2013; Layne 2014; Little 2015). These racialized stereotypes limit the sexuality of Black women and may be internalized by them (Stephens and Phillips 2003). Furthermore, sexualized controlling images reflect and reinforce the marginalization of underprivileged Black women (Windsor et al. 2011).

In spite of these obstacles, Black women do exhibit sexual agency and there are a growing number of texts "that address and illuminate black female sexual desires marked by both agency and empowerment and pleasure and pain in order to elucidate the ways black women regulate their sexual lives" (Melancon 2015: 3). For example, Lee (2010: xiv) recognizes cultural icons such as Beyoncé as "erotic revolutionaries" who "effectively wage war against the politics of respectability" by simultaneously representing erotic freedom and (strategically) conforming to heteropatriarchal expectations. Stallings employs the figure of the trickster to show how Black women create space for expressing their sexual desires while resisting labels and heteronormativity. She argues for "languages of sexual rights that Black females need to know and embrace for their own sake" (2007: 293), which has been interpreted as a call for a Black feminist politics of pleasure (Nash 2012). Garvey (2015) argues that same-gender loving Black women provide models of agency and empowerment for younger Black women traumatized by the norms and biases of dominant culture. The strength and authenticity of their relationships can be understood as an erotic form of healing that helps younger women realize the wholeness of their identities. Black women's narratives of their sexual decision making and the different ways they seek sexual pleasure represent empowerment and contestation of interconnected inequalities.

Methods

Data for this chapter comes from the qualitative study "Heterosexual Black Females: Socialization and HIV Risks in Scripts and Practices," which is based on in-depth interviews with low-income, heterosexual, substance-using women in New York City and was funded by the National Institutes of Health. Trained ethnographers recruited 99 women 18–50 years old who self-identified as Black and heterosexual, had four or more lifetime sexual partners, and at least two sexual partners in the two past years, and had an annual income below $35,000. Women who had sexual relations with only one mate in the past two years were recruited as a monogamous comparison group. Staff went to various New York City Housing Authority housing developments and low-income neighborhoods, local social events, community centers, and medical clinics, where they handed out fliers and spoke to residents about the study. Snowball sampling was also used to tap into networks of potential participants. Study participants gave written informed consent and invented code names for themselves and for any sexual partners mentioned. They then completed in-depth individual interviews that covered demographics, socialization, sexual scripts/partnering, safe sex and condom use, drug involvement, and parenthood. The interviews took two or more meetings to complete and were held as often as possible in participants' homes to gain a sense of their environments. Ethnographers also took extensive field notes of participants' surroundings and interviews.

The mean age of study participants was 32. Nearly one-third did not live with their main sex partner and 18% did not have a primary sex partner. More than one-quarter had at least some college education, but 30% did not complete high school. Public benefits were the primary source of income for 43% of the women (see Table 16.1). Participants are located at the juncture of racial, gender, and economic inequalities. In addition to being low-income, 67% have experienced violence in their intimate relationships; at least 11% disclosed sexual abuse during childhood; about 40% are single parents, and 67% have been involved with the criminal justice system. The women in this study experience multiple and overlapping oppressions at the structural and individual levels and these inequalities impact their health. For example, 5% are HIV positive and 12% rely primarily or substantially on disability benefits.

Table 16.1 Demographics

Characteristic (N=99)	%
Relationship status	
Has no primary partner	18
Not living with main partner	32
Living with main partner (non-monogamous)	34
Monogamous (comparison group)	15
Education	
Attending now	13
Less than high school	30
GED	14
High school diploma	15
Some college	19
College degree	8
Primary source of income	
Public benefits	43
Legal employment	25
Family/friends	12
Hustling (drug sales, sex work, braiding hair, e.g.)	7
Off-the-books work	6
Other	6

Interviews were audio recorded, transcribed, and entered into FileMaker Pro, a relational database program that the research team has used successfully to manage qualitative data. This chapter focuses on analysis of narrative responses to questions concerning sexual behavior, including same-sex experiences and sources of sexual pleasure. Data was analyzed using a grounded theory approach (Charmaz 2006), led by the first author and corroborated by the second. Initial analysis began with two reviews of a sample of full transcripts (50%) in order to identify emerging themes. This involved underlining key phrases and constructing case summaries for each participant that included notes on relationship status, partner selection, and sexual behavior. The authors noted unexpected repetition of phrases related to seeking sexual pleasure and sexual autonomy. Based on this tentative finding, the second stage of analysis included a systematic review of all responses to specific questions regarding same-sex behavior, multiple sex partners and what sexually arouses participants. Both authors independently analyzed data and created codes and categories that reflected study participants' statements and behaviors. They then compared codes and noted where they coincided and differed. In instances of discrepancies, both authors re-analyzed the data under consideration and met again to build one set of codes and categories.

Participants most often expressed sexual agency within four broad areas: consumption of pornography, attendance at exotic dance clubs, multiple sex partners, and same-sex behavior. Authors were able to detect patterns but limited data prevented further in-depth analysis. The goal of the larger study was to understand the sexual scripts women used to negotiate sex with multiple male partners and findings on sexual autonomy emerged after data was collected.

Results

Same-sex encounters

An unexpected finding was the high rate of same-sex behavior among women who self-identified as heterosexual. During interviews, 57% of respondents reported sexual relationships or encounters with women. This suggests that sexual attraction among Black women, as among others, is fluid and that sexual behavior and identity may not always neatly align (Diamond 2008). Despite being at increased risk for STIs/STDs and HIV (Muzny et al. 2011; Lindley et al. 2013; Muzny et al. 2013), behaviorally bisexual Black women are virtually invisible in the literature. They may also experience shame in their families and larger social environment (Alexander and Fannin 2014; Henderson 2009), some as a result of religiosity. For example, Hill argues that, "As the black community tends to be more connected to faith-based traditions and have higher church attendance, religious traditions and values also influence expression of support, or lack thereof, for black LGBT people" (2013: 212). The politics of respectability may also be at work, where homophobia is seen as an attempt to distance the Black community from stereotypes of Black sexuality as deviant and reckless (Cohen 1999). Interviewees in this subsample may not have labeled themselves lesbian or bisexual, but their sexual relationships with women are still considered stigmatized practices. Asserting their sexuality was therefore a form of resistance against converging inequalities.

Women in this subsample demonstrated a wide range of sexual experiences with women. For example, 21% reported that their initial same-sex encounter occurred during childhood or as a teenager. Bossy's (age 18) same-sex debut occurred "my freshman year in high school . . . that's my baby, I love her . . . even though we're not together." Brownie (49) said that she had a relationship with a woman "when I was younger." They were together for about a year: "As a matter of fact, we still friends. She lives in Florida. When I go down there, I see her." They are no longer intimate: "[W]e just talk and talk about the past." Some participants (9.4%) began same-sex relationships during incarceration and a small group (6%) stated that their sexual experiences with women were paid.

Like Alexander and Fannin (2014), we discovered that emotional connectedness was a motivating factor for having sex with another woman: about 36% of our subsample said that they had been in a same-sex relationship.

Harmani (23), for example, had a sexual relationship with "my ex-wife, I love her." The last time they had sex was "last year, that's still my girlfriend but I ain't see her in a while cause she got locked up, she just came home." Cynthia (23) described her same-sex experience:

> When I started dating my children's father, when I was 17, I was actually with another girl for a couple of months because she was living with me. I was going through a phase in my life where I just wanted to go out with girls so I went out with her for like eight months.

Interviewees who formed romantic and emotional sexual partnerships with women resisted heteronormative cultural ideals.

Another group of participants (28%) reported only a single sexual experience with a woman. Many of these encounters, like Susie's (20), were motivated by curiosity:

> When I was younger, you know how they say everyone is bi-curious, everyone wants to know if they like a female or they don't? So one day there was this girl, we went to her house, me and my cousin. I never knew she liked me . . . So when I got there my cousin put me on like, "Yo, you know she likes you" and I'm like, "Okay?" I am not gay, though. I don't like females. And she was like, "Alright, just talk to her" and I was like "Alright." But in my head I was like, I want to see if I like girls, I just want to know. So I started talking to her . . . and that night I received oral sex from her."

The women in this category were curious about experiencing sexual pleasure outside penetrative sex and by acting on this desire challenged the "coital imperative" (Jackson and Cram 2003; McPhillips et al. 2001). This is the dominant discourse that the only type of heterosexual sex that matters is vaginal/penis intercourse despite the potential that non-penetrative sex has for preventing the spread of HIV/AIDS (McPhillips et al. 2001). Oral sex with a woman not only questions heterosexual sex as the sexual norm, but also the view that sexual pleasure must involve penetration.

A similar number of women (28%) had more than one same-sex experience but were not interested in forming committed relationships with female sex partners. Women in this group challenged the traditional three-category model of sexual orientation (i.e., heterosexual, homosexual, bisexual). They identified as heterosexual but had several same-sex encounters, demonstrating "that there are many genders and sexualities, but too few existing narratives for the multitude of them" (Stallings 2007:4). Jada (23) said her encounters are random occurrences . . . [T]he last time, we were drunk at a party, it was like funny. We were kissing and dancing together and we were like, "You know what? We are going to go home and leave the party together" and then we went home together.

She would not have a relationship with another woman "because it would be weird. Like, my emotions mixed with another female's emotions would kind of cloud us in our own way because we would both be extra emotional. And I don't think that is a good thing." Cookie (34) echoed this sentiment: "No, I don't deal with relationships, not with girls. They too much like me. It's too much headache." While these women push the boundaries of heterosexuality, they also exhibit internalized gendered notions that women are the same at the emotive level and having a relationship with one would lead to negative consequences for both partners.

Pleasure and sexual satisfaction were motivations for having sex with women. Lucy (21) said it well:

I love having sexual intercourse with a female . . . because a female knows exactly what another female is looking for and it's . . . so much better, like I don't know, just the way like you're a female like when someone touches [you] that the whole body tingles. You just imagine another beautiful woman's body touching like all that tingling and stuff is just running through you . . ..

Lucy's comment echoes Walker's (2014) findings among heterosexually identified women who had sex with women. One reason for seeking out sex with other women was the idea that females are skilled lovers who naturally know how to sexually please other women.

At least 49% of this subsample had male sex partners at the time they had sex with women. Participants in the larger study often had a main sex partner (MSP) and a secondary sex partner (SSP). Other women had non-committed sexual relationships with male sex partners (SP). We found that heterosexual and same-sex sexual relationships often overlapped. For instance, Sexy (23) had two male SPs in addition to a female partner: "I kind of live with my girlfriend . . . I'm straight . . . I just like women, they're hot, sexy. Women know where it's at. But men know more." Olivia (24) was with her MSP for over two years. She spoke about her sexual experience with a woman: "Months ago, I guess. It was my first time, me just having fun, talking to her and stuff like that. We had sex one time; it's a possibility for a next time." Olivia's same-sex encounter took place while she was still in a relationship with her MSP.

Overall, participants' same-sex experiences reflect the fact that "variability in the emergence and expression of female same-sex desire during the life course is normative rather than exceptional" (Diamond and Savin-Williams

2000: 298). They illustrate the "continuous nature of sexual orientation" (Vrangalova and Savin-Williams 2012: 96) and question the exclusivity of a heterosexual identity. In other words, having a heterosexual identity did not preclude most study participants from having sex with women.

The sexual autonomy expressed by participants illustrates resistance to gendered and racial oppression historically experienced by Black women. We recognize, however, that resistance can be contradictory and limited. For instance, 23% of participants who had same-sex experiences did so under the influence of alcohol and/or drugs. Perhaps this lowered inhibitions and made it easier to breach heterosexual norms, as Nicki (23) explains:

> Like usually I have to be like—I don't know. Like I have to be drinking. Like maybe I am attracted to women, but on a sober note I'm not bold enough to say it or do something like of that nature. But when I'm drinking and you're out in a club, and you with your home girls, and y'all dancing on each other, or she smack your butt, then you might be a little more subjective to those type of things.

Research on "nondiscordant" heterosexually identified women has found higher levels of binge drinking and substance use than among those who were concordant (Nield et al. 2015). Young adult bisexual women are more at risk for alcohol abuse than those who identify as heterosexual; consuming alcohol may be one strategy for coping with heterosexism (Gruskin et al. 2001). Among the women in our study who spoke about having sex with women while under the influence of alcohol and/or drugs, 67% were under 30 years old. They may not have yet developed other strategies for contending with internalized and externalized homophobia.

A small number of women (six) reported only receiving oral sex. They were uncomfortable with the idea of performing oral sex on another woman. Tamara (28), for example, talked about her sexual encounters with women:

> I always feel disgusted by them afterwards 'cause I'm not gay. It was just because they were fiendin' and it was easier to take advantage of them. But at the end of the day, "ughhh," I'm not gay . . . I never do it back so it make them mad but I take it. I took it in my life . . . but ughhh, I don't trust they vagina.

Tamara reflects negative historical constructions of female genitalia that associate it with ugliness, unattractive odor, and uncleanliness (Braun and Wilkinson 2001; McDougall 2013). Internalized ideas of female genitalia as disgusting limited the same-sex sexual repertoire for women in this subgroup.

Pornography and Strip Clubs

Participants were asked about their sexual desires and what stimulates them, including whether they consume pornographic media and attend strip clubs. Mainstream feminist research on pornography has focused historically on debates over the extent to which sexually explicit media content objectifies women, incites male violence against women, and should be legally proscribed or heavily regulated in order to protect women (see review in Crawford 2007). Beginning in the 1990s, third-wave feminism, while acknowledging pornographic exploitation of women, also emphasized women's consumption of pornography as a source of pleasure that is vital to their sexual health (Crawford 2007; McElroy 1995).

Against this backdrop, our participants' consumption of pornography for sexual pleasure may be examined as potential evidence of resistance to domination and silencing. Forty-four percent of the women in our sample said they watch pornographic videos either on DVDs or on adult-content Internet sites. This is not necessarily surprising, given research that shows up to one-third of pornography consumers are women (Crawford 2007). More recent analysis of national survey data found that women who consumed pornography, compared with non-consumers, had more sexual partners in the past year and past five years, and were more likely to have engaged in extramarital sex and in paid sex. They were also likely to be younger and non-white (Wright et al. 2013).

Participants who watch pornographic videos say they often watch them with their male partners and sometimes alone, and they use both DVDs and Internet sites. Many said they watch the videos as an aid to sexual arousal—to put them in the mood for sex—or to enhance the sexual experience. Some watch videos if they are in the mood for sex, but they are not with a male partner. Samantha (28) explains:

> I go look at porn sites if I'm horny . . . and I'm just, like, "OK, I'm doing it myself. So I'm just gonna look at a few seconds and I'll [be] back to normal." [Interviewer: So you masturbate after this?] "While I'm watching it."

Participants expressed a preference for lesbian pornography. Velvet (42) said, "I like to see two girls . . . I'm more turned on by that than anything else." Malya (22) is definite about her preference: "I can't watch, like, a man and a woman have sex; it doesn't do anything for me." Niki (23) watches "girl-on-girl porno" because she identifies too much with the women in heterosexual videos: "If I watch regular, like, guy and girl, I don't really like to see like a beautiful woman doing this ugly-ass man. Like I'm more upset for her than getting turned on." These findings are consistent with a recent survey indicating that women prefer lesbian pornography over heterosexual pornography because lesbian actors more often appear to experience pleasure and because oral sex is more prominently featured (Dickson 2014).

Only one participant said she explicitly avoids pornography because she thinks it is abusive toward women. In contrast, two others said they prefer videos that may be considered abusive. When asked what type of pornography she watches, Bossy (18) said: "Gang banging. Umm, I don't know. I mean, I be bored . . . Even though I would never get gang—I wouldn't wanna get gang banged; I don't know, I just watch that . . . It's usually many umm, men on women." Bossy seems unable to explain clearly why she prefers this type of video, which could be interpreted as exploitive or as a fantasy representation of female sexual power. Angel's (25) preferences include "people getting beat . . . I don't watch regular porn. I think it's so fake." Angel's preference for pornography that includes violence appears to be problematic as a form of resistance. Alternatively, perhaps coupled with her rejection of heterosexual pornography, her choice could be interpreted as a liberated act of consuming and enjoying a cultural product that may also be degrading (Crawford 2007).

The practice of attending strip clubs also may be investigated as a potential act of resistance to sexual stereotyping and heteronormative oppression. In recent years, the number of women patronizing female strip clubs has increased, perhaps reflecting growing social acceptance of fluidity in sexual identities and behaviors. Most research on strip clubs concerns venues with female dancers that cater to heterosexual men (see review in Frank 2007). As with pornography, research has focused on questions of gendered power, particularly with respect to women who work in the clubs and the complexities of their efforts to negotiate power. For women of color, racial and hypersexual stereotypes diminish their opportunities to convert erotic capital to economic capital (Brooks 2010; Hakim 2010). The imagery of these venues and their dancers is commonplace in hip hop songs, videos, and reality television shows and contributes to depictions of sexual relations "as transactional in nature; that is, men pay for access to women's sexual services" (Hunter 2011: 25). Black women in particular are characterized as hypersexualized and available for consumption.

Attention to the characteristics and motivations of strip-club patrons has increased in the past decade or so and is generally focused on male customers in clubs with female dancers. There is still very little literature on women as female strip-club customers. We are aware of only one study, based on participant observation and qualitative interviews, which found that women were not taken seriously as customers in an environment designed to appeal to men's sexual pleasure (Wosick-Correa and Joseph 2008). This was partly because women were presumed to have less money than men and partly because some dancers were uncomfortable approaching women. Another reason was the fact that female patrons and dancers shared the women's rest rooms, which de-mystified the dancers and removed for women the element of fantasy that inspires men to purchase drinks and lap dances.

Thirty-one percent of our participants reported going to strip clubs, mostly to venues with female dancers. Some go with friends, some with male partners. When asked what they like about strip clubs, participants most often said they liked the dancers. As Velvet (42) said, "I watch women. I will do everything the guy do—put money down their thing, give them a lap dance, everything." Malya (22) describes an appeal that is not necessarily erotic:

> [W]hen you think of strip clubs you think, like, these nasty women . . . but this strip club I went to majority of them their bodies were like on point . . . and they were doing these tricks that I couldn't even understand how it's possible to do that in the human body . . . [T]hese girls climb up the poles that high and twirl around and do tricks . . . with no harness, no like safety net above them and they make it look so effortless.

More frequently, participants did emphasize the dancers' erotic appeal. Cookie (34) was enthusiastic when she said, "Strip spots is the best spots ever . . . 'Cause it's girls all over the pole. Shit. Ass and titties everywhere. It's so much scattered ass . . . You know, that turns me on." Several participants said they liked not only looking at the dancers' bodies, but touching them, purchasing lap dances and perhaps more, as Angel (25) suggests:

Interviewer: What's it like, if you're in a strip club in the VIP room? What does that mean?

Angel: Some VIP rooms you have sex in. And I've never been to one where you don't have sex, unless it's a real strip club.

By "real strip club," Angel appears to mean one that enforces restrictions on interactions between dancers and patrons. Yet even in such places, monitors have been found to exercise less supervision over women customers with female dancers, enabling more intimate encounters (Wosick-Correa and Joseph 2008).

The limited research on women as strip-club customers indicates that going to the clubs and even buying lap dances is not related to sexual orientation. Rather, the venues may be places where same-sex experimentation is possible and situational (Wosick-Correa and Joseph 2008). That may be true for some of our participants, although a large majority of those who went to strip clubs reported having same-sex encounters at other times and places, with varying degrees of intensity and interest. Their bisexual behavior is also situational, but it may exclude or at least not be limited to the strip-club setting.

Multiple Sex Partners

A major theme in interviews was concurrent partnerships with men. As one criterion for participating in the study, all participants (except the monogamous comparison group) reported having had two or more male sex partners two years prior to the interview and four or more in her lifetime. Analysis of transcripts indicated that 47% of all participants were in concurrent opposite-sex sexual relationships at the time of the interview: 27% had two concurrent partners, 9% had three, 5% had four, and another 5% had five or more sex partners. Previous research suggests that urban Black women might be expected to uphold traditional gender roles and experience lack of power in their sexual relationships (e.g., Bowleg et al. 2004; Ortiz-Torres et al. 2003; Paxton et al. 2013). We found, however, that most respondents demonstrated sexual agency with male partners.

Thirty percent of interviewees reported having a MSP and one or more SSPs. These relationships were extra relational because monogamy was assumed and/or asserted by participants and their main partners. Dominant cultural norms in the U.S. define this situation as infidelity. This term is applied here because it is the most often used in the literature and is not meant to stigmatize or critique participants in any way. Women's motivations for engaging in extra-relational sex fell into four dominant themes: sexual pleasure, partner infidelity, sex exchange, and past main partners. They expressed varying incentives and desires within each broad theme. Sexual pleasure was often cited as a reason for engaging in extra-relational sex. For instance, Violet (18) had a MSP but was also having sex with another man because "the sex is good." Velvet (42) lived with her MSP and was having sex with another man. She told us, "I . . . always want something that I don't have . . . I want a difference, a change sometimes." Pinky (19) had two SSPs because her MSP wasn't fulfilling her sexually. The frequency and quality of their sex had declined since she had given birth to her baby and they had not had sex in months. "He doesn't satisfy me anymore," she told us, "so I have to find somebody else to satisfy me." Articulating and acting on sexual desire were forms of resistance to the sexual double standard (Jackson and Cram 2003).

Money was an additional reason for having SSPs. Angel (25) had a boyfriend and participated in paid sex exchanges because "I need the money and I need things for me and my kids and my boyfriend." Despite her instrumental motive, she admitted feeling pleasure during these exchanges. Sassy (45) had a MSP and two long-term SSPs. She received money and gifts from all of them:

Sometimes I think about it and I know the things I am doing is not right, but I have to do what I have to do to pay a bill. You know, it could help me pay my car insurance or whatever. I know it's not right but I am going to do what I have to do to survive.

309

Sassy and Angel actively managed their sexual relationships to meet their financial goals.

Other women were motivated to step outside the bounds of their relationship because of MSP infidelity. Similar to Nunn et al.'s (2012) study of a sample of heterosexual Black women in Philadelphia, we discovered that lack of trust was one factor contributing to concurrent partnerships. Cookie had a MSP and one other male sex partner: "My man was playing me so now it's time for me to play him." She and others who fell into this group had SSPs in order to create some sort of equilibrium in their main relationships, to relieve themselves of some of the pain caused by their mate's cheating, and to assert their sexual independence.

Another group of women (25%) did not have MSPs. Instead, they had one or more sex partners and did not consider themselves committed to them. Pleasure and sexual variety was an ongoing theme in several of these interviews. Lucy (21), for example, stated that she had multiple sex partners, "Because I don't like being bored." Jada had three sex partners "for the experience, seeing what I like and I don't like and what I would like in a man." Dizzle (37) had only one sex partner when she was interviewed but said, "I don't consider him my mate, I consider him my fuck buddy." The older women in this category claimed that being faithful was "boring" and not "fulfilling enough." Several of the younger women spoke about sexual freedom and having multiple sex partners until they entered a committed relationship. For example, Aneesa (26) said, "I don't have anybody to respond to, I don't have to pick up my phone if I don't feel like it, I can do whatever I want . . . I'm committed to nobody." Several women in this category reported money as a motivating factor. For example, Sandy (46) and Lolita (40) had paying sex partners and no other partners outside their sex work. Angela (50) said of her two sex partners: "It's just a money thing . . . most of the time when I do it with them it really be a money thing." She had been having sex with the same two men for two to three years.

Feelings about having multiple sex partners differed from actual practice. Four main narratives materialized from interviews: negative, neutrality, discomfort, and positive. The largest group (33%) conveyed negative feelings about having sex with multiple men. A few women felt guilty about being unfaithful to their partners: Violet (18) said "I feel like I need to stop . . . I feel guilty [about] what I'm doing to Kevin." Ms. Mookie (40) had similar feelings: "Sometimes I feel guilty about it. But then other times I didn't . . . I'm cheating on my mate . . . and I don't think that he's doing the same thing . . . so sometimes the guilt . . . plays a part." A number of participants in this subgroup mirrored gendered ideas of proper femininity. Blueberry (23) put it starkly: "I feel just like a slut. I feel like a hoe. I feel dirty. I feel like this is not what it should be, but it's like what society is . . . I don't know." Cookie (34) asked, "I mean if you ain't a freak, then what are you doing it for?" Sandra (50) tried not to think about it, "because I know it's wrong . . . to be having sex with two guys at the same time . . . it's a moral deficiency."

Women who exchanged sex for money also had negative opinions. Alectra (29) created a boundary between her sex work and her personal life:

> It sucks . . . [I]n my personal life I'm a good girl, I think. So when I'm an escort I fuck a bunch of men for money. But as a regular normal life, this is me, I don't want to be fucking these niggas out here.

Harmani (23) had also exchanged sex for money: "I feel bad sometimes but it's like I needed to do what I have to do to get what I gotta get." These responses indicate a contradiction between behavior and the meanings applied to them. Participants displayed agency by having various sexual relationships with men but their adverse sentiments reflected difficulty with and sometimes distress about transgressing cultural rules of female propriety.

The next largest group (27%) was relatively neutral on the subject. Chanel's (27) comment was representative of many: "It doesn't bother me none. It's my satisfaction." Luscious (28) felt a similar way: "It doesn't bother me too much, I'd rather get it out of my system now than to be still doing this when I am married." Cleo's (50) response illustrated agency when she answered, "It's my pussy, I can do as I want with it." Dizzle's (47) reaction was located between pride and guilt: "I don't have no shame, I don't feel guilty. I'm not proud of it but I'm not guilty about it either." They did not emphasize their sexual autonomy, neither did they experience shame.

Several study participants (12.5%) did not express a strong negative reaction but did exhibit a certain level of discomfort and contemplation. Niki (23), for example, said "[S]ometimes I wish I could've made smarter decisions about who these partners were." Tanya (18) also questioned her choice of partners: "I don't regret any of them, but I would be like: why did I do that?" S.I. Stacy (18) told us, "I don't feel like it's that bad but like if I wanted to stop I would, so." There was a certain level of reflection and perhaps doubt about their sexual choices, but this did not move them to convey guilt over their actions. The smallest group of women (8%) communicated positive reactions to having concurrent sex partners. Sexy (23), for example, stated feeling "wonderful about it. Because I've learned so much about myself." Bronx-Brownie (30) had a comparable opinion:

> I just feel like I either learned—experienced whether it's oral sex, or back side or whatever it is, I learned something from each and every one of them . . . and it made me better at something I couldn't do before.

Others expressed empowerment: D.D. (34) explained that "some people feel shamed or whatever. I feel good, proud about it." Ms. Jackie (29) claimed that "I felt good, I felt like I was running shit." The small number of women voicing positive feelings about their multiple sexual relationships reinforces past research on the persistence of the sexual double standard; women who resist dominant sexual scripts are vulnerable to social stigma (Lyons et al. 2011; Rudman et al. 2013). The silencing of sexual pleasure in the lives of Black women influences how they think about their sexual relationships.

Discussion

The Black, low-income women in our study are located at a particularly vulnerable intersection of race, gender, and class. A majority have histories of intimate partner violence and criminal-justice involvement, and several reported experiencing sexual abuse as children. They were socialized into a sexual milieu in which Black male partners were in short supply and presumed to hold the balance of power in heterosexual relationships. Yet despite their experiences, or perhaps because of them, these women appear to conduct their sexual lives with considerable autonomy. The vast majority have multiple male sex partners and more than one-quarter have had concurrent female sex partners as well. Although we recognize the importance of the literature that links multiple sexual relationships to increased risk for HIV/AIDS and STIs (Adimora et al. 2011; Adimora et al., 2006), we also suggest that framing sexual concurrency only in terms of risk overlooks the sexual agency of women who have been historically marginalized and sexually exploited. In particular, it is important to recognize sexual pleasure as a motivating force behind maintaining multiple partnerships, consuming pornography, and patronizing strip clubs. On a superficial level, these behaviors flirt with hypersexual stereotypes of Black women, but on closer examination, they become acts of resistance against silencing and may even reflect changes in the meaning of respectability. Growing social acceptance of bisexual behavior and of women watching pornography and exotic dancers suggests that these behaviors are becoming less transgressive than they once were.

That is not to say, however, that the sexual agency exercised by the women in our study constitutes unalloyed resistance. Rather, their experiences demonstrate agency with contradictions. For example, the increased popularity of strip clubs among women makes it easier for participants to pursue sexual pleasure openly in a traditionally male-oriented domain, but the extent to which that popularity is tied to misogynistic hip hop culture renders the outings problematic. There is also the problem of supporting a part of the sex industry in which Black female workers experience discrimination (Brooks 2010). A similar issue arises in consuming pornography, also known for exploiting women and perpetuating patriarchal dominance. Yet perhaps this is mitigated somewhat by participants' preference for female pornographic videos, in which women fare better than in traditional heterosexual pornography, and which constitute a growing share of pornographic production (Dickson 2014; May 2011).

Recounting sexual encounters and relationships with female partners, participants described experiences that enabled them to experiment and to realize physical gratification in a way they could not with male partners, while maintaining their heterosexual identities. Growing public acceptance of the separation of identity from behavior in the sexual realm helps to normalize these acts of resistance. Yet there is contradiction here, too, in the fact that the vast majority of participants expressed a preference for receiving oral sex and several voiced disdain for giving oral sex, based on revulsion toward female genitalia.

Having multiple male partners is a way in which Black women demonstrate sexual control in a gender-imbalanced environment that favors men. Our participants talked about their varied motivations for having these relationships, ranging from survival to the simple pursuit of pleasure. Here the contradiction is found in how they say they *feel* about these arrangements, for most of the women were highly self-critical. Many described themselves in terms that suggest they have internalized oppressive norms of respectability, as when Blueberry calls herself a "hoe," a term that is "an amalgamation of various destructive tropes used to describe black women" (Little 2015:90). There is pursuit of sexual pleasure in spite of dominant sexist discourses that limit Black women's sexuality, but the meanings participants give to their sexual experiences represent complicated agency.

Our findings suggest individual rather than collective resistance. This may be a result of our behaviorally based interviews, as we did not ask participants how they related their sexual decision making to a broader community of Black women. On the other hand, our findings may reflect continued invisibility for Black female sexuality: it may more permissible today for Black women to act on their sexual desires but these experiences must be singular and private rather than public. Consequently, marginalized women run the risk of looking "away from the importance of the erotic in the development and sustenance" of their own power (Lorde 2007: 59). Black female sexuality is powerful and bringing it out from the margins challenges structures of oppression.

In this chapter, we have applied intersectionality to a sexual health study. We link sexuality and by extension, sexual health, to overlapping and interrelated oppressions. Race, class, and gender together have shaped Black women's sexual choices and opportunities, very often in damaging ways. We attempt to delineate how racism and sexism in particular have impacted Black women's sexuality and how they have confronted these inequities. The ability to incorporate structural constraints into sexual health research is one of the strengths of intersectionality. There are also obstacles that future research can resolve, such as: how to select which structural categories to use (Bowleg 2012); moving beyond "the trinity of race, class, gender"

(Hankivsky 2012: 1717); limited options for methodology (Bowleg 2008), and a wide "gap between conceptions of intersectional methodology and practices of intersectional investigations" (Nash 2008: 89).

What does it mean that other women have such a large role in the ways in which our participants seek sexual pleasure? Women are valued as occasional sex partners (even if only for oral sex), and they are the actors in the pornographic videos participants prefer to watch and the dancers in the strip clubs participants visit. Participants speak frankly about the appeal of female bodies even as they maintain their heterosexual identities. They are living sexual freedom as a right, embodying the promise of a Black feminist politics of pleasure (Nash 2012), and they do so for the most part un-self-consciously.

We have recorded how the actions of study participants exemplify resistance to oppression via their sexuality, but more research is needed on the meanings they give to these acts. Understanding these meanings provides a multidimensional portrayal of how their sexual desire and autonomy undoes racist and sexist oppression. This research also illustrates the importance of including sexual pleasure in sexual health interventions and research. Risk-reduction programs should incorporate sexual satisfaction and enjoyment in their health curriculums because pleasure, often denied to Black women through stereotypical symbols, was a strong impetus for pursuing various forms of sexual fulfillment among our participants.

Discussion Questions

1 What is intersectionality theory and how is it applied in the reading?
2 How has the historical experience of Black women in the United States shaped their sexuality?
3 Do you agree that sexual assertiveness (generally) is a form of resistance to structural constraints of race, gender and class? Why or why not? What is it about Black female sexuality specifically that might challenge structures of oppression?
4 What do we learn about Black men's sexual agency through the perspectives of the women in this chapter?
5 In what ways were the expressions of resistance to structural constraints described in this paper contradictory? What do you believe are the reasons for these contradictions? How might sexual pleasure be integrated into HIV/STD intervention programs?

Suggested Readings

1 Childs, E. C., Page, E., Dickerson, B., Rousseau, N., Hunter, M., Guerrero, M. . . . and McCune, J. (2009). *Black sexualities: Probing powers, passions, practices, and policies*. New Brunswick, NJ: Rutgers University Press.

2   Collins, P. H. (2004). *Black sexual politics: African Americans, gender, and the new racism*. New York: Routledge.
3   Hammonds, E. M. (1997). Toward a genealogy of Black female sexuality: The problematic of silence. In *Feminist Genealogies, Colonial Legacies, Democratic Futures* (pp. 93–103). New York: Routledge.
4   Lee, S. (2010). *Erotic Revolutionaries: Black Women, Sexuality and Popular Culture*. Lanham, MD: Hamilton Books.
5   Melancon, T., Braxton, J. M., Harris-Perry, M., Brown, K. J., and Patterson, C. J. (2015). *Black Female Sexualities*. New Brunswick, NJ: Rutgers University Press.
6   Mullings, L., and Schulz, A. J. (2006). Intersectionality and health: An introduction. In *Gender, Race, Class, and Health: Intersectional Approaches*. San Francisco, CA: Jossey-Bass.

Suggested Media

1   *Silence: in search of black female sexuality in America*. Director: Mya B., 2004
2   *Dreams deferred: the Sakia Gunn Film Project*. Director: Charles B. Brack, 2008
3   *The life and times of Sara Baartman: "The Hottentot Venus."* Director: Zola Maseko, 1998

Acknowledgments

This research was funded by the National Institute of Child Health and Human Development (NICHD 5R01HD059706-04) to study socialization and HIV risks in scripts and practices of heterosexual Black females. The authors would like to thank Deborah Murray, Michael Pass, Sharayu Salvi, and June Townes for their contributions to this paper as well as all the respondents who participated in this research. The authors declare that they have no conflict of interest.

References

Adimora, A. A. and Schoenbach, V. J. (2005). Social context, sexual networks, and racial disparities in rates of sexually transmitted infections. *Journal of Infectious Diseases*, 191, S115–S122.
Adimora, A., Schoenbach, V. J., Martinson, F. E., Coyne-Beasly, T., Doherty, I., Stancil, T. R., and Fullilove, R. E. (2006). Heterosexually transmitted HIV infection among African Americans in North Carolina. *JAIDS Journal of Acquired Immune Deficiency Syndromes*, 41(5), 616–623.
Adimora, A. A., Schoenbach, V. J., Taylor, E. M., Khan, M. R., and Schwartz, R. J. (2011). Concurrent partnerships, nonmonogamous partners, and substance use among women in the United States. *American Journal of Public Health*, 101(1), 128–136.

Alexander, K. A., and Fannin, E. F. (2014). Sexual safety and sexual security among young black women who have sex with women and men. *Journal of Obstetric, Gynecologic, and Neonatal Nursing*, 43, 509–519.

Andrasik, M. P., Nguyen, H., George, W., and Kajumulo, K. (2014). Sexual decision making in the absence of choice: The African American female dating experience. *Journal of Health Disparities Research and Practice*, 7(2), 66–86.

Black Women's Blueprint. (2012). The Truth Commission on Black Women and Sexual Violence: Sexual violence against Black women in the United States. Retrieved July 9, 2015, from www.blackwomensblueprint.org/wp-content/uploads/SexualViolenceAgainstBlackWomen-BWB-FactSheet-6-11-15.pdf

Bowleg, L., Lucas, K., and Tschann, J. (2004). The ball was always in his court: an exploratory analysis of relationship scripts, sexual scripts, and condom use among African American women. *Psychology of Women Quarterly*, 28, 70–82.

Bowleg, L. (2008). When Black + lesbian + woman ≠ Black lesbian woman: The methodological challenges of qualitative and quantitative intersectionality research. *Sex Roles*, 59(5–6), 312–325.

Bowleg, L. (2012). The problem with the phrase women and minorities: Intersectionality—an important theoretical framework for public health. *American Journal of Public Health*, 102(7), 1267–1273.

Bowleg, L., Teti, M., Malebranche, D. J., and Tschann, J. M. (2013). "It's an uphill battle everyday": Intersectionality and the implications of social-structural factors for sexual HIV risk among Black heterosexual men. *Psychology of Men and Masculinity*, 14(1), 25–34.

Braun, V. and Wilkinson, S. (2001). Socio-cultural representations of the vagina. *Journal of Reproductive and Infant Psychology*, 19(1), 19–32.

Bredström, A. (2006). Intersectionality: A challenge for feminist HIV/AIDS research? *European Journal of Women's Studies*, 13(3), 229–243.

Brooks, S. (2010). *Unequal Desires: Race and Erotic Capital in the Stripping Industry*. Albany, NY: State University of New York Press.

Carby, H. V. (1992). Policing the Black woman's body in an urban context. *Critical Inquiry*, 18(4), 738–755.

CDC (Centers for Disease Control and Prevention) National Center for HIV/ AIDS, Viral Hepatitis, STD, and T. P. (2015). HIV among African Americans. Retrieved from www.cdc.gov/hiv/pdf/HIV-AA-english-508.pdf

Charmaz, K. (2006). *Constructing Grounded Theory: A Practical Guide Through Qualitative Analysis* (p. 208). London: Sage Publications.

Cohen, C. (1999). *The Boundaries of Blackness: AIDS and the Breakdown of Black Politics*. Chicago, IL: University of Chicago Press.

Collins, P. H. (2000). *Black Feminist Thought: Knowledge, Consciousness, and the Politics of Empowerment* (2nd ed., p. 335). London: Routledge.

Collins, P. H. (2004). *Black Sexual Politics: African Americans, Gender, and the New Racism*. New York: Routledge.

Collins, P. Y., von Unger, H., and Armbrister, A. (2008). Church ladies, good girls, and locas: stigma and the intersection of gender, ethnicity, mental illness, and sexuality in relation to HIV risk. *Social Science and Medicine*, 67(3), 389–397.

Crenshaw, K. (1989). Demarginalizing the intersection of race and sex: A Black feminist critique of antidiscrimination doctrine, feminist theory and antiracist politics. *University of Chicago Legal Forum*, 140, 139–167.

Crawford, B. J. (2007). Toward a third-wave feminist legal theory: Young women, pornography and the praxis of pleasure. *Michigan Journal of Gender and Law*, 14, 6–31.

Diamond, L., and Savin-Williams, R. (2000). Explaining diversity in the development of same-sex sexuality among young women. *Journal of Social Issues*, 56(2), 297–313.

Diamond, L. (2008). Female bisexuality from adolescence to adulthood: Results from a 10-year longitudinal study. *Developmental Psychology*, 44(1), 5–14.

Dickson, E. J. (2014) Pornhub stats reveal women are primarily watching gay porn. www.dailydot.com/lifestyle/women-porn-gay-pornhub/ September 22, 2014. Retrieved July 8, 2015.

Doyal, L. (2009). Challenges in researching life with HIV/AIDS: an intersectional analysis of black African migrants in London. *Culture, Health and Sexuality*, 11(2), 173–188.

Dworkin, S. (2005). Who is epidemiologically fathomable in the HIV/AIDS epidemic? Gender, sexuality, and intersectionality in public health. *Culture, Health and Sexuality*, 7(6), 615–623.

Fisher Collins, C. (2006). Introduction: commentary on the health and social status of African American women. In C. Fisher Collins (Ed.), *African American Women's Health and Social Issues*. Westport, CT: Praeger.

Frank, K. (2007). Thinking critically about strip club research. *Sexualities*, 10(4), 501–517.

French, B. H. (2013). More than jezebels and freaks: Exploring how Black girls navigate sexual coercion and sexual scripts. *Journal of African American Studies*, 17, 35–50.

Garvey, J. (2015). "Embrace the Narrative of the Whole": Complicating Black Female Sexuality in Contemporary Fiction. In T. Melancon and J. Braxton (Eds.), *Black Female Sexualities* (pp. 159–179). New Brunswick, NJ: Rutgers University Press.

Griffith, D. (2012). An intersectional approach to men's health. *Journal of Men's Health*, 9(2), 106–112.

Gruskin, E., Hart, S., Gordon, N., and Ackerson, L. (2001). Patterns of cigarette smoking and alcohol use among lesbians and bisexual women enrolled in a large health maintenance organization. *American Journal of Public Health*, 91(6), 976–979.

Hakim, C. (2010). Erotic capital. *European Sociological Review*, 26(5), 499–518.

Hammonds, E. M. (1997). Toward a genealogy of Black female sexuality: The problematic of silence. In *Feminist Genealogies, Colonial Legacies, Democratic Futures* (pp. 93–103). New York: Routledge.

Hankivsky, O., Colleen, R., Cormier, R., Varcoe, C., Clark, N., Benoit, C., and Brotman, S. (2010). Exploring the promise of intersectionality for advancing women's health research. *International Journal for Equity in Health*, 9(5), 1–15.

Hankivsky, O. (2012). Women's health, men's health, and gender and health: Implications of intersectionality. *Social Science and Medicine*, 74, 1712–1720.

Henderson, L. (2009). Between the two: Bisexual identity among African Americans. *Journal of African American Studies*, 13(3), 263–282.

Higgins, J. A., Hoffman, S., and Dworkin, S. (2010). Rethinking gender, heterosexual men, and women's vulnerability to HIV/AIDS. *American Journal of Public Health*, 100(3), 435–445.

Hill, M. (2013). Is the Black community more homophobic?: Reflections on the intersectionality of race, class, gender, culture and religiosity of the perception of homophobia in the Black community. *Journal of Gay and Lesbian Mental Health*, 17(2), 208–214.

Hunter, M. (2011). Shake it, baby, shake it: Consumption and the new gender relation in hip-hop. *Sociological Perspectives*, 54(1), 15–36.

IDVAAC (Institute on Domestic Violence in the African American community) (2008). Intimate Partner Violence (IPV) in the African American Community. Retrieved July 9, 2015, from www.idvaac.org/media/publications/FactSheet. IDVAAC_AAPCFV-Community Insights.pdf

Jackson, S. M., and Cram, F. (2003). Disrupting the sexual double standard: Young women's talk about heterosexuality. *British Journal of Social Psychology*, 42, 113–127.

Layne, A. (2014). Now that's a bad bitch!: The state of women in hip-hop. Retrieved from www.hamptoninstitution.org/women-in-hip-hop.html#.U1_MvfldWSo

Lee, S. (2010). *Erotic Revolutionaries: Black Women, Sexuality and Popular Culture*. Lanham, MD: Hamilton Books.

Lindley, L. L., Walsemann, K. M., and Carter, J. W. (2013). Invisible and at risk: STD among young adult sexual minority women in the United States. *Perspectives on Sexual and Reproductive Health*, 45(2), 66–73.

Little, M. A. (2015). Why don't we love these hoes? Black women, popular culture, and the contemporary hoe archetype. In T. Melancon and J. M. Braxton (Eds.), *Black Female Sexualities* (pp. 89–99). New Brunswick, NJ: Rutgers University Press.

Lorde, A. (2007). *Sister Outsider*. Berkeley, CA: Crossing Press.

Lyons, H., Giordano, P., Manning, W., and Longmore, M. (2011). Identity, peer relationships, and adolescent girls' sexual behavior: An exploration of the contemporary double standard. *Journal of Sex Research*, 48(5), 437–449.

May, C. (2011). Porn made for women, by women. *Guardian*, March 22. Retrieved July 8, 2015, www.theguardian.com/lifeandstyle/2011/mar/22/porn-women

McDougall, L. J. (2013). Towards a clean slit: how medicine and notions of normality are shaping female genital aesthetics. *Culture, Health and Sexuality*, 15(7), 774–787.

McElroy, W. (1995). *XXX: A Woman's Right to Pornography*. New York: St. Martin's Press.

McGruder, K. (2006). Pathologizing Black sexuality: The U.S. experience. In J. Battle and S. L. Barnes(Eds.), *Black Sexualities: Probing Powers, Passions, Practices, and Policies* (pp. 101–118).

McPhillips, K., Braun, V., and Gavey, N. (2001). Defining (hetero) sex: How imperative is the "coital imperative"? *Women's Studies International Forum*, 24(2), 229–240.

Melancon, T. (2015). "somebody almost walked off wid alla my stuff": Black female sexualities and Black feminist intervention. In T. Melancon and J. Braxton (Eds.), *Black Female Sexualities*: (pp. 1–9). New Brunswick, NJ: Rutgers University Press.

Mullings, L., and Schulz, A. J. (2006). Intersectionality and health: An introduction. In idem (Eds.), *Gender, Race, Class, and Health: Intersectional Approaches*. San Francisco, CA: Jossey-Bass.

Muzny, C. A., Sunesara, I. R., Martin, D. H., and Mena, L. (2011). Sexually transmitted infections and risk behaviors among African American women who have sex with women: Does sex with men make a difference? *Sexually Transmitted Diseases*, 38(12), 1118–1125.

Muzny, C. A., Whittington, L., Richter, S. S., Jones, M. G., Austin, E. L., and Hook, E. W. (2013). Sexually transmitted infections (STIS) vary among African American women who have sex with women based on exposure to male sexual partners. *Sexually Transmitted Infections*, 89, A25.

Nash, J. (2008). Rethinking intersectionality. *Feminist Review*, 89, 1–15.

Nash, J. (2012). Review: Theorizing pleasure: New directions in Black feminist studies. *Feminist Studies*, 38(2), 507–515.

Newsome, V., and Airhihenbuwa, C. (2013). Gender ratio imbalance effects on HIV risk behaviors in African American women. *Health Promotion Practice*, 14(3), 459–463.

Nield, J., Magnusson, B., Brooks, C., Chapman, D., and Lapane, K. (2015). Sexual discordance and sexual partnering among heterosexual women. *Archives of Sexual Behavior*, 44(4), 885–894.

Nunn, A., Dickman, S., Cornwall, A., Kwakwa, H., Mayer, K. H., Rana, A., and Rosengard, C. (2012). Concurrent sexual partnerships among African American women in Philadelphia: results from a qualitative study. *Sexual Health*, 9(3), 288–296.

Ortiz-Torres, B., Williams, S., and Ehrhardt, A. (2003). Urban women's gender scripts: Implications for HIV prevention. *Culture, Health and Sexuality*, 5(1), 1–17.

Paxton, K. C., Williams, J. K., Bolden, S., Guzman, Y., and Harawa, N. T. (2013). HIV risk behaviors among African American women with at-risk male partners. *AIDS and Clinical Research*, 4(7), 1–8.

Roberts, D. (1997). *Killing the Black body: Race, Reproduction, and the Meaning of Liberty*. New York: Pantheon Books.

Rudman, L., Fetterolf, J., and Sanchez, D. (2013). What motivates the sexual double standard? More support for male versus female control theory. *Personality and Social Psychology Bulletin*, 39(2), 250–263.

Stallings, L. H. (2007). *Mutha is Half a Word: Intersections of Folklore, Vernacular, Myth and Queerness in Black Female Culture*. Columbus, OH: Ohio State University Press.

Staples, R. (2006). *Exploring Black Sexuality*. Lanham, MD: Rowman and Littlefield Publishers, Inc.

Stephens, D., and Phillips, L. (2003). Freaks, gold diggers, divas, and dykes: The sociohistorical development of adolescent African American women's sexual scripts. *Sexuality and Culture*, 7(1), 3–49.

Telfair Sharpe, T., Voute, C., Rose, M., Cleveland, J., Dean, H., and Fenton, K. (2012). Social determinants of HIV/AIDS and sexually transmitted diseases among Black women: Implications for health equity. *Journal of Women's Health*, 21(3), 249–254.

Vrangalova, Z., and Savin-Williams, R. (2012). Mostly heterosexual and mostly gay/lesbian: Evidence for new sexual orientation identities. *Archives of Sexual Behavior*, 41(1), 85–101.

Walker, A. (2014). "I'm not a lesbian; I'm just a freak": A pilot study of the experiences of women in assumed-monogamous other-sex unions seeking secret same-sex encounters online, their negotiation of sexual desire, and meaning-making of sexual identity. *Sexuality and Culture*, 18(4), 911–935.

White, E. F. (2010). *Dark Continent of Our Bodies: Black Feminism and Politics of Respectability*. Philadelphia, PA: Temple University Press.

Windsor, L. C., Dunlap, E., and Golub, A. (2011). Challenging controlling images, oppression, poverty and other structural constraints: Survival strategies among African American women in distressed households. *Journal of African American Studies*, 15(1), 290–306.

Wingood, G., and DiClemente, R. (2000). Application of the theory of gender and power to examine HIV-related exposures, risk factors, and effective interventions for women. *Health Education and Behavior*, 27(5), 539–565.

Wosick-Correa, K. R., and Joseph, L. J. (2008). Sexy ladies sexing ladies: Women as consumers in strip clubs. *Journal of Sex Research*, 45(3), 201–216.

Wright, P. J., Bae, S. and Funk, M. 2013. United States women and pornography through four decades: Exposure, attitudes, behaviors, individual differences. *Archives of Sexual Behavior*, 42, 1131–1144.

17

RAISE YOUR BANNER HIGH! MOUNTING A TAKE BACK THE NIGHT EVENT

Civic Engagement and Feminist Practice on a University Campus

Colleen Denney

In a senior-level/graduate course on "The Visual Culture of Women's Activism," I embedded a service-learning/civic engagement component in order to mount the annual "Take Back the Night" event on the University of Wyoming campus. My goal was to help students put their knowledge of the history of women's activism into practice in their conceptualization of the march and in the march's visual, educational, and emotional impact. Simultaneously I launched a Smart Girl Program at our University Lab School and was able to dovetail some events for those girls with our activist work for the march (William and Ferber 2008). Here I detail how we put the students' activist, artistic, and/or artisan skills to work in communicating a feminist agenda to the university, secondary schools, and town communities through a historical feminist practice. As an academic who was new to putting activist history into a praxis mode, I was often conflicted about the balance of knowledge/production we achieved. As Rhonda L. Williams and Abby L. Ferber articulate, "Knowledge gained in the university classroom is often disconnected from action and from the practices of women working for change in the community" (2008: 47). While I will discuss here the ways we were able to take knowledge to the streets and community, I will also discuss the ways I was conflicted that represent the dilemmas of a feminist professor in a civically engaged classroom who employs the four themes involved in doing feminist work: reflexivity, action orientation, attention to affect, and use of the situation at hand (Fonow and Cook 1991; qtd. in Williams and Ferber 2008: 47).

Within the thematic framework of pedagogical methods, production, reflection, and impact, I will address the value of

1) Feminist civic engagement;
2) Negotiations and collaborations with Recognized Student Organizations (RSOs) and community co-sponsors;
3) Honoring and including different communities in our planning and production;
4) Securing funding, and
5) Controversies, outcomes and future considerations.

Background

Take Back the Night has been an event on our campus for over ten years. It has, in the past, been organized by our student affiliate group, Women's Action Network (WAN). This year we wanted to let WAN pursue other endeavors so I took on the event in conjunction with my students; however, WAN still applied and received some of the funding to help mount the event. We always co-sponsor with the community, domestic violence shelter, SAFE Project and, starting this year, we now have a STOP Violence Project (Student Training, Orientation, and Prevention of violence against men and women) on campus that addresses sexual assault/violence on college campuses and which works to educate about healthy sexual relationships as well as doing advocacy work. They became a new co-sponsor. In addition, I worked with the Student Activities Council (SAC) who agreed to co-sponsor and fund some of our entertainment costs. Also, I had preparatory meetings with faculty in Family and Consumer Science and the Art Department, to determine students with appropriate skills for the course. We would need textile specialists with sewing skills and graphic designers, along with students who could do printmaking and painting. These professors also helped me visualize our banners in terms of the materials and the construction methods we would need to use. It helped that I sew so I could envision some of the ideas they presented. I expected to spend some significant hours at my sewing machine. Before the class even met, then, I already had four co-sponsors in place, a guest speaker, select students for the course, a clear vision of the materials for the march, and had met with WAN members and members of a new affiliate group, Queer Advocacy Network (QAN) to discuss ways they could go for funding to supplement some of our costs. I also had identified several other groups to march with us under designated banners. (The students eventually added more to this list and we enlarged our community group invitations as well.) Further, I had met with the Student Leadership and Civic Engagement office (SLCE) to discuss other sources of support and funding. I was working with them on the Smart Girl Program at the same time.

My goals in launching both projects were manifold: As the then-director, I was often forced to be self-serving, promoting the program and giving it visibility to the community but I was, and am, more altruistic than those motivations might otherwise suggest: I wanted to use this event to honor our program's feminist pedagogy of "creating change to improve women's lives" (Williams and Ferber 2008: 47). As a program, we needed to begin to make more connections with the secondary schools and others in the community, partly for recruiting purposes, partly to start a dialogue about activism, partly to have better communication than had existed previously, partly to begin addressing healthy relationship skills at an early stage through raising awareness about gender issues. Through these plans, I hoped I would not only teach my students about activism, but also "enable them to use this knowledge to work for social justice" (Williams and Ferber 2008: 47). Further, past renditions of the Take Back the Night event had met with serious critique from students in my History of Women Artists course; in that course, we brought our activist dialogue up to the present and spent considerable time on women artists' activism, culminating with our own attendance at the Take Back the Night event in 2011. As art students, they wanted to see much more visual unity to the event than they experienced during the march. It was due, in part, to their concerns that I began to envision a different look for the march.

I received funds from the SLCE office through their service-learning grant to cover costs of the march, including materials for our banners, sashes, and graphics. At the same time, I received a Wyoming Community Foundation Grant, along with additional funds from the Arts & Sciences Dean's Office, the Office of Student Affairs, and the SLCE office, to cover the costs of starting a Smart Girl Program at our University Lab School, targeting the middle-school girls. We received in-kind contributions from the school district and the Smart Girl Program to make it possible to train eight of us (counselors, university professors, graduate/undergraduate/high school students). The Office of Student Affairs had one condition: that we have a recruiting day on campus for the Smart Girls. Our hope was to bring what the college students learned into sync with what the Smart Girls would be learning, inviting them either to an event about such activism and/or to have them join in the march itself.

Pedagogical Methods

My pedagogical method in terms of putting theory into practice was to expose students to the visual history of activism in historic suffrage marches—the first activist marches ever mounted—and help the students to duplicate the visual unity and dignity of those events. Further, I addressed the historic reasoning for the feminist engagement in "Take Back the Night" marches and other examples of artistic activism and community activism, in order to apply, where the students felt it was appropriate, some of the most effective tactics of those groups.

Students in Visual Culture of Women's Activism would be learning about the history of activism, a missing component in our Gender and Women's

Studies curriculum, which is surprising considering how, historically and today, our students have maintained activist agendas on this campus and once they leave the university. We have just changed the major so that it now requires a course in women's history. Through the construction of this method I was cognizant both of research without action and action without research. As Donna M. Bickford and Nedra Reynolds explain in their critique of service learning: "The push to include volunteer work in the curriculum tends to ignore the work that has been done in women's studies on grassroots organizing and coalition building" (2002: 232).

This course satisfies that requirement in a unique way, since our mission in Gender and Women's Studies is to put feminist theory into practice, making a service-learning component on activism essential. Not only would students learn the motivations for activism, but also they would put it into practice by researching and mounting their own march which, I hoped, would help them generate ideas for other activist events. Further, I wanted students to understand the importance of civic engagement in terms of the benefits of creating connections in the community. The Smart Girl project at the UW Lab School was one such opportunity, a place to help in exposing girls to ways they could work with near-peer mentors in order to empower themselves and others through self-esteem and team-building exercises; in this way we hoped they would begin to find their own activist voices.

I am aware that I have used the term "activism" specifically, instead of "service-learning" in the above explication. As Bickford and Reynolds point out, many discourses on service-learning are uncomfortable with the word "activism," citing that it is more commonly used in women's studies programs than in, say, the field of composition. They recognize that service-learning "while it can be activist, is too often infused with the volunteer ethos," yet they argue that activism "as a name and a practice . . . works *with* service-learning." My goal in the classroom, one readily apparent among the students, many of whom self-identified as campus activists, was the same as Bickford and Reynolds's: "[T]hat a more historical and geographic approach to activist learning projects [would] give learners a broader understanding of dissent and [would] encourage them to envision themselves as actors or agents in political arenas" (2002: 230).

History Coming Alive

Students in the course learned the history of women's activism globally, but with a particular focus on the United States and England, through the lens of visual materials such as banners, posters, and other ephemeral propaganda that have promoted women's causes. We started the class with a showing of the film, *Iron-Jawed Angels* (Garnier et al. 2004), which details Alice Paul's fight for U.S. suffrage for women and her struggle with the more established feminist groups, important background information to which the students returned again and again, often asking, "What would Alice Paul do?" and keeping in their minds the ways even feminist groups can form factions based on their different visions. We then worked through 19th- and 20th-century imagery within different activist groups and engaged in two well-spent weeks on Gail Collins's book, *When Everything Changed* (2009), which gave students strong historical grounding in civic engagement and action and let them understand their own histories. We brought this study up to the present with articles on activist groups; two groups particularly intrigued the students: Gran Fury, who agitated for AIDS research in the 1980s, and Suzanne Lacy, the feminist performance artist who herself emulated suffrage tactics in protests against sexual violence (Meyer 1995; Kelley 1995). A model we used for each class was to ask the following questions of these various movements/groups:

1) The goals of such activism,
2) What motivates such activism,
3) How such activism is implemented (tactics),
4) The pros and cons of such implementation, and
5) Changes the students might make in the same situation in terms of leadership and production.

Students shared their reflections in class discussions with the goal of looking for ideas they could implement for the march; in this moment, we brought history and application together through the generation of ideas, articulation of our goals, best practices, analysis of benefits, and areas for further thought.
Through this classroom practice, we were addressing Bickford and Reynolds's call to create a space for consciousness-raising:

> Students need to understand the power and necessity of activism in achieving social change. For many traditional college-aged students, the passionate activism of the civil rights era is ancient history. They are often completely unaware of earlier social change movements . . . [T]hey seldom appreciate what drives social change movements (in terms of needs, impetus, and historical specificity), know how to assess their accomplishments and shortcomings, perceive what still needs to be done, and so on.
>
> (2002: 239)

Our work on Alice Paul, our readings, and our practical questioning of those readings gave us a strong base for translating history into activism. Collins's book was particularly useful since she literally brought activists to life through interviews, selecting individuals who either helped to create legislative change or who benefited from it and who were empowered by the work of the grass-roots groups. This aspect of our work together was gratifying from a feminist academic's standpoint. Students were well aware of the Occupy movement but, once they had read these other materials, they were able to connect the Occupy movement's tactics to a historical framework of street activism, thus bringing together their world and the historical one.

While the students in the course understood the importance of the feminist, historical precedent, what was more frustrating was that many of our co-sponsors did not have this background. This unevenness created a task for my students: they became the educators for the other groups. That was a good experience for them, but I was left with a bittersweet taste in my mouth, wondering if student affiliate groups needed some similar feminist training in their own history. It was clear from what was to follow that they would have been much better able to understand our vision if they had more solid background themselves.

Production

While we were grounding ourselves in the history, we also had to plan the production piece, which meant we had to determine students' skills and how they wanted to be involved. Students had to visualize how we were going to create and execute designs for banners, sashes, graphic advertising (posters, flyers, t-shirts, program booklets), as well as manage the logistics of how to mount a procession and be involved in all of the planning in a way that duplicated the historical standard of feminist collaboration and leadership. In my lecture portion of the class, I had gone over many different examples of such materials and the students had direct access to these historical examples for further study. I split the students into two main groups with a leader for each group: administration and production. The administrative group consisted of students who were already activists on campus, who would be contacting our co-sponsors and other university/campus groups for participation, as well as organizing tables in the Union, starting a Facebook page, and recruiting and managing assistance from other groups. On the production team I had several students who, as one of them said, "lettered in Home Ec in High School," so we had textile experts in place. We had two advanced, graphic design students, two painting students, and one printmaker, all of whom worked together on the visual materials. I also had several students with strong research backgrounds so I gave them the task of putting together historical information and statistics that would go in our march program, informational sheets, as well as on our flyers. I had one student who was pursuing a social studies secondary education degree; new to activism but incredibly enthusiastic, she wanted to be our Smart Girl liaison, working with the girls and their guides/coaches on a plan to incorporate them into our event. I had a few students like her, who wanted to help with everything, so they floated between groups readily.

In many service-learning situations, students do the work on their own. But I felt from the beginning that I would need to be part of the production as well as being the overseer for all activities. While I was a member of the sewing group (and we turned my dining room into the sewing production arena for two months), I was also working with our SAFE and STOP Violence co-sponsors on advertising the event and organizing the rally portion that would precede the march. The painters worked on posters that we would carry, while the graphic designers/printmaker had the lion's share of the work of banners, posters, t-shirts, button designs, while the administrative team produced the buttons and made sure our event logistics/entertainment/rally plans were in order.

As the instructor of the course, I was often torn between our historical work and getting updates/sharing ideas in terms of production. For example, as part of our planning in terms of grounding us, I had to make time to have STOP Violence come to class to present on issues of sexual violence on campus. Also, we had a class-planning meeting with our SAFE co-sponsor. Once we moved into full production mode, we were seldom all together, but scattered at various sites. I did a lot of communicating by e-mail and phone with students and, on many class days, I had to be at several sites at once, to make sure everything was going according to plan.

Student Vision of the March

Based on our questioning/inquiry mode within our historic examination, the students decided they wanted to do a silent march. They had become intrigued by the power of Suzanne Lacy's performance piece, *Three Weeks in May* (1977), in which a group of women stood silently, dressed in black, as a symbolic representation of the recent rape victims in their city, Los Angeles (Kelley 1995). The students wanted everyone to wear mouth coverings to symbolize the silence to which sexual violence survivors are often subjected within the criminal justice system or, more important, the fact that the majority of victims never tell anyone of their victimization. The students had learned this information from a new national survey, the *American College Health Association/National College Health Assessment II Survey [ACHA NCHA II Survey]* (2011) that STOP Violence shared with us. Further, they wanted to honor the suffrage marches not only visually, but also symbolically, since those early marchers did so in silence, to show their dignity and their desire to be taken seriously as potential citizens. The printmaker designed an image of an anguished face, with a mouth covering, which appeared on our t-shirts, banners, and poster. We had also determined a color scheme to emulate the symbolic colors of the suffrage groups; we chose teal, already the color for Sexual Assault Awareness Month, and white, which for us meant hope. We also asked some marchers, in emulation of Lacy's work, to wear black in honor of sexual assault survivors. The students' slogan for the march: "Stop the Violence, Stop the Silence" appeared on our main banner as well as on our poster, among other materials.

Community Needs Addressed

Take Back the Night has traditionally been the place where UW comes together with SAFE Project to raise awareness about sexual violence on campus. We hoped, through extensive advertising and contacts we made, to educate the larger university and community about the need for change. I was able to communicate our plans most readily to the SAFE Board since I am a member, so I recruited board members and their constituents to march with us.

Meanwhile, the students developed leadership skills with distinct but equally important groups in the community, learning how to educate a public about the need for both social change and public policy change and, further, how to conduct research/develop relationships in order to bring that education to fruition. Students had the opportunity to voice their passions and goals to diverse audiences on issues that were of critical importance to them. For example, two students were prominent activists on campus as well as part of Associated Senators of the University of Wyoming (ASUW), the student governing body. We were in the midst of elections while mounting the march and one student and his election mate had sexual assault awareness as one of their main campaign goals. Another presented our plans to the Board of Trustees. Several students canvassed the march route prior to the event, with informational sheets in hand, to welcome community members to come out and support us. One rather subversive endeavor involved emulating Gran Fury's news intervention; they created "The New York Crimes" and covered the *New York Times* with them, detailing information on lack of AIDS research (Meyer 1995). The students wanted to do something like that with our flyers, which cited very hard-hitting statistics. We borrowed a slogan from Gran Fury, "This is to enrage you," because the students wanted their readers to rise up out of anger, as had so many groups they had studied, to bring about social change. For the flyers, they chose a new name for themselves: Canvass Campus Interventionists for Take Back the Night. We canvassed the campus and the community with these flyers a week before the event and the students gave them out at the Union tables. They also became a prominent piece of our promotion video, created by Ali Grossman, UW videographer, which aired on Wyoming PBS (Grossman 2012).

Further, plans for the march became a moment to create positive mentorship both among students in the classroom and with middle-school/high-school/other college students (specifically those involved in the Smart Girl project). There is a dire need globally for community services that address girls' futures; students in the class and among our affiliate groups provided positive role models of activism and leadership.

As Williams and Ferber explain, one of the best practices of the Smart Girl Program is the way it allows for community building activity with benefits that go far beyond the program's impact on the girls and women involved. Implementing the Smart Girl Program has brought together faculty, administrators and students from across the campus, working with middle school and high school students and staff as well as interested members of the community to create positive social change.

(2008: 62)

Specifically, working with our Smart Girl coaches and guides, my student organized a pizza lunch for UW Lab School girls, including those in the Smart Girl Program, as well as Lab School faculty and administrators. She contacted various women activists on campus to present to the girls during the lunch after she gave an overview talk on Youth Activism and on our march plans. I also talked about the Smart Girl Program. We used this event as a way to recruit new Smart Girls but, more important, as a way to expose girls to future possibilities for activism.

The Event

Our rally gathered around 200 attendees to whom we gave sashes and programs. Our SAFE Project leader welcomed everyone, then I gave a brief explanation of our vision for the march and why we would march silently. Our guest speaker, Nancy Schwartzman from the Line Campaign, talked about her own experiences as a survivor and how she has empowered herself and us, being the recent winner of the White House Apps Against Abuse Tech Challenge for its iPhone application called the "Circle of 6," creating a ready network of friends for safety.

For the march that followed, we were most excited to procure a white horse and rider, who would portray Joan of Arc, for the head of our march, this in emulation of the suffrage marches, the students most familiar with Inez Milholland Boissevain taking on this role for Alice Paul's march on Washington in 1913. With the administrative team, I had designed an order to our march, designated marshals from our group and from volunteer groups, and included an order of march within our program. Our marshals gave out banners and posters and organized everyone for the march. Our march route mirrored our goals of reaching the community and honoring our history as we processed silently toward downtown from campus, walking past the statue of the first woman voter, Louisa Ann Swain, Wyoming being the first state to grant women suffrage in 1869. We completed the march on the steps of the campus Union after finishing our walk through town neighborhoods, with a group chorus of "Will the Circle Be Unbroken" (lyrics included in the program) to end the silence. The students chose this song as it was the one Alice Paul's comrades sang in prison in her honor.

With this song, we broke the silence and literally gave voice to our passion for change. We then went back to the Union for food, music and dancing.

Conflicts and Resolution

Anyone who has put together an event of this kind knows it does not happen without some conflict and negotiation. Our original vision of marching silently with mouth coverings met with serious consternation from some members of various groups, some of whom were survivors and felt triggered by the idea of marching silently, stating instead that they should be able to chant and manifest their anger. This conflict was not easy to resolve since many of the students in the class felt marching silently, and with the coverings, would send a strong message that we were performing the silence that many victims encounter. Through conversations with the groups, and in concert with the students in the class, we decided to go with one student's idea to break the silence with the song at the end of the march, and, to compromise further, we did not march with the mouth coverings. Our marshals wore them, instead, on their arms. Further, our SAFE Project advocates identified themselves through their own t-shirts in case anyone felt triggered by any of the events and needed assistance. The students' desire to resolve the conflict speaks to Fonow and Cook's emphasis on feminist work being sensitive to the situation at hand (qtd. in Williams and Ferber 2008: 47). In this circumstance, our overarching feminist agenda of addressing sexual violence conflicted with community experiences of such violence. Yet, part of the disagreement was due to the fact that while the students had learned the activist history to allow them to make sense of their vision, the groups with whom we were negotiating did not have that same history under their belts. While we did explain that history, and the groups in question had the benefit of my explanation of my vision for the march prior to the class's work, when it came to the march itself, they were unable to process that information due to the emotional level at which they engaged the impact of the march. As Bickford and Reynolds recognize:

> With activism, as with service-learning, there are potential trouble spots. Students may have emotional reactions to social change work, including anger, outrage, pity, and contempt. Educators need to deal with these reactions in a way that encourages students to continue their work.
>
> (2002: 246)

In our post-event debriefing, we discussed this circumstance and others that came up where our vision and tactics were questioned. We had a heated discussion, one that was necessary so students could air their frustrations. One particular student was outraged that anyone would stand in the way of allowing us to air the sobering statistics on sexual violence, suggesting we have a post-dialogue during which we shared more disturbing information. It took a lot of courage for him to share that information in class, but we had to temper that suggestion by realizing we were not the only group involved in this process. The class would end with students presenting their reflections; they originally wanted the groups in question to attend that session but, we realized, based on our own passionate response to the event, that it might devolve into a shouting match and we wanted to be constructive in how we decided to go forward rather than continuing to air grievances about which we thought we had already compromised. Further, I needed to evaluate the students' contributions and their reflections. I could not dedicate class time to this dialogue without compromising the time I needed for evaluation.

Yet this particular incident started a very important conversation for the students, one which we had not found time to address in the classroom previously because I was trying to ground them in the history or we were busy with production. As Sheila Radford-Hill reminds us, "Implicit in the articulation of a feminist ideology . . . is the promise of a mediation structure, a set of actions and practices that are directed toward the empowerment of women" (1986: 159). My students certainly recognized this central component of feminism as they attempted to be sensitive to the other groups' voices and experiences.

Further, some of our students are heavily involved in Greek Life on campus and had to face some angry Greek members over some of the statistical information on our flyers, which we pulled directly from the *ACHA-NCHA II Survey*. Panhellenic was unhappy with our flyer that read: "This is to enrage you. Women living in sorority houses have three times the risk of being raped as students living off campus." While the students felt this particular statistic would encourage Greek members to be more diligent, with this particular group it backfired. First, they thought we had made up the statistic; this misunderstanding was partly due to our failure to cite the national survey on our flyers, a moment when aesthetics got in the way of academicism. They were irritated because they felt such statistics would impair their ability to recruit women to Greek life—a misplaced anger in my students' opinions. The one student who had to explain our goals very ably suggested to them that if they wanted to be different from the statistic, then they should join us in the march, which they eventually did.

However, we originally had another hard-hitting statistic about the fact that fraternity men were three times more likely to commit sexual violence than non-fraternity men. In consultation with one of the graphic designers, I decided to suppress this flyer. In retrospect, two of the students felt we should have included this statistic because what we had unintentionally done was to victimize women rather than show how men needed to be part of the change. We did have many men in the class and many men marching with us, including a large section of fraternity men. It was hard for me to justify such a harsh piece of information in light of the fact that, historically, we had worked hard to get the fraternity men to march with us. In the end, it was my call as the person with the institutional history and I felt that, while the sorority information was impacting, it did not point fingers at the Greek community in the way the one about fraternity men did. Yet, what we had done was to buy in to a legal code which Wendy Brown characterizes as "male sexual rapaciousness and female powerlessness," a process which "desexualizes and depowers women in its assignment of responsibility to the state for women's fate as objects of sexist sexual construction" (1992: 9). Further, we had been guilty of silencing women, a method construed by some of our groups as a patriarchal move. As Brown explains, it would look like we were

> seeking protection against men from masculinist institutions, a move more in keeping with the politics of feudalism than freedom. Indeed, to be 'protected' by the very power whose violation one fears perpetuates the specific modality of dependence and powerlessness marking much of women's experience . . .
>
> (1992: 9)

While we could intellectualize the ways the offended groups would perceive that we might be engaging in such a practice, we were cognizant of trying to perform a resistance narrative, using the oppression to protest it.

Further, we were in a bind in terms of identity discourse, particularly what Ellen Messer-Davidow calls "grievance discourses":

> [O]n one hand, "You have oppressed me" or "You have marginalized my people"; on the other, "I didn't" or "Oh my god, I did and I'm sorry." This modality generates antagonisms that make it very hard for people to form coalitions and work together. In fact, people may withdraw because they're just too frightened to engage in ongoing conflict [which] undercuts the work of political change in two ways. First, the affiliational issue: how do you form alliances if you're constantly reminding people that you've been victimized and they've been the victimizers? Second, the practical issue: how can you take on time-consuming work of planning a change project and choreographing the action if you're expending your energy on generating grievances?
>
> (Messer-Davidow et al. 2004: 5)

The students and I did feel exhausted and it was our perception that the groups' members in question could not get past the victimization model. In fact, while the Greek community did march with us, a member of another key group withdrew, choosing not to join us in the march, even with our compromises. Yet, we were doing our job of educating the larger community about the devastating facts of domestic and sexual violence in a very impactful way, with flyers that launched a conversation and contributed to furthering everyone's concern about how to address such issues on our campus and in our community.

Reflection

Students were able to analyze critically the experience of activism and its benefits to self, others, and the community, as well as articulate ideas for improvement for future such events through their final oral presentations to the class and to some of our co-sponsors. In groups they self-selected, based on their roles in production, they addressed the pros and cons of our implementation and changes they might make in leadership and production. I asked them to consider the value of civic engagement and what it meant to them in terms of the community contacts and experiences they created and how those contacts might benefit them in the future. Within this presentation, students evaluated the service-learning component and whether or not it increased their level of knowledge on activism and its application in a real-world environment. In this way, we responded to Bickford and Reynolds's understanding that "acts of dissent demand a more process-oriented method of evaluation, which includes the framing of the activity in advance as well as reflection on its level of success once completed." But what I became increasingly aware of, as the students shared their presentations, was whether or not I had too singlehandedly controlled our vision. As Bickford and Reynolds admit (2002: 246), "We walk a fine line. How can we expect our students to engage in activism without imposing our own ideological agendas on them?" And, as a feminist teacher, is it *ever* possible *not* to operate with a feminist agenda? There was a moment when I was able to step out of that dilemma with one of the WAN organizers. She was responsible for working with the equestrian team to secure a horse and rider to portray Joan. She aired her concern to me that she did not feel like they would support a feminist cause. I replied, "Would they say they were against sexual and domestic violence? That's all you have to ask them." They did join us on that score. Sometimes we had to be subversive in our feminism and just not call it that! Yet this incident begs for a large feminist critique, one which responds to challenges we face as feminist teachers and activists in both making feminism palatable (or debating about whether or not that should be one of our goals) and, simultaneously, yet genuinely, explaining its core components and values.

Many students started their presentations by saying, "I have never done any activism prior to this class, but now . . . " and it was always a positive "now" experience of enlightenment. Many happy outcomes included my Youth Activism student along with three others wanting to train for Smart

Girl/Smart Guys, exemplifying what Sara L. Crawley et al., determine as one of the great values of the Smart Girl Program, how it becomes a "model for systemic change" and also works across disciplines (2008: 6). For example, while the students all now have feminist backgrounds, they come from such diverse programs as Elementary Education, Political Science, Disability Studies, and History. Smart Girl is a place where the goals of Take Back the Night might actually take form: Williams and Ferber, in addressing feminist education as an activist project have had success with Smart Girl in providing girls with necessary confidence and self-esteem to allow them to begin considering work in the STEM fields (2008: 50). From our perspective, if the program can provide such benefits through confidence building, it can provide others, such as preparing girls to handle relationships with a more empowering sense of how to protect themselves from sexual violence, walk away from bad relationships, and be change agents in this regard themselves.

Further, many students will submit their visual work for design competitions on activism. Students were doing a research paper prior to the production, during which they chose an artist activist or visual activist agenda. One student decided to research and create a design board for Dove's Beauty campaign, during which she conflated our work on activism with feminist work on body image in relation to issues of sexual violence. Also, four students planned to present our service-learning experience at an activism conference.

While it was gratifying to hear the students voice a new-found or continuing call to activism through this service-learning experience, and we have various success stories of students taking it to the next level, it was less clear that they understood how to evaluate the impact of what we had done in the communities at large. How would we measure our impact? Bickford and Reynolds cite this dilemma as endemic to engaging in activist work (2002: 246). Not only had we done a historical reenactment, but also we had feature articles in the town newspaper (two, along with front-page coverage of the march itself), and the campus newspaper (similarly, two, along with front-page coverage of the march itself), a UW website article, and radio and television coverage. These less conventional sources of dissemination meet the challenges we face as academics trying to do activist work: Finding venues where we can address public audiences, cognizant of what Brenda Daly asserts, that "our discourse doesn't go where it is needed" (Messer-Davidow et al. 2004: 10). For the future, we have determined that STOP Violence will spearhead the event; in concert with them, we hope to track sexual assault statistics/reporting before and after the march. A pre- and post-survey may also tell us more about the impact of the event.

Further, none of the students were satisfied with our conflict resolution, either the process or the product. Many of them wished we would have marched with the mouth coverings, our actual silence not enough of a message in their minds. In a nice follow-up, however, our QAN group used the mouth coverings for their Day of Silence demonstration a week later.

Because we felt we wanted to work through the dialogue that the initial conflicts generated, we decided we would organize a group panel to address co-sponsors' reflections on the event and ways to go forward. This is a positive move, one that contradicts Bickford and Reynolds' critique of service-learning versus activism, in which they suggest that our classrooms need to be places where we challenge students "to examine their resistance to activism and consider what is at stake in recognizing the power of and the need for dissent" (2002: 247). While this questioning is certainly a valid form of inquiry, my experience with this particular group of students was that they had already bought in to activism. Perhaps their proactive attitude is a product of what Dan Butin determines to be a "substantial spread of service-learning over the last ten years [which] mirrors" higher education's embrace of a "scholarship of engagement" (2006: 473). And we have come a long way from where we were ten years ago, when I can remember colleagues who worked with activist student groups asking us, as the Women's Studies faculty, to be more present in our activism. We looked puzzled, exclaiming, "But, we're academics. How do we do activism outside of our research and our example of being feminists in the classroom?" We were living through Messer-Davidow's argument in *Disciplining Feminism* (2002) that women's studies programs were too removed from activism, seeing it as a "change-oriented activity outside of academia" (qtd. in Messer-Davidow et al. 2002: 1). Rather, what we are encouraged to do now is to follow Jesse Lemisch's example, to "stay and fight" (2003). Yet, in many women's studies programs, 56% according to Jeni Hart, there are "still no faculty lines and [they] struggle to create scholarship and curriculum that the institution values and rewards, placing activism on the margins" (2008: 186). It's what she calls the "thinking-(i.e., knowledge production) doing (i.e., activism) dichotomy." In my 2012 classroom, on day one I looked at the group of thirteen students and knew I had several Gender and Women's Studies majors and minors, a handful of SAFE volunteers, several campus activists, and others who, in the first-day survey for class, revealed their excitement to work on this project. Perhaps signing up for a Gender and Women's Studies class now means, for students, that they assume an activist agenda will be central. Perhaps they saw my poster advertising the class, a NOW photograph from an early 1970s march, with women marching, arms raised, voices engaged in a chant. Perhaps I just got lucky in the mix of students I gathered and in being part of a program to writes activism into its research expectations. Yet, Bickford and Reynolds's question will be the first one off my tongue in future renditions of the course.

Discussion Questions

1   This project involved many partnerships. In your community/campus, who might make good partners for activist/service-learning work and why?
2   What is present or missing from your campus/community to support student activist/service-learning voices? What other group formations might you add?
3   Part of this project involved partnering with mentors/middle-school girls through Smart Girl. Do you have Girl Activist programs at your secondary schools? If not, what do you see as needs in your education community in terms of empowering girls?
4   What kind of projects might you create to connect your classroom learning to action in your community?
5   We faced inevitable conflicts in organizing our march. What would you have done differently in the same situation? What conflict resolution tools might you use? What leadership models would you use?
6   This project focused on visually based messages. What ideas do you have for other creative displays? How might the work we did be compared to the visual displays and other ephemera of the Women's March globally in January, 2017?
7   What are the limitations of Take Back the Night events not addressed in the article?

Suggested Readings

1   Butler, Cornelia et al. 2007. *WACK! Art and the Feminist Revolution.* Los Angeles, CA: Museum of Contemporary Art; Cambridge, MA: MIT Press.
2   Broude, Norma and Mary D. Garrard, eds. 1996. *The Power of Feminist Art: The American Movement of the 1970s, History and Impact.* New York: Abrams.
3   Huneault, Kristine. 2002. *Difficult Subjects: Working Women and Visual Culture, Britain, 1880–1914.* Aldershot, Hants, England: Ashgate.
4   Lippard, Lucy R. 1984. *Get the Message? A Decade of Art for Social Change.* New York: E.P. Dutton.
5   McAdam, Doug and David A. Snow, eds. 2010. *Readings on Social Movements: Origins, Dynamics and Outcomes.* 2nd ed. New York: Oxford University Press.
6   Tickner, Lisa. 1988. *The Spectacle of Women: Imagery of the Suffrage Campaign 1907–14.* Chicago, IL: University of Chicago Press; London: Chatto and Windus.
7   Tilly, Charles and Lesley J. Wood. 2009. *Social Movements, 1768–2008.* 2nd ed. Boulder, CO: Paradigm.

Suggested Media

1   *Suffragette.* 2015. Focus Features, Pathe, Film4, and BFI. Universal City, CA: Universal Studios Home Entertainment.
2   *Milk.* 2009. Focus Features. University City, CA: Universal Studios Home Entertainment.

References

**American College Health Association-National College Health Assessment II Survey (ACHA-NCHA II Survey, 2011).* 2001. Accessed June 8th, 2012. www.achancha.org.

**Bickford, Donna M., and Nedra Reynolds. 2002. "Activism and Service-Learning: Reframing Volunteerism as Acts of Dissent." *Pedagogy* 2 (2002): 229–252.

**Brown, Wendy. 1992. "Finding the Man in the State." *Feminist Studies* 18 (1992): 7–34.

**Butin, Dan W. 2006. "The Limits of Service-Learning in Higher Education." *Review of Higher Education* 29 (2006): 473–498.

**Collins, Gail. 2009. *When Everything Changed: The Amazing Journey of American Women from 1960 to the Present.* New York: Little, Brown and Co.

**Crawley, Sara L. et al. 2008. "Introduction to 'Feminist Pedagogies in Action: Teaching Beyond Disciplines.'" *Feminist Teacher* 19: 1–12.

**Fonow, Mary Margaret, and Judith A . Cook, eds. 1991. *Beyond Methodology: Feminist Scholarship as Lived Research.* Bloomington, IN: Indiana University Press.

**Garnier, Katja von, Sally Robinson, and Jennifer Friedes. 2004. *Iron-Jawed Angels.* New York: HBO Video.

**Grossman, Ali. 2012. *Take Back the Night, University of Wyoming.* UW TV production. www.youtube.com/watch?v=HiMV08InvUg&feature=share&list=PL B63857A1563FC891

**Hart, Jeni. 2008. "Mobilization among Women Academics: The Interplay between Feminism and Professionalization." *NWSA Journal* 20 (2008): 184–208.

**Kelley, Jeff. 1995. "The Body Politics of Suzanne Lacy." In *But is it Art? The Spirit of Activism,* ed. Nina Felshin, 221–249. Seattle, WA: Bay Press.

**Lemisch, Jesse. 2003. "2.5 Cheers for Bridging the Gap between Activism and the Academy; Or, Stay and Fight." *Radical History Review* 85 (2003): 239–248.

**Messer-Davidow, Ellen, et al. 2004. "Women's Studies and Activism: An Interview with Ellen Messer-Davidow." *NWSA Journal* 16 (2004): 1–14.

**Meyer, Richard. 1995. "This is to Enrage You: Gran Fury and the Graphics of AIDS Activism." In *But is it Art? The Spirit of Activism,* ed. Nina Felshin, 51–83. Seattle, WA: Bay Press.

**Radford-Hill, Sheila. 1986. "Considering Feminism as a Model for Social Change." In *Feminist Studies, Critical Studies,* ed. Teresa de Lauretis, 157–172. Bloomington, IN: Indiana University Press.

**"Smart Girl Program." Accessed June 8th, 2012. www.Smart Girl.org

**Williams, Rhonda L., and Abby L. Ferber. 2008. "Facilitating Smart Girl: Feminist Pedagogy in Service Learning in Action." *Feminist Teacher* 19: 47–67.

18

INSISTING ON
INTERSECTIONALITY IN *THE*
VAGINA MONOLOGUES

Erin Heisler

In an effort to eliminate oppression and violence against women, *The Vagina Monologues* by Eve Ensler has been produced as part of the V-Day movement in cities around the world since February 14, 1998. With 715 productions of *The Vagina Monologues* taking place in 2015, the play continues to serve as a reliable resource for these aims (Sherman 2015).[1] Throughout the play, Ensler creatively utilizes the vagina as an outlet to retell the stories of women and pushes to unify women through their experiences with their vaginas. While the play excels in raising public consciousness about ways in which women are oppressed, as well as funds to end specific cases of violence occurring around the world, it fails to address the gender binarist, racist, nationalist, ageist, and capitalist ideological structures at play, and as such much of its potential for achieving its final goal. As part of the V-Day movement "to end violence against women and girls," the play must challenge the range of hierarchies that are used to oppress women—not just gender-based, but also age-, race-, national-, and class-based hierarchies. By analyzing the play through Nancy Fraser's three-pronged theory of justice, I will show that Ensler appropriates trans identities within the cultural dimension, naturalizes class identities thus failing to address issues of distribution and exploitation in the economic dimension, and silences older, intersex, non-white, non-Christian, and global voices that must be given recognition within the political dimension of feminist struggles. As audience members, actors, and activists with a vested interest in ending violence against women and girls, we have witnessed the power of *The Vagina Monologues* to start necessary conversations for justice.[2] We must appreciate *The Vagina Monologues* for what it accomplishes, but *we* cannot be lulled into accepting where it falls short. As a living text and movement, the play still holds potential to affect change, but this potential relies on an evolution in the manner in which future productions of the play are created and produced, as well as future manifestations of the V-Day movement and new advocacy plays that choose to mirror the format of *The Vagina Monologues*.[3] It is my hope that this critique will provide a critical framework to insist on an intersectional approach to the play and the movement for justice that has built upon the play's momentum.

The Vagina Monologues began as a play that sought to educate and empower women through vivid accounts of women's experiences with sexuality and violence. Influenced by the feminist projects that preceded it, the play focuses on empowering and liberating women, much like the work of many second-wave feminists, through an adaptation of methods used by feminist theatre groups during the 1970s and early 1980s.[4] It builds pride and creates moments of celebration for women through first-person heartfelt accounts of first orgasmic experiences and vagina facts such as "[the clitoris] is the only organ in the body designed purely for pleasure" (Ensler 2008: 51). Through renditions of women's orgasms and first menstruation stories, the play focuses on events that are uniquely female—showing how moments of joy and exhilaration can also be frightening due to a woman's lack of control over her own body. Finally, with appalling accounts of violence and rape, as well as facts about genital mutilation, it brings to light the atrocities that threaten women individually and as a community around the world. Throughout the show, unifying messages about the commonalities of women are juxtaposed with provocative accounts of violence perpetrated against them; as a result, the audience is implicitly challenged to seek ways to fight the patriarchy that makes this violence against women—and potentially, themselves, or the women in their lives—possible.

The play's provocative messages and powerful call-to-action garnered public attention, and on February 14, 1998 the one-woman show quickly transformed into a feminist powerhouse: the V-Day movement. "At a juncture in the history of feminism when the media was rife with exposés about the death of feminism and when there was much hand-wringing in feminist circles about the so-called postfeminism of younger generations of women," V-Day burst onto the scene touting celebrity and university productions of *The Vagina Monologues* whose engagement levels were in apparent opposition to this postfeminist narrative (Cooper 2007: 730–731). Every year since then, the show has been performed by a multitude of women in different areas around the world—uniting community members with students and audiences with actors in a movement for change. Dedicated to ending all violence against women and girls, V-Day leadership explains that the movement

> is grounded in three core beliefs: that art has the power to transform thinking and inspire people to act; that lasting social and cultural change is spread by ordinary people doing extraordinary things; and that local women know what their communities need and can become unstoppable leaders.[5]
>
> (Ensler 170: 2008)

To further its efforts to empower and protect women, proceeds from the play and V-Day events—over $100 million in 17 years—are donated to both international and local organizations that fight violence against women and/or provide safe spaces for the victims of violence ("About" 2014).

On a practical level, raising money for these organizations helps address the problematic effects of patriarchy. But Ensler acknowledges that the act of "raising money to stop violence against women makes it something other, something separate from the human condition, from every moment of our daily lives" (2008: xxi). The act of raising money to end violence allows the violence to become something separate from the person who is raising/donating the money because the philanthropic act serves as the antithesis of the violence in so far as the funds become the answer to "the problem." Moreover, this false equation has detrimental side effects: it allows the person to view the violence as the problem in and of itself, rather than seeing it as a symptom of the larger problem—the ideological structures that make that violence acceptable—and thus allows the person to deny his/her role in the violence as a member of a society that adheres to said ideologies. So to succeed at its goal, V-Day must do more than raise money for anti-violence organizations; it must also challenge the ideologies that make this violence possible.

In addition to raising funds and the support of anti-violence organizations and safe houses that comes with these funds, the short-term goals of *The Vagina Monologues* and V-Day can be deduced through what Ensler deems victories of the movement in the "Introduction to the Tenth Anniversary Edition." These include: the increase in women "reclaiming their bodies" and sharing their stories; women "finding their power, their voice, and their leadership," and the ability to "point to places where violence has been reduced or stopped altogether or where the consciousness has most clearly shifted" (2008: xiv, xvii). Although these victories are worthy of celebration, they must not distract from the lofty end goal of eliminating violence against women and girls. As evident through the play's history, the increase in sharing the stories of women and raising consciousness does not precipitate the eradication of violence. It makes society aware of the atrocities occurring, but fails to point to *why* they exist. Furthermore, the act of empowering women and helping them find their voice leads women to action, but would require a world or society in which women's actions are equal to men's and capable of creating the systemic changes necessary to meet their goals. While the struggle for empowering women goes hand-in-hand with the struggle to create this equal society, it must be acknowledged that the former cannot be fully achieved without advancements in society that address the institutionalized ways in which women's actions are denied equal consideration and weight. As Ensler notes:

we have reclaimed our stories and our voices, but we have not
yet unraveled or deconstructed the inherent cultural underpinnings
and causes of violence. We have not penetrated the mindset that,
somewhere in every single culture, gives permission to violence,
expects violence, waits for violence and instigates violence.

(2008: xix)

Herein Ensler acknowledges the shortcoming of *The Vagina Monologues*.
Without deconstructing the hierarchies and cultural underpinnings perpetuated by patriarchy, capitalism, gender binarism, ageism, racism, and
nationalism that make the violence possible, there can be no end to violence
against women and girls.

Ensler argues that

the trick [to the success of *The Vagina Monologues*] has been to lay a
certain groundwork—i.e., the play, the intention of the movement—
and then to trust individuals and groups to bring their own vision,
culture, and creativity to the experience.

(2008: xiii)

This has proven effective in not only increasing the accessibility and reach
of play productions, but also for allowing specific productions of the play
to introduce intersectionality to their shows.[6] For instance, performers
Meredith Talusan (2015) and Julie Rei Goldstein (2014) write about the
support and belonging they experienced as transwomen during productions of the play. This denotes the play's ability to fight hierarchies that
place transwomen below cisgender women. Furthermore, shows that utilize actors of all ages, such as those I performed in at the University of
Wisconsin-Marathon, challenge the intersections of ageism and patriarchy.
Similarly, shows that engage actors of various races, or those that take place
in non-Western countries, have the potential to challenge not only patriarchy, but also racial or nationalist undertones within the play's text.

Yet, the success of these productions relies on deliberate choices by
the directors of each show to counter forms of systemic injustice in the
performance of the piece. And, the directors' ability to expand on intersectional notions is bound to the parameters established in the groundwork
laid by Ensler. This foundation is centered on essentialist ideas of woman
and the vagina, and thus falls into the trap of flattening the discourse it
attempts to create. Norma Alarcón argues: "with gender as the central
concept in feminist thinking, epistemology is flattened out in such a way
that we lose sight of the complex and multiple ways in which the subject and object of possible experience are constituted" (qtd. in Hennessy
1993: 69). Because the play's groundwork focuses on sex (as defined by

the binary based in male/female anatomy),[7] it inadvertently simplifies the knowledge of and discussions around patriarchy and minimizes the intersection of patriarchal systems with the ideologies of racism, classism, ageism, nationalism, and gender binarism. As such, U.S. or Western productions that do not (or cannot, based on the demographics of the actors available) cast women in order to highlight the intersectionality of power structures, will inadvertently strengthen a simplified discussion of patriarchy that is threatened by ideological pitfalls that weaken its ability to end violence against women and girls.

In order to identify these pitfalls for the sake of removing them from the current play and V-Day movement, addressing them in individual productions of the play, or avoiding them when creating new advocacy pieces that are inspired by *The Vagina Monologues*, it is useful to turn to Nancy Fraser's theory of justice, because the fight to end violence against women and subvert the ideologies of patriarchy is a fight with the realm of justice. Fraser's theory illuminates how the concept of justice is utilized by societies to determine the following: what is right and wrong, who can make claims to justice, and who can decide whether justice has been served. Fraser "situate[s] gender struggles as one strand among others in a broader political project" and offers a way to "unflatten" epistemology, to identify the complex intersections that create women's experience and identities and points to how justice is a complicated concept—one that has unjustly excluded some identities from its purview (2013: 161).[8] In order to avoid these exclusions, she argues: "the theory of justice must become three-dimensional, incorporating the political dimension of representation alongside the economic dimension of distribution and the cultural dimension of recognition" (Fraser 2013: 13; emphasis removed). This theory of justice insists on intersectionality by requiring parity of participation across each dimension and showing how each facet of justice is interconnected with and affected by the others. Fraser notes that "each lens brings into focus an important aspect of status subordination, but [none of them are singularly] sufficient on [their] own" (2013: 162).[9] Therefore movements for justice must address and consider ideologies that are perpetuated within and interconnected between all three.

When looking at the ideological arguments of *The Vagina Monologues* with this in mind, it is necessary to consider the following: the cultural dimension that establishes the values associated with particular characteristics and societal norms in order to place women as lesser than men, minority races as lesser than whites, elderly as lesser than youth, etc.; the economic dimension that determines where divisions of labor are created in order to justify lower compensation or value for a particular group's work, and the political dimension that determines which persons have a right to representation within the fight to change the injustices of the former two dimensions. It is also important to keep in mind what varying types of injustices fall under the umbrella of "violence against women and girls." This "violence" can come in many forms: not only as rape, abuse, murder, sex trafficking, genital mutilation, or forced childhood marriages, but also as the societal structures and ideas that allow these explicit forms of violence to exist relatively unchecked—for instance, failure to prosecute perpetrators of the formerly mentioned acts, "slut-shaming" or other methods of silencing, imbalances of power between women and men in homes, work places, and governments, and the exacerbation of these injustices faced by women who identify with other minority statuses.[10] In order to combat both explicit and covert forms of violence, a multidimensional form of justice must be used. In the analysis that follows, I will show that, however sincere Ensler's intent may be, the groundwork she develops within *The Vagina Monologues* fails to address aspects of each dimension of justice and thus fails to provide space for the dialogue and action needed to free women from the oppressive ideological systems that make gendered violence possible.

For the purposes of clarity, in this chapter I will explore each dimension separately, but it is important to keep in mind that all three intersect with and overlap each other. Therefore, macro-level consideration and application of these dimensions cannot be compartmentalized. It is natural to start with the cultural, because a large part of the ideological struggle found in *The Vagina Monologues* takes place within the cultural dimension of recognition. Fraser argues that "the essence of misrecognition [is] the material construction, through the institutionalization of cultural norms, of a class of devalued persons who are impeded from political parity" (Fraser 2013: 180). In the case of gender relations, this would be the establishment of cultural norms and ideologies that devalue women and femininity and thus prevent women from parity of participation. As a result, women are unable to participate equally in decisions about new laws and the interpretation, prosecution, or amendment of existing laws; or, in the very simplest of measures, they are unable to vote on the representatives who make decisions. Fraser explains that "participatory parity is 'intersubjective.' It requires that institutionalized patterns of cultural value express equal respect for all participants and ensure opportunity for achieving social esteem" (Fraser 2013: 164).

In order to engage with this condition of participatory parity, *The Vagina Monologues* works to build respect for women by recoding and strengthening the power of the word "vagina" and ideas surrounding it. When "vagina" is a word to be feared or, worse, ignored, and when bodily actions associated with the vagina such as orgasms and menstrual cycles are things to be ashamed of, women are devalued and their political voice is silenced. As a result of this devaluation and other forms of diminishing women, Fraser argues that injustices of misrecognition are made possible:

women suffer gender-specific forms of *status subordination*, including sexual harassment, sexual assault, and domestic violence; trivializing, objectifying, and demeaning stereotypical depictions in the media; disparagement in everyday life; exclusion or marginalization in public spheres and deliberative bodies; and denial of the full rights and equal protections of citizenship.

(2013: 162–163)

Thus, Ensler's work to fight violence is seen as a fight against forms of status subordination; and, upon first consideration, her work to recode the vagina in an effort to correct its cultural misrecognition appears to be an appropriate method of addressing this status subordination within the cultural dimension.

However, this form of addressing the cultural dimension fails to acknowledge the ways in which gender is socially constructed and valued in conjunction with a person's sex. When explaining Ensler's conflation of femininity and woman through the vagina, Christine Cooper argues: "Rather than a metaphor, which reveals difference as much as resemblance between two ideas, the vagina becomes a metonym—a part of the body and a particular subset of experience standing in for the whole of female consciousness" (2007: 732). Instead of empowering women by revaluing the vagina, the extended trope threatens to pigeonhole the gender "woman" to a place where it is only understood through the singular sex identifier: the vagina. This fails to address the differing ways in which gender is experienced on an individual level. Fraser notes that "a major feature of gender injustice . . . androcentrism [is] an institutionalized pattern of cultural value that privileges traits associated with masculinity, while devaluing everything coded as 'feminine' paradigmatically—*but not only women*" (2013: 162; emphasis added). As such, recoding the values associated with the female sex alone, rather than feminine characteristics or actions that have been societally associated with the gender "woman," will not result in cultural political parity because it will never fully address the injustices that transwomen or other feminized marginalized populations experience.

In an attempt to address this concern, Ensler worked with transwomen to create the monologue "They Beat the Girl Out of My Boy . . . Or So They Tried." The play gives voice to women who are born male and the anxiety and violence they experience as a result of not conforming to gender expectations. The speaker recounts: "I always knew I was a girl / They beat me for it / . . . In the park they smashed my Magic Marker painted nails / They punched my lipsticked mouth" (Ensler 2008: 143). The attack on her "Magic Marker painted nails" and "lipsticked mouth" is not just a physical assault on her person, but a direct attack on her femininity and (trans)womanly actions. It is her feminine attributes in combination with her sex that wrongfully authorize this violence. Yet the speaker argues that sex is arbitrary: "They assigned me a sex / The day I was born / It's as random as being adopted / or being assigned a hotel room on the thirtieth floor / It has nothing to do with who you are" (Ensler 2008: 142).

But this argument in the monologue simultaneously folds in on itself, because the monologue adheres to the trope found throughout the play: that the vagina acts as a synecdoche for the speaker's identity. The monologue starts with the by-then-familiar emphasis on the vagina as the speaker recounts that when she was five years old and saw her sister's vagina, she realized: "I wanted one / I wanted one / I thought it would grow / I thought I would open" (2008: 141). As she explains her desire for a vagina, repetition cues the reader into the vehemence behind her words. Then as she imagines her vagina, the repetition remains in the core structure of her lines, but key words are altered. By keeping the phrase "I thought . . . would" and replacing "it" with "I," Ensler conflates the identity of the vagina and the speaker, furthering the idea that one's vagina can stand in for one's identity. The speaker recounts embodying gendered female actions— wearing lipstick, crocheting socks—but yearns "to be completed" until her sex change (Ensler 2008: 142). Without a vagina, her identity is not whole. This emphasis on the physical anatomy, or sex, being essential to her identity is in direct opposition to the idea that sex "has nothing to do with who you are." If having a vagina is essential to a person's identity as a woman, then having a penis is essential to a person's identity as a man. But the speaker of this monologue has already established that her physical anatomy did not determine her identity when she had a penis, so the essentialist notion that a woman's vagina is (key to) her identity rings false. Furthermore, a belief that a person's physical anatomy must fit his/her gender in order to have a fully formed identity fails to acknowledge intersex or transgender people who are not transsexual.

This incongruity between an emphasis on the vagina and the varied experiences of trans and intersex communities is indicative of a larger dismissal of difference within the play. When analyzing an intersex monologue, Kim Q. Hall argues that

> The normativity of "Western," "American," and "white" is secured, not disrupted, by their ability to appropriate nondominant difference. Similarly, the narrative force of *The Vagina Monologues* is the ability of the normative vagina to appropriate different women's experiences and yet still produce the same story of the "normal" female body with a vagina.
>
> (2005: 108)

Although the monologue Hall is addressing was removed from the play shortly after it was introduced, the appropriation she describes continues to apply to "They Beat the Girl Out of My Boy . . . Or So They Tried." By focusing on the power of the vagina even in cases when a woman was not born with one, the play appropriates the experiences of women that do not have a (normal) vagina, and Ensler is able to create a movement that appears inclusive of transwomen without acknowledging essential moments of misrecognition—i.e., moments in which trans and intersex people are denied cultural recognition—that can become the means for forms of status subordination.

Along with a failure to address the misrecognition of transwomen, the play neglects to address the economic realities of the women in the monologues and that the movement seeks to empower. Instead, as Cooper argues in her analysis of "The Little Coochie Snorcher That Could," "no evidence of the woman's circumstances (mental, physical, or economic) at the time of Ensler's interview appears within [the monologue]" (2007: 742), an argument that applies to all of the monologues in the play. Fraser explains: "Not only is gender 'difference' constructed simultaneously from both economic differentials and institutionalized patterns of cultural value, but both maldistribution and misrecognition are fundamental to sexism" (2013: 163). By maldistribution, Fraser is referencing the economic structures that deny individuals parity of participation in the economic realm of justice and as such deny them the material means to make claims for their "independence and 'voice'" within the cultural dimension (2013: 164).[11] Because of this, women's inability to claim participatory parity is shown to not only be caused by cultural ideologies that devalue their sex and femininity but also as a result of an accumulation of ways in which women are denied the material conditions to make their voices heard: when women are paid less than men, or denied jobs altogether, their ability to have equal power in decisions within their household, and furthermore the government, is hindered.[12] Patriarchal ideologies must be understood and addressed with consideration of their interconnection with capitalist ideologies:[13] capitalism benefits from cultural norms that naturalize lesser pay for women than men as well as unpaid labor that is conducted within the home, while patriarchal ideologies are reinforced by this unequal distribution.[14] Yet, Ensler fails to provide the material realities of the women's lives as she tells their stories and, as part of that omission, removes the context necessary to understand the economic structures that have created each woman's oppression, and the tools needed to appropriately address the multiple ideological structures at work.

The play not only removes essential information about the women's economic realities, but furthermore promotes the capitalist structures that need to be questioned. One monologue curiously asks, "If your vagina got dressed, what would it wear?" (Ensler 2008: 15). While the answers vary from the childish "tutu," to the branded "Armani only," to the protective "electric shock device to keep unwanted strangers away," (2008: 16), the question is rooted within the social relations through material goods that is perpetuated by the fetishization of commodities and the alienation experienced in capitalism.[15] Marx argues that the fetishization of commodities allows for "the relations connecting the [labor] of one individual with that of the rest [to] appear . . . [as] material relations between persons and social relations between things" (1978: 321). By fetishization of commodities, he is referring to the process that allows the value of a commodity to be removed from the raw materials and labor that were needed to produce it, so that they are instead valued by the value of the items with which they can be exchanged—in many cases, money. This allows a commodity to become a material with no connection to the work of the wo/man required to create it. Having his/her labor removed from the value of commodities, the worker then turns to the possession of items to represent his/her (labor) value in society. Through this, the worker is alienated from his/her labor in that the labor takes on "an *external* existence" outside of the worker (Marx 1978: 72). As a result, members of society fail to connect their work with the objects they create because the objects become something outside of the workers' material existence due to fetishization. Furthermore, due to their alienation, they misrecognize their interconnectedness through the material goods each member possesses. By identifying people by what they own, and building social relations based on these materials, their identities are defined and strengthened based on class. Thus, through the question, "If your vagina got dressed, what would it wear?", the women are asked to turn to commodities to represent themselves accurately to others—reinforcing the fetishization of commodities within capitalism and a form of alienation that acts counter to the goal of solidarity.

Additionally, this question silences voices of the lower class and/or laborers who produce these goods. Many of the items that are selected for vaginal adornment are items only the privileged have access to: "a leather jacket, silk stockings, mink (2008: 15). When commenting on this monologue, Delia Aguilar asks, "Where does this put those of us, members of the non-elite, living in the 'Third World?'" (2002: 22). As an empowerment exercise, asking women to identify themselves through commodities effectively fails to recognize those who do not have the capital to purchase these goods. Furthermore, because fetishization has removed the role of the worker, it fails to acknowledge the person who creates these goods. To the Third World factory worker, the question "If your vagina got dressed, what would it wear?", in many cases, does not provide empowerment not only because she is denied the capital to purchase these commodities, but also because her exploitation takes on an exponential characteristic in which her labor creates a material commodity *and simultaneously* a commodity of empowerment. In both, her labor is not recognized by the person being empowered (i.e., the role of the Third World woman in the First World woman's empowerment is erased).

The fetishization present in the question "What would your vagina wear?" is in many cases used for comedic effect, and a critic may therefore question the weight of its ideological ramifications; however, Ensler also relies on material goods as a means to communicate personal growth within a more serious monologue. The speaker of "The Little Coochie Snorcher That Could" describes her underwear in multiple moments throughout her monologue. The audience is told that at age five, she "sleep[s] with three pairs of happy heart-patterned cotton underpants" (Ensler 2008: 78) in a fit of anxiety to avoid touching herself; at ten, she's trying on her "new white cotton bra and panties" (p. 79) when her father's best friend rapes her; and at thirteen, she dismisses her "white cotton bra and underpants" in a moment of insecurity, and "Then [her lover] dresses [her], slowly, in [a] satin teddy" (p. 81). While upon an initial reading, the satin teddy may seem unimportant, it is a significant part of the speaker's growth. The satin teddy is what makes her sexy; it is associated with the moment when she appreciates her vagina and begins to love her (sexual) self. It is also in deep contrast with the cotton panties, which along with being associated with a lower class, are also associated with points of anxiety in her life. Through this, the hierarchy of expensive commodities is reinforced and applied to the extended metaphor of the vagina as self. The pricier the underwear, the more value the speaker gives herself as a sexual being. Additionally, the more expensive underwear is associated with a desired sexual experience, versus the avoided or unwanted sexual experiences that occur with the cotton (i.e., cheaper) underwear. If expensive underwear represents the ability to protect oneself or enjoy one's sexual experience, women who live in areas where these commodities are unavailable, or do not have the material means to purchase these commodities, are denied this empowerment and awakening. Thus, whether the play expresses empowerment or sexual enlightenment through material goods, in each depiction, the poor do not receive parity of participation, for they do not have the material means to fight for recognition in this manner. Through this, in *The Vagina Monologues* Ensler recreates and naturalizes the material hierarchies that deny women parity of participation within both the economic and cultural dimensions of justice.

In addition to looking at the cultural dimension of recognition and economic dimension of distribution, it is essential to consider how *The Vagina Monologues* approaches the third dimension of justice: the political. Fraser explains:

> The political . . . furnishes the stage on which struggles over distribution and recognition are played out. Establishing criteria of social belonging, and thus determining who counts as a member, the political dimension of justice specifies the reach of those other dimensions: it tells us who is included in, and who excluded from, the circle of those entitled to a just distribution and reciprocal recognition.
>
> (2013: 195)

Unfortunately, the established criteria of social belonging within *The Vagina Monologues'* fight for women's right to representation offers an extremely narrow definition of the women it is speaking for, and thus creates a framework for the political dimension within the play that replicates the silencing structures that exclude many women from justice in their societies.

The political dimension of *The Vagina Monologues* is defined by the framework established by Ensler. Fraser argues that

> Frame-setting is among the most consequential of political decisions. Constituting both members and nonmembers in a single stroke, this decision effectively excludes the latter from the universe of those entitled to consideration within the community in matters of distribution, recognition, and ordinary-political representation.
>
> (2013: 197)

As part of a movement to end violence against women and girls, it could be assumed that the frame for *The Vagina Monologues* would mean to constitute all individuals who identify as women or girls as members of the political dimension. Yet this is not the case. In an interview with Howard Sherman about Mount Holyoke's decision to discontinue *The Vagina Monologues* because it has been deemed non-inclusive, Ensler argues:

> This is my perspective on it: *The Vagina Monologues* is a play. It's one play. It was never meant to speak for all women and it was never a play about what it means to be a woman. It was a play about what it means to have a vagina. It was very specific. I don't think I ever said that the definition of a woman – that a woman is defined by having a vagina.
>
> (Sherman 2015)

While her argument that this is one play is valid in so far that it cannot be expected to encompass every person's story, her assertion that the play is "about what it means to have a vagina" points to the narrow and contradictory frame she has set. If the play were only meant to depict the experience of having a vagina and to empower women through these depictions, then this frame would be acceptable. But the play is meant to be a tool to end violence against all women and girls and as such, the frame must be wide enough to encompass even those who do not have a normative vagina.

Before looking at how the frame of "what it means to have a vagina" unjustly excludes women from the political dimension of the play, it is essential to look at how, even within the frame she created, Ensler fails to provide political parity to menopausal and postmenopausal women. Although Ensler explains that she "interviewed a group of women between the ages of sixty-five and seventy-five," there are no monologues about the experience of menopause or the postmenopausal stage in a woman's life (2008: 23). Instead, the only monologue with an identifiable postmenopausal speaker, "The Flood," describes the woman's traumatic first orgasm in her youth. Because this monologue is dedicated to an interviewee, it cannot be assumed that the speaker is telling the story of the interviewee's lived experience, but only that Ensler was inspired by the interviewee's story and created "The Flood" in response. In this act, Ensler effectively erases the postmenopausal woman, for her story is not worth telling—yet a created story about her imagined youth is deemed worthy.

However, the physiological marker of menopause is essential to understanding a woman's experience with her vagina. Just as first menstruation (an experience addressed through the collective monologue "When I Was Twelve, My Mother Slapped Me") denotes the start of her physical experience with her bleeding body and mental understanding of her fertility, menopause denotes the end of this vaginal experience. Simone de Beauvoir explains:

> whereas man grows old gradually, [in menopause] woman is suddenly deprived of her femininity; she is still relatively young when she loses the erotic attractiveness and the fertility which, in the view of society and in her own, provide the justification of her existence and her opportunity for happiness.
>
> (qtd. in Young 2005: 105)

This passage is problematic because it assumes that a woman's perception of herself is the same as society's perception of her, or assumes that all women identify with their ability to have children—excluding women who have no plans to become mothers. However, it is useful for elucidating the fears that some women may experience during this time. For those who connect their fertility with their sexuality or are affected by the societal messages to this effect, menopause can become a clear demarcation of old age. Unlike men who maintain their fertility, and thus their sexuality, as they mature, women are faced with a distinct point in which their fertility ends. Once their fertility is gone, their sexuality and attractiveness are assumed to disappear as well. On the other side of the spectrum, Beauvoir argues that menopause can also demarcate the time when a woman "is delivered from the servitude imposed by her female nature . . . she is no longer the prey of overwhelming forces; she is herself, she and her body are one" (qtd. in Young 2005: 105). After menopause, a woman is no longer restrained by the monthly bleeding over which she had no control, but rather becomes one with her body and can relish in a freedom she has not experienced since her youth. For these reasons, menopause is shown to be both an empowering yet emotionally taxing moment in women's lives. Given that Ensler's political framework includes women's experience with menstruation, sex, vaginal exams, and childbirth, her failure to include stories about how menopause is understood and experienced by women unjustly excludes older women from political parity in so far as they are not allowed to fight for cultural recognition of their experiences in old(er) age. They can speak of their experiences in youth, but they are not allowed to fight as women during or after menopause for a "justification of [their] existence" that counters societal messages or personal fears.

The political framework of the vagina furthermore unjustly excludes intersex and transgender women who are not transsexual. In an open letter to V-Day, an intersex audience member describes her experience with the play: "walking through a crowd of women talking to each other about how empowered they felt. We felt invisible, it presented horror stories about genital mutilation occurring in other continents, as if we do not experience them here" (qtd. in Hall 2005: 105). Intersex individuals, who are born with a variation of the anatomical genitalia that would typically be used to identify them as male or female, often undergo the surgical creation of normative genitalia when they are too young to understand their gender identities or to consent to operations. Yet, the intersex woman is made invisible and silenced by the play because a frame has been established that excludes her identity and experience because she does not have a vagina. By framing violence against women and girls as violence against the vagina, the genital mutilation of girls in Africa with vaginas is depicted as an atrocity, while the genital mutilation of intersex individuals around the world (including in the U.S.) is ignored.[16] These women are not provided political parity within the play to explain this violence and fight for cultural parity that would acknowledge that a normative vagina is not necessary to understanding themselves as women. This erasure of identities of women who do not have vaginas can also be applied to transwomen who are not transsexuals: women who experience violence specifically because they challenge the frame set by society, and *The Vagina Monologues* in conjunction with V-Day, that defines the gender "woman" with the vagina.

The lack of intersectionality in the political framework of *The Vagina Monologues* is further complicated by considering that just as trans and intersex women are appropriated by the normative vagina, the positive experiences of women of color or non-Western women are subsumed and silenced by the identity of the privileged white woman. Cooper argues that the introductory notes about some character's race or accent "[encode] a seemingly arbitrary array of differences, marking these voices as other to the presumed normative voice of American whiteness" (Cooper 2007: 744). The preliminary notes—"Southern woman of color," "Jewish, Queens accent," and "a slight English accent"—establish this American whiteness by assuming a knowledge of American geography, to the extent that the director and actor would understand the variation that distinguishes a Jewish accent from the Queens borough of New York, and by only noting the race of one of the speakers, which establishes the precedent that the other speakers do not break the non-white mold unless there are geographic indicators in the narrator's introductions to the monologues (2008: 77, 25, 43).[17] These differences are not noted to the audience, but can only be conveyed through the director's choice in casting or the actor's depiction. The effect of this is to make the racial identity of the person interviewed for the monologue a type, or surface detail, rather than to acknowledge the real ways in which her race affects her experience as a woman in the world. Cooper argues that "the literary quality of the personal 'I' in *The Vagina Monologues* tends to be lost on or overlooked by viewers, even as its aesthetic appeal—the entertaining message—is what holds the promise of shifted mindsets and future feminist activity" (2007: 729). The audience is not asked to respect or value the racial identity of the speaker, but rather to look past this element of the "personal 'I'" in the hopes of empowering her through the singular identity of woman. Through this, in Hall's terms, the speaker's nondominant racial trait is appropriated to create an identity of unified sexual awareness. The "Southern woman of color" can then conclude her monologue with an experience that transformed her "coochie snorcher[18] and raised it up into a kind of heaven" (Esler 2008: 82), mirroring the sentiment of another woman (who is potentially of a different race and has lived in very different material conditions) who proclaims, "I began to swell, began to feel proud. Began to love my vagina . . . " (p. 57). These similar conclusions provide unity to the play and to the audience, but deny the African American woman the political parity to voice the ways in which she experiences different forms of cultural misrecognition that have greatly impacted the experiences she had before and during her sexual enlightenment.

Furthermore, the monologues involving a single voice within the main piece establish a violent correlation based on this normative racial identity: the white women experience negative/undesirable moments as they learn about and work to accept their sexual identities; while the identified non-white, non-Western women (the Southern woman of color, the Bosnian woman, and African girls who experience genital mutilation as noted in one of the narrative "Vagina Fact" asides) experience negative/undesirable moments as they become victims of transparent forms of violence and rape.[19] This correlation is only furthered by the spotlight monologues that Ensler has written to bring attention to "a situation in the world where women [are] totally at risk, where they [have] been raped or murdered or dismissed or simply not allowed to be" (Ensler 2008: 127). Through dedications prefacing each piece, all but one of these monologues specifies that the women facing these life-threatening forms of violence are either non-white or non-Western; the monologue that escapes this non-normative criterion based on race is that of the transwomen who have been identified as non-normative based on their sexual anatomy as outlined above. Through this,

The Vagina Monologues fails to give non-white, non-Western women political parity by omitting any stories that describe their empowerment outside of this violence; it is only through overcoming violence, if at all, that they can come to know their power. Moreover, this disclaims the political representation Western (and white) women need to voice their experiences with overt violent acts. These women are presumed to have surpassed the need to fight for their own safety within the political dimensions of the play, and are thus silenced as their lived experiences of violence are relegated to the lives of their non-Western or non-white Other.

One of the spotlight monologues that depicts violence perpetrated against the Western woman's Other is "Under the Burqa." The piece, like a few of the other spotlight monologues, does not depict a woman's experience with her vagina, but rather focuses on her violence and oppression.[20] A parenthetical note prefaces the monologue: "This piece is not about the burqa per se. Wearing one is obviously a matter of culture and choice. The piece is about a time and place where women had no choice" (Ensler 2008: 135). Yet, unless the individual shows' directors make a conscious decision to read this, this disclaimer is not shared with the audience and perpetuates a custom that is execrable to many Western audience members. The monologue opens: "imagine a huge dark piece of cloth / hung over your entire body / like you were a shameful statue / imagine there is only a drop of light / enough to know there is still daylight for others" (p. 135). These lines ask the audience to imagine the oppression a woman experiences *as she lives under a burqa*. Although later references to the violent oppression of her society indicate that the monologue "is about a time and place where women had no choice," this is not the focus at the start of the piece. As such, the monologue pushes the audience to first accept the custom of wearing a burqa as a form of oppression in and of itself and fails to acknowledge those who choose to wear a burqa for religious reasons. Although talking about men speaking *of* the subordinated person rather than *for* him/her, Gayatri Chakravorty Spivak explains that when the British created laws that criminalized the self-immolation of Indian widows "the dubious place of the free will of the constituted sexed subject as female was successfully effaced" (Spivak 1988: 98). Likewise, when a woman's choice to wear a burqa is subsumed by a description of the practice as inherently oppressive, she is, in principle, silenced. Thus the Muslim woman who chooses to wear a burqa is denied political parity to explain why she follows the religious practice, as, simultaneously, the Western feminist's definition of female free will is strengthened.[21]

An effect of cosmopolitan feminism, a form of feminism that Ensler seems to embrace, is the narrow depiction of the dichotomy between Western and non-Western women and their definitions of and calls for empowerment within their localized and global movements. Wendy S. Hesford defines feminist cosmopolitanism as

feminist formations of global citizenship particularly as these formations inform human rights advocacy, and the privileging of Western
feminist cosmopolitans' encounters with women and children of
Third World countries, namely those construed as non-Western or
marginalized U.S. subjects.

(2010: 54–55)

Within cosmopolitan feminism, non-Western or marginalized women are
no longer provided the political parity to tell their own stories, but instead
their stories are defined by the privileged, Western feminists' experience
with them. As a result, the non-Western woman becomes an object to
be defined by the Western feminist. This form of feminism allows the
Western woman to use violence against her female Other as a rallying cry:
"Spectacular representations of sexual violations against women and girls
continue to attract the international media, in part because such stories
ascribe to Western myths of deserving victims and to the shaming tactics of
human rights organizations" (Hesford 2010: 56). This rally cry relies on the
reaffirming message that the Western woman has the power to identify violence, and that said violence depicted occurs *over there*; it asks the Western
feminist to be appalled by this violence and oppression, but not to see herself
as a likely victim in solidarity with the non-Western woman, and furthermore not to see how her own ideologies could be further victimizing her
non-Western Other. In her analysis of Ensler's work, Hesford points out
that the non-Western woman's story instead becomes a tool, or a method,
through which the Western woman can save herself:

> Seeing the newly built rescue center two years later, Ensler realizes
> that she is no longer waiting. As she puts it, "We get rescued by
> giving what we need the most. What we are waiting for has always
> lived inside us."
>
> (Hesford 2010: 57)

In this assumption, the Western woman does not need to fight for political
parity, because she is assumed to already have it. Instead, she gives "what
she needs most" to the non-Western woman—her political parity by telling the stories of the women who cannot tell their own, or her economic
parity to build safe houses or organizations to "save" the non-Western, or
marginalized, woman. However, this does not provide the non-privileged
women political parity, but merely allows the privileged women to act as
delegates with their own assumed political parity. Through this Hesford
argues *The Vagina Monologues* builds up "a cosmopolitan feminist bildung-
sroman, which privileges individual transformation over and above an analysis of structural injustices and the contradictions of globalization" (Hesford
2010: 58). By not emphasizing the need to guarantee the political parity

of all women, *The Vagina Monologues* focuses on the transformation of the individual, rather than solidarity across differences, and therefore, fails to provide the tools to effectively empower women globally.

While the ideological faults of *The Vagina Monologues* continue to undermine the efficacy of the play in moving toward its stated goal, the V-Day movement has started to evolve and embrace intersectionality. In the last three years, the V-Day movement has shifted its focus away from *The Vagina Monologues* and toward its One Billion Rising campaign.[22] The One Billion Rising campaign "began as a call to action based on the staggering statistic that 1 in 3 women on the planet will be beaten or raped during her lifetime" ("What" 2015). This adds up to more than one billion women and girls, providing further motivation to continue fighting to end violence against women and girls worldwide. Its efforts include productions of *The Vagina Monologues*, but now further emphasis is placed on regionally organized events, workshops, flash mobs, strikes, and various forms of resistance. What is important about this shift is the focus on the fourth core belief of V-Day: "One must look at the intersection of race, class and gender to understand violence against women" ("Four Core Beliefs" 2014). Because of the localized and intersectional nature of One Billion Rising, events in 2014 included fights for economic parity of participation:

> risings in Bangladesh focused on labour rights in the wake of the Rana Plaza factory collapse, where more than 1,000 garment workers died; [and] in Hong Kong, thousands joined an event focusing on the plight of domestic workers after a young Indonesian maid, Erwiana Sulistyaningsih, was allegedly abused by her employer.
>
> (Khaleeli 2015)

These events highlight the intersection between the material conditions of women's lives and the violence they experience: by protesting the violence that domestic workers face in Indonesia, activists show that domestic workers do not have the cultural and economic parity to stand up against their employers but insist that this maldistribution and misrecognition must change—furthermore, the link of this protest to the One Billion Rising events illuminates the connection of these labor issues with gender violence. Likewise, because the events are organized by regional and local activists, the One Billion Rising structure lessens the potential for the appropriation of non-Western voices by Western voices. The structure allows people to "[interpret] revolution in different ways" and ensure that localized voices are provided the political parity to determine what causes are the most important to them within the V-Day fight for justice (Khaleeli 2015). However, as Homa Khaleeli notes, "inevitably, the celebrity-heavy events in cities such as London or New York gain the most attention" so continual (re)evaluation must occur to ensure that celebrity-endorsed events, or those taking place in Western countries, do not inappropriately influence the events in lesser privileged locations.[23] This is obviously not an exhaustive analysis of the One Billion Rising campaign—a further look would require consideration of its inclusion of women with non-normative female bodies, as well as deep analysis of the manner in which individual events around the globe are developed and executed—but rather, this highlights how V-Day can and is continually adapting its methods—an act that would be strengthened with further consideration of Fraser's theory of justice.

The Vagina Monologues and the V-Day movement have successfully engaged over a billion activists in the cause to end violence against women and girls globally. But even with this success, the movement and play are not immune to ideological pitfalls. Without an intersectional approach, the play threatens to silence voices within the movement. In its current state, The Vagina Monologues fails to provide cultural and political parity to individuals who do not have a normative vagina by emphasizing the stories and value of the vagina; it fails to acknowledge the ways that race and nationality affect fights for cultural, economic, and political parity by silencing non-Western and non-white women and homogenizing their experience; and it reaffirms structures of economic maldistribution by emphasizing the value of commodities for understanding and empowering women's identities. Yet, these shortcomings do not signal the demise or irrelevance of The Vagina Monologues and V-Day. Because of the malleability of its structure, changes can be made to expand its framework beyond "what it means to have a vagina" to offer a more inclusive tool for the fight to end gender violence around the world. Such changes would require the inclusion of voices and experiences that have not yet received participatory parity within the play—for instance, those of intersex, transwomen, international, and postmenopausal women. Additionally, it would require Ensler to make changes for justice in the economic dimension. For instance Ensler could add a monologue immediately following "If Your Vagina Got Dressed, What Would It Wear?" from the perspective of a Third World factory worker. This monologue could nuance identification with commodities at the moment in the play when it is most poignant, as well as provide women who suffer from maldistribution an example of empowerment by explaining how a Third World factory worker experiences her identity as woman outside of the purchase of commodities.[24] Additionally, individual production directors can immediately work to make deliberate casting choices that challenge the ideological implications that are inherent in the current work. As V-Day continues to engage the One Billion Rising campaign, consideration of Nancy Fraser's theory of justice can offer activists a method to evaluate the ideological success of the movement. The goal to end violence against women and girls is considerably large. But, by learning from the past and thoughtfully engaging in an intersectional approach in the future movement, it is possible to imagine a world in which this violence is greatly attenuated.

Discussion Questions

1   In what ways can Eve Ensler's *The Vagina Monologues* lead to social change?
2   According to the author, what are the main limitations of *The Vagina Monologues*?
3   In what ways does Nancy Fraser's theory of justice aid the author in illuminating the multitude of voices silenced in *The Vagina Monologues*?
4   How can an intersectional approach enhance the play's capacity to act as a tool for ending oppression against women?

Suggested Readings

1   Ensler, Eve. 2013. *In the Body of the World.* New York: Henry Holt.
2   ———. *Vagina Monologues, The.* 10th Anniversary ed. New York: Villard, 2008.
3   Fraser, Nancy. *Fortunes of Feminism: From State-Managed Capitalism to Neoliberal Crisis.* New York, Verso, 2013.

Notes

1   The popularity of this play after 17 years warrants continued critical analysis. However, this number also represents a sharp decline in productions. In 2011, the V-Day website "About V-Day" page noted that there were 5,400 performances in 2010.
2   I had amazing experiences performing in *The Vagina Monologues* in 2004 and 2005—I will always cherish the memories and the "Vaginas Unite" credo that continues to influence my actions today.
3   One example of productions mirroring the work of *The Vagina Monologues* can be found in Jenny Kutner's article (2015) on the Mount Holyoke decision to discontinue productions of the play. To explain the decision, Mount Holyoke's Project Theatre Board states: "At its core, the show offers an extremely narrow perspective on what it means to be a woman ... Gender is a wide and varied experience, one that cannot simply be reduced to biological or anatomical distinctions ...." In its stead, the group plans to "put on a more trans-inclusive production of its own in a similar style to 'Vagina Monologues.'"
4   For a deep look at how the methods of feminist theatre groups in the 1970s and early 1980s were appropriated and adapted by Ensler, see Shelly Scott's "Been There, Done That: Paving the Way for *The Vagina Monologues*" (2003).
5   A fourth core belief, "One must look at the intersection of race, class, and gender to understand violence against women" has been added as the movement evolved beyond that envisioned in the Tenth Anniversary Edition quoted here, but changes to the original three beliefs, and changes to the play to address this fourth belief, have not been made. ("Four Core Beliefs")
6   Throughout my analysis, I mirror contemporary feminist outlets' use of the term "intersectionality" as a call for an intersectional approach that encompasses more than gender. This term is also used by Kimberlé Crenshaw to reference the ways in which the oppression and discrimination a person experiences is compounded if s/he embodies more than one "minority" demographic. For instance, a black woman will experience worse discrimination because she is a woman *and* black,

than would a white woman or a black man who embody one of these two identifiers (Brodkey 1996: 162–163). While this insight is poignant when applied to aspects of this analysis, I will not use "intersectionality" to reference this phenomenon in this chapter.

7 Alarcón uses "gender," but I am intentionally utilizing "sex" so as not to conflate the two concepts within this analysis.

8 For instance, she points to the "Keynesian-Westphalian frame" of justice that defines the "who" of justice claims by their national borders. Within this frame, claims for justice must be heard and resolved within the nation state and systems, and as such, claims for justice made outside of the national citizenry cannot be addressed because they cannot be solved within the boundaries of the nation state; subsequently, these claims are excluded from the realm and idea of justice (Fraser 2013: 189–191).

9 She makes this argument when addressing the economic and cultural dimensions of justice, years before she conceptualizes and argues for the third dimension of the political. However, this interconnection between all three dimensions remains necessary with the addition of the political.

10 This list is not meant to be exhaustive, but rather to offer a few examples of how violence encompasses more than the overt forms that are typically referenced.

11 Although Fraser does not specifically call for an end to capitalism, she argues that "social arrangements that institutionalize deprivation, exploitation, and gross disparities in wealth, income, and leisure time" are precluded from the potential to reach participatory parity within the economic dimension (2013: 164). Because capitalism relies on exploitation of the worker and the continued accumulation of wealth which increases disparities between peoples, I would argue that justice in the economic dimension is impossible within the capitalist system.

12 This inequality is intensified when households are forced to choose who will stay home rather than work, to take care of children or elderly family members, for instance. Women will many times be the member to quit working because it will have a smaller economic impact on the household. As a result, they will lack the material conditions for participatory parity within their household. Then, as they seek to reenter the work force or, more directly, a position in government to make their voice heard, they will lack the material condition—work experience—that the men applying for the same position hold, thus providing justification for their dismissal and exacerbating the imbalance of participation further. This example, of course, assumes a society in which women would have the potential to apply for such positions.

13 This intertwined and mutually reinforcing relationship between ideologies can also be seen within other ideological structures; for instance, the connection between capitalism and racism can be witnessed in the unequal pay between minority and white citizens in the U.S.

14 Silvia Federici provides a thorough explanation of how "the exploitation of [woman's] unpaid labor and the unequal power relations built on her wageless condition were pillars of the capitalist organization of production" within her text, *Revolution at Point Zero: Housework, Reproduction, and Feminist Struggles* (2012: 11). Nancy Fraser also outlines how second-wave feminist struggles for gender equality have been appropriated by and benefited capitalist structures in her chapter "Feminism, Capitalism, and the Cunning of History" (2013).

15 When I attended a 2015 production of *The Vagina Monologues*, a portion of the audience laughed at the response "an electric shock device to keep unwanted

strangers away," indicating a removed understanding that this individual is threatened by violence so much so that this protective device would be necessary. Although I doubt this response was Ensler's intention, and the response to lines and monologues varies by show, it highlights that the manner in which the message of the play is received is largely dependent on the group dynamics of each production and, in this case, the juxtaposition of this serious and devastating admission with more comical responses failed to give the audience enough time to experience emotional solidarity with the speaker.

16 The genital mutilation of an intersex girl to create a normalized vagina was valorized in the 2002 productions of *The Vagina Monologues* and at the time that Hall and the Intersex Society of North America were critiquing it. I was unable to find a copy of this monologue for analysis. But content aside, the removal of the intersex monologue without a replacement of a more inclusive version of the monologue can be read as a transparent form of the political frame setting that excludes non-normative female bodies from the play.

17 It must be acknowledged that the original play was written with the expectation that it would be produced off-Broadway in New York City, and wouldn't become the global phenomenon that it is now. However, given that Ensler talks about interviewing women from around the world as part of this project, and there have been numerous variations published and produced since then, additional variations of identities could have been introduced to challenge the establishment of this normative identity.

18 The term the speaker uses for the vagina.

19 There is reference to violence against white women occurring in the past, but, as Hall points out, these forms of violence are presumed to be abolished in modern Western culture.

20 A choice that counters Ensler's assertion that the play is "about what it means to have a vagina" (Sherman 2015). This, however, highlights the malleability of the play's framework, and it's potential to move beyond "what it means to have a vagina" with the inclusion of other experiences.

21 Spivak notes that she is not advocating for the killing of widows through her analysis (1988: 97). I likewise am not taking a stance on the custom of wearing burqas. As a non-Muslim woman, it is not my place to speak to this custom. Instead this should be read as a call for an acknowledgement of the various perspectives on this practice from the women who subscribe to it and an understanding of how the one-sided portrayal in "Under the Burqa" exemplifies one way in which non-Western women are denied political parity within the work.

22 This is evident in the set-up of the website. Visitors to the vday.org page first enter a splash page that, when clicked, redirects them to onebillionrising.org. It is only by scrolling down to the hyperlinks at the bottom of the splash page that visitors can go to the vday.org site.

23 Attention must be paid to the localized movements to ensure that local activists are not being denied political parity by the regional V-Day activists, as was evidenced in Clara Eugenia Rojas's explanation of the Juárez, Mexico protests in "The V-Day March in Mexico: Appropriation and Misuse of Local Women's Activism" (2005).

24 This monologue is a hypothetical suggestion based in a desire for a monologue that meets the needs of this movement for justice. The specific details would be determined by women's interviews with Ensler, however I believe it would be possible to find stories to this effect if Third World factory workers were interviewed.

References

"About V-Day." *V-Day.* n.p., 2014. Web. March 5, 2015.

Aguilar, Delia D. "On Vagina Monologues." *Kritika Kultura* 2 (2002): 22–23.

Brodkey, Linda. "On the Intersection of Feminism and Cultural Studies." *Writing Permitted in Designated Areas Only*, Vol. 4. Minneapolis, MN: Minnesota University Press, March 1996.

Cooper, Christine M. "Worrying about Vaginas: Feminism and Eve Ensler's *The Vagina Monologues.*" *Signs* 32:3 (Spring 2007): 727–758.

Ensler, Eve. *In the Body of the World.* New York: Henry Holt, 2013.

———. *The Vagina Monologues*, 10th anniversary ed. New York: Villard, 2008.

Federici, Silvia. *Revolution at Point Zero: Housework, Reproduction, and Feminist Struggle.* New York: PM Press, 2012.

"Four Core Beliefs." *V-Day.* n.p., 2014.

Fraser, Nancy. *Fortunes of Feminism: From State-Managed Capitalism to Neoliberal Crisis.* New York, Verso, 2013.

Goldstein, Julie Rei. "I've Never Found the V-Day Conversation to Be Dependent on Genitalia." *Time.com*, January 19, 2014.

Hall, Kim Q. "Queerness, Disability, and the Vagina Monologues." *Hypatia.* 20:1 (Winter 2005): 99–119.

Hennessy, Rosemary. *Materialist Feminism and the Politics of Discourse.* New York: Routledge, 1993.

Hesford, Wendy S. "Cosmopolitanism and the Geopolitics of Feminist Rhetoric." in Eileen Schell and K. J. Rawson (eds.), *Rhetorica in Motion*. Pittsburgh, PA: University Press of Pittsburgh, 2010, 53–70.

Khaleeli, Homa. "One Billion Rising: how can public dancing end violence against women?" *TheGuardian.com*, Guardian News and Media, February 13, 2015.

Kutner, Jenny. "Women's college will no longer perform 'Vagina Monologues' because it isn't 'inclusive.'" *Salon.com*, 15 January 15, 2015.

Marx, Karl. *The Marx-Engels Reader*, Robert C. Tucker (ed.). 2nd ed. New York: Norton, 1978.

Rojas, Clara Eugenia. "The 'V-Day' March in Mexico: Appropriation and Misuse of Local Women's Activism." *NWSA Journal.* 17.2 (Summer 2005): 217–227.

Scott, Shelly. "Been There, Done That: Paving the Way for *The Vagina Monologues.*" *Modern Drama*, 46:3 (Fall 2003): 404–423.

Sherman, Howard. "Of Vagina Monologues and Dialogues, On Stage and On Campus." *HESherman.com*, January 17, 2015.

Spivak, Gayatri Chakravorty. "Can the Subaltern Speak?" in C. Nelson and L. Grossberg (eds.), *Marxism and the Interpretation of Culture*. Basingstoke: Macmillan Education, 1988, 66–111.

Talusan, Meredith. "Performing in 'The Vagina Monologues' as a Transgender Woman." *Buzzfeed.com*. March 13, 2015.

Young, Iris Marion. *On Female Body Experience: "Throwing Like a Girl" and Other Essays.* New York: Oxford, 2005.

"What is One Billion Rising?" *1 Billion Rising.* n.p., 2015.

INDEX

361